Anansi's Gold

Anansi's Gold

The Man Who Looted the West, Outfoxed Washington,
and Swindled the World

Yepoka Yeebo

BLOOMSBURY PUBLISHING

NEW YORK · LONDON · OXFORD · NEW DELHI · SYDNEY

BLOOMSBURY PUBLISHING
Bloomsbury Publishing Inc.
1385 Broadway, New York, NY 10018, USA

BLOOMSBURY, BLOOMSBURY PUBLISHING, and the Diana logo are trademarks
of Bloomsbury Publishing Plc

First published in the United States 2023

Bloomsbury Publishing Plc does not have any control over, or responsibility for, any third-
party websites referred to or in this book. All internet addresses given in this book were
correct at the time of going to press. The author and publisher regret any inconvenience
caused if addresses have changed or sites have ceased to exist, but can accept no
responsibility for any such changes.

LIBRARY OF CONGRESS CATALOGING-IN-PUBLICATION DATA IS AVAILABLE

ISBN: HB: 978-1-63557-473-9; EBOOK: 978-1-63557-475-3

2 4 6 8 10 9 7 5 3 1

Typeset by Westchester Publishing Services
Printed and bound in the U.S.A.

To find out more about our authors and books visit www.bloomsbury.com and sign up
for our newsletters.

Bloomsbury books may be purchased for business or promotional use. For information
on bulk purchases please contact Macmillan Corporate and Premium Sales Department at
specialmarkets@macmillan.com.

For my grandparents, Felicia Naa-Yeye Agoe (née Nortey) and John Obodai Coffie-Agoe, who told the best stories. Nyɛ yiwala dɔŋŋ kɛ sadzi kpakpai kɛ adesai ninyɛ ta mi lɛ. Nyɛ woa yɛ hedzolɛ mli.

CONTENTS

CAST OF CHARACTERS

Lynne Abraham: Philadelphia judge who carried a gun, drank three cups of coffee a day, and presided over the trial of Robert Ellis in 1986–87.

Ignatius Kutu Acheampong: Ghana's lean, stern head of state between 1972 and 1978. He seized power in a coup d'état. He was the first head of state to issue a diplomatic passport to John Ackah Blay-Miezah.

Jewel Ackah: Blay-Miezah's personal pop star—a musician and leader of the Butterfly Six. He recorded "Akaraka-Chi," Blay-Miezah's impossibly catchy anthem.

Ebenezer Ako-Adjei: One of Ghana's founding fathers, and the minister of foreign affairs in Kwame Nkrumah's government. He became a prominent supporter of Blay-Miezah.

Kwesi Amoako-Atta: Minister of finance in Nkrumah's government, he let Ghana's reserves dwindle to less than a million dollars. He would enable Blay-Miezah for decades.

Joe Appiah: Ghanaian lawyer and activist who was one of Nkrumah's closest friends, and later one of his fiercest rivals. He prosecuted Blay-Miezah in 1979.

Emmanuel Ayeh-Kumi: Ghanaian businessman who was imprisoned by Nkrumah on charges of corruption. After Nkrumah was deposed, Ayeh-Kumi claimed that Nkrumah had stolen millions. Ayeh-Kumi became an ally of Blay-Miezah.

Jacob Badu: Shared an apartment with Blay-Miezah in Philadelphia while studying at the University of Pennsylvania. Years later, he discovered that the university had put Blay-Miezah's name on his degrees.

Gladys Blay-Miezah: John Ackah Blay-Miezah's glamorous wife, a fashion designer and one of the few people who could stay one step ahead of him. Friends nicknamed her "Columbo" due to her ability to track down Blay-Miezah's girlfriends.

John Ackah Blay-Miezah, a.k.a. John Kolorah Blay, a.k.a. Doc, a.k.a. Nana Ackah Nyanzu the Second, a.k.a. Our Man: Architect of the Oman Ghana Trust Fund, and one of the greatest con artists of all time.

Ed Bradley: American journalist and host of *60 Minutes*, he interviewed Blay-Miezah in 1988 for a segment called "The Ultimate Con Man."

Steven Burbank: General counsel for the University of Pennsylvania—and a surprise witness at Blay-Miezah's trial in 1979.

Richard Butera: Attorney and businessman who invested in the Oman Ghana Trust Fund. He introduced his friend Ed Bradley to Blay-Miezah.

Ben Bynum: Owner of some of Philadelphia's iconic bars and clubs, friend of Gladys Knight and Aretha Franklin, and investor in the Oman Ghana Trust Fund.

Ebenezer Moses Debrah: Ghanaian diplomat and civil servant who attempted to stop Blay-Miezah's scam in 1974–75.

Krobo Edusei: Minister in Nkrumah's government who was epically corrupt and proud of it. Husband of Mary Edusei, who bought a gold-plated bed from Selfridges, triggering his political demise. He was subsequently one of Blay-Miezah's closest allies.

Robert Ellis: Blay-Miezah's partner in the Oman Ghana Trust Fund, and Robert Redford to Blay-Miezah's Paul Newman. A dapper, roguish Philadelphian citizen of the world, who seemed to know everyone and everything.

Benjamin Forjoe: Feared, Israeli-trained director of Ghana's Special Branch under Nkrumah who first met Blay-Miezah in 1963.

Barry Ginsberg: Philadelphia attorney and investor in the Oman Ghana Trust Fund.

Kwame Gyawu-Kyem: Editor of the *Ghanaian Times* and one of Blay-Miezah's most important allies in the media.

Walter Hajduk: New Jersey businessmen who made a fortune in metal fabrication and lost a fortune to Blay-Miezah.

Ben Hayford: Manager of the Oman Ghana Trust Fund's London office in the 1980s.

Gordon Kells: London doctor known for his underworld connections who became Blay-Miezah's physician.

Henry Kissinger: U.S. secretary of state between 1973 and 1977, he ordered investigations into Blay-Miezah and the Oman Ghana Trust Fund.

Bashiru Kwaw-Swanzy: Attorney general of Ghana between 1962 and 1966, he ordered Blay-Miezah's detention, then went on to become Blay-Miezah's personal lawyer.

Charles Lowenthal: Disgraced American lawyer with delusions of grandeur who forged documents—inexpertly—for Blay-Miezah.

Georges Mayer: Manager at Union Bank of Switzerland who was tricked by Blay-Miezah into supporting the story of the Oman Ghana Trust Fund.

John Mitchell: U.S. attorney general in Richard Nixon's administration who was jailed for his part in Watergate. Subsequently, he went to work for Blay-Miezah.

Arno Newman: Belgian banker, convicted fraudster, and ally of Blay-Miezah.

Fathia Nkrumah: Kwame Nkrumah's Egyptian wife. After Nkrumah's death, Blay-Miezah told his investors that she was a supporter of the Oman Ghana Trust Fund.

Kwame Nkrumah: Ghana's first prime minister, and subsequently first president, he led the fight for independence from Britain. Famously incorruptible, he was deposed in a coup d'état in 1966.

Elizabeth Nyaniba: Nkrumah's beloved mother. She would outlive her son.

George Padmore: Writer and activist who became friends with Nkrumah in London. He moved to Accra after independence to run the Bureau of African Affairs.

Kofi Bentum Quantson: Blay-Miezah's former schoolmaster and subsequently a member of Ghana's Special Branch. He was tasked with investigating Blay-Miezah on several occasions.

Jerry John Rawlings: Ghana's head of state in 1979 and 1981–2001. He was responsible for multiple coups d'état and countless atrocities. He granted Blay-Miezah government support and a diplomatic passport.

Barry Rider: Chief commercial fraud officer at the Commonwealth Commercial Crime Unit in London, he began investigating Blay-Miezah in 1983.

Peter Rigby: Ran a video studio in Muswell Hill, London, and met Blay-Miezah in 1981. He subsequently became Blay-Miezah's bagman, smuggling cash and guns into Ghana for him.

Abraham Sackey: Police officer and member of Ghana's Special Branch. Blay-Miezah accused him of corruption.

Joshua Kwabena Siaw: Ghanaian industrialist, self-made millionaire, and a major investor in the Oman Ghana Trust Fund. He lost a large sum investing in Blay-Miezah. The rest of his fortune was stolen by the regime of Jerry Rawlings.

Ezra D. M. Stephens: Officer in Ghana's Bureau of National Investigation who surveilled Blay-Miezah during the 1980s.

Shirley Temple Black: Onetime child star who was appointed U.S. ambassador to Ghana in 1974. She spent much of her time in office monitoring Blay-Miezah.

Kojo Tsikata: National security adviser to Jerry Rawlings and a fearsomely effective spymaster. He watched Blay-Miezah closely throughout the 1980s.

James Edward Woodruff: Radical priest who marched from Selma to Montgomery with Dr. Martin Luther King Jr. He would spend years working with Blay-Miezah, hoping that the Oman Ghana Trust Fund would bring about economic liberation for people in the United States and Ghana.

Anansi's Gold

Chapter 1

Our Man

1974

In a castle by the sea in Accra, our man was telling his story.

Outside, the sky was so bright it was almost white. In the shallows next to the castle, the waves were pale gray with white caps. Farther out to sea, they turned a shimmering blue. Huge fishing canoes rocked gently, close to shore. On the horizon, container ships lined up, waiting to dock. The air smelled of salt and smoke and brine. The castle—Osu Castle—was cut off from the rest of Accra by palm trees and checkpoints. It was a maze of archways and staircases and parapets, patched together over four centuries. Some of its walls were brightly whitewashed. Others were gray concrete, slick with algae. Ancient cannons and soldiers with assault rifles lined the castle's walls. Even without stepping into its underground dungeons, you could tell that unspeakable things had happened here. In a heavily guarded room at the heart of the castle, a haze hung in the air as our man began.

The history of Ghana, he said, had a secret chapter. Kwame Nkrumah, the country's first president, had revealed it on his deathbed in 1972.

Over his years in power, President Nkrumah had hidden away millions of dollars in cash and gold. At that very moment, tens of thousands of gold bars were sitting in vaults in Switzerland. But Nkrumah was not a thief. He was a visionary. He hid the gold to make sure it did not fall into the wrong hands. And he ensured that, when the time was right, it would be handed back to Ghanaians. The money would be used to transform the nation. It would give every Ghanaian their birthright.

Nkrumah had known that he could lose power at any moment. Toward the end of his time in office, it was hard to keep track of the plots to overthrow him: Ghanaian plots, British plots, and American plots. There had been countless assassination attempts. So Nkrumah made a plan to ensure that Ghana's enemies could not steal the nation's wealth. Slowly, carefully, using a network of confidants, he moved some of Ghana's gold reserves abroad. Once he had gotten the gold out, Nkrumah placed it under the control of a trust: the Oman Ghana Trust Fund.

Years later, Nkrumah was dying of cancer. His former friends and allies had abandoned him. There was only one man left in the world he could count on: our man, Dr. John Ackah Blay-Miezah. Blay-Miezah and Nkrumah were like father and son. Nkrumah knew he could rely on Blay-Miezah to do what was best for Ghana. So he put Blay-Miezah in charge of the Trust Fund.

Now, two years after Nkrumah's death, Blay-Miezah was ready to fulfill the president's dying wish. He could bring eighty-six million dollars of the gold home to Ghana immediately. And that was just the beginning. As soon as he had satisfied the conditions of Nkrumah's trust, Blay-Miezah, with the help of his foreign associates, could bring the rest of the money home. And Ghana's future would be golden.

Imagine it, Blay-Miezah said. Every Ghanaian "has a good home to live in, and good pipe-borne water to drink. He has good electricity. He has a good clinic or hospital to attend. He has a good school to educate the children. Good textbooks. Good roads. New cars. New industry. Heavy employment." Blay-Miezah knew that people would say he was a fantasist or a con man. "Some people are just trying to stop what is real. Please, let us open our eyes," Blay-Miezah said, "so this country does not lose this beautiful chance. So this country does not lose this wonderful chance."

IN THE CASTLE, our man, Dr. John Ackah Blay-Miezah, sat back, his story at an end. From the other side of a huge desk, Ghana's head of state, Colonel

Ignatius Kutu Acheampong, took the measure of his visitor. Blay-Miezah looked good. He wore polished loafers and a crisp white leisure suit. It had been pressed, and it was spotless. He had a boyishly charming face and sat ramrod straight, like he had been in the army. He was shaved and showered and fresh.

Blay-Miezah's story sounded absurd. But Ghana was broke. A couple of years earlier, Colonel Acheampong had quietly staged a coup d'état. At the time, he had been commander of the country's First Infantry Brigade. It was Ghana's second successful coup, the first being the one that toppled President Nkrumah. It would not be the last.

One of the colonel's first acts as self-appointed head of the new military government had been to announce that the country would not pay off many of its debts. Ghana was spending more money servicing its loans than on anything else, and the economy was in trouble. There were food shortages, and people were suffering. Acheampong announced that if a loan had come with kickbacks to politicians, he would not be paying it. "We have told those who had helped to tie the massive foreign debt like a noose around our necks: 'Yentua eka hunu.' We won't pay any bad debts." Genuine debts, the colonel said, would be honored when Ghana was in a position to do so.

The approach had worked for a couple of years, but by 1974, the economy had slowed again. So when Blay-Miezah sat down in his office, Colonel Acheampong was happy to give him a hearing. Blay-Miezah's millions would fill Acheampong's coffers again. He might actually be able to restart all the factories that had been mothballed since the first coup d'état. With that kind of money, Acheampong could make Ghana the envy of the world. He told Blay-Miezah that if the money existed, he should bring it home. For the time being, though, he had to keep its origins quiet.

It was a deal. There were, Blay-Miezah said, just two more things he needed from the colonel. He needed a diplomatic passport. Also, he would be very grateful if Acheampong would let him out of jail.

Blay-Miezah was, at the time, a resident at Ussher Fort, the most notorious prison in Accra. He had been charged with fraud, escaped police custody, then had been locked up again. Outside Acheampong's office, guards were waiting to escort him back to jail.

Blay-Miezah walked out a free man.

Within days, stories about the mysterious fortune were all over the newspapers. The eighty-six million dollars was the talk of Accra parties. Everyone was trying to work out where the money had come from, whether it actually existed, and, if it did, when they would get their cut.

OSU CASTLE AND Ussher Fort were in the oldest part of Accra, along the shoreline of the Gulf of Guinea. Surrounding them were ancient family compound houses, and palaces arranged around two lagoons, the Korle and the Klottey. Nearby, slapped-together colonial-era buildings moldered in the sea air. The modern metropolis of Accra grew up in concentric circles around the old city.

There were sprawling, whitewashed bungalows in planned communities, built for middle-class families and their rosebushes. And there were the soaring, modernist structures that the Nkrumah government constructed in the 1950s and 1960s: government offices, lavish hotels, and factories that had been shut for years. People would look up at these crumbling edifices and get a feeling, like a punch to the gut, that something had gone horribly wrong.

There was an air of decadence everywhere in Accra. Dancing girls with names like Sexy Pepsi Yana (who was "back from Britain with lots of sophistry," one ad proclaimed) performed at legendary nightclubs inside state-owned hotels. There were brightly lit casinos serving lobster, where the champagne flowed even when the electricity did not.

Soon after his meeting with Colonel Acheampong, Blay-Miezah was sitting by the pools at Accra's grandest hotels. He was the guest of honor wherever he went. After all, rumor had it, he was Ghana's richest man.

Foreign diplomats, particularly the Americans, were baffled by Blay-Miezah. At the time, the American ambassador to Ghana was Shirley Temple Black, the former child star. Her controversial appointment had been greeted with a mixture of amusement and resignation. She did, however, know more about Africa than the secretary of state, Henry Kissinger. In a meeting at the State Department, when Kissinger got confused about what or where Namibia was, Temple Black pointed it out to him on a map.

Temple Black watched Blay-Miezah with intense interest. A series of Americans had begun to show up at her embassy, often unannounced, claiming to be Blay-Miezah's American business partners and demanding meetings with the ambassador. Confidential diplomatic cables flew back and forth between her embassy and Washington all year.

"Those who believe Blay-Miezah a fraud," she wrote in a cable to Kissinger, "are worried he might just have the money and then they would look extremely foolish."

GHANAIANS LOVE THEIR con men. It's the national sport. There's an appreciation for the con, for the sweetener, for getting one over on someone, for kalabule. There have been government crusades against kalabule. One military leader killed people accused of it. But Ghanaians delight in the kind of man who can talk himself out of a bind or into a fortune. (Less so when a woman does it.) In hard times, all you have is your wit, and Ghana has seen a lot of hard times.

When Ghanaian children are young, their parents often tell them stories about Anansi. Sometimes a man and sometimes a spider, Anansi is a trickster. He is wise, but also greedy and lazy. He uses stories to deceive, or cheat, or steal from someone bigger or stronger than him.

As the legends have it, Anansi knew the power of stories—and his stories were so good, they changed the world. If he told a story about a mountain, the next morning people would look outside and see the mountain. If he told a story about some hidden treasure, people would dive to the bottom of the sea in search of it. If he told a story about being a king, people would bring him a crown.

Anansi's stories made people feel special: like they knew a great secret or were part of an amazing adventure. Sometimes he got away with his cons. More often, he got greedy. And because, in Ghana, Anansi stories are used to teach children not to be like Anansi, he would often fall into one of his own traps. There would be consequences, and Anansi would be humiliated. But after that, Anansi's stories wouldn't go away. The mountain would still be there. People would keep searching for the treasure. Anansi would still be remembered as a king.

John Ackah Blay-Miezah was Anansi. His story of Nkrumah's secret fortune rewrote Ghana's history and made him fabulously rich. Then it destroyed him. But the story outlived Blay-Miezah. Decades after his death, people are still telling his story and are still hunting for Nkrumah's gold.

BLAY-MIEZAH WAS A precocious child. He noticed—and remembered— almost everything. People thought he had supernatural abilities and started asking him for advice. The young Blay-Miezah quickly learned that if you told people what they wanted to hear, they would give you anything. He grew into a charming young man who liked the high life and paid for it by scamming his way around West Africa and the United States. He left a trail of angry diplomats, hotel managers, and investigators in his wake. Each time he got caught, Blay-Miezah found a bigger story, a better con, and ever-more-powerful associates to bail him out. One day, he turned a combination of half-remembered news bulletins, CIA propaganda, and prison-yard gossip into the Oman Ghana Trust Fund.

Very soon, Blay-Miezah was selling the Trust Fund to businessmen in Philadelphia and industrialists in Accra. Lawyers and politicians, distinguished and disgraced, lent the operation their gravitas. Millions of dollars poured in.

To keep the investors coming, Blay-Miezah promised them returns of ten to one, twenty to one, or even a hundred to one. He would take money from poor widows in South Philadelphia and millionaires in Achimota. He ran for president of Ghana, smuggled money and guns, and made himself indispensable to crooked bankers, corrupt officials, and, eventually, the most brutal regime ever to hold power in Ghana. By the mid-1980s, the Oman Ghana Trust Fund had become one of the largest frauds of the twentieth century.

Over the years, the trail of destruction behind Blay-Miezah kept growing. He sacrificed one ally after another. His supporters and investors lost their homes, their businesses, and their families. Law enforcement agencies on three continents began to investigate him. Blay-Miezah started looking for a way out, but he realized that his story had trapped him too. So he staked everything on one final bet and tried to con the entire world.

At the heart of Blay-Miezah's con was a country ripped apart by colonialism, then given no time to heal. Before Ghana could mourn its losses, or rebuild, it was set upon by vultures from around the world and destroyed from within by opportunistic crooks. These were Blay-Miezah's people: military dictators, unscrupulous businessmen, ruthless spies, and corrupt politicians.

This is a story of how lies change history. And it is a story that comes with a warning. If a lie is big enough—if enough people profit from it—that lie will not just change history: it will become history.

The Oman Ghana Trust Fund never existed. The story of President Nkrumah's secret fortune was a lie. But it—and Blay-Miezah—shaped the modern history of Ghana. This is the story of a lie that changed the world.

Chapter 2

Kerosene Boy

1941–1962

O ur man was born in 1941 in a village called Alengenzure. His parents, Maame Elizabeth Kongyea Agyili and Papa Blay Cudjoe, did not think they would be able to have another child. Their new baby was a gift, destined for great things. They named him for his grandfather: John Kolorah Blay.

The village was named Alengenzure for the river running through it. Once, the river had been home to basks of Nile crocodiles. By the time Blay was born, the crocodiles had retreated upstream, all the way to the evergreen rainforests north of the village. The river flowed through the east of the village, where it was choked with mangroves, then ran through a culvert into a pristine stretch of coastline on the Gulf of Guinea. The way the elders told it, gold used to wash up in every river in Ghana. If it rained hard enough, you could scoop a fortune out of a stream with your bare hands.

Blay's village did not yet have electricity, or piped water, but it was astonishingly rich with natural resources. It was surrounded by forests and dense, lush coconut groves. The southern edge of the village was a white sand beach dotted with monumental, jagged rocks. The waters were quiet; there were never more than two canoes fishing. At night, above the orange haze of cooking fires and flickering kerosene lamps, it was so dark you could see entire constellations, bright and clear, curving off into the darkness above the Atlantic Ocean.

Alengenzure was in Nzema country, in what would become the Western Region of Ghana. In 1941, Ghana was under British colonial rule and was known as the Gold Coast. Nzemaland stretched over a thousand square miles on the southwest coast and across the border into Côte d'Ivoire. Many families lived between the two countries, speaking Nzema and Akan as well as French and English.

A hundred years before Blay was born, foreigners called Nzemaland "Appollonia," although nobody remembered why: perhaps it was a misunderstanding by the Dutch, or something to do with a ship called the *Great Apollo*. The kings of Nzemaland had been the mightiest rulers in the western Gold Coast. And the most powerful of them all was Awulae Kaku Aka. His kingdom was strong and well run. The way dazed nineteenth-century travelers told it, the streets were paved with gold. King Kaku Aka had gold armor. He had a tiger cast in gold. His ceremonial cutlasses and swords had gold handles. There was even a gold cannon.

The British wanted his gold, and they wanted his land. But the kingdom of Awulae Kaku Aka was entirely independent, trading with surrounding nations and foreign merchants. And King Kaku Aka made it clear that he would not tolerate nonsense. If the British encroached, he told his people, take their heads, and bring them to me. I will reward you with gold.

The British encroached. In 1848, an official named Francis Swanzy sent messengers into King Kaku Aka's realm, demanding that he submit to British authority. Swanzy made his money trading. He had recently been accused of violating the Slave Trade Act of 1807 by selling supplies to sailors planning to kidnap and sell people. When he applied for a post with the Colonial Office in London, he was judged to be entirely unemployable, in any role. So he made other plans.

Swanzy's messengers to King Kaku Aka disappeared. Swanzy was thrilled. He had the excuse he needed to go in and plunder—"to bring" King Kaku Aka "to his bearings," he said. Swanzy had been planning the war for six years: in 1842, he stood before a Parliamentary committee in London and urged the annexation of Nzemaland.

Now, Swanzy accused King Kaku Aka of enslaving and exploiting his people—the practices that had built much of Britain's wealth. Swanzy's real aim was to increase his profits: he needed new markets and goods for his trading firm. He intended to take those things from King Kaku Aka. Swanzy led six thousand troops down the coast, into the Nzema kingdom. King Kaku Aka was betrayed by one of his advisers and died a British hostage.

In their greed, the British decimated Nzemaland and killed countless people. After the massacre, Swanzy's sanctimony evaporated: there was loot to be had. It was "difficult to make even a fair distribution of the spoils," he wrote, in a vainglorious account published in a London magazine. "I have a gold skull-cap, and there are gold handled cutlasses, swords, and a variety of articles, the Governor has a handsomely carved chair and a sword." King Kaku Aka's gold tiger was sent to Queen Victoria. It was a pattern repeated across the world, throughout the history of the British Empire.

Despite being delighted by how much they had been able to loot, the British had not found what they were looking for: King Kaku Aka's ancestral wealth, the royal treasure of Nzemaland. "We have in vain endeavored to persuade the king to disclose the spot where he has concealed his treasure, which must be very considerable," Swanzy wrote. But the British would never find it. "The king's treasure has never been discovered," Swanzy admitted, months later. "It is supposed that he buried it when alone, and out of sight of his attendants."

When Swanzy retold the story of the war, he was the hero—liberating King Kaku Aka's people from "one of the most cruel of tyrants." But Swanzy's

Awulae Kaku Aka I's ceremonial cutlass, stolen by Francis Swanzy in 1848, and currently held in the British Museum.

attempt to make a name for himself was an abject failure. Henry Grey, Earl Grey, Britain's secretary of state for the colonies, was furious when he heard about the invasion. The governor of the Gold Coast detailed Swanzy's venality and incompetence in multiple reports to London. Swanzy, having been frustrated in his attempt to steal King Kaku Aka's ancestral wealth, was said to have robbed the British instead. The governor suspected that Swanzy had stolen gold dust from the British reserves at Osu Castle.

In place of Kaku Aka's strong, well-ordered kingdom, the British—as they had throughout their empire—brought anarchy, violence, and plunder. They built a counterfeit society that existed purely to be emptied of anything and everything valuable. They turned the kingdom of Awulae Kaku Aka into one big mine. And for more than a hundred years, the people of the kingdom, and their descendants, dedicated themselves to getting the British out.

The dream of the lost kingdom of Awulae Kaku Aka would haunt Blay for his entire life. What if that lost wealth could be restored? His people could take a quantum jump forward: from dirt roads to monorails. From kerosene lamps to a fully electrified city. Blay would even name himself after the great king: later in life, he would call himself John Ackah Blay-Miezah. Blay would swear, until the day he died, that all the things he did—the lies he told, the people he hurt—were in pursuit of this one goal, to turn his home back into a kingdom of gold, a modern wonder of the world. "That call," he would say, "is vibrating with the pulse beat of my heart, every moment."

EVEN AS A child, Blay was an absolute charmer. That way some small children look at you—the way that makes you want to do anything for them? Blay had that quality. He had a round, open face and deep dimples in each cheek. As he grew, he developed the ability to look either wide-eyed and innocent or startlingly distinguished. The young Blay also had a phenomenal memory. He would see someone on the street, pick up on the tiniest thing—the kind of watch they wore, the honorific others used to address them, things no one else noticed—and remember that detail for years.

When Blay was old enough, his parents sent him to Takoradi, the nearest big city, which was about two hours away. He lived with an uncle named Papa Blay Morkeh and went to a nearby Presbyterian primary school. Takoradi was home to the port where most of Ghana's gold and timber was shipped out of the country. It was a boomtown, full of people newly arrived from the countryside to work in the mines, mills, and harbor: dockworkers and gold miners who had followed the money to a town that wasn't ready for its new residents. There were so few homes available that, for years, landlords converted their kitchens and latrines and rented them out as rooms.

In 1956, John Kolorah Blay enrolled at Bishop O'Rorke, an Anglican middle school in the city. Children frequently stopped and started school, according to whether their parents could afford the fees. Some were in their late teens by the time they reached middle school. Blay was determined to stay in school, whatever it took. In the afternoons, he worked to help pay his fees, hawking kerosene in glass bottles. All the kids at school called him "Kerosene Boy."

Bishop O'Rorke School was a traditional colonial-era institution. It was designed to crush children's spirits. Pupils were disciplined with the lash and called their teachers "master." One of Blay's schoolmasters, a twenty-three-year-old fresh out of training college named Kofi Bentum Quantson, "wielded the cane with vigor," he wrote. "If it were these latter days, I would have been prosecuted." He even beat children for things they did outside school hours: parents brought children to him for punishment.

By contrast, Quantson thought Blay was an angel. Blay was the star of Middle Form Four. Always polite, obedient to a fault, fastidiously dressed, and—Quantson thought—a bit of a kiss ass. He had an almost supernatural ability to discern what Quantson wanted. So, Quantson later wrote, after he had made the transition from feared local schoolmaster to feared secret policeman, "he did the right thing." Or at least he appeared to.

Blay also served as an altar boy at the church. He liked the ritual of High Anglican services: the candles, the robes, the chalices, the choir. He liked the way the incense went up in plumes and left a fragrant haze in the air. He liked that the services were sometimes solemn and sometimes serene. He liked the Victorian hymns, unchanged for a hundred years. One, by James Russell Lowell, stayed with him for the rest of his life:

Once to ev'ry man and nation
Comes the moment to decide,

In the strife of truth and falsehood,
For the good or evil side;
Some great cause, some great decision,
Off'ring each the bloom or blight,
And the choice goes by forever
'Twixt that darkness and that light.

Mostly, though, Blay liked being the center of attention. In a place built to crush him, he had found a way to thrive and to be noticed.

Within a year, this had paid off: he won a scholarship to attend Fijai Secondary School, skipping the rest of middle school. At Fijai, while the other kids played football, Blay cultivated a reputation. He told everyone he was "gifted in more senses than five." He could cure ailments with herbs and had dreams that let him glimpse the future. The headmaster at Fijai Secondary School, Timothy Ansah, heard about this and suggested an arrangement. After school, Blay held court at the house of one of his teachers. Soon, people—women, especially—were coming from far and wide for the teenager's counsel. Whether he had spiritual abilities or was simply adept at noticing things most people did not, Blay had found a source of power. Soon he was making more money selling stories than kerosene.

In the summer of 1959, a few years after Ghana declared independence, Blay told his friends and family he had won a scholarship to study at the University of Pennsylvania, just like the country's prime minister, Kwame Nkrumah. Everyone Blay knew turned up to bid him farewell at Takoradi Harbor on August 3, 1959.

His old teacher, Quantson, would remember that day for decades. He went to the harbor to see Blay off and soon realized that he was not alone. An entourage of women dressed in white had also come to bid Blay farewell. Quantson was baffled. The women were not Blay's family, or his teachers, so who were they?

Blay embarked on the *African Glade*, a down-at-heel former Second World War freighter. It called at Monrovia, Liberia, before crossing the Atlantic to New York. Blay was the only passenger.

Back in Takoradi, Quantson was still trying to figure out the mystery of the women in white. He asked around and found out that they were Blay's "clients." His former pupil had been helping them with their problems, physical and spiritual, for a fee. That was news to Quantson. It was not the first time that Blay had surprised him, and it would not be the last.

On August 15, 1959, the *African Glade* steamed past Staten Island. Construction on the Verrazzano-Narrows Bridge, linking Staten Island with Brooklyn, had begun two days earlier. In the distance, Blay could see the Statue of Liberty and the towers of Manhattan. The *African Glade* docked at the less glamorous surroundings of Brooklyn's Thirty-Third Street pier: a warren of railyards, industrial plants, and rusting ships. Blay stepped off the gangplank and into America.

HE WAS SOON in Philadelphia and moved into a redbrick row house at 4037 Locust Street. It was a short walk from the University of Pennsylvania campus in West Philadelphia and was already home to a number of Ghanaian students, including Rudolph von Ballmoos and Jacob Badu, who were at the Wharton School of Commerce and Finance. Blay told his housemates that he planned to study medicine.

As more African nations fought for and won their independence, the number of students from the continent in American colleges grew. In the 1950s, Lincoln University in Pennsylvania had more African students enrolled than any other college in the United States. The Ghanaian students in Blay's Philadelphia house were different from most of the kids he had known in Takoradi. They were from rich and prominent families: they had grown up in Accra, had gone to boarding school abroad, and seemed worldly and confident. In 1957, while Blay was still at school, von Ballmoos, dressed in Kente and smiling broadly, had unfurled the flag of Ghana, the world's newest nation, in front of the Liberty Bell, flanked by a city councilman and two other members of the All-African Students Union of Greater Philadelphia.

Philadelphia in the 1950s was beautiful and broken. On some blocks, you could hear a dozen languages. In the Free Library on Logan Square, teenagers and music critics argued about jazz. At the Mayfair Diner, on Frankford Avenue, the pie and coffee were just as good as when it first opened in 1932. But there was never enough money to fuel the city's ambitions. Corrupt

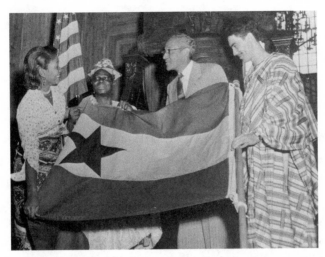

Rudolph von Ballmoos (far right) unfurls Ghana's flag in front of the Liberty Bell.

politicians and the Mafia stole much of the money that was left. Philadelphia's population was declining. Grand townhouses stood empty or were turned into cheap boardinghouses. Factories began to close. Streets caved in. And the Phillies kept losing. People needed hope.

Philadelphia was also a brutally racist place, in ways that shocked the students. Many wrapped themselves in their Africanness like armor. Some were actual African princesses and princes. Most were not, but claiming they were made navigating Pennsylvania a little easier.

Oliver St. Clair Franklin, an African American student at Lincoln University at the time, watched it all unfold with amusement. As soon as people realized the advantages of being an African prince, he remembered, the campus was suddenly awash with them. "All these African princes had the ability to go over to Swarthmore and Bryn Mawr and get these white girls, who were rich and had cars, to drive their Black butts back to Lincoln."

The African princes were so ubiquitous that the All-African Students' Union even put on a play about the phenomenon. It was narrated by von Ballmoos and "pointed up the problems facing a young African prince who comes to America and marries a Negro girl." It was favorably reviewed by the *Philadelphia Tribune*.

In July 1959, the *Tribune* had also covered von Ballmoos's wedding to Miss Agnes Nebo of Liberia, a recent graduate of the Philadelphia Conservatory of Music. They married at St. Mary's Church, a couple of blocks over from the row house where von Ballmoos lived. "The bride wore a French brocade lace princess-style gown, with a sweeping chapel train, a bodice of short sleeves with a scoop neckline trimmed in tiny pearls and from elbow to wrist matching gloves." The bouquet was twenty-four white roses and a single orchid. The bridesmaids and the maid of honor wore long pastel gowns. At the reception, two dinners were served, and Saka Acquaye and his African Ensemble supplied the music for a choreographed waltz.

Blay arrived a month later and went on to seduce one of the young women who had attended the wedding. Once again, just like when he was at school, everyone apart from Blay seemed to live in a glamorous, carefree world— enabled, of course, by their very wealthy families. For Blay—for Kerosene Boy—it was jarring, and instructive. He wanted what they had, and eventually, he would take it.

Blay seemed to all the world to be a gregarious, popular student. He could belt out the Penn fight song as loudly as any frat boy and was well liked on campus. Most of the other students didn't realize that he had never enrolled in the University of Pennsylvania. While Blay's roommates were studying and having lavish weddings, he was working. He had found a job at a private club in Center City, the Union League of Philadelphia.

The Union League was a venerable institution in a grand, redbrick building that took up a whole short block on South Broad Street near City Hall. In the early 1960s, it was one of the most exclusive places in the United States: a coven of old money and power brokers, where cigars were smoked and deals were done. It was a natural habitat for rich Republicans like John Mitchell, a lawyer who would become infamous as President Richard Nixon's attorney general. Blay worked as a busboy, clearing tables, cleaning dishes, listening closely. After about a year at the Union League, Blay was fired for unsatisfactory performance.

To everyone who met him, Blay looked like a regular teenager, a world away from home, learning to live in a new city for the first time. But Blay was not learning in university lecture halls. Instead, at dinner parties and at the

Union League, he studied what money and power looked like. He was learning how to be the center of attention in any room he walked into.

Later, Blay would put what he learned, and the people he met, to work in ways none of them could have dreamed of. Soon, he would have more money, and more power, than any of the students at the rooming house—and any of the old men at the Union League.

Like Prime Minister Kwame Nkrumah before him, Blay had found in Philadelphia what he had been missing: opportunity.

Chapter 3

Legends and Lies

1909 or 1912

The story of Kwame Nkrumah unfolds like a legend.

Nobody is exactly sure when he was born. It was in a village called Nkroful, which was a two-hour drive west of Takoradi. His mother, Elizabeth Nyaniba, remembered it was September, around the time of the Kundum Festival. She kept track of Nkrumah's age by the number of Kundum Festivals since his birth.

Decades later, when Nkrumah became the leader of Ghana, he was writing his autobiography, and he tried to figure out the exact date of his birth. He asked his mother, who said she remembered two major events.

The first was his grandmother's death. Nyaniba had been in labor around the time Nkrumah's grandmother was being buried: she remembered hearing drums the entire time. Most of the family was at the grave, so few people noticed the commotion when she gave birth. The baby showed no signs of life. Nyaniba thought he was dead and started mourning all over again. News of the stillborn infant quickly reached the funeral. Her family rushed to the house where the baby lay.

It looked like he was not breathing, so they tried to make him cry by clashing cymbals and making loud noises. When that did not work, they realized they had to help him inhale. Someone used a banana to gently open the baby's mouth and throat, and he finally coughed and drew breath. They handed him back kicking and screaming to Nyaniba. Nkrumah's grandmother had died in 1912: that was one possible date for his birth.

But there was another story. The second thing Nyaniba remembered was a shipwreck, which happened when Nkrumah was a toddler, and the family had moved west along the coast, closer to Half Assini and the border with Côte d'Ivoire. Late at night, a gigantic cargo ship called the *Bakana* got caught in heavy surf just off the coast. The storm tossed it closer and closer to the shore, driving its propeller into the seabed until it was lodged in five feet of sand. It came to rest about a mile offshore, near the mouth of the river Ama Azule.

In the evenings, when the family sat around the fire, Nkrumah would ask to hear the story about the ship, over and over again. That fateful night, Nyaniba would tell him, the God of one river, Ama Azule, decided to visit the Goddess of the next river, Awianialuanu. The God needed a ship for the journey, so he took the *Bakana*. "Look, son, how the boat he chose for the journey is slowly being dragged closer and closer to the mouth of his river." After the ship was wrecked, she said, people would see the lights of the *Bakana*, seemingly setting out to sea, night after night. The *Bakana* sank in 1913. If Nkrumah was three or four then, that would mean he was born around 1909.

To this day, Nkrumah has two dates of birth, from two different stories. And as Nkrumah became more prominent, the stories about him multiplied.

IN 1935, NKRUMAH left Ghana for Lincoln University in Pennsylvania, about fifty miles from Philadelphia. He had been working as a teacher to save for his tuition, but his savings and some money he borrowed were barely enough for his passage to America. By the time he arrived, he had about two hundred dollars to his name.

While he was a student, Nkrumah visited Philadelphia with a friend, but they had no money for lodgings. They had planned to pass the night on the wooden benches at Thirtieth Street Station, but they were immediately hassled by the police. So Nkrumah and his friend walked to a nearby park, and as they finally fell asleep, it began to rain. It was miserable. Nkrumah was homesick. "To sleep under the stars in my native Africa was, in spite of the raiding mosquitoes, a far happier prospect than sleeping out in the cities of America," he later wrote.

At Lincoln University, Nkrumah was always short of money. To pay his way, he labored. At school, he charged a dollar apiece to write book reports in sociology and economics. He also tried to get work at the Hershey Chocolate Company. He thought that he would be a good candidate because much of the cocoa they used came from Ghana. Instead, they sent him out through the back door, without a job. He had more success at the Sun Shipbuilding & Dry Dock Company in Chester, Pennsylvania, which hired him for the graveyard shift. Sometimes it was so cold Nkrumah's hands would stick to the steel. In winter, he worked dressed in every stitch of clothing he possessed. When his shift was over, he slept for a few hours, then went back to studying. It nearly killed him. One morning, Nkrumah woke up in an oxygen tent at a nearby hospital: he had contracted pneumonia.

During university vacations, Nkrumah sometimes stayed with a friend in New York, up in Harlem. To make money, every morning they would go down to Fulton Fish Market near the Brooklyn Bridge to buy seafood wholesale and spend the rest of the day on a corner uptown, trying to sell it.

When Nkrumah needed an evening's entertainment, he would go to revivalist meetings. His favorite was the International Peace Mission Movement of the Reverend Major Jealous Divine. You could get a haircut for ten cents and a good chicken dinner for half a buck. "Poverty and need drive one to surprising ends," Nkrumah later wrote. Father Divine was one of the great preachers of the twentieth century. He believed in his own divinity, civil rights, and good food, which he subsidized through grocery stores and restaurants. These had sustained countless people, ever since the Depression. Father Divine baptized hundreds of people at a time with a fire hose. Nkrumah was fascinated. But mostly, he was grateful for the haircuts and hot meals. Father Divine's preaching was less captivating.

Some evenings, Nkrumah did not have a friend to stay with, so he would sleep on the subway. He would buy a five-cent ticket and spend the night riding back and forth between Harlem and Brooklyn, waking up to change trains and sleeping when he could.

Nkrumah graduated from Lincoln in 1939. He took a position as an assistant lecturer at the college and joined the theological seminary. At the same time, he enrolled at the University of Pennsylvania and moved to Philadelphia. He hoped to save money by doing two graduate degrees at the same time. On Sundays, Nkrumah preached in Black churches. He learned how to hold people spellbound, how to give them hope, and how to inspire belief in a better world.

Nkrumah started to realize that America was built to keep certain people poor. He endured segregation at his jobs, on buses, in restaurants, and in public. He traveled below the Mason-Dixon line. A white American waiter refused to serve him water in Baltimore. "When I compared this racial segregation with the modernity and advancement of the country it made my heart sink." It was all so familiar.

In Philadelphia, Nkrumah saw the many ways in which people resisted. People—Black Americans especially—were boundlessly kind. The city was still reeling from the effects of the Depression. Nkrumah would see people rummaging through trash cans, searching for something to eat, and think that were it not for the generosity of his landlady, he would probably be doing the same. Nkrumah started to think, a lot, about what it truly meant to be free.

In 1945, Nkrumah left America, sailing from New York to Britain. As he looked up at the Statue of Liberty, it seemed as if it were bidding him farewell. "A mist covered my eyes. 'You have opened my eyes to the true meaning of liberty,' I thought. 'I shall never rest until I have carried your message to Africa.'"

NKRUMAH SPENT JUST two years in London. He had enrolled at Gray's Inn to study law, and University College London for philosophy, but would not complete the degrees. Instead, from the day he arrived, he was drawn into politics: the writer George Padmore picked him up from Euston Station and took him straight to a meeting.

Nkrumah spent much of his time with friends such as Joe Appiah, who also studied law and was regularly to be found at Speakers' Corner in Hyde

Park, telling everyone within earshot that the British Empire's days were numbered. Nkrumah had contrarian, antiestablishment sensibilities, and he reveled in them. He would take great pleasure in running down the steps of Holborn Underground station with the rush hour crowd, and sitting in a tube carriage surrounded by businessmen in bowler hats reading the *Daily Telegraph*, the *Times*, and the *Manchester Guardian*. Slowly, and with several flourishes, he would open the only British newspaper he could stand to read: the Communist Party's *Daily Worker*. He spent his free time in working-class cafés in Camden Town, nursing a single cup of tea for hours and debating the other patrons or, if it was cold, walking around London in search of lumps of coal dropped from merchants' lorries.

At the Fifth Pan-African Congress in Manchester, Nkrumah met and became firm friends with the American scholar and activist W. E. B. Du Bois. Together, they wrote declarations asserting "the determination of colonial peoples to be free" and condemning "the monopoly of capital and the use of private wealth and industry for personal profits alone." Because of this, British authorities began monitoring Nkrumah and his associates closely while actual threats slipped through the cracks: at the time, several high-ranking members of the British intelligence and diplomatic services were working for the Soviet Union. The methods British intelligence employed were not subtle. More than once, Nkrumah and Appiah arrived at their office to find it had been ransacked, their files strewn about. The building was a few steps away from a police station, and the police offered absolutely no help. "We went and reported the matter," Appiah wrote. "The sergeant's only comment was 'Curious, ain't it?'" The sergeant knew exactly who had broken in.

IN 1947, A man named Ebenezer Ako-Adjei wrote to offer Nkrumah a job. They knew each other from Lincoln University; Ako-Adjei's room had been opposite Nkrumah's. After graduating from Lincoln, Ako-Adjei studied at Columbia and the London School of Economics, and qualified as a lawyer. He returned to the Gold Coast in 1947 and became one of the first members of a political party called the United Gold Coast Convention. It had been founded by wealthy Nzema merchants and politicians, and it was dedicated—mostly—to getting rid of the British. The party needed a general secretary. Nkrumah accepted.

Nkrumah left Britain soon after, on a boat sailing from Liverpool. At the docks, he was questioned for a long time. The authorities seemed thrilled that he was going back home, instead of fomenting revolution in London cafés. But they were concerned about his plans.

Nkrumah anticipated the same treatment at Takoradi Harbor. When he arrived, a stern-looking immigration officer examined his passport, then motioned for Nkrumah to follow him. Nkrumah was sure he was about to disappear forever. But once everyone was out of earshot, the immigration officer's demeanor changed entirely. He shook Nkrumah's hand enthusiastically. They had heard all about him, he said—they had heard about the people planning to wrest their country back from the British.

The first thing Nkrumah did was find a telephone and call a distinguished barrister named Robert Samuel Blay. (No relation to our man, though our man would soon muddy those waters.) R. S. Blay had been born in the Nzema district; after he graduated from the University of London in 1926, he went straight back to Ghana, where he eschewed his destiny—to be a dutiful colonial administrator—and became the third person to join the United Gold Coast Convention. R. S. Blay drove Nkrumah from the port to his home village, to see his mother for the first time in more than a decade.

The beginning of Nkrumah's life was shrouded in legends. The rest of his life, and his legacy, would be choked by lies. And no one would tell more lies about Kwame Nkrumah than John Kolorah Blay.

DURING THE SECOND World War, millions of people from across the empire helped Britain fight for freedom—the same freedom Britain had stolen from them. After the war, the servicemen who won freedom and democracy for the rest of the world would return home, ready to take it for themselves.

The servicemen of the Gold Coast—around sixty-five thousand—fought bravely and became some of the most highly decorated soldiers of the Second World War. Officially, their victories were celebrated. In 1945, a memorandum from the Colonial Office in London triumphantly stated: "They defended British West Africa from attack from Vichy territory, helped take Madagascar, and went to the Middle East as Pioneers and to the Far East to fight Japan." But those servicemen were also paid a pittance—British soldiers who served alongside them were shocked by how "underpaid" they were. They were housed in inferior quarters, fed truly disgusting chop, and were arbitrarily punished in ways that one serviceman said "looked like hell."

There was even a ban on African officers in the Royal West African Frontier Force. To justify this, a British colonel asked a serviceman, R. M. Asante, to write a letter that stated Africans did not have the qualities required of officers. Asante refused to do this, because it was a lie. He remembered that during one battle, he had seen a British officer run away from his platoon, "panting for breath and shouting for whisky," while an African soldier took charge, bringing the surviving troops back safely. "We didn't like the way they were treating us," wrote one Ghanaian soldier. "So there we even decided to do something for ourselves when we came back."

After the war ended, servicemen who had been ready to lay down their lives for British independence discovered that independence for themselves, and their families, and their countries was still out of the question—and the full machinery of colonial repression was there to make sure no one forgot that.

Veterans returned home to Ghana to learn that the British also intended to cheat them out of their pensions. They organized boycotts and parades. Their protests overlapped with several other campaigns for independence, including one mounted by the United Gold Coast Convention. On February 28, 1948, a group of veterans marched toward Osu Castle in Accra to deliver a petition to the governor. Colonial police officers tried to turn them back, but they declined: they had the right to demonstrate. The police opened fire. Three veterans—Sergeant Cornelius Francis Adjetey, Corporal Patrick Attipoe, and Private Odartey Lamptey—were killed.

News of the murders spread around Accra. In what seemed like minutes, there were protests everywhere. The United Gold Coast Convention had not planned the veterans' march, but colonial officials had the party's leaders arrested at gunpoint anyway. They were initially taken to a prison in

Kumasi, but campaigners led by a young radical named Krobo Edusei made very public plans to free them. The British had to move the party leaders north to Tamale, where, Nkrumah remembered, their bus was met by weeping protestors.

Colonial officials blamed the unrest on communist incitement, rather than three veterans being murdered for asking for their pensions. The British concluded that they needed more spies: the Special Branch of the Gold Coast Constabulary. Special Branch's activities were so grubby that colonial officials who received their reports were directed to destroy them "by fire" and to "complete and return" a certificate confirming the destruction. Even after independence, Special Branch would forever be defined by its origins: an organization founded to repress people, under the guise of keeping them safe. (Special Branch was not set up to investigate actual crimes. In later years, our man would take full advantage of this.) But the harder colonial officials tried to suppress the protests, the larger the protests grew.

"Accra," Nkrumah wrote, "became the scene of persecution. At this period a number of people disappeared and were never accounted for."

In 1951, Nkrumah was once again in prison. While in jail, he stood for election as the leader of a newly created political entity called the Convention People's Party. The party was funded largely by the women who ran the trade in commodities at Accra's markets, and in particular by the queen of the flour trade, Rebecca Naa Dedei Aryeetey. Aryeetey would be one of the party's biggest donors. Because of women like her, Nkrumah did not have to worry about the mucky business of raising money for the struggle for independence. To the enormous embarrassment of the British, his party won thirty-four of the thirty-eight seats in the country's assembly.

Soon after the election, the prison warden sent for Nkrumah. He was a free man and had an hour to pack up. It took Nkrumah only a few seconds to gather his possessions: pencil stubs and some sheets of toilet paper he had used to smuggle messages to supporters outside. He told the warden he was ready to leave immediately.

News of Nkrumah's release had spread rapidly. People flocked to the prison gates to see him. Nkrumah had never seen such a dense crowd; everyone wanted to get as close to him as they could. "I was too bewildered to do anything but stand and stare." Nkrumah was hoisted shoulder-high and carried to a car. He became the head of Ghana's government later that day.

LATER THAT YEAR, Lincoln University conferred an honorary doctor of laws degree on Nkrumah. It had been just six years since he had left Pennsylvania. He went on a brief, triumphant tour of his old haunts. He was given the key to the city of Philadelphia. He visited his former landlady, Effie Borum, who had kept him fed. "Nkrumah appeared at her home about midnight, kissed her, gave her $100, saying: 'Mom, I can't pay you for all you've done.'" *Jet* magazine reported that Nkrumah "told her that he was 'going to raise hell when he got home,' and that 'one day he would bring freedom to his country or die.'" From his room at the luxurious Bellevue-Stratford Hotel, high above the city, Nkrumah thought about the night he had tried to sleep on the benches at Thirtieth Street Station.

Chapter 4

One Big Cocktail Party

1957

The Gold Coast won independence on March 6, 1957. Nkrumah had spent the last six years raising hell, just as he had promised. While outwardly supportive of independence, the British had sabotaged him at every turn. Informants reported his every move to the security services. Special Branch kept twenty-eight of the thirty-seven members of the Legislative Assembly under surveillance. His old friends, such as George Padmore in London, had their mail opened. As independence drew closer, the British did everything they could to rewrite history, whitewashing centuries of looting and exploitation. When Nkrumah planned a speech to set the record straight—with, a panicked intelligence officer wrote, in a top-secret memo, "two whole pages which dealt with such items as the slave trade and were in remarkably poor taste"—officials were so alarmed that the British governor was woken up in the middle of the night. Even in its dying days, colonialism seeped into everything and tried to poison it. But now, in spite of it all, Ghana had won.

"At long last, the battle has ended!" Nkrumah told a cheering crowd in Accra. "And thus Ghana, your beloved country, is free forever."

The early days were like a gigantic cocktail party. There were grand balls in the State House, where Nkrumah, Nelson Mandela, and Oliver Tambo danced and drank far into the night with W. E. B. Du Bois, Ralph Bunche, and Martin Luther King Jr. Nkrumah wanted everyone to know that the world had changed. June Milne, who edited many of his books, noted that "Nkrumah saw to it that King was accorded the same VIP treatment as Vice-President Richard Nixon, the official representative of the American government."

Genoveva Marais met Nkrumah at one of the independence balls. She was from a wealthy South African family and had been recruited to work at the Ghanaian Ministry of Education while studying at Columbia University. She looked like a 1950s spy, straight out of central casting, complete with beehive. When she met Nkrumah, she was wearing an evening gown she had modeled in New York, at a fashion show for President Harry Truman's campaign. It was so tight that she was dizzy and could barely curtsey.

Marais and Nkrumah soon became close friends. "This man's friendship was dear to me, but not for the usual reasons," she wrote. "I was alone, in a job I thoroughly enjoyed, and gained before ever I had come to Ghana, and needed no special strings to be pulled."

Hans Buser, a Swiss salesman who spent time with Nkrumah and Marais, remembered meeting Marais for the first time. She breezed into his showroom to collect her government car, an Opel Rekord. Marais took one look at the Opel, then another look at the Chevrolet next to it. She told Buser: "I am used to big cars—I'll take the Chevrolet." The Chevrolet cost twice as much as her government allowance but, she told Buser, "Daddy in Bloemfontein" would pay the difference. As negotiations were ongoing, a steady stream of Buser's colleagues trooped into the car showroom to gawk at her.

With Marais, Nkrumah could relax and let his guard down. They played tennis. He tended roses. For a while, anything seemed possible.

After independence, Nkrumah asked George Padmore to come to Ghana to advise him on African affairs. In December 1957, Padmore and his wife, Dorothy Pizer, moved into a house surrounded by bougainvillea in Accra. Padmore immediately started organizing a conference of independent African states and supporting liberation movements across the continent. His office helped create the Bureau of African Affairs, where liberation fighters and students who had been forced into exile by their own countries could live, work, and learn. Accra soon became a refuge for liberation movements across

Africa. "Padmore," the journalist Cameron Duodu wrote, "took care of Africa, enabling Nkrumah to devote himself to Ghana." Unsurprisingly, the CIA took considerable interest in what Padmore and Nkrumah were up to.

JOHN KOLORAH BLAY would tell the story of 1957, again and again, in the decades to come. As Blay told it, almost immediately after independence, Nkrumah began sending Ghana's gold out of the country in secret. Stored in the vaults of Swiss banks, it became the nucleus of the Oman Ghana Trust Fund.

Just after independence, there really was a plot to take Ghana's gold reserves out of the country. It did involve secret files, double-dealing, and betrayal. But it was not a plot made by Nkrumah. It was made by the British.

At independence, Ghana's gold reserves were held in London. With Britain's economy still struggling to emerge from the shadow of the Second World War, the British depended on Ghanaian gold to prop up the value of their currency. But in May 1957, Nkrumah and his cabinet began to discuss bringing Ghana's gold home. Nkrumah wanted to establish a truly national Ghanaian gold reserve.

At the time, the deputy governor of the Bank of Ghana was Douglas F. Stone, who had been seconded from the Bank of England. One of Stone's responsibilities—unknown to Nkrumah—was feeding top-secret information on Ghana's financial plans to the British government. When Stone heard about Nkrumah's proposed independent gold reserve, he immediately alerted his handlers.

"Stone tells me in confidence," wrote a British diplomat in Accra, "that the Prime Minister and his chief lieutenants—[Kojo] Botsio and [Komla] Gbedemah—are in favour of Ghana retaining her gold, all of which is exported to London at present, and in 1957 was worth some £9.6m."

The British were horrified. Without Ghana's gold, Britain's currency might have to be devalued. Stone's report—with "Keep his name out of it" scribbled next to his name—was soon the subject of urgent discussion across London. "It would be most important not to reveal that we have had this information from him, since he is in the employment of the Ghanaian government," noted a secret memo to Britain's chancellor of the exchequer.

The plot to get Ghana's gold out of the country was, in fact, a very British affair.

ON NEW YEAR'S Eve 1957, Nkrumah married Fathia Rizk, who had grown up in Cairo. It was a political marriage. Rizk was a glamorous figure who could not speak any Ghanaian languages, while Nkrumah could not speak Arabic. The wedding was a simple ceremony at the Castle, with just a few guests: some government ministers and Nkrumah's mother, Elizabeth Nyaniba. Before Rizk left her homeland, the Egyptian president, Gamal Abdel Nasser, had summoned her to ask if she was sure she wanted to marry Nkrumah. She replied, "I would like to go and marry this anti-colonial leader." She had read his autobiography, and she was impressed. "I know of his trials and tribulations, of his struggles during his student days in America and Britain." Still, none of this prepared her for what was to come.

President Kwame Nkrumah and Fathia Nkrumah in 1963.

Kwame Nkrumah had pulled together all the nations that made up the Gold Coast—each with its own distinct history and culture and language—and united them in a common cause: independence. People had banded together to give the new nation of Ghana an identity, one that could grow beyond four hundred years of mourning.

But Nkrumah's Ghana was fragile. From the moment independence was declared, it was under attack, from without and from within. Corrupt businessmen, war criminals, and spies from all over the world descended on the country, looking to hide out or make a killing. They would find ready allies in some of Nkrumah's ministers, men who cared more about their own enrichment than the country they had founded and promised to serve. These men did not just steal money from Ghana—though they did plenty of that. They stole the dream of liberty that so many people had given their lives for. They stole the hope of a bright and prosperous future. And eventually, they would teach our man John Kolorah Blay everything they knew. Some of them would stand beside him for the rest of their lives.

When the party was over, the hangover would last for decades.

IN 1958, PRIME Minister Nkrumah and a delegation went on an American state visit. One of the stops was the Hershey Chocolate Company in Pennsylvania. Nkrumah arrived at the factory with his entourage. A red carpet was laid out, and the company officials were waiting to greet him. As the prime minister got out of his car, instead of walking straight down the red carpet, he turned to his secretary, Erica Powell, and said: "Do you know—about 15 years ago—I came to this very same factory, right here where I'm standing, hoping to find a job." He almost doubled over laughing.

In America, too, the vultures were circling. Hungry businessmen descended on Nkrumah's delegation, hoping to make a quick fortune from the new country. Powell noted that almost everybody she encountered during the state visit claimed to be an old friend of Nkrumah. When the delegation arrived in New York, it seemed like the whole city wanted to see him. Some people phoned, some wrote letters, some arrived at the Waldorf Astoria hotel in person, unannounced. A few of them actually were friends of Nkrumah; the vast majority were opportunists or con men. Powell kept as many of them from seeing him as she could—though that did not stop countless people telling stories for decades about their intimate conversations and confidential business deals with the prime minister. Nkrumah himself, meanwhile, was growing tired of being feted with big dinners and just wanted a hamburger with ketchup and a Pepsi-Cola. The Waldorf didn't serve hamburgers, but the Secret Service knew a place.

The last stop of the state visit was Chicago. "One of Chicago's most spectacular welcomes" awaited Nkrumah. Cheering crowds lined the entire route from the airport to the Drake Hotel. As rain fell, in a light drizzle, some, notably the older women and men, were openly weeping. "Others stood as if stunned," Powell wrote, "unable to believe in miracles, that they would ever live as witness to such honour bestowed on one of their own colour."

In Chicago, Nkrumah was whisked from one grand hotel to another. Mayor Richard J. Daley kept him well away from the crowds. Minnie Curtwright, a retired nurse, told the *Chicago Defender* that Nkrumah "should not be kept away from the people who need his inspiration most. Preparations should have been made long ago for a mammoth mass meeting for him where he could tell us what the future holds for Africa and her descendants who are suffering in foreign soil."

NKRUMAH WOULD LATER write about how empty much of Ghana was when he came to power, and how much had to be built to make it a modern country. Hundreds of years of wars and colonialism had destroyed almost everything.

Ghana was relatively rich for a new country. Newspapers across the world reported that the country had hundreds of millions of dollars in its reserves at independence. But as Nkrumah would soon discover, those reserves were not what they seemed to be.

In the decade before independence, Britain siphoned off more than £150 million (more than $400 million) from Ghana. Officials claimed that it was being held in reserve in London. By contrast, total British investment in Ghana during this period was £1.5 million, or $4 million, less than 1 percent of the funds extracted from the country.

After independence, Nkrumah and his finance minister, Komla Gbedemah, wanted to know where the money was. The British were evasive. So Nkrumah sent Gbedemah to London to investigate. When Gbedemah found out what had happened to Ghana's reserves, he was horrified. The British had mismanaged Ghana's funds so badly that they had lost twelve million pounds, or thirty-three million dollars, on government securities alone. The reserves of Ghana's Cocoa Marketing Board had lost another ten million pounds, or twenty-eight million dollars, about 25 percent of their value.

Almost all the remaining money was locked up in securities that would not mature for over a decade. Nkrumah and Gbedemah had been relying on those funds to finance development projects in Ghana. But because of Ghana's British accountant general, and the British Crown Agents who had handled the investments in London, the money that was supposed to build Ghana after independence was building Britain. It was as if the colonial era had never ended.

The story that Britain generously left Ghana with hundreds of millions was as much of a lie as the Oman Ghana Trust Fund.

Nkrumah and Gbedemah were furious—or, as the classified British files on the incident put it, "extremely cross." British civil servants scrambled to contain the damage. "It is true that the Ghana Government is not the only overseas government that has suffered in drops in the value of its investments in London," noted one British civil servant, in a secret memo. "But if they start blaming either the Crown Agents or expatriate officers for losses in the value of their sterling funds, this could have grave political consequences." Officials asked the Bank of England to help the Crown Agents cover the situation up, but the Bank concluded that the Agents' actions were "open to various criticisms which it might well be hard to refute. The alleged rejoinder—if only they [Ghana] had spent their reserves more slowly, it would have been all right—seems neither demonstrably true nor tactful to give to a newly independent country with big development needs."

So Britain decided to act as if nothing had happened. At the bottom of the Bank's letter, a scribbled note advised the government to write "a pretty candid and confidential letter to the [British] High Commissioner [in Accra], explaining why we think it would be impolitic to get into any argument and advising him to stonewall if the Ghanaians return to the charge." Civil servants were instructed to keep a close eye on the newspapers and report any coverage of the scandal immediately. "Nothing new has come out," one reported, with relief.

This would not be the last time the Crown Agents were embroiled in scandal. In 1977, the British government commissioned a report into the firm's activities. It revealed a pattern of "clear failures" going back years and "ill-advised and disastrous speculative involvements." The report concluded that the Crown Agents "lacked competence and good judgment" and that their activities represented "a most severe failure of public accountability." Criminal proceedings for corruption were brought against two employees.

Nkrumah and Gbedemah eventually succeeded in moving Ghana's remaining reserves out of the British government's grasp. The securities were gradually sold. But this parting perfidy—the colonizer's squandering of riches held in trust on behalf of the colonized—would later fuel a further betrayal of the people of Ghana: Blay-Miezah's story of the Oman Ghana Trust Fund.

The search for Ghana's lost reserves—complete with conspiracies, duplicitous bankers, and missing millions—was the truth that Blay-Miezah would later weave into his web of lies. Ghana's ancestral wealth had indeed been secretly shipped out of the country and lost in a mire of financial trickery.

As a Ghanaian government investigation into the affair concluded, "The main loss which the Government of Ghana had suffered through 'extravagance' arose out of the way its reserves had been invested in Colonial times by the United Kingdom government. In the interests of preserving good relations with the United Kingdom, the Government of Ghana had up to this point refrained from publicizing the fact that no less than £15 million of Ghana's reserves had been squandered by the United Kingdom." Where was the money? The British took it.

EVEN BEFORE INDEPENDENCE, Nkrumah's government had been making plans to build an entire nation's worth of infrastructure. To fund it, the government had focused on Ghana's biggest cash crop, cocoa. It invested in farm equipment and disease-resistant varieties that led to bumper crops while the price of cocoa was high. This had helped the government build the substantial reserves that Britain secretly frittered away. "Those who would judge us merely by the heights we have achieved," Nkrumah wrote, "would do well to remember the depths from which we started." The government built the Akosombo Dam, an enormous hydroelectric power plant on the River Volta. It built an aluminum smelter, a harbor, an industrial area and a brand-new city at Tema, sugar refineries, textile plants, railways, the Bui Dam, glass factories, printworks and presses, hotels, universities and hospitals, and schools across the country.

This was often a dirty business. Each project presented an opportunity for graft. Nkrumah's government was plagued by monumental levels of corruption. Ghana's institutions—holdovers from the colonial era—enabled a familiar style of looting everywhere. Nkrumah himself lived simply and did not take bribes. But that did not matter. Corrupt businessmen descended on his ministers with envelopes full of cash. While many indignantly refused the money, some, inevitably, succumbed.

Ghana became a magnet for all kinds of shady characters. Malcolm X remembered sitting in the dining room of his hotel in Accra, listening to Americans "discussing Africa's untapped wealth as though the African waiters had no ears." The United States and the Soviet Union had spent the last decade recruiting Nazi scientists. Many of the Nazis no one else wanted tried their luck in Ghana. Horst Schumann was a Nazi physician who had attempted to use X-rays to sterilize Jewish prisoners at Auschwitz. He had overseen tens of thousands of murders. He told foreign reporters that Nkrumah had appointed him as a senior medical officer in Ghana's National Health Service. Nkrumah had not.

After a certain point, you could say anything about Nkrumah, and people would believe you—especially if you painted him, Ghanaians, and Africans in general as greedy, short-sighted, and easy to manipulate. Nkrumah wrote extensively about his work, and much of what he did as a politician was well recorded, yet he came to be defined by the lies of other people. Those lies had one thing in common: they powered greed. People smuggled diamonds in Nkrumah's name. Dozens of opportunists, from all over the world, would simultaneously claim he had given them exclusive rights to the country's gold mines. The lies would, in time, swallow up the truth about who Nkrumah was and what he believed in.

OF ALL NKRUMAH'S ministers, few enabled more crooks and monsters than Krobo Edusei. John Kolorah Blay would transform from a small-time grifter to a man whose stories changed history, thanks in great part to Edusei's patronage. Edusei was a gregarious and popular member of cabinet. At a young age he had become an icon in the battle for independence; he had led the group of young rebels who in 1948 had publicized their plans to break Nkrumah and the United Gold Coast Convention leaders out of jail. Edusei was partly responsible for getting the Akan, Ghana's most populous and most powerful nation, to support Nkrumah. "Edusei was, for all these reasons and his obvious ruthless bravery, intensely popular," Genoveva Marais wrote. He became minister of the interior, and his power kept growing, along with his wealth. "When I receive my salary," Edusei said to *TIME* magazine, "am I expected to throw it into the sea?" Marais remembered that "Krobo used to say something like 'the line between myself and starvation is very long.'"

In 1957, Edusei introduced the Preventive Detention Act, which allowed the government to "imprison, without trial, any person suspected of activities prejudicial to the security of the State." When it was written into law, Edusei immediately started using it against his enemies. "I love power," Edusei said in an interview with the *Washington Post*. "Anybody who gives a speech to the discredit of the Government will be removed to a detention camp . . . Any civil servant or politician who plays the fool will be cut down at once."

Edusei liked to tell bawdy, boastful stories. He had one about the first time he was bribed (in a big hotel in London, someone handed him an envelope stuffed with ten-pound notes). He had one about his very first trip to London, before independence (he was released from prison, borrowed a fine suit, and before he knew it he was at a reception at Buckingham Palace, telling King George: "King, life is great! Two weeks ago I was cleaning out latrines in Kumasi Prison. And tonight, I'm having a drink with the King of England"). He also had one about his first visit to a London brothel (right after that audience with the king). Edusei was so charming, and so shameless, that he could get away with almost anything.

Soon after independence, Edusei started setting up meetings for a man named Michael Marion Emil Anacletus Pierre Savundranayagam, otherwise known as Emil Savundra. Savundra said that he wanted to invest a great deal of money into businesses in Ghana and needed government permits. But in fact he was a well-known swindler from Ceylon. He specialized in getting people to pay real money for fake things. Savundra would make deals to supply commodities, use those deals to get a line of credit with Swiss and Belgian banks, and then take the money and run. The commodities would never arrive. In 1950, he had made more than a million dollars from a fake deal to supply oil to China, and $750,000 on an imaginary cargo of rice. Whenever authorities got too close, Savundra would fake a heart attack and slip away.

In 1958, Savundra appeared in Ghana claiming to be a representative of a Colorado-based gold mining company called Camp Bird. But his reputation had preceded him. When Edusei tried to make introductions, other politicians recognized Savundra, publicly mocked him, and then had him deported. This did not stop Savundra (just like many other fortunate businessmen) from telling the British press that he had been granted the exclusive rights to all of Ghana's gold mines.

For months after Savundra's visit to Accra, whenever Edusei stepped into the Executive Chamber of Parliament, he was met with peals of laughter. By now, Joe Appiah, the lawyer and activist who had been one of Nkrumah's closest friends in London, was a leading member of the opposition. He had moved back to Ghana in 1954 to join Nkrumah's cabinet, then fallen out with Nkrumah. "Joe Appiah used to watch the entrance to Parliament House carefully," one journalist remembered, "and as soon as he spotted Krobo Edusei making his way into the House, would raise his arm, point to Edusei and shout: 'SAVUUUUU!'" The opposition knew what to do next. All together, they would answer: "SAVUUUUUNDRA!"

All this ended abruptly when most of the opposition, including Appiah, were jailed without charge, under Edusei's Preventive Detention Act. They were sent to Nsawam Prison. Edusei was not a subtle man. He grew so brazenly corrupt that Nkrumah eventually moved him to another post.

Edusei exhibited the same lack of subtlety in his personal affairs. He was frequently pictured in the society pages with a woman who was not his wife. When Mary Edusei grew tired of her husband's dalliances, she retired to the

The gold-plated bed bought by Mary Edusei.

family's home in London. It was nearby, in the window of Selfridges department store in March 1962, that Mary Edusei saw a gold-plated bed, with a gold canopy, upholstered with gilded brocade. And she had to have it.

A salesman at the store later told reporters that this had come as a surprise, because the bed itself was technically not for sale. It was the centerpiece of a furniture show that had been turned into part of the window display. The salesman, however, accompanied Mrs. Edusei into the display, where she sat on the bed to test its springs. The store was more than happy to take a check for the equivalent of $8,400 and deliver the bed to her home nearby in Mayfair.

Someone immediately tipped reporters off about the golden bed. When the news reached Accra, there were protests. Edusei made a big show of telling his wife to send the bed back at once. Instead, Mrs. Edusei invited a reporter to her home and sent her husband a very public message: "Every wife will know how I feel," she said, archly. "I am just a woman. I don't understand politics." She did not, she told the reporter, see her diamonds as often as she would have liked: they had to stay at the bank, because they might get stolen. But who, she said innocently, would steal a bed? "People may think I'm extravagant, but I can enjoy the bed every night."

Back in Accra, Krobo Edusei, for the first time in his career—and apparently his marriage—finally faced some consequences. He was stripped of his ministerial post and detained under the Preventive Detention Act, in Nsawam Prison. Later that year Nkrumah signed an order releasing members of several opposition parties detained by Edusei, including Joe Appiah.

Nkrumah miscalculated by assuming that politicians like Edusei were more patriotic than greedy. He filled his cabinet with ministers and advisers who had already made it clear where their priorities lay: with themselves. At the time it was expedient; he needed their support. But it was a fatal mistake. Every time a prominent minister got caught out, people lost a little more trust in the government. And it became a little easier to believe that everyone in power—especially Nkrumah—had to be on the take. Many of the people who had fought for independence by Nkrumah's side, like Appiah, were sickened.

"My hatred for the regime grew to such proportions," Appiah wrote, "that I was prepared now to risk everything I possessed in this world, including life itself, for the total destruction of this abominable Frankenstein monster that my poor country had created in all sweet innocence."

Chapter 5

Crooks and Heroes

1963–1966

In December 1963, Ghana's attorney general, Bashiru Kwaw-Swanzy, sent John Kolorah Blay to Nsawam Prison under the Preventive Detention Act.

Blay had returned to Ghana earlier that year. He told everyone he had just graduated from the University of Pennsylvania and was in Ghana briefly for some important business: he had to meet with President Nkrumah. Blay claimed to have had a prophetic dream: there was about to be an attempt on Nkrumah's life. There would be a shooting at the presidential palace at Flagstaff House.

Benjamin Forjoe was the feared, Israeli-trained director of Ghana's Special Branch. Forjoe would later claim that, after a 1963 meeting with Nkrumah at Flagstaff House, the president introduced him to a visitor to his office, John Kolorah Blay. This was not impossible—Nkrumah met countless people every day, and it was typical Ghanaian hospitality to make introductions. By 1963, Nkrumah's long-serving gatekeeper, June Milne, had been sidelined. Forjoe said that he gave Blay a place to stay for a couple of days, until he heard that Blay had been detained. Forjoe ought to have known about the detention earlier—the officers who detained Blay worked for him. In other versions of the story, Blay and Nkrumah never met. The security services concluded that Blay was either a threat or a kook, and he was not allowed anywhere near the president.

IN THE EARLY 1960s, the prices of Ghana's main exports, gold and cocoa, started plunging, which triggered a recession. Cocoa, which had sold for £500 ($1,400) a ton in 1954, fetched less than £100 ($280) a ton in 1965. Despite Ghana's industrial output more than doubling as a result of Nkrumah's investment, the budget deficit began to grow. Western countries were going out of their way to support the crooks who were looting the country—and to avoid supporting Nkrumah. "Intensive efforts," ran an American memo, "should be made through psychological warfare and other means to diminish support for Nkrumah within Ghana." The worst elements were about to win out: the country's hopes for a bright future would be swallowed up by lies, greed, and violence. It was terrible news for Ghana, but it was great news for John Kolorah Blay.

The American journalist Charles P. Howard, writing for the *Gazette and Daily* in York, Pennsylvania, realized just how much Ghana's economy was being hobbled when he tried to buy a radio in Accra. The British-owned "Kingsway stores, their U.T.C., and their other large trading operations absolutely bar certain Ghana manufactured goods from their shelves." Each one "refused to sell me a Ghana made radio," any furniture manufactured in Ghana, or even a Ghanaian bar of chocolate. "If Ghana is in economic distress, and it is not proven that it is, the people who are responsible for it are the Britains and the Americas [sic] who have dominated that economy and milked it of every last drop that they could extract."

The West German government said that Ghana's deficit was caused by "the careless expenditure policy of the Ghanaian government." Behind the scenes, West Germany's actual concern was that Ghana planned to cut the deficit by importing fewer products from countries like West Germany.

The Germans had been propping up one crooked businessman in particular: a Romanian named Noe Drevici. With the help of Krobo Edusei, Drevici was awarded government contracts to build "a flour mill, a vegetable oil plant, a fish cannery, and fish meal factory and a tin can manufacturing plant," the Associated Press reported. German authorities considered Drevici a crook, but an able one, and that was all that mattered. Each new contract he signed, no matter how suspect, was celebrated by German diplomats. Eventually Drevici had signed so many contracts that other governments started to worry he was engaged in a single-handed corrupt takeover of Ghana's economy—which would, of course, stop them from doing the same thing. The most controversial of Drevici's projects was a chocolate factory in Tema. It was a chance for Ghana, the world's biggest cocoa supplier, to finally produce industrial quantities of chocolate. But like the rest of his projects, the plant never really got off the ground—and the only person who benefited from it was Drevici himself. It would take many years, and Drevici's departure, for the factory to begin producing chocolate.

Nkrumah made the same mistake, over and over again. He concerned himself with issues more lofty than the day-to-day management of the economy, trusting that his advisers, and the ministers he appointed, were doing their jobs and being honest when they briefed him. Some were doing everything in their power to keep the country going. Others were not. And it takes only a few people in high places, who care about enriching themselves above all, to bring an entire country down.

Kwesi Amoako-Atta, an economist and former deputy governor of the Bank of Ghana, was minister of finance in early 1965. He was as incompetent as he was venal: he would go on to lend his credibility to John Kolorah Blay's scam. By February 11, 1965, Amoako-Atta realized that the economy was heading for disaster. He let the country's reserves dwindle to less than a million dollars before announcing the news in a cabinet meeting. Within weeks, the government would be unable to pay its bills. After they heard the news, Nkrumah and the rest of the cabinet sat in silence for fifteen minutes.

The government appealed for foreign support to stop Ghana plunging into a crisis. Help was not forthcoming. People in Ghana began to starve. But for many countries, this was less important than the opportunity to undermine Nkrumah. A weak Ghana was easily exploitable. "Other Western countries (including France) have been helping to set up the situation by ignoring Nkrumah's pleas for economic aid," a staffer from the United States National

Security Council wrote, in a memo that was read by President Lyndon Baines Johnson. "All in all, looks good."

GHANA'S NATURAL RESOURCES were still almost exclusively controlled by British and American companies. Nkrumah began to talk about national- izing gold mines and letting the Soviet Union in. Western companies, which had been making easy profits for years, stood to lose a fortune. The British and American governments did not like Nkrumah's growing closeness to the Soviets or his threats to their corporations' profits. They paid opposing factions to undermine him. Then they paid for assassination attempts.

There had been attempts to assassinate Nkrumah since at least 1954, when the Special Branch uncovered intelligence that a bomb would be placed at his home at Kokomlemle in Accra, but did not tell him or intervene. And in 1962, Ghana's minister of foreign affairs, Ebenezer Ako-Adjei—who had known Nkrumah since they were both at Lincoln—was imprisoned after being accused of involvement in planning one of the ugliest attempts on Nkrumah's life.

Nkrumah was traveling back to Accra from a meeting with the president of Burkina Faso. His motorcade stopped in the village of Kulungugu near the border, where children holding bunches of flowers had lined up at the roadside to welcome him. As one of the children, a little girl named Eliza- beth Asantewaa, approached Nkrumah to offer him a bouquet, one of the president's aides heard ticking. He threw Nkrumah to the ground, jumping on top of him, just as the bomb exploded. Nkrumah and his aide were hurt but survived. Elizabeth Asantewaa lost one of her legs, and many of the other children were horrifically injured. After the attack, Nkrumah visited Asantewaa in hospital, sat by her bedside, and wept. Maya Angelou, who was living in Accra, wrote that "the springs burst and the happy clock stopped running" after Kulungugu. It seemed that "the spirit of Ghana was poisoned by the news."

Ako-Adjei joined Edusei and Blay in Nsawam Prison.

Blay had been making the most of his time there. By the time he arrived, Nsawam was packed to the rafters with Ghana's biggest men. Along with Edusei, and many of the opposition, were a number of Ghana's

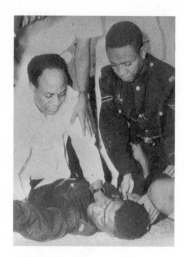

Nkrumah checking the pulse of Superintendent Salifu Dagarti, who died shielding him during an assassination attempt.

most distinguished politicians. Some were there under the Preventive Detention Act. Others—like Ako-Adjei—had been accused of involvement in attempts to assassinate the president.

Some inmates at Nsawam were not crooks but heroes. J. B. Danquah, a brilliant scholar and lawyer, was regarded as one of Ghana's founding fathers. In 1960, he stood against Nkrumah in the presidential election. In 1964, an attempt on Nkrumah's life at Flagstaff House killed a bodyguard named Salifu Dagarti. In the aftermath, Danquah was sent to Nsawam under the Preventive Detention Act. "I find myself," Danquah wrote to Nkrumah, "locked up at Nsawam Prison in a cell of about six by nine feet, without a writing or reading desk, without a dining table, without a bed, or a chair or any form of seat, and compelled to eat my food squatting on the same floor where two blankets and a cover are spread for me on the hard cement to sleep on." Danquah was allowed out of his cell for only a few minutes a day. Otherwise, "I am required to sleep or keep lying down on the blankets and a small pillow for the whole 24 hours of the day and night," he wrote, "with my talents, such as I possess, going waste." Danquah would die in Nsawam in February 1965.

In Nsawam, Blay lived and ate with people whom he would not otherwise have got anywhere near. Blay heard their stories. He befriended them. Just like when he was a child, he picked up the details that no one else noticed: how a powerful man should sit, how he should nod his head, how he should take up space in a room—even if that room was a prison cell. Soon, Blay started to look like one of the big men.

John Kolorah Blay walked into Nsawam prison a nobody. But day by day he was growing into a new role, one he would play for the rest of his life: he was no longer Kerosene Boy in Takoradi or the poor kid in Philadelphia.

Within a few years, many of the big men in the prison, Nkrumah's former ministers—and even the attorney general who sent him to prison, Kwaw-Swanzy—would be working for him. Our man was somebody special.

JOE APPIAH WAS RELEASED from Nsawam. His telephone was tapped, and he was followed wherever he went. One night, Nkrumah invited his old friend to Flagstaff House. Nkrumah was increasingly isolated: many of the people who had fought alongside him for decades, such as George Padmore, had died. Others were in prison. "Joe, Ghana is in pieces," Appiah remembered Nkrumah saying. "My people have let me down; they fed me on lies and enriched themselves. This is not the country you and I dreamt of and fought for. I should have listened to you long ago. Joe, it's never too late to mend." But none of the plans Nkrumah and Appiah made that night, to set things right, ever made it to the light of day. The president was about to be deposed.

"It is," wrote the British high commissioner, A. W. Snelling, "in the interests of Britain that Nkrumah should cease to rule Ghana." On the instructions of the prime minister, British officials deluged Ghana with propaganda attacking Nkrumah and his advisers, in the name of the "Freedom for Africa Movement," which did not exist. "For your own sake, Kwame, we tell you to beware," one pamphlet threatened. When Nkrumah published a book exposing the dirty secrets of American businesses in Africa, it was, according to one State Department staffer, "the straw that broke the camel's back."

"The plotters are keeping us briefed," wrote a staffer at the United States National Security Council. "[The] State [Department] thinks we're more on the inside than the British." The CIA had been determined to topple Nkrumah for some time: officers even considered raiding the Chinese embassy in Accra in blackface, in the hope that this would somehow trigger a coup d'état. Instead, the decision was made to fund disgruntled local military officers and policemen.

On February 24, 1966, when Nkrumah was on his way to China, his young family woke to the sound of artillery fire and explosions. They could hear the lions at Accra Zoo roaring. The children were terrified. Fathia Nkrumah told them not to be afraid, over and over again. She called the Egyptian embassy. Just after she put the telephone down, the lines were cut. Outside, there was a pitched battle for Flagstaff House going on. Military and police officers had staged a coup d'état.

Eventually, Egypt sent a plane to evacuate Fathia and Nkrumah's children. Their bags were confiscated on the way to the airport. The soldiers even took family photographs, letters, and souvenirs. Nkrumah's family were ordered to leave Ghana with just the clothes they were wearing. Before they were allowed on the plane, they were all interrogated at police headquarters. Fathia, her son remembered, "seemed fearless, berating the soldiers and reproaching them for their ingratitude." The family fled to Egypt.

Hundreds died, and Accra was turned upside down. After dark, the streets were deserted, patrolled by jumpy soldiers in armored cars. Anyone who resisted "was brutally shot," Nkrumah wrote. "Women, children and old people were driven out into the streets. Many of the women were raped. A woman with a child on her back was shot, and both mother and child were thrown to the ground from a three-storey [sic] window."

Government buildings were looted—some randomly, others systematically. "At Flagstaff House, troops dashed from one room to another, smashing windows and furniture, tearing up papers, ripping telephones from desks, and destroying anything they could lay their hands on. My own office was singled out for special treatment." Thousands of documents were disappeared. The home where Nkrumah had been born was razed. His mother, Elizabeth Nyaniba, was held by soldiers for nine days. They wanted her to say that Nkrumah was not her son and was not Ghanaian. She refused. "When I was released," she later said, it was "with only the clothes I had on. The possessions I gained over 80 years' time were all gone."

The Americans were delighted. When the secretary of state, Dean Rusk, was told the news, a member of his staff saw him break "into an ear-splitting grin. I've never seen him look so happy." Charles P. Howard attended a State Department briefing where officials "made no attempt to cover up their great satisfaction over the over-throw [sic] of African Governments through military coups here lately, and reported openly to their hearers that 'now the climate for American investors in Africa is better.'" "Nkrumah was doing more to undermine our interests than any other black African," an aide wrote in a memo to President Johnson. The new regime, the memo exulted, was "almost pathetically pro-Western."

THE MEMBERS OF Ghana's new ruling junta called themselves the National Liberation Council. The junta raided every office they could think of. They gathered up Nkrumah's papers, searching for evidence of corruption that they could use to retroactively justify the coup d'état. Many of those documents eventually disappeared into the maw of the military base at Burma Camp. Some were never seen again, and others would end up for sale. In just a few chaotic days, much of Ghana's history was destroyed, so that it could be rewritten.

The junta began to release prisoners held under the Preventive Detention Act. Blay was a free man, along with the corrupt politicians and crooked businessmen he had been imprisoned with. Within a few years, they would stop mentioning their jail terms. After a few more years, streets would be named in their honor, statues would be erected, and their faces would be emblazoned on the currency. If they ever mentioned their time in Nsawam prison, they would blame it on the people around them or on Nkrumah himself. They would teach Ghana to make heroes out of crooks by making crooks out of heroes.

THE NATIONAL LIBERATION Council soon discovered that the foreigners who had paid them to upend their own country did not intend to fund them any further and that it was difficult to run a country without an economy. They sold off many state-run corporations and abandoned infrastructure projects. "Foreign multinationals, which had been held firmly at arm's length by Nkrumah, swiftly took control of much of the production sector." "It may come as a shock" to the council, Howard wrote, "but the Americans, the British and their associates didn't use them to overthrow Nkrumah, and thus take over the Ghana economy, to turn around and give it back to them. It isn't like that." "The country," the council admitted, "is on the brink of national bankruptcy." This was awkward: the council had promised things would get better once Nkrumah was deposed, and things soon got much worse. Factories were closed. Building sites were abandoned. For some, it would be decades before work began again. Others were shuttered forever. Ghana's economy ground to a halt.

The junta blamed Nkrumah. They claimed that he had bankrupted the country, not by paying for infrastructure, but by physically emptying the treasury of cash and gold. They claimed that Nkrumah had fled to China with suitcases full of gold bars, that he had eight mistresses, that he owned houses in Cairo and Rabat, and that his five- and six-year-old children had Swiss bank accounts. That he had lied about attending Lincoln University and the University of Pennsylvania. The junta promised they would bring home the fortune salted away by the former president. They also threatened to kidnap Nkrumah and bring him back to Ghana to stand trial.

Investigators would look for proof of Nkrumah's secret fortune for decades. They found nothing.

Across the world, newspapers from Ghana's *Daily Graphic* to the *New York Times* devoted dozens of column inches to increasingly hysterical speculation about millions of dollars missing from Ghana's treasury. In Britain, the *Guardian* claimed that Nkrumah had "accepted a bribe of £1.5 million" and had "two accounts in Swiss banks." In America, newspapers spread rumors about "gold plated Cadillacs, personal jet planes, and strings of mistresses." The Associated Press reported that "Nkrumah is estimated to have a personal fortune of $7 million"—then, a few weeks later, upped it to "a fortune of more than $132 million." But British and American authorities knew that none of these stories were true. In recently declassified files, British civil servants admitted that Nkrumah "would not take a bribe."

In Accra, "the newspapers, television and radio," reported Howard, "run a 24-hour campaign against Nkrumah. Some white man came over radio one night saying they had to get African history straightened out." It was a concerted smear campaign. It also laid the groundwork for Blay's scam. For decades, these reports propped up his story about Nkrumah's hidden millions.

For now, Blay—fresh out of prison—was working in a provincial marriage bureau, which let him build an intimate knowledge of official documents and how they were drawn up. He still worked as a spiritual healer. But his ambitions were growing.

THE NATIONAL LIBERATION Council needed to convince people that Nkrumah was a crook. So it allowed some of the businessmen and politicians who had been charged with corruption to hold prison press conferences. At one, a prominent businessman and government adviser named Emmanuel Ayeh-Kumi claimed that President Nkrumah had a $7 million fortune and solid-gold bathroom fixtures. Ayeh-Kumi said that when he had tried to warn the president about excessive spending, he was told to "shut up and was given books on Marxist economics to study." (Another businessman, in jail for taking a multimillion-dollar kickback, said Ayeh-Kumi had told him Nkrumah actually had $132 million, hidden away in foreign banks.)

Edusei had a particularly improbable story to tell. At a press conference— where he had to fend off questions about the gold bed—"asked if Dr. Nkrumah were corrupt, Mr. Edusei shouted, 'More than anybody else! He is so greedy and so corrupt that he likes money even more than he likes his mother.'" Edusei claimed that he "had conveyed 13 boxes containing gold bars valued at over £520,000 to Cairo," allegedly for Nkrumah's wife, Fathia. In the early 1960s, gold was valued at around £12.55 per ounce. This would mean that Edusei had transported well over a U.S. ton of gold out of the country, without anyone noticing.

The worst of Nkrumah's ministers and hangers-on discovered that they had a literal get-out-of-jail-free card: the National Liberation Council would release them and wipe their reputations, leaving them free to loot Ghana again—as long as they condemned Nkrumah first. At least initially, it must have seemed like their lies were relatively harmless. After all, Nkrumah was no longer in the country. What consequences could there possibly be? As soon as those lies started circulating, however, the people named in them became targets of extraordinary violence and cruelty.

At Ayeh-Kumi's press conference, he claimed that Nkrumah's friend and adviser Genoveva Marais was in fact his mistress. The president "maintained a villa with gold bathroom fixtures" for her, Ayeh-Kumi asserted. *Life* magazine reported that Marais "was questioned briefly by the police and released early this week. However her red Thunderbird convertible was impounded." In fact, Marais had been imprisoned by the new regime and treated with particular brutality. A number of American newspapers ran with the story that Marais and Nkrumah were lovers, that he kept her in lavish style and had bought her a red Thunderbird. The new regime staged a photo shoot with Marais in the passenger seat of a convertible, her eyes defiantly downcast. *Life* claimed, with no evidence, that the Thunderbird was bought for her with government funds. After she was released from prison, Marais was forced to leave Ghana.

Marais had always paid her own way: she came from a rich family and worked for a living. The truth was, she drove a ten-year-old gray Chevrolet, which made odd noises and had been taken apart multiple times. But the lie—that Nkrumah had bought her gold taps and a luxury convertible—was far more interesting. Even years later, when the lie had outlived its usefulness, it still drowned out the truth.

In 1966, the junta staged an inquiry into the missing millions. Like many other commissions set up in the aftermath of the coup, it was designed to confuse history, not to clarify it. Edusei spent months testifying on his financial affairs. His claims always seemed credible, but almost every fact he introduced—including the address of his home in London—collapsed under the slightest scrutiny. Edusei explained that there was no paper trail for his claims because "I am an international man. All these papers are deposited in the Zurich bank vaults, so that if I am dead my children can get the money." When asked which bank his papers were kept in, Edusei stalled: "I have known all along that the life of a politician is like that of a film star. You can die at any time. I have therefore got all these papers in Zurich. That is how I deal internationally." Asked again for the name of the bank, Edusei came up with "Swiss Credit Bank," a studied mangling of Credit Suisse. Regrettably, he said that he could not remember his account number.

The police conducted hundreds of interviews but could find only a handful of people willing to claim Nkrumah had been corrupt: the crooked businessmen and politicians recently released from Nsawam. And then, even in front of a panel determined to find evidence that Nkrumah had done something wrong, their claims got smaller and stopped adding up. No one could provide any proof that Nkrumah had been emptying the treasury or acquiring solid-gold automobiles.

Instead of $132 million, Ayeh-Kumi started talking about hundreds of thousands in kickbacks to Nkrumah—which just happened to have been received by Ayeh-Kumi himself. He claimed to have run at least two bank accounts as trusts for President Nkrumah, including one at a branch of Midland Bank in London. This had a balance of a little more than £8,800. He also claimed that in 1965, he had invested £170,000 (then £85,000—his story changed) on Nkrumah's behalf at Swiss Bank Incorporated in Zurich. There was no evidence that Nkrumah had anything to do with these two accounts. (Swiss Bank Incorporated also did not exist, although nobody at the inquiry pointed this out.) Nor did Ayeh-Kumi explain why the president would need a trustee or would have appointed a man he had imprisoned as that trustee.

Ayeh-Kumi's lies were credible enough for the panel to assert that they were likely true, and for newspapers to publish them. But they fell apart on closer inspection. The accounts in London and Switzerland were not trusts: they were personal bank accounts and were both in Ayeh-Kumi's own name. Ayeh-Kumi had admitted to taking public money and stashing it overseas, but because he blamed Nkrumah for his own crimes, he got away with stealing a fortune.

Years later, a judge recommended that Ayeh-Kumi be banned from holding public office. He responded indignantly that this was "uncalled for and unjustified." Ayeh-Kumi also said he had every intention of returning the money he stole, but he had not been "permitted to travel overseas to repatriate any balance standing on our accounts." (In fact, Ayeh-Kumi had recently traveled to Switzerland with Blay, whom he would also go on to work for.)

It takes only one lie to change the world. And once Edusei, Ayeh-Kumi, and the others told that lie, countless people were convinced that President Nkrumah had stolen money and put it in a Swiss bank account. Within a few years, that lie would be written into Ghana's national history.

AT THE TIME, Nkrumah was living in a crumbling colonial-era villa in Conakry, Guinea, as a guest of President Ahmed Sékou Touré. It was a modest, white-painted place, with a roof of ochre tiles, surrounded by "orange and mango trees, flowering shrubs and other plants." The house was "built on two levels," wrote Nkrumah's editor, June Milne, who visited several times between 1966 and 1971, "with a lower terrace which jutted out onto the beach. At high tide, the sea lapped against three of its walls. From the seafront, Nkrumah could see the off-shore islands, and the distant shore of so-called Portuguese Guinea, where a fierce liberation struggle was being fought, led by Amilcar Cabral."

The trappings of power had disappeared. The president spent his days writing at a desk out on the terrace and receiving visitors. "These visitors, freedom fighters and members of progressive organizations, have discussed their problems with me," Nkrumah wrote.

In 1969, Stokely Carmichael moved to Guinea and announced that he planned to help Nkrumah return to power. Britain's Information Research Department—a propaganda division that officially did not exist—was alarmed. The department was instructed to create "differences between United States and Caribbean Black Power advocates and Africans." In 1970, it drafted a rambling pamphlet, ostensibly written by "all African lovers of freedom and democracy," insinuating that Nkrumah and Carmichael were focused "not on the Africa we know, but the Africa which Nkrumah failed once and is now again trying to create—that is the premature unification at any price of our continent." Realizing that many actual Africans were in favor of a union, British officials crossed out "premature unification at any price" in a draft of the pamphlet and replaced it with "domination by one man." The rest of the hysterical draft was peppered with embarrassing stabs at authenticity: Carmichael was asked to go "elsewhere to do his thing."

Nkrumah, meanwhile, survived on modest royalties from his books and the tinned sardines Milne sent him from London. A small refrigerator held biscuits, water, and chocolate. Nkrumah's family remained in Egypt: he "feared that they might be hijacked on their way to or from Guinea." He never saw them again. When it rained, Ghana's founder moved his bed to the other side of the room and put a pan down.

The years went by, Ghana's economy remained stalled, the national debt soared, and the treasury stayed empty. Despite the fact that it had been producing gold for centuries, Ghana was still poor. Ghanaians wanted to know where all that gold had gone. For decades, the answer was: Nkrumah took it.

Chapter 6

Three Hotels

1971–1972

John Kolorah Blay began to hone his most indispensable skill: leaving town right before things got complicated. Blay would blow into a city, make money, wreak havoc, and then, in the blink of an eye, disappear. He would reappear months later, in a different country or another continent entirely, often with a slightly different name.

Blay began 1971 as a small-time hustler. He had left the marriage bureau behind. He continued to work as a healer, but now he also posed as a banker, defrauding businessmen around West Africa of a few hundred here and there, offering to deliver loans for an up-front fee. But Blay was aiming higher. And soon, his cons would begin to match his ambitions.

Even when Blay was small-time, woe betide you if you had the misfortune to get caught up in one of his schemes. By the time you realized that you'd been had, he would be long gone. Blink and you'd miss him waving goodbye, a fistful of your hard-earned cash crammed into the breast pocket of his spotless linen leisure suit.

Blay began to traverse so much territory so quickly that he seemed to defy the laws of physics. He gave marks, police officers, and even Interpol the slip, effortlessly. But as elusive as Blay was, he had one habit he could never kick, a pattern he repeated over and over again. He loved hotels. The more luxurious, the better. In every city Blay visited, he would find the poshest, most let-them-eat-cake hotel and make it his pied-à-terre, his operational nerve center.

In one city after another, he wafted in on a wave of seemingly boundless power and wealth—sometimes ensnaring old associates, sometimes new ones. Each time, he quickly amassed a crowd of admirers and a reputation. Then he left the bill for someone else to pick up. Eventually this habit—and the people left holding the bills—would catch up with him. But until then, Blay seemed to be on a roll.

IN THE SUMMER of 1971, Blay was in Accra. He made himself at home at the Star Hotel. The Star was one of President Nkrumah's success stories. It was that rare combination: luxurious, state-owned, and profitable long after the president's administration so abruptly ended. The government built it in 1960 near the center of Accra, with every modern convenience: spacious rooms, air conditioning, and chalets on the grounds (for guests who needed discretion).

The hotel instantly became a popular, well-patronized society haunt. One year, it even held its own beauty pageant, Miss Star Hotel. Ramblers International, a band that played a fusion of Accra high-life and Liverpool Merseybeat, and frequently toured both Ghana and England, provided the music. Herr Sanday San, international limbo dancer and fire-eater, displayed both of his talents. Guests were invited to compete for the title of "fastest gentleman smoker."

By 1971, Accra was the epicenter of West Africa's music scene. "Ghana was really swinging," Tony Allen, Fela Kuti's drummer, later wrote. "There was more music in Ghana than in Lagos. More clubs too." The biggest events in the scene were midday concerts called Afternoon Jumps, where musical combinations like Fela Kuti's band would perform. The Star Hotel played host to many an Afternoon Jump.

Kofi Bentum Quantson—Blay's former schoolteacher and now a member of Ghana's Special Branch—was a frequent attendee. ("Actually, there was no physical jumping," he once wrote. Quantson was there for the music, the beer, the kebabs, and the crowd.) One Afternoon Jump, on a sticky summer

Saturday, would change the course of Quantson's life. The terrace of the hotel was bathed in blue-white afternoon sunlight. There was a thick blanket of humid heat, lifted, occasionally, by a sweet sea breeze from the shore at Osu. The terrace smelled of perfume and the meat and charcoal from a colossal grill.

Then Quantson looked up from his beer and saw his favorite pupil walk in. He hadn't set eyes on John Kolorah Blay since seeing him off at Takoradi Harbor in 1959. Now, it seemed, Blay had graduated and was back from Philadelphia. The boy was much taller—a little thicker in the waist too. His clothes were still immaculately pressed. He looked prosperous now. On his way to becoming a big man. In eighty-degree heat on a terrace bar packed with people, he was the only one who apparently hadn't broken a sweat.

Blay spotted Quantson immediately. They greeted each other loudly. They hugged. They had a lovely reunion in the middle of the packed bar while the band played high-life. Blay said something vague about being back in Ghana on business. He was staying right there at the Star Hotel, he said, and he insisted that his old teacher come back the next day and see him.

As Quantson left the bar that evening, he noticed that Blay had quite the crowd around him. He was holding court, unrolling loud stories, and everyone around him was laughing. His student was, apparently, still great at knowing what people wanted to hear.

Quantson was not the only ambitious young policeman whom Blay was cultivating. Abraham Sackey, who was also a member of Special Branch, heard that a powerful man had taken up residence in the Star Hotel, an herbalist, occultist, and spiritualist who was healing people. Sackey's mother had been sick since 1959, and doctors had not been able to help her. So Sackey went to Blay. Blay "performed some rituals and told Sackey that his mother would not ever be healthy again, but he could prolong her life." He also gave him some powder for his mother's bathwater. Blay said that his fee was usually one thousand cedi, but he charged Sackey only two hundred cedi "because he liked him and wanted to be his friend." Sackey would live to regret this friendship.

The next day, Quantson met Blay at the bar of the Star Hotel. Blay told him he was now an executive with the African Development Bank. His work took him all over West Africa; he had just been to Liberia. He was back in

Ghana to meet with local industrialists seeking loans from the African Development Bank.

But Blay had something else on his mind. He implied that it was a little delicate. And he leaned toward Quantson before confiding in him. Some terrible things had happened while he was a student in Philadelphia. He had been falsely arrested and imprisoned. Eventually, Blay said, he had prevailed. When all the unpleasantness was over, he had been awarded millions of dollars in restitution. Blay was looking for the best way to bring it back to Ghana. He looked at Quantson expectantly.

Quantson was immediately skeptical. He had never heard of anyone having trouble bringing dollars into Ghana. On top of that, he had a nagging doubt. Something about what Blay said was not quite right. And something Quantson half-remembered about him made him uneasy. Everything seemed so grandiose: "He was full of big talk, and big money." Quantson made a noncommittal reply, and Blay dropped the subject. Later, as Quantson was getting up to leave, Blay asked for a lift. He was going ten minutes down the road to see an old friend, a naval officer who was stationed at Burma Camp, the nearby military base.

On Sundays, Accra was almost eerily quiet. Even after church services ended, when everyone was heading home in their Sunday best, there was very little traffic. So it did not take Quantson long to notice that when he and Blay pulled out of the Star Hotel, someone seemed to be following him. That made no sense. Quantson was the chief analyst on the political desk of Ghana's Special Branch. If there was a person under investigation in his car, he would be the first to know about it. So Quantson dropped Blay off at Burma Camp and thought nothing more of it. He should have known better.

On Monday, nursing a headache, Quantson went to the Criminal Investigation Department at Ghana's police headquarters, to follow his hunch about John Kolorah Blay. Sure enough, his suspicions were correct: his favorite pupil had recently jumped bail on a petty fraud case. Quantson later wrote that he immediately knew something was going horribly wrong.

He grabbed a detective and told him where to pick up Blay. Then Quantson went to his own office at Special Branch headquarters, and his headache immediately got worse. The director of Special Branch wanted to see him right away. It was about a coup d'état.

After independence, Special Branch, along with the entire colonial police force, found itself in the awkward position of protecting the people they had been hired to subjugate. The transition was not smooth. Quantson had been recruited to the Special Branch under Nkrumah. He was dismissed after the junta took over. He petitioned to stay and agreed to take the police entrance exam and go through the academy. His family was horrified. They thought he would spend his days attacking people with a truncheon. His uncle offered him the same salary to stay home and manage a coconut farm. For a highly trained analyst like Quantson it had been humiliating. By the time he was called into the director's office in June 1971, he had sacrificed a great deal for his job.

Now, the director of Special Branch was demanding to know what Quantson had been doing over the weekend. He was immediately offended. "What a question! Where I went that weekend was not the business of the director." Then his boss explained that Prime Minister Kofi Abrefa Busia had just called a special cabinet meeting, to decide whether Quantson should be charged with treason. Quantson felt as if the floor were falling out from under him.

On Saturday, at Afternoon Jump at the Star Hotel, Quantson had noticed Blay loudly holding court. He had not realized that Blay was telling the people he was drinking with—as well as everyone within earshot—that he was about to launch a coup d'état. There was a lot of ridicule and laughter as he detailed how he was going to overthrow Busia's government. But the mockery got quieter and quieter as Blay explained that he had a friend at military head-quarters, and an inside man at Special Branch.

One of the people who overheard him immediately left the Star Hotel and reported Blay to Special Branch. This person had also seen Blay loudly and effusively greet his former schoolmaster and had immediately concluded that the inside man was Quantson, Special Branch's head of political intelligence. By Sunday morning, Quantson was under surveillance. His suspicions had been correct: he was being followed.

Quantson was saved by the fact the first thing he had done that Monday morning was tell the detectives at the Criminal Investigation Department where to find bail-jumping Blay. Quantson explained it all to the director. He had run into his old student by chance. Blay had tried to run a con on him. When that didn't work, Blay had tricked him into driving to military headquarters. Quantson couldn't quite believe that he had been manipulated and outsmarted by an old pupil and was dismissive: Blay had to be "crazy or fraudulent, or possibly both."

The prime minister was apparently greatly relieved to hear that one of his chief analysts had not been plotting against him with a petty criminal who was just turning thirty. Quantson, meanwhile, was deeply shaken by the whole affair. He had no idea what Blay was trying to achieve by pretending to stage a coup d'état. He did some digging and found out that Blay was also in the middle of trying to con a prominent businessman who believed that Blay was genuinely working for the African Development Bank.

Blay was arrested and taken to Cape Coast, where he was kept in police custody to await a trial. The next thing Quantson heard was that he had left the country.

In fact, Blay had escaped. While he was in custody, he faked a heart attack and asked to be taken to the hospital. On the way there, he asked the officers accompanying him to stop at a bank so that he could withdraw money to pay the hospital bill. When they got to a branch of Ghana Commercial Bank in Takoradi, Blay asked to use the water closet. Then, the police officers later testified, he miraculously disappeared.

The water closet at the bank contained no water. Instead, there was a sturdy latrine, a wooden box on a platform with a hole cut in the top, and a toilet seat screwed to it as a concession to comfort. It was—after all—a bank. There was a deep pit below the box, which was emptied through a trap door in the back. Blay had gone in to use the facilities, removed the seat, lowered himself into the pit latrine, crawled out of the trap door, and vanished.

THREE MONTHS LATER, in September 1971, a low-ranking Ghanaian diplomat ushered a doctor into the Ducor Intercontinental Hotel in Monrovia, Liberia. The diplomat had met Dr. John Kolorah Blay at the embassy just hours earlier. Now he was vouching for him.

Letters for Blay had been arriving at the embassy for two years prior to his arrival. When he finally appeared there to pick up his mail, he said that he was the eldest son of an icon of Ghanaian history, the prominent barrister

Robert Samuel Blay. He asked to speak with the ambassador, Augustina Obetsebi-Lamptey.

Blay was, of course, a wanted man in Ghana. So it took audacity for him to walk into the Ghanaian embassy and talk his way into the ambassador's office. It's also hard to overstate how big a swing our man was taking by claiming to be related to Robert Samuel Blay, the distinguished lawyer who had picked Kwame Nkrumah up from the port when he returned to Ghana in 1947. R. S. Blay was said to be Ghana's first Nzema lawyer, and his name carried weight. So when Dr. Blay made his grand entrance in Liberia in 1971, touting a connection to the great man, Ambassador Obetsebi-Lamptey was more than happy to meet with him for a few minutes.

The young Blay was wearing a fashionable suit and a kipper tie. He smelled like cologne. He said that he had just returned to West Africa after medical school at the University of Pennsylvania. He had started forwarding his mail to the embassy because he planned to teach at Cuttington University in Monrovia. When he smiled—a deep, charming grin, revealing dimples—the ambassador thought that he looked too young to be a doctor, let alone a lecturer.

On his way out, Blay struck up a conversation with the ambassador's secretary, Nii Ashrifi Nunoo. This was unexpected: Nunoo was not used to being noticed by her excellency's guests. But for Blay, getting his attention was more important than meeting the ambassador.

Blay told Nunoo he was staying in a modest hotel for a few days while he waited for his father, Robert Samuel Blay, to wire some money over so that he could move to the five-star Ducor Intercontinental. Nunoo ended up lending him money to pay off the first hotel bill, then driving him to the Ducor and introducing him to the manager. Nunoo even gave the hotel manager his card and told him to get in touch if he ever needed anything from the embassy.

The Ducor was a white modernist pile, perched on a hill in the center of the capital. When Blay arrived in 1971, it was in its prime. The rooms had grand, sweeping views of the Atlantic and rattan furniture. Blay found it to be exceedingly comfortable. He made liberal use of the restaurant, which was known for its jollof, served sometimes with roast beef, overcooked in the style of the English. The rice was just okay, nowhere near as good as the jollof at home. The pastry chef made a curious papaya pie, served à la mode. There were seemingly bottomless bottles of Châteauneuf-du-Pape and Laurent-Perrier Grand Siècle. Blay was satisfied with the offerings. Being a doctor with friends in high places suited him very well. He decided to keep the title.

Nunoo, the man from the embassy, frequently dined with him. When Blay asked for a few favors, Nunoo was only too happy to oblige. He typed up Blay's curriculum vitae. He even gave Blay stationery from the embassy, for the doctor's new job at Cuttington University (he never asked why blank embassy letterhead was required). After a few weeks, Blay got busier, and they spent less time together. Nunoo didn't realize that the doctor was not who he claimed to be.

It was at this point that the hotel manager dug out Nunoo's card. He asked him when the embassy would be paying Blay's bill. Nunoo was surprised. There must have been some confusion. Nunoo told the manager that Blay would be paying his own hotel bills. Then he went up to Blay's suite and demanded an explanation. Blay assured him that the money was about to arrive, his father would cover everything, and Nunoo had nothing to worry about. In fact, there was a great deal to worry about.

Shortly afterward, Ambassador Obetsebi-Lamptey was surprised when the manager of the Ducor Hotel asked to speak to her on a matter of great delicacy. This matter turned out to be young Blay's ever-expanding hotel bill. The ambassador declined to pay: she had not instructed him to lodge at the most expensive hotel in town. In fact, she had not instructed him to lodge anywhere. He was not a diplomat. The manager then apologetically showed her a letter. It said Blay's bill should be forwarded to her; the embassy would be paying. Her signature had been forged. The letter was typed on her embassy's letterhead. The hotel manager explained that a Ghanaian diplomat had escorted Blay into the hotel and personally vouched for him. The ambassador called the authorities.

Nunoo saw Blay one last time, at the offices of Interpol in Monrovia. The doctor maintained that it had all been a big misunderstanding. Soon after, he disappeared.

Nobody knows for sure what happened next, but decades later, investigators all over the world would trade stories: Blay was said to have washed up in New York, been a guest at the Waldorf Astoria, and left Bergdorf Goodman with several fine, tailored suits that would never be paid for. When he was not enjoying the luxuries of the city that never slept, he was apparently getting very friendly with a clerk at the Ghanaian UN mission in Manhattan.

IN JANUARY 1972, a car with fluttering diplomatic flags pulled up to the entrance of the Bellevue-Stratford Hotel in Philadelphia. The gigantic beaux arts building was once known as the "Grande Dame of Broad Street." Now, it was the polished, old-world heart of a crumbling city.

Outside the hotel's doors, Philadelphia was in the middle of one of the most precipitous urban declines of the century. The region used to make everything from Campbell's Soup to Stetson hats to warships. The decline had started around the Depression. It had gotten worse during the Second World War. Now, the slow, steady drain of people and jobs had become "a torrent." Over the course of the 1970s, Philadelphia would lose 140,000 jobs. Once-grand buildings had been converted into halfway houses. Entire blocks lay derelict. The newspapers were full of advertisements for get-rich-quick schemes and business owners selling out after decades. The Bellevue-Stratford would soon hit hard times as well. In 1976, an American Legion convention at the hotel triggered the first known outbreak of a pneumonia-like illness later named Legionnaires' disease. But in 1972, the Bellevue-Stratford was still the center of its own gleaming universe. The lobby was all marble and polished brass. Higher up, the rooms had sweeping views of the city.

Dr. John Ackah Blay-Miezah stepped out of the limousine onto an icy stretch of Broad Street. Blay had arrived in Philadelphia with a brand-new name. He was welcomed by a frigid, bright winter day. Glancing up Broad Street, he looked, with some satisfaction, at the redbrick Union League Club, then to the marble and granite grandeur of Philadelphia City Hall, all the way up to the statue of William Penn perched on the roof. The cold air caught his throat and made him feel alive. He had arrived.

He ambled into the lobby of the Bellevue-Stratford, introduced himself as a member of Ghana's delegation to the United Nations, and charmed the desk clerk. The doctor also presented a letter. It explained that he was a diplomat and that any charges would be settled by the Ghanaian embassy in Washington, D.C. The diplomat was escorted to a large suite. He rather liked looking down on the city from his perch high up in the hotel, biting on an unlit cigar.

Dr. Blay-Miezah settled into life at the Bellevue-Stratford. He spent his days being driven around in the limousine with diplomatic flags, trailing a full retinue, and running small-time cons all over Philadelphia. His chauffeur would open the door, and he would step out into the snow, draped in heavy ochre Kente cloth, and just stand there like he had all the time in the world, the quiet center of a flurry of activity. Traffic would halt. Passers-by would stop dead in the middle of the sidewalk and gawk. For years afterward, people would talk about the African prince who came to town and took meetings with some of the wealthiest and best-connected residents of Philadelphia. He was said to be selling gold, straight from the motherland. And he apparently had a great number of takers. Wealthy investors would hand over large sums of money, and to celebrate, the prince would show them a great time in Philadelphia. They apparently had no idea he was entertaining them with their own money.

In the evenings at the Bellevue-Stratford, the tables were laid with silver, and the dining-room was lit with flickering candles and chandeliers. Philadelphia's high society gathered for dinner in the Hunt Room, the women with their bouffant hairdos and the men in their double-breasted blazers, to remind themselves that despite what was going on outside, they still had a great deal of money. Blay-Miezah made fast friends and reminisced about his days at the University of Pennsylvania. Sometimes, he would lead the other guests in the Penn fight song. Dinner was served on gold-rimmed china. At the top of each plate, inside a gilded wreath, were the letters B.S.

Dr. Blay-Miezah's bill was mounting, but the manager of the Bellevue-Stratford had not yet called the Ghanaian embassy. So he never discovered that on January 13, 1972, the day after Dr. Blay-Miezah checked into his hotel, the Second Republic of Ghana had been ended by force.

Prime Minister Busia had been overthrown. Not by Blay-Miezah, but by soldiers under the command of a lean, stern lieutenant colonel named Ignatius Kutu Acheampong. There had been a military coup d'état while the prime minister was in London for a medical procedure; Busia would remain there indefinitely, in exile. The National Liberation Council was no more; Colonel

Acheampong established the National Redemption Council and, as its chairman, became Ghana's de facto head of state.

Back in Philadelphia, after a month, someone at the hotel did finally call the Ghanaian embassy in Washington to present Dr. Blay-Miezah's $2,700 bill. It was discovered that there was no Ghanaian diplomat staying at the Bellevue-Stratford. The manager of the hotel called the police, but it was too late: Dr. Blay-Miezah was nowhere to be found.

Chapter 7

The Crew

1972–1973

A few days later, on February 16, 1972, Blay-Miezah reappeared. He turned himself in at a Philadelphia police precinct, looking every bit the aggrieved diplomat. His lips were pursed, his chin held high. He wore a pressed white shirt and a paisley tie. He looked like he had been interrupted on his way to work and had every intention of going straight back. There was, however, no sign of the car with diplomatic flags or the retinue. While there was no way to tell from his appearance, Blay-Miezah was in over his head.

He was initially charged with "defrauding an innkeeper." Blay-Miezah and his lawyer Filindo Masino could explain everything. The police had, surely, seen news of the recent coup in Ghana? It had been so unexpected. Even Prime Minister Busia himself did not seem to believe it. There Busia was, on TV, in his trademark acetate glasses with the wire rims, telling a reporter that he was still the democratically elected leader of Ghana: "There has only been an adventure by a small band of the military people stationed in Accra."

But the coup was very real. Three days after seizing power, Colonel Acheampong had thrown the entire Busia administration in jail and frozen their assets. Blay-Miezah's accounts had been frozen too; the new military regime, Masino explained, considered Blay-Miezah an enemy. In consequence, his

Arrest photograph of Blay-Miezah, taken in Philadelphia in 1972.

client's rightful attempt to bill the Ghanaian embassy in Washington, D.C., had been rejected.

To save the Commonwealth of Pennsylvania the time and expense associated with a trial, Masino suggested that Blay-Miezah plead guilty and offer to settle the hotel bill at the first hearing. Masino could then use this noble act as leverage to get a promise that Blay-Miezah, as a person spurned and threatened by the current leaders of his home country, could stay in the United States.

When Blay-Miezah walked into his hearing, at Philadelphia's Court of Common Pleas, everything seemed to be going to plan. But our man had not just acquired a double-barreled name and a taste for the high life. He had also amassed colossal hotel bills and an increasingly aggrieved following of diplomats, law enforcement agencies, and hotel managers. And the story that he and Masino had told the Philadelphia police would take only one telephone call to refute.

In the brief time Blay-Miezah was a wanted man, police officers investigating him had gone to the University of Pennsylvania and searched the registry for his file. There he seemed to be, listed as a graduate with a bachelor's in commerce from the Wharton School and a master's degree in international relations. They pulled a picture from the file.

Unfortunately for Blay-Miezah, the police found out some other things about him as well. The Ghanaian embassy in Washington, D.C., also had a file on Blay-Miezah, whom they had already established to be John Kolorah Blay, wanted for escaping custody in Ghana, and Dr. John Kolorah Blay, wanted for fraud in Liberia. The diplomats were tired of sending and receiving telegrams about his exploits. By this point Blay-Miezah had variously introduced himself as a diplomatic aide, a newly qualified doctor, a banker, a Harvard lecturer, and a part-time consultant for the United Nations' Children's Fund. Each persona had created new problems for the embassy. Then there was everything he had been up to in Monrovia and Accra. The embassy was happy to provide the prosecutors in Pennsylvania with full details. "He's full of lies," said a Ghanaian diplomat at the embassy. "He's not a reliable person, he's a wanted person."

In the Court of Common Pleas, Blay-Miezah—convinced he could talk his way out of anything—insisted on his innocence. But there was too much evidence against him; his lawyer's strategy fell apart. Judge Joseph T. Murphy found Blay-Miezah guilty of cheating by fraudulent pretenses, defrauding an innkeeper, and conspiracy to do an unlawful act. The judge handed down an unusually harsh sentence: one to two years at the State Correctional Institute at Graterford.

Barely an hour's drive from the Bellevue-Stratford, Graterford lay amid frost-covered fields and bare trees. It was a bleak place, surrounded by a high concrete wall and guard towers. Blay-Miezah was marched through the metal gates, down foul-smelling, fluorescent-lit corridors. He was photographed, made to strip off his fine clothes, and issued with his prison uniform.

Graterford was hell. Inside the long, low cell blocks, men shivered in their quarters. When Blay-Miezah arrived, it was so cold that fifteen inmates had just filed a civil suit against the superintendent of the prison, alleging cruel and unusual punishment. Even the food was served cold. Guards randomly subjected Black inmates to forced haircuts and solitary confinement in an entirely empty, filthy cell called the "glass cage."

Graterford was designed to break people. But the prison's racist, abusive atmosphere had the unintended effect of uniting many of the prisoners. They were desperate, but they were determined to stand up for one another and for themselves. Some tried protesting. Eventually the residents of Pennsylvania's penal system started a union. "Since when," wrote one inmate at Graterford, "is it a crime of the first magnitude, to want to be treated as a human being?"

For Blay-Miezah, this was rock bottom.

But he remembered the big men at Nsawam Prison back home. He remembered how they made the crowded, fetid jail feel like a private club. And he got to work making friends with other prisoners, guards, and even the chaplains. He got to know the prison library, hoovering up news about everything, but especially about what was going on in Ghana, now that Acheampong was in charge. He comported himself exactly as he had at the Bellevue-Stratford: as a doctor and diplomat. He told his story to everyone who would listen—how he had been wrongly jailed by uncultured and unworldly prosecutors, and how the American legal system was clearly unjust. A prison psychiatrist thought Blay-Miezah was suffering delusions: "I feel this man cannot distinguish reality from fantasy."

IN THE EARLY hours of April 27, 1972, soon after Blay-Miezah's arrival in Graterford, President Nkrumah died. He was sixty-two. He had been diagnosed with cancer and had traveled from Conakry, where he was in exile, to Bucharest, Romania, for treatment. His nephew and his bodyguard had remained by his side from the moment his plane landed, even sleeping beside Nkrumah's bed, wrapped up in hospital dressing gowns. President Ahmed Sékou Touré of Guinea announced his death.

Nkrumah left almost nothing in his will: mostly the royalties from the books he wrote about the struggle for independence, which he bequeathed to his family.

There was a state funeral in Guinea. "For two long days, at the Palais du Peuple in Conakry, mourners from all over Guinea, South African anti-Apartheid activists and freedom fighters, and representatives of foreign governments paid tribute to Kwame Nkrumah." Nkrumah's family was shocked by the sight of his emaciated body. Then the handful of people who had remained with him since the coup d'état, and Joe Appiah, who was one of Acheampong's closest aides at the time, flew President Nkrumah home. Appiah still thought highly of his old friend. He had, Appiah thought, always loved power too much, but never "for the acquisition of wealth for himself."

There was no state funeral in Ghana. Instead, Nkrumah's body was flown by military helicopter to Nkroful for a grand, traditional funeral. Thousands of people marched in procession behind the family. A modest mausoleum of wood and concrete was erected where his mother's house had stood before it was destroyed in the first coup. Nkrumah's mother would not believe that her son was dead until her hand was placed on his coffin.

NKRUMAH WAS BACK in the news in America—and this was especially true in Pennsylvania. "Many Philadelphians will remember the dead statesman, since he was a prominent figure in Philadelphia while a student at Lincoln University and at the University of Pennsylvania," wrote a columnist at the *Philadelphia Tribune*.

Blay-Miezah saw his opening. The last few months had been humbling. But his mistake had not been running a con. It had been running a *small* con. He had been aiming too low. He needed to be bigger, more ambitious. But he couldn't do it alone. He needed allies: people who knew Philadelphia. He needed a crew.

BLAY-MIEZAH'S LIBERATION WOULD come at the hands of the Reverend James Edward Woodruff, a radical Episcopal priest. Another clergyman called him "the Malcolm X of the Episcopal Church." Woodruff would get Blay-Miezah out of jail, and he would introduce him to the people who would seal his destiny, transforming Blay-Miezah from a small-time hustler to someone whose stories changed history.

Woodruff had marched with the Reverend Dr. Martin Luther King Jr. from Selma to Montgomery in 1965. When the Episcopal Diocese of Pennsylvania came calling, Woodruff was the chaplain for two Black colleges in

Tennessee. He was also running classes for local children, teaching them about Black history and culture. The local police, concerned that such lessons would teach the children to "hate whitey," shut Woodruff's school down.

Woodruff was posted to Philadelphia in 1967, to help run what the Episcopal bishop called an urban mission. There was no church. Instead his job was community outreach: to bring in the Black Christians whom his church had previously "persecuted, abandoned and malignantly ignored," as one of Woodruff's fellow priests put it. (During the Civil War, a group of Episcopal bishops had cast their lot in with the enslavers, calling the Abolitionist movement "a hateful and infidel pestilence.") The reverend took to the role immediately. He campaigned for reparations and held "confrontations with white people" in the suburbs. "We've got to talk about the redistribution of wealth," Woodruff said. "The American Dream is a nightmare." He spoke frankly about racism and police brutality in Philadelphia.

Woodruff "was like a breath of fresh air when he came to the city," another Episcopal priest remembered. "Woodruff quickly won the trust of the city's black dissidents by delivering impassioned speeches in street language, unafraid to use words that some might have considered vulgar or profane," one local paper reported. And Woodruff did it all dressed in a long liturgical robe with a hood and sandals, sometimes accessorized with a dashiki and beads. People called him Friar Tuck, so he took to wearing a weight belt "to tighten his abdominal muscles while he worked."

The urban mission was deeply unpopular with many white Episcopal leaders. The Diocese of Pennsylvania was already in turmoil, split by racism and infighting over whether to support or protest the war in Vietnam. Members of the church tried to get Woodruff fired. The bishop refused. But a conflict in the summer of 1969 would drive a wedge even deeper into Woodruff's relationship with the church.

The conflict revolved around Cookman United Methodist Church in North Philadelphia, a dying institution with just over thirty regular congregants. Among them was a woman named Ethel Coy, the only African American member of the congregation. Cookman had been built when the neighborhood had mostly white residents. It was a huge compound, containing a skating rink, swimming pool, gymnasium, and several classrooms. But none of those facilities were available to the new Black residents of the parish. For most of the week, the church's grounds were entirely vacant. The Methodist Church decided that it would rather see an entire parish die out than welcome Black parishioners.

So local activists from the Philadelphia Black Economic Development Conference, a civil rights organization, staged a takeover. They opened the doors and opened the classrooms. Within days, there were four hundred children in Cookman United Methodist, learning about African art and history and mathematics. There was indoor skating and a nap room. The occupation had injected "life and love into a decaying North Philadelphia neighborhood," a local paper said. Woodruff led Sunday service, but only one member of the regular congregation—Ethel Coy—attended.

After eight days, the activists were tipped off that the police were coming. Commissioner Frank Lazzaro Rizzo was dubbed "the Idi Amin of Pennsylvania" by the NAACP. Rizzo's contempt for the rights of Black Americans was matched only by the brutality of his officers' tactics. These were later the subject of federal investigation and included "placing a telephone book on a suspect's head and hammering it with a heavy object (to prevent telltale marks)." There was a good chance that no one in the church would survive an encounter with his police force. So the activists and children left, and eight ministers, including Reverend Woodruff, strode into the church and chained the doors closed behind them. The president of the city council called it "the worst thing that has ever happened in Philadelphia," despite the fact that the activists had harmed no one, had kept the neighborhood children safe, and had not damaged a single piece of church property. He recommended that the ministers be thrown out and stepped on.

Rizzo insisted on arresting the priests himself. He arrived, trailed by a hundred and fifty police officers, and stormed the church. The eight ministers were kneeling, their heads bowed in prayer. Rizzo interrupted to tell them he was delivering an injunction: they were ordered to leave the church. Reverend Woodruff declined, telling Rizzo: "This is a house of God and for all people. We are human beings and therefore we have a right to be here." All eight clergy members were arrested, but none were charged.

Soon after, Father Woodruff took six months' leave from his post. Many thought he had left Philadelphia. "Father Woodruff dropped out of sight. It was as though he had never been here," wrote one newspaper columnist.

But Woodruff was still ministering to his flock. He officiated a wedding where Stevie Wonder was the best man and Aretha Franklin and Lou Rawls were in attendance. He held rap sessions with the comic and civil rights activist Dick Gregory. And in April 1972, as the news broke that President Kwame Nkrumah had died, Reverend Woodruff was also ministering to inmates at Graterford.

IN THE AFTERMATH of Nkrumah's death, Blay-Miezah approached Woodruff. The prison chapel at Graterford was an unexpectedly airy room, with tall ceilings and stained glass that tinted the sunlight in jewel tones. Blay-Miezah sat in a worn pew and told Woodruff his new story.

Six years ago, in 1966, Nkrumah was president of Ghana. In February of that year, Nkrumah got word of the coup d'état that would unseat him. When the president heard the news, Blay-Miezah had been right by his side. "Nkrumah and I were more than brothers, by tribe and by politics," Blay-Miezah said. (For the story to work, he added twenty years to his own age.) Blay-Miezah ended up in Guinea with Ghana's president in exile. He was, and always had been, a staunch loyalist.

In 1969, Blay-Miezah said, he was called back to Ghana. The government was looking for someone to help steer the Ministry of Health in a new direction. Dr. John Ackah Blay-Miezah, who had trained in Dublin and London, was just the man. In two short years, he had turned the ministry around. He was so successful that Prime Minister Busia reassigned him to a more pressing task: boosting Ghana's trade revenue. The government needed Blay-Miezah to find a home for some of Ghana's exports. So he made plans to leave Accra for Philadelphia, via New York.

When he was in New York, Blay-Miezah heard that Busia had been unseated by a coup. He was devastated, but he decided to stay the course. When he arrived in Philadelphia, he did not realize that he was out of favor at home, and his accounts, and access to government support, had been cut off. The same thing had happened to all of Busia's allies; perhaps Reverend Woodruff had read about it in the papers? When the bill came to be settled at the Bellevue-Stratford, everyone, Blay-Miezah said, assumed the worst of him. They were not, sadly, as well versed in revolutionary West

African politics as Woodruff. Before he knew it, Blay-Miezah was in Graterford.

He told Woodruff that he had to get out of prison urgently because he had an important, deeply secret task to complete in memory of President Nkrumah. "Nkrumah liberated his people politically," Blay-Miezah said. "I am going to liberate them economically."

Woodruff had long believed that America—and the world—needed "to establish a tradition of black heroes." And Blay-Miezah was urbane and persuasive. He hinted to Woodruff that even though he was a prisoner now, he had access to fabulous wealth. "Where do you find our precious metals? It's always in the dirt. Look at a man like St Francis of Assisi. This man was a leper, this saint." The former altar boy's story worked like a charm.

Woodruff preached a very specific form of liberation, which was largely economic. He believed that communities would have to work to regain centuries' worth of wealth stolen by colonialism and enslavement. He believed that Black Americans needed "the power to force fair and equal distribution of resources." When Blay-Miezah told Woodruff that he had been a confidant of President Nkrumah and that he controlled the kind of wealth that would transform entire nations, it was as if all of Woodruff's dreams had come true. This was what he had been searching for. Later in his career, Blay-Miezah would position himself as an economic liberator, using language stolen directly from Woodruff.

Woodruff was soon hard at work trying to get Blay-Miezah out of Graterford. He had a remarkable network of contacts. He knew everybody from two-bit scammers to captains of industry to civil rights heroes. He went looking for someone with money and connections in Philadelphia—and someone who might be down with the cause. He went to Robert Ellis.

ELLIS WAS ROGUISH and magnetic, with bright eyes. He seemed to know everyone in Philadelphia. He was brought up in a foster home. By the time he turned sixteen, he was fending for himself and had dropped out of school. An associate told reporters that Ellis was always hustling: he had to learn to think faster than anyone else. "You always had the feeling with Bob that he was a step ahead of everybody trying to figure out how he could use someone to better himself. He was networking before the word was ever coined." And wherever he was, whatever he was doing, he was always impeccably dressed.

Ellis started his working life driving a soda truck. By 1972 he was running Industrial Dynamics Incorporated, with his business partner, Wylie Stevens. Initially, it was not clear to outsiders what Industrial Dynamics did. Ellis said the company was founded in April 1971, and just ten months later—after the company constructed some highly profitable town houses in South Philadelphia—it was worth $1.5 million. This, Ellis said, made Industrial Dynamics the most successful minority-owned company in the entire state of Pennsylvania.

Ellis and Stevens told people that Industrial Dynamics wasn't just a construction company. It was an engine of economic liberation. "Both of us grew up in the city's ghetto, like many black men of our generation. We saw the critical need for good housing, and we saw what's being done to unsuspecting poor people, so we decided to do something about it," Stevens told a reporter from *Black Business Digest*.

And they had big plans: a nightclub, a $400,000 medical center, sixty-seven (then six hundred) upper-income town houses in Bensalem (to be sold at $30,000 each), and a 174-acre waterfront development in Atlantic City. Ellis and Stevens said none of this was funded by banks: the partners raised money from small investors. A group of Black professionals helped them raise the first $50,000. Then they raised another $250,000 by selling shares at $1 apiece, which, the *Philadelphia Inquirer* said—with ham-fisted racism—the "ghetto-bred partners" did "especially to appeal to ghetto dwellers."

In one publicity photo, Ellis and Stevens stood on a muddy construction site in South Philadelphia, flanking a worker in a flat cap with a cigarette tucked behind one ear. Ellis looked entirely too dapper, in a dark peacoat and flared trousers. Stevens wore a light double-breasted jacket and muttonchops. In another shot, Ellis and Stevens were poring over what looked like blueprints. Only if you looked closely would you see anything strange about this picture. Both Ellis and Stevens wore shoes freshly polished to a gleam: they hadn't been on the construction site too long. Around them, there were no tools, no building materials, no workers in hardhats and tool belts. The site looked abandoned.

Robert Ellis (left) and Wylie Stevens (right) at a construction site in Philadelphia.

Ellis was happy to help Woodruff. To pay off Blay-Miezah's Bellevue-Stratford bill, he called in a favor with Ben Bynum, a friend who owned the legendary Cadillac Club on Germantown Avenue in North Philadelphia with his wife, Ruth. Bynum's first job was at Sun Shipbuilding in Chester, Pennsylvania, where Kwame Nkrumah had worked the night shift. During the Second World War, Bynum was one of the Montford Point Marines, the first African Americans to serve in the Marine Corps. After the war, he returned to Philadelphia and built up a nightlife empire, starting with small bars: the Cosmo Club and the Big Moose. The Cadillac Club had opened in 1965. Gladys Knight and the Pips and George Benson regularly performed there. Aretha Franklin stayed with the family when she passed through the city; the Queen of Soul had her ears pierced by Ruth Bynum. In 1973, Billy Paul released an entire Philadelphia Soul album dedicated to its ambiance: *Feelin' Good at the Cadillac Club.*

Blay-Miezah was out of prison by February 1973. He went into business with Woodruff, Ellis, and Bynum.

IN AUGUST 1973, Blay-Miezah and Ellis opened the American offices of the Bureau of African Affairs and Industrial Development. It was an import-export company with a dozen directors, including Father Woodruff. Another director was none other than Emmanuel Ayeh-Kumi, the Ghanaian businessman who had taken kickbacks, stashed the money in a Swiss bank, and—when he was caught—said his personal account actually belonged to President Nkrumah. Blay-Miezah was calling in his favors: his old friends from Nsawam Prison, and corrupt Nkrumah-era officials, joined the bureau.

Offices were in suite 455 of a fashionable new business district called Decker Square, just outside Philadelphia in Bala Cynwyd. They were furnished with plush red carpet, soft plump chairs, and citrus trees. The offices impressed the hell out of visitors. Blay-Miezah hired a small, discreet, and very well-paid staff, including Mary Lou Valinote, a soft-spoken and glamorous secretary.

Business appeared to be booming. The bureau had, Blay-Miezah claimed, obtained a license to import seven hundred thousand tons of timber from Ghana, which was worth an estimated three million dollars a year. More prosaically, the company also sold a line of promotional greeting cards and 45 rpm records in honor of President Kwame Nkrumah, and filed to copyright a notepaper folder with a portrait of the president on it.

The new company was intended to resemble—but had nothing to do with—another Bureau of African Affairs. This one had been set up by President Nkrumah, with the help of George Padmore, his activist friend from London. Their aim, according to Padmore's biographer, was to turn Accra into the "chief meeting site for anti-colonial nationalists." Nkrumah's bureau supported groups fighting for independence all over Africa, and is said to have sent out agents to assist African independence movements. After the attempt to assassinate Nkrumah at Kulungugu, the Bureau of African Affairs began gathering intelligence, "assisting the State apparatus in unearthing plans and exposing the wicked intentions of people both within the country and outside," as one of Padmore's staffers put it, in a letter to Nkrumah. After the coup d'état, the Bureau of African Affairs was closed, and the people working there were arrested. Needless to say, Nkrumah's Bureau of African Affairs never sold greeting cards, or timber, or 45 rpm records.

In Philadelphia, whenever investors—or reporters—asked about the Bellevue-Stratford incident, Blay-Miezah explained away his little brush with the law. It had all been a big misunderstanding because of the coup d'état, he said. "Nobody understood me," Blay-Miezah told the *Philadelphia Tribune*. He sat behind his fancy new desk, surrounded by floor-to-ceiling windows, oozing injured innocence. "They thought I was telling lies." The stress had given him hypertension, so he missed his chance to appeal. (A doctor was ready to swear that Blay-Miezah had indeed been hospitalized.) Blay-Miezah said that he had been so shaken by the ordeal—and being cast aside by his own government—that he had requested political asylum in the United States.

But since then, Blay-Miezah said, he had cultivated a better relationship with the new government. "I'm a good politician." Then he pitched readers some premium African imports, including three million railroad ties "made of heavy African woods that blunt the teeth of American termites." He told the *Philadelphia Evening Bulletin* that his company had so many orders they couldn't handle them all. Regrettably, he could not take on any new business for the foreseeable future.

BLAY-MIEZAH MET JEANNINE West at a party and charmed the hell out of her. West was a widow. She was raising nine children in West Philadelphia and working as a teacher's aide. He told her that he was a forty-nine-year-old doctor and that his father was the chief of the Nzema tribe. West fell for him immediately, and they planned to get married. The wedding would, incidentally, solve Blay-Miezah's ongoing immigration issues: he was currently fighting deportation proceedings, due to his time in Graterford. He promised to be a father to her children and to buy his wife a home.

The two were married in front of a Catholic priest on April 18, 1973. It was not a good union. "I married him in April, and I divorced him in September," Jeannine said. "I cut him out of my life . . . He only used me to be in America."

IN SEPTEMBER 1973, the Bureau of African Affairs held a banquet to commemorate President Kwame Nkrumah's birthday. Blay-Miezah, whom the press described as "a close associate and a fellow tribesman of the late Ghanaian statesman," invited one hundred guests to the Marriott Hotel on

City Line Avenue, which was known for its distinctive tiki bar, with a real waterfall. The guests included several diplomats, a professor from Lincoln University, and two Philadelphia city commissioners. The Arthur Hall Afro-American Dance Ensemble performed a musical number in tribute to the president, called "The King Is Dead." The event reportedly cost $1,200.

Many of the people at the banquet were not there for the tiki drinks or the jumbo shrimp. They were there because Blay-Miezah had sold them a story. Those plush offices in Decker Square appeared to be busy. But Blay-Miezah never sold a single railroad tie or truck body. The Bureau of African Affairs was not actually in the import-export business. It was in a different business: the business of Nkrumah.

Blay-Miezah told visitors to his offices about the secret of President Nkrumah's fortune, lying hidden in bank vaults in Switzerland. His tone was confiding and cautious: he was letting them in on a deep secret, and he implored them to keep it quiet. Nobody could know. He told them how Nkrumah had set up the Oman Ghana Trust Fund—Oman meant "our nation" he explained patiently—to protect Ghana's ancestral wealth. Then Blay-Miezah dropped in some convincing numbers, even more impressive than the ones he would later give to Acheampong.

The Trust Fund controlled twenty-seven billion dollars in cash and diamonds and thirty thousand gold bars. All of it was hidden in Swiss banks.

Most of Nkrumah's money, Blay-Miezah said, was to develop Ghana. To build farms and factories and railways. The rest of the money? Well, Blay-Miezah could do what he liked with that.

Sometimes, Blay-Miezah would produce yellowed documents that were seemingly signed by Nkrumah himself. Those battered pieces of paper, Blay-Miezah would reveal, gave him power over untold wealth. At this point, he would loftily explain the ways of the financial world. "Every day in New York, from eleven o'clock to about five minutes past eleven, over five hundred billion dollars leaves that city, into the world," he said. "Ninety percent of that money came from documents like this," he added.

But, Blay-Miezah would say, there was a catch: before the Swiss would release the money, Blay-Miezah had to show that he had met all the conditions Nkrumah set up to govern the Trust Fund. And for that, he needed funding. "Don't let it slip through our fingers," Blay-Miezah said. To the naysayers: "The majority can never always be right. Sometimes only the minority can possess a truth."

So Blay-Miezah wanted to make a deal. Anyone who invested in his firm, and helped him return the gold to the good people of Ghana, would earn ten dollars for every dollar they put in. They'd get their money back in months—maybe weeks, guaranteed. "Whatever I promise," Blay-Miezah told them, "I will deliver."

This was what the Bureau of African Affairs was really selling, and the money was rolling in. The investors were businessmen and lawyers. There were accountants, insurance salesmen, at least one cop, and a lady who sold tickets from a shop in the lobby of the Marriott Hotel. All of the American directors of the Bureau of African Affairs had invested. Many of them would put more money in over the next two decades. Their investments would range from a few hundred dollars to millions.

Before parting with their money, some prospective investors tried to check out Blay-Miezah's story. Was it actually true that millions of dollars had gone missing from Ghana's treasury? At Philadelphia's Free Library, investors would have found countless newspaper stories, from across the world, claiming that President Nkrumah had stolen millions while he was in office. If the investors dug a little deeper, they might have found one of Charles P. Howard's stories from the *Gazette and Daily* in York, Pennsylvania. Howard told his readers about the millions that had disappeared from Ghana's reserves at independence. Wherever you looked, and whomever you chose to believe, the message was the same: a fortune really had vanished from Ghana.

Blay-Miezah and Ellis were not just selling shares; they were selling a dream. To Black people, they were selling liberation: a chance to repair the wounds of colonialism. To everyone else, they were selling the chance to loot an African country's ancestral wealth—which is to say, they were selling colonialism. "What Blay-Miezah and Ellis sold," Claude Lewis, a columnist at the *Philadelphia Inquirer*, later wrote, "was the mystery of Africa, along with the promise of billions in gold and riches."

Chapter 8

The Longest Con

1596

The inheritance scam has a long and ignoble history. It starts with a promise: you are about to become bountifully rich, thanks to a bequest from a distant relative, or a leader who has been unseated, or a long-dead ancestor. But first: there are a few small fees to settle. Our man's particular incarnation of the con had its roots hundreds of years earlier, with the death of Sir Francis Drake.

Before Drake, England was a poor, mostly rural country that lagged behind the Portuguese, the Dutch, and especially the Spanish when it came to trading with resource-rich parts of the globe and—on the way home—stealing everything in sight.

Drake robbed the robbers. He started in Panama, with Spanish silver miners. Then—equipped with a letter of marque licensing him to pillage England's enemies—he set sail as a privateer. He raided the king of Spain's treasure ships and attempted to kidnap innocent bystanders to sell them into slavery. His enterprising attitude and complete lack of morals were both remarkably lucrative.

Most of the spoils of Drake's raids went to the young Queen Elizabeth, who, because her coffers were empty at the time, was an admirer. When one of his captains protested his increasingly violent methods, Drake put him on trial for witchcraft and had him beheaded. Drake made the English realize that they too could sail to tropical countries and rob, kill, and enslave with impunity. He became one of the first English heroes of the colonial age. The queen rewarded him by making him a knight in 1581.

Drake died a national hero on his ship, in January 1596. He was thought to be unimaginably rich. And he left no direct heir. This was when the new con began.

For the next three hundred years, people prowled the English country-side telling tales of Drake's fortune. The smoke-sellers, foggers, and jack-in-the-boxes claimed that they had found Drake's rightful heir. But the poor boy was illegitimate. He needed help to wrest his ancestral fortune from the Crown. They were taking donations to aid him. For every shilling you invested, a hundred would be returned. These tales drew countless takers.

By 1900, the Drake swindle had reached the shores of the New World. Hucksters all over America scoured directories for people named Drake. They wrote the Drakes letters, telling them they were entitled to a share in Sir Francis's estate back in the old country. The Drake scam was so successful that flimflammers, swizzlers, and Sam Slicks started going after anyone who made a good mark, even if they were not named Drake.

By 1909, the most successful Drake huckster was a woman named Oseida Whittaker. She brandished a sheaf of faded documents, tied with ribbon and sealed with wax. Wherever Whittaker went—Iowa, Indiana, Missouri, Kentucky, even California—she collected tens of thousands of dollars in a matter of weeks. Her accomplices fanned out across the country behind her, looking for new pigeons. In 1914, two of them sat down at the kitchen table at Oscar Hartzell's family farm in Madison County, Iowa, and told the tale.

The rightful heir to Drake's fortune, they said was a humble man named George Drake, who lived in Roarchport, Missouri. (Neither George Drake nor the city of Roarchport existed, but if anyone thought to check, there was a Rocheport, Missouri. Close enough.) Drake's ancestors had left England for the New World during the Revolutionary War, they said. The American Drake heir was just a simple farmer, like the Hartzells. He didn't have the money to go up against the king of England, in an English court, so his friends were raising money to help him out. For $25, the Hartzells could buy a share in Drake's treasure. For "every dollar you invest to help free this treasure, a hundred will be returned to you," the men told Mrs. Hartzell. In addition, after it was all over, she would own part of an ancient, walled city in England called Plymouth. Mrs. Hartzell, her son Oscar later claimed, gave the men every last cent she had saved: $6,500.

Weeks later, Oscar Hartzell caught up with the Drake scammers. Hartzell was a stout man with a florid complexion and a winning smile. He always had a cigar between his teeth. When he finally tracked the scammers down, they confessed that they'd made sixty-five thousand dollars in just two months. Hartzell burst out laughing.

"You took small pickings," he told them. "Why, my mother still believes your scheme will come through. So does everyone else I talked to who fell for your line. Thousands! Hell, there's millions in this racket. But you can't go sneaking around like alley rats. You've got to come out in the open. Make it respectable, legitimate. Open an office."

Throughout history, the most successful con men have looked, to all the world, like pillars of society. They carried on their business in plush offices, surrounded by credible people, bankers and industrialists. They often looked more like respectable businessmen than the respectable businessmen they scammed. Some of them never got caught. They were running the most American con of all: fake it till you make it.

Chapter 9

Girard Bank

1776, 1974

I n Philadelphia, Blay-Miezah was the man who could make dreams come true. To some, he was a liberator—a man who was about to turn Ghana into a shining beacon for Black people all over the world. To others, he was someone who could open up vast, unsaturated markets for their businesses and transform them from moderately successful to obscenely wealthy, almost overnight. As business grew at the Bureau of African Affairs, Blay-Miezah learned to fleece people with their own fantasies.

But Blay-Miezah was making too many promises, too quickly, to people who expected results immediately. The more promises he made, the more investors he signed up, the more precarious his house of cards became. Soon, he had to make a decision: Should he keep scamming and hope that his cons would bring in enough money to keep him one step ahead of his investors, or should he turn himself into a legitimate businessman and try to do all the things he had promised? There were two major problems with going legit: Blay-Miezah had no ins with Colonel Acheampong, and the money that was meant to power the Bureau of African Affairs and transform Ghana—President Nkrumah's fortune—did not actually exist. Blay-Miezah, however, thought he saw a way out. It would prove to be one of his costliest mistakes.

Blay-Miezah wrote to organizations all over Africa—from the Timber Board in Accra to the Ministry of Education in Zambia—and to companies across America, asking for trade information. All at once, diplomats and businessmen from across the world began contacting Ghanaian and American embassies to ask about this new firm out of Philadelphia. What, they wanted to know, was the Bureau of African Affairs up to?

Diplomats at the Ghanaian embassy in Washington wrote to several American companies considering doing business with Blay-Miezah to warn them about his previous incarnations. Blay-Miezah caught wind of this and was livid: this threatened to bring down his entire operation. He called the embassy and made some veiled threats. Diplomats started to look into extraditing Blay-Miezah to Ghana for escaping police custody and jumping bail on the fraud charge back in 1971. Around the same time, Secretary of State Henry Kissinger wrote a memo to every American diplomatic mission in the world, warning that the "'Bureau [of] African Affairs and Industrial Development' is [a] front organization which Blay-Miezah has used in attempting [to] arrange several apparently fraudulent business transactions which have come to [the] department's attention."

Some of his investors got wind of the Kissinger memo, and Blay-Miezah's record in Ghana, and began asking questions. But the surge of people eager to work with Blay-Miezah and claim a piece of Ghana's ancestral wealth for themselves showed no sign of abating.

In February 1974, Blay-Miezah's investors started visiting Accra. By rights, this should have been the end of his scam—instead, it turned the investors from believers to evangelists. Two Philadelphia businessmen, Samuel Canale and Robert Brandon, in a display of brazen opportunism, announced a plan to barter tractors, earthmovers, and log skidders for cocoa, timber, and minerals. They didn't specify which timber or minerals, but the commodities in question were likely worth far more than heavy machinery gathering dust in a warehouse in West Conshohocken. Canale and Brandon told a diplomat at the American embassy in Accra that they had, so far, spent ten thousand dollars setting up the deal, with the help of former Ghanaian interior minister Krobo Edusei (he of the golden bed).

Canale and Brandon believed that the Ghanaian government was about to appoint Blay-Miezah to an important diplomatic post. In preparation,

Canale had been paying for lawyers back in Philadelphia. They were planning to clear Blay-Miezah's criminal record and restore his reputation.

Soon after, the attorney general of Ghana, Edward Nathaniel Moore, wrote a letter telling the Ghanaian embassy in Washington, D.C., to drop all plans to extradite Blay-Miezah. It was an order from the top, according to diplomatic chatter: "other influential Ghanaians also involved in effort reabilitate [*sic*] Blay-Miezah."

The letter was leaked to Blay-Miezah. He showed it to his investors: proof that the government was dropping all charges. Blay-Miezah's lawyers even brandished it at a deportation hearing in Pennsylvania. The Ghanaian government was, Blay-Miezah assured the court, so confident in his good standing that he was also being considered for the post of consul general. This set off a scramble at the State Department, which asked the Ghanaian embassy to send a letter to the Immigration and Naturalization Service stating that Blay-Miezah was not actually about to be made a senior diplomat.

TO STAND UP his illusions, Blay-Miezah needed money. The Bureau of African Affairs still amounted to little more than a ritzy rented office suite in suburban Pennsylvania and a growing number of investors who expected to trade their rusty tractors for gold. Just one of the massive deals he had been talking about—for timber, heavy machinery, and minerals—would need more cash up front than all his investors combined had given him so far.

First, Blay-Miezah tried forgery. On January 18, 1974, he opened an account at Central Penn National Bank. He got a bank statement and a checkbook. He deposited ten dollars, took the checkbook, and went on his way. Back at the office, someone took the bank statement and doctored it. Under the first deposit, they typed the date January 26 and a larger deposit: $15,578,000. Blay-Miezah showed investors the statement as proof things were moving along—even if they were slower than promised.

But Blay-Miezah needed some real money. So he planned, in the most subtle way possible, to rob a bank.

In February 1974, Gerald Smith, an assistant manager at a branch of Girard Bank on Sixtieth Street and Ludlow Street in Philadelphia, allegedly visited the offices of the Bureau of African Affairs and Industrial Development. He took with him five blank treasurer's checks: these were checks issued by the officer of a bank, on the bank's own account.

While Smith was sitting there in the plush offices in Bala Cynwyd, Blay-Miezah handed the five checks to a secretary (leaving his fingerprint on one of them). The secretary typed "$50,000" into the amount box of each check and took them back into Blay-Miezah's office, where they were signed "Michael Smith." All the checks were made out to Edusei.

A couple of days later, Blay-Miezah sent a teletype message to a branch of Deutsche Bank in Cologne, Germany. In the message, Blay-Miezah said he had $250,000 in an escrow account numbered 3-664-067, at a West Philadelphia branch of Girard Bank. He would be transferring the money to a business associate in Germany, Edusei, in the form of treasurer's checks. One of Edusei's employees would be visiting the bank to cash the checks.

Girard Bank was not just a mark. It was, for our man, an institution that deserved to be taken. The story of Girard Bank was wrapped up in the original long con—the same long con that pulled every strand of Blay-Miezah's story together: colonialism.

STEPHEN GIRARD WAS born in France and settled in Philadelphia in 1776. Following in the footsteps of his father, Pierre Girard, he held plantations in

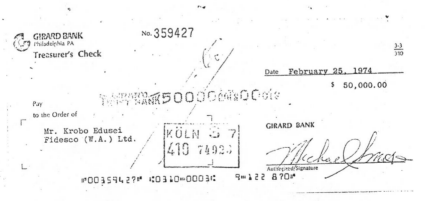

One of the Girard Bank treasurer's checks presented to Deutsche Bank in Cologne, Germany.

Saint-Domingue—a French colony in the Caribbean—and had enslaved people to work on them. Like Francis Drake, Stephen Girard was a privateer. He helped fund American raiders in the War of 1812, which outmaneuvered and plundered the slower, heavier British fleet, just as the British had outmaneuvered the Spanish in the time of Drake.

In 1886, after Girard's death, a lawsuit was brought in the Court of Common Pleas in Philadelphia. Madame Rose de Laulanie said that she was a descendant of Toussaint L'Ouverture, the man who liberated Saint-Domingue. L'Ouverture was a master tactician who would defeat—in a great tangle of allegiances—the British, the Spanish, and the French. He would abolish slavery in what would become Haiti, and eventually on the entire island of Hispaniola, and become governor-general of the island. After he retired, he was kidnapped by men working for Napoléon Bonaparte, who was keen to see to it that people on the island were enslaved again. L'Ouverture died in France in 1803.

Madame de Laulanie alleged that before her ancestor was kidnapped by Napoléon's men, he had entrusted the fortune he had amassed as a military leader and governor-general—about two million dollars—to Stephen Girard, who immediately left for Philadelphia, with the money. "Girard, it is averred, sailed to this port, retaining all the valuables," a newspaper reported in 1886.

At the trial, lawyers representing Girard's estate claimed that he had never met L'Ouverture and had no dealings in Saint-Domingue at the time (which was not the case). In the end, neither side could produce enough proof of their claims. The truth of the case had disappeared, and only stories were left. Girard's heirs insisted that he was blameless, but for the next century and beyond, people in Philadelphia would talk about how Girard swindled Toussaint L'Ouverture and the people of Haiti.

The story was particularly plausible because Girard was the kind of man who had enslaved people and made a fortune from their labor, but piously claimed that he had never owned any plantations. Even to his last breath, his public acts of charity were built on a foundation of petty cruelty toward anyone who wasn't white. Before Girard died in 1831, as well as founding Girard Bank, he bequeathed six million dollars to found a school in Philadelphia. He specified everything: the curriculum, the lunches, and, most important, that the school was to educate "poor, white orphan boys only."

By the 1950s Girard College was a massive compound. It contained an armory, two swimming pools, and a library with ninety thousand books. None of the other schools in its North Philadelphia neighborhood even had a library. Residents protested: the law, and the neighborhood, had changed, so Girard College had to follow suit. The school refused to admit even one Black student.

In 1957, local residents won a landmark Supreme Court case against the school. In response, city officials and the school's trustees performed ever more arcane legal maneuvers to avoid obeying the law. By 1965 there were regular protests by the National Association for the Advancement of Colored People. At the first one, there were twenty people on the picket line, and eight hundred police officers. That summer, several leaders of the civil rights movement joined the picket line, including the Reverend Dr. Martin Luther King Jr.

Even after all that, it was the better part of another decade before the school finally began to admit Black children. Girard, and everything he stood for, remained anathema for many in Philadelphia. The bank he founded was fair game.

BLAY-MIEZAH'S FIVE TREASURER'S checks made their way over the Atlantic to Cologne. It seemed like he and Edusei were about to be $250,000 richer. But there was a problem. The Germans were puzzled by the teletype message they had received from Philadelphia: it was most unorthodox and, a Deutsche Bank employee would later testify, "not understandable."

Staff in Cologne made the unusual move of contacting Girard Bank in Philadelphia for further instructions. They quickly discovered that there was no escrow account and no $250,000 deposit. As soon as it became clear that something had gone wrong, Blay-Miezah left Philadelphia for New York, supposedly to take meetings.

Gerald Smith was arrested by an FBI agent; the woebegone bank manager's bail was set at $5,000. Bail for Blay-Miezah was set at $150,000. Someone else posted his bond. Blay-Miezah would never return to Philadelphia. (Ten years later, the case against Blay-Miezah was dropped, as is standard. But, because he skipped bail, there is to this day an active bench warrant for him in Philadelphia.)

In court, Smith said that he had been conned. The checks, he testified, were never meant to be deposited in a bank: they were just for show—props, for Blay-Miezah. Otherwise, why would Smith have signed them with a pseudonym—Michael Smith—so close to his actual name? Why would he let his telephone extension be used on the teletype message to Cologne? In court, his attorney told the judge that Blay-Miezah "could sell a Toyota to the president of General Motors."

Blay-Miezah's time in New York was brief. He spent it opening accounts for the Oman Ghana Trust Fund at five different banks: Chemical Bank, Manufacturers Hanover Trust Company, Bankers Trust Company, Chase Manhattan, and American Bank and Trust. He left each bank with a brand-new checkbook.

Blay-Miezah next flew to Brussels, where he deposited five enormous checks, totaling $150 million. Then he traveled to Accra. News of his fortune was spreading: the crowd welcoming him at the airport was as big as the one that had seen him off from Takoradi port in 1959. But shortly after his arrival in Ghana, Blay-Miezah was arrested. His next meeting would be with Colonel Acheampong.

Chapter 10

Multi, Multi, Multi

1974

I n front of Acheampong, Blay-Miezah laid out the story of the Oman Ghana Trust Fund. He promised that he could repatriate tens of millions almost immediately—if only Acheampong would let him out of jail.

Acheampong had heard so many rumors about missing millions that when Blay-Miezah turned up to sell the story of the Oman Ghana Trust Fund, his tale, while ridiculous, was far from the strangest one Acheampong had encountered. There had been rumors that Ghana's reserves had been impossible to wrest from the British, rumors about mysterious Swiss bank accounts, rumors about gold being secretly shipped overseas. But multiple inquiries had been able to find only a few kickbacks in the London accounts of a few politicians. Acheampong was sure that there had to be more of Ghana's money out there. Even if Blay-Miezah's story was bunkum, as long as there was a chance his money was real, Acheampong was willing to let him out of jail. But he would be watching closely.

Blay-Miezah had sold the story of President Nkrumah's gold to Ghana's head of state. A few years earlier, he had been running short cons. As he walked out of Osu Castle, a free man, even Blay-Miezah himself could barely believe he had done it.

Our man set to work.

Blay-Miezah needed to look exactly like the wealthy businessman he had convinced Acheampong that he was. And he needed people to vouch for him: people like Krobo Edusei and his other old cellmates at Nsawam Prison, men who had known President Nkrumah but whose principles were for sale. Finally, Blay-Miezah needed friends in the Castle ready to tell him if the colonel got suspicious. So our man began plotting a truly byzantine scheme that would keep Acheampong happy and—with luck—make Blay-Miezah very rich.

Our man needed to keep up the elaborate fictions of both the Oman Ghana Trust Fund and Dr. John Ackah Blay-Miezah. He needed to keep his American investors happy and bring in more investors. He had proved that he could con almost anyone into almost anything. He was starting to believe that he could actually deliver on even his most outlandish promises. With Acheampong on his side, he could sign timber deals, buy minerals, and sell earthmovers. He might be able to get government contracts for his investors. With access to the treasury, he could even pay them back and emerge as a legitimate businessman. All he needed was money and power.

Blay-Miezah was building a stage set, on three continents, for the story of the Oman Ghana Trust Fund. A bank box in Zurich was rented and salted with a trust document apparently signed by President Nkrumah.

Edusei helped Blay-Miezah rent a sprawling home in Airport Residential, a neighborhood full of ritzy, modernist, pastel-colored mansions, surrounded by manicured lawns and high walls topped with barbed wire and broken glass. Blay-Miezah charmed the landlord, S. K. Mainoo. Mainoo was a contractor, and a notoriously corrupt one. He and Edusei knew each other well. When Mainoo was awarded a major government contract, the work was so slapdash and dragged-out that his contract was canceled. Soon he, too, had invested in the Oman Ghana Trust Fund and was funding Blay-Miezah's lifestyle. He even lent him several cars.

The Trust Fund opened an office in the Labone neighborhood, directly opposite the American embassy. Once he had the mansion, and the chauffeured cars, and the office, Blay-Miezah worked hard to court his old friends from Nsawam Prison and to show them how far he had come.

Less than a decade after the coup d'état that unseated Nkrumah, men like Edusei and Ayeh-Kumi had successfully laundered their reputations. The charges of corruption and treason were largely forgotten. Their prison terms were brushed aside. Like Blay-Miezah, they were quick to align themselves with Nkrumah's legacy and play the elder statesmen, the nation's fathers. Blay-Miezah knew that if these men surrounded him, he could put their reputations to work: he, too, could be a statesman.

Just as he had in Philadelphia, Blay-Miezah built himself a network of allies. He met with businessmen and lawyers and newspaper editors and sold them all on the story of the Trust Fund. With most people he was artfully vague about where the money had come from. But rumors began to circulate that the fortune Nkrumah had spirited out of the country had finally been found. Blay-Miezah charmed more of Nkrumah's former ministers, men like the incompetent finance minister Kwesi Amoako-Atta. Blay-Miezah also took particular care to court the chiefs in the Western Region, people who could eventually make him a chief too. He cultivated relationships with officials at the Castle and in the government. When he couldn't charm people, he promised them money.

Blay-Miezah was suddenly a celebrity. It was hard to miss him. Everywhere he went, he would draw a crowd. He was chauffeured around town in large, expensive-looking American cars. The Continental Hotel threw a party in his honor. The pool had been filled with foam, and there was a dancer swimming around doing acrobatic tricks. Blay-Miezah sat at a table by the pool, taking it all in. The party's host made a big show of introducing him as "a multi, multi, multi, multi, multimillionaire." With each "multi" Blay-Miezah shook with laughter and seemed to grow taller in his chair.

But without realizing it, Blay-Miezah had already made a powerful enemy.

EBENEZER MOSES DEBRAH WAS ONE of Ghana's most distinguished diplomats. He had been in the country's civil service for as long as it had existed. He was a fierce defender of President Nkrumah's reputation: he had been shielding the president against lies since the early 1960s, when Debrah was an attaché at the embassy in Washington, D.C., and the American press began making up stories about what the president of Ghana was doing and why he was doing it. Debrah was with Nkrumah in China when the latter was told about the coup d'état. The changes of government since then had not shaken Debrah's loyalty: in his office, he kept a photograph commemorating a visit Nkrumah had made to his home in Accra.

In 1967, Debrah was appointed ambassador to the United States. He immediately became one of the most popular diplomats in D.C., pictured in the papers giving lively speeches, wearing a short Afro parted on the side and a woven tie. He told rapt audiences that "Africa was called dark because others did not want to understand it, failed to understand it, and worked hard not to appreciate it." Debrah also gave legendary parties where militants would dine with diplomats. Ethel Payne, who wrote about the civil rights movement for the iconic, Black-owned newspaper the *Chicago Defender*, described watching the Kente-clad ambassador greet a guest wearing a dashiki and an Afro with "the authentic black power handshake and top it off with a snap of the fingers." At these shindigs, Debrah's staff would serve Ghanaian food. One menu included Nkrumah's favorite groundnut soup, a diced chicken dish made famous at a nightclub in Ghana called Tema Point, and, for dessert, a tongue-in-cheek reference to Ghana's most infamous prison: compote Nsawam.

The ambassador held events for New York congresswoman Shirley Chisholm and organized fundraisers for historically Black colleges and universities. One Christmas he hosted a luncheon for forty inmates from Lorton Reformatory in Virginia. *Jet* magazine said that the function showed Ambassador Debrah was Washington's leading diplomat. Debrah regularly invited African American businesses to invest in Ghana. His aim, he often said, was to bring African Americans and Africans closer together.

It was in 1974—when Debrah was secretary to the National Redemption Council, Colonel Acheampong's junta—that the ambassador started to pick up chatter about Blay-Miezah and the colonel. As a political insider, Debrah was one of the few people to hear the story about Blay-Miezah inheriting his legacy from President Nkrumah. He was appalled. The story was an obvious lie. Blay-Miezah was running a con on the entire country by playing a funhouse mirror version of the person Debrah had worked so hard to be: a man who had been one of Nkrumah's closest confidants, and who had dedicated himself to building connections between African Americans and Ghanaians. Blay-Miezah was mocking everything Debrah stood for. Debrah vowed to put a stop to it.

BLAY-MIEZAH MADE THE exact size of the Trust Fund seem like a closely guarded secret. He claimed that Amoako-Atta—Nkrumah's former finance minister—pressured him to say that his fortune was smaller, more credible. "Just put $150 million down," Amoako-Atta had reportedly said, "because if we mention a lot of money, they may not believe it. For our record purposes, this will do." But in confidence, Blay-Miezah told people he was actually worth far more than $150 million. By the early 1970s, Amoako-Atta's ineptitude was almost forgotten; the man who had allowed Ghana's foreign reserves to dwindle to almost nothing was now considered a brilliant financial mind. His support for Blay-Miezah was unwavering. "I am prepared to stick out my neck and face the firing squad," Amoako-Atta reportedly said, "if at the end of the whole investigation it is proved that Ackah Blay-Miezah's legacy is false." With Amoako-Atta behind him, Blay-Miezah looked like a legitimate businessman. Doors in government began to open to him.

Amoako-Atta was, at the time, also working as a consultant to the country's first properly Ghanaian brewery, Tata Brewery. It was owned by Joshua Kwabena Siaw. By 1974, Siaw *was* a multimillionaire. And he had built it all from nothing. But Siaw was about to fall, hard, for Blay-Miezah. It would eventually cost him everything.

Siaw was born into a family of cocoa farmers in Obomeng, a small town in the Eastern Region. It took years for him to convince his father to let him go to school: the fees were high, and Siaw was needed on the farm because he had a head for numbers. Siaw was finally enrolled at a Presbyterian school in 1935, at the age of eleven.

As soon as he got settled, cocoa prices fell steeply. Then the trees on the farm got hit by the swollen shoot disease. It almost ruined the family. Siaw's father could not afford to pay the fees and pulled him from school. But the child knew how to turn a profit, and if there was no cocoa to sell, he would put a markup on something else. So he started making baskets. Soon he had saved enough to enroll in school again. At school, Siaw was sharp with mathematics but struggled with everything else. He had started puberty before he started his formal education, and it was hard to make up that kind of time. He had wanted to be a professional—a lawyer or a pharmacist—and make his parents proud, but he couldn't get into university with his grades. So he worked. First as a teacher, then as a sanitary laborer at the mines near Bogoso in the Western Region. Then he started trading, first in cocoa—where in just four months he turned a loan of fifty pounds into six hundred pounds of profit—then, for eight years, in the enamel trade. When President Nkrumah banned enamel imports, Siaw shifted to importing textiles, then beverages. When he saw the markups on alcohol, he decided he had to open up a brewery.

That was unheard of. At the time, beer was a cutthroat corner of the import trade. Until independence, it had been run by a cartel of European trading firms. Alcohol was shipped into the country in vats, then sent to bottling plants. To keep costs down, bottles were recycled. You went to a bottle store, bought your Guinness by the crate, then returned the crate of empties. The company recycled the bottles, and you got your deposit back. In 1935, a Swiss company set up a brewery in the Adabraka neighborhood of Accra, between the industrial area and the Ministries, and began producing the first local brew: Club Beer. It was instantly popular, and it triggered a turf war with the importers. For five years, European importers sent employees to buy massive quantities of Club, then empty and destroy the bottles. Production at the Accra brewery ground to a halt, and the plant almost went out of business.

Colonialism was about exploitation: exploiting resources like cotton and gold and cocoa and the human labor required to produce them. Raw materials were extracted, shipped to the colonizing country, turned into finished goods, and then shipped back—at a massive markup. Local manufacturing capacity was systematically suppressed. Colonized people were captive consumers. For people in countries such as Ghana, it was like being robbed—twice. But it kept the factories everywhere from Liverpool to Scranton to Milan going.

"If African countries were permitted to industrialize," wrote Charles P. Howard, the American journalist, "to build their own factories, to modernize their agriculture, they could take their raw materials, manufacture them into needed consumer goods and not have to buy them at terribly inflated prices from outside sources. However, if this were permitted then the continued flow of cheap raw materials from the African producers to the Western manufacturers would be broken. And the ever-expanding market for manufactured goods would be lessened."

The idea that colonized nations would want to produce their own teacups or pilsner was deeply troubling. It would mean competition. Prices would go down, and the cost of raw materials and labor would go up. It could ruin entire industries on the other side of the world. Siaw—a multimillionaire who had started school at the age of eleven because his father never got a fair price for the cocoa he grew—was keenly aware of this. He became almost evangelical about building Ghana's first Ghanaian brewery. He didn't just want to make beer: he wanted to help people make a decent living and send their children to school.

It took Siaw close to a decade to get the license for the brewery. He toured beer-loving countries—West Germany, Denmark, Belgium, the United States, Sweden, the Netherlands, and the United Kingdom—to buy machinery and hire technicians. The brewery was finally opened in Achimota, a leafy suburb of Accra, on Siaw's fiftieth birthday, with Colonel Acheampong presiding. Siaw named it Tata, after his mother, Adwoa Taata. In 1974, the brewery could churn out forty thousand cartons of beer a day. And Siaw made good on his promise to be a decent boss. He built a clinic with an in-house doctor, the employees had a subsidized canteen, and they negotiated—successfully—for a thousand apartments near the complex, more than enough to house every member of the staff. Siaw was also a great philanthropist: he bought machinery and medicine for Korle-Bu Teaching Hospital.

To Siaw, Blay-Miezah looked like a man after his own heart. He, too, seemed to have built a successful business from nothing. He, too, had navigated the politics of making a fortune. And he, too, had big plans that would change Ghana for centuries to come. On the advice of Amoako-Atta, Siaw invested between a quarter of a million and half a

An advertisement for Tata beer in the Ghanaian press.

million cedi—well over a hundred thousand dollars—in the Oman Ghana Trust Fund.

ACROSS THE ROAD from Blay-Miezah's Accra office, in the embassy of the United States, Ambassador Shirley Temple Black was trying to get to the bottom of the stories about him.

When Temple Black was posted to Accra, the *Chicago Defender* made jokes about the government choosing to appoint the former child star rather than hiring "a truly qualified Black." But Temple Black made herself right at home, visiting Makola Market dressed in kaba and slit, looking very much like a middle-class Ghanaian woman going to market. She spoke frequently of "the fortitude, ingenuity and enterprising spirit of Ghanaian women," and how many of the businesses at Makola, and all over the city, were owned by women: tro tros, fishing boats, and stalls in every market.

Out at Accra dinner-dances, Temple Black and Debrah traded the latest gossip about Blay-Miezah. Both of them thought that he was drawing far too many Americans and Ghanaians into his schemes. The potential embarrassment for the United States and Ghana—and for them personally—was too great.

Neither Debrah nor Temple Black thought that it would be difficult to find something on Blay-Miezah that would get him jailed for a long time. They were sure they could run rings around him: he was nothing more than a two-bit crook, after all. They didn't realize who they were dealing with.

BLAY-MIEZAH DIDN'T CARE if Debrah, Temple Black, or the whole world was watching. Life was good. And better yet, he had met someone.

Gladys Desbordes was a secretary. She came from a sheltered, middle-class home in Tarkwa, in the Western Region. Her father worked on the railways that took manganese from the mines at Tarkwa and gold from the mines at Prestea to Takoradi. She had just gotten her diploma at Takoradi Polytechnic. Her first job was at the Timber Marketing Board in Takoradi, then she moved to the board's office in Accra. She planned to go back to school and become a lawyer. When Blay-Miezah visited the offices (perhaps to source the railroad ties "made of heavy African woods that blunt the teeth of American termites" he had claimed to be selling in Philadelphia), he took an instant liking to her. He started calling her at the office, "bombarding [her] on this rotary phone," asking to take her out. Each time, Desbordes turned him down.

Her boss, who enjoyed taking an active role in his employees' lives, sometimes listened in on his extension when Blay-Miezah called. He couldn't believe Desbordes was turning Blay-Miezah down: Did she know who he was? "Is it not that fat man?" she replied. Desbordes didn't know anything about Blay-Miezah and wasn't into politics, so even if she had seen his name in the newspapers, it would not have meant anything to her. Her boss was incredulous: "You mean the millionaire?"

Her boss had his car brought around. He was going to drive her over to Blay-Miezah's office that very moment. Desbordes was dressed simply. Her watch was broken, but she was wearing it, just for show; her boss made her take it off. "I can't believe your watch is stopped and you're taking it to a millionaire's office," he said. He gave her his large, expensive one to wear instead.

At Blay-Miezah's office, Desbordes and her boss sat down to wait. She noticed that reception was full of beautiful, impeccably dressed young women. Eventually, Desbordes and her boss went into Blay-Miezah's office. He was captivating and told her he fell in love the moment he saw her. She realized, years later, that she had been very much the ingenue. "I was just green," she said.

Blay-Miezah needed to look respectable. For that, he needed a spouse. Because Desbordes was naive, he thought, he could carry on doing whatever he wanted and seeing whomever he wanted, and she would sit at home, the picture of the proper wife.

On the drive back to the Timber Marketing Board, Desbordes's boss was ecstatic. He was sure he'd found his secretary a husband. Then—because he was curious about Blay-Miezah too—he asked her whether she'd been able to figure out what, exactly, Blay-Miezah was a doctor of. Desbordes was incredulous; it was so obvious: "Didn't you see all those women in his office? He's a gynecologist." Her boss laughed so hard he swerved the car. A giant rain gutter, several feet wide, ran parallel to the road. He drove right into it.

Desbordes married Blay-Miezah later that year. They had a traditional wedding. Blay-Miezah, flush with Ghanaian investors' money, made a show of increasing the dowry by 1,000 percent; it was the talk of the Western Region. Edusei spoke at the wedding, and several Nkrumah-era ministers attended. Two years into the marriage, Blay-Miezah—who never missed a detail—asked her: "Where is that borrowed watch you brought to my office?"

BLAY-MIEZAH'S PLAN—TO launder his reputation and emerge as a legitimate businessman and potential statesman—was proceeding apace. His new friends had been calling in some favors. In June 1974, someone at the Ghanaian embassy in Washington sent the State Department a note that read like it was dictated by Blay-Miezah himself: "The Government of Ghana has now decided that all criminal charges pending against Dr John Ackah Blay-Miezah in Ghana should be forthwith withdrawn as they have been found groundless. Dr John Ackah Blay-Miezah has now been issued Ghana diplomatic passport No. 000065 and is now considered a worthy citizen of Ghana." It was technically true that there were no pending charges against Dr. John Ackah Blay-Miezah in Ghana. All the charges had been against John Kolorah Blay.

Blay-Miezah's Philadelphia investors were thrilled. While Blay-Miezah was building up his operation in Accra, Robert Ellis had been busy bringing in new investors and reassuring the existing ones. Now, Samuel Canale asked his banker to take over the transfer of $160 million from the Trust Fund to Ghana. The banker was ecstatic: his previous experience in high finance involved transferring money from North Philadelphia to South Philadelphia.

The banker flew to Accra and tried—and failed—to get a meeting with Colonel Acheampong. Much to his frustration, when he called on Ghanaian officials and announced that he would be bringing the country's ancestral wealth home, no one seemed to take him seriously. The vast majority of government officials were intensely skeptical of Blay-Miezah's claims. Eventually, the lawyer contacted the State Department, which told him that he had almost certainly been caught up in a hoax.

Inside the State Department, though, they weren't quite so certain. Officials had been looking into whether there was some truth behind Blay-Miezah's story since he emerged in Philadelphia. "No luck to date finding any trace of mid-sixties research on missing funds," Kissinger told the embassy in Accra. Notably, no one in the State Department took seriously any of the stories about Nkrumah's corruption and his missing millions, which had been appearing in American newspapers for years.

Canale's banker had arrived in Accra at around the same time as a man named Matthew Coppolino. Coppolino was a lawyer from Philadelphia and, until 1972, a Republican member of the Pennsylvania House of Representatives. Coppolino claimed that he had actually met Colonel Acheampong, who told him he would grant Blay-Miezah diplomatic status if that was what he needed to bring back Nkrumah's money.

Coppolino also spent a lot of time with Blay-Miezah. Our man was so open, so trusting, Coppolino said. Blay-Miezah had offered to grant the lawyer power of attorney so that he could go to Zurich and see President Nkrumah's secret trust document for himself. Now officially smitten with Blay-Miezah, Coppolino went to Zurich along with Alija Dumas, one of our man's American investors and also a former member of the Pennsylvania House of Representatives. Dumas ran a detective agency in Philadelphia and was vice president of a branch of the NAACP. After a few days in Switzerland, Coppolino flew back to Philadelphia wide-eyed. He said he had seen the documents. The Oman Ghana Trust Fund was real. And he could not believe how many zeroes there were. The State Department tried to find out as much as possible about what Coppolino had seen—and whether Blay-Miezah's fortune was actually real.

Blay-Miezah, was, incidentally, said to owe Coppolino and his associates one hundred thousand dollars in fees.

BLAY-MIEZAH'S LIST OF allies kept growing: he seemed to be able to win over everyone in his path. Debrah and Temple Black realized that he would not be as easy to squash as they had thought. They considered extraditing Blay-Miezah back to the United States to face charges for his part in the

Girard Bank scam. Debrah had not been able to find much on Blay-Miezah in Ghana. "It is doubtful GOG [Government of Ghana] can muster anything more serious than misuses of passport or similar miscellaneous low-level charges," Temple Black cabled Kissinger. "They might well be glad to get rid of him." This suggestion was met with a shrug.

So Debrah went directly to Colonel Acheampong and tried to stop him taking Blay-Miezah seriously. Debrah was persistent. He brandished a copy of President Nkrumah's modest will, showing that the former president had died with little more than the royalties from his books to his name. He also reminded the colonel of Blay-Miezah's extensive history as a con man. When that didn't work, Debrah revealed one last thing: Blay-Miezah was about to be indicted for bank fraud in Pennsylvania. That got the colonel's attention.

BLAY-MIEZAH DECIDED THAT Accra was becoming a little too hot for him. He made plans to decamp to Brussels, ostensibly to meet with bankers. He asked a friend at the Ministry of Foreign Affairs to call the Ghanaian embassy in Brussels and tell them he was on his way. He wanted the embassy to cover his bills. It was an evolution of the trick he had played in Philadelphia, except now he had a diplomatic passport.

When Debrah heard what Blay-Miezah was up to, he was livid. The Ministry of Foreign Affairs sent out an emphatic memo to all Ghanaian missions, warning them to steer clear of Blay-Miezah. "His hotel and other expenses are his own private matter . . . Missions should NOT repeat NOT grant loans or guarantee bill." Debrah asked his contacts at the Belgian embassy in Accra to look out for Blay-Miezah.

Blissfully unaware, Blay-Miezah went to the Belgian embassy with Siaw, the managing director of Tata Brewery, and Edusei in tow, to make sure that he got the most deferential reception possible. They were shown into the office of the chargé d'affaires. Blay-Miezah said that they were in a rush to get to Belgium to complete a bank transaction for $160 million and needed emergency visas. They had to catch a plane in a matter of minutes. Forewarned by Debrah, the Belgians turned him down. Blay-Miezah might have gotten away with it if he hadn't overplayed his hand with the Ministry of Foreign Affairs.

Blay-Miezah was stuck in Accra. But he had learned to always have a backup plan. And his backup plans were always bigger than his original schemes. Now, as he could not fly to Brussels, he planned to put on a show in Accra: the kind of show that would draw media attention and make it look as if everything were proceeding as planned. The money was coming, Blay-Miezah told everyone, but he needed official cooperation to bring it home. Soon, people across the country were petitioning the government to do the right thing and back him. Meanwhile, Blay-Miezah tried to set up multiple government officials to take the fall when the money failed to materialize, as he knew it would.

First, Blay-Miezah went to see the commissioner for economic planning, Colonel Roger Felli, and told him the story of his fortune, and the projects he wanted to fund. Felli was noncommittal and somewhat skeptical. He reminded Blay-Miezah that he was free to do whatever he wanted with his own money, but he would need government approval for any infrastructure projects. Blay-Miezah asked for this in writing. Felli looked over his suggested wording. It implied that the government was working with Blay-Miezah directly and acknowledged that his fortune was real. The commissioner declined.

Undeterred, Blay-Miezah held another meeting with the chiefs of the Western Region. He told them that Acheampong had given him almost everything he needed to bring the fortune home. All that was left was the cooperation of the commissioner for economic planning, and the land he needed for industrial plants. Blay-Miezah thought that he could put pressure on the commissioner and negotiate for enough land up front to keep his investors happy. The chiefs weren't about to give the land under their protection away for free, but they did—in principle—support his plans. Chiefs and leaders from all over the Western Region started petitioning the commissioner for economic planning. However, Acheampong's government later claimed in a press release, "The Ministry of Economic Planning was careful to ensure that these requests from local people did not get government involved in the operations of the Oman Ghana Trust Fund."

So Blay-Miezah played his next card. A few weeks later a man named Arno Newman arrived in Accra. Newman said he was the president of Geoffrey's Bank in Brussels. Blay-Miezah made sure that his favorite newspaper editor, Kwame Gyawu-Kyem at the *Ghanaian Times*, covered Newman's arrival.

Newman was, Blay-Miezah made it known, the financial mastermind who would complete the task of transferring the money over the next few weeks. The appearance of a distinguished-looking banker from Europe was designed to convince his critics that they were wrong, and to impress everyone else. Blay-Miezah was pleased with how things were taking shape. This was a miscalculation.

IN EARLY DECEMBER, Blay-Miezah held a press conference at the Western Regional House of Chiefs. He was surrounded by businessmen and Nkrumah-era politicians who had invested in the Trust Fund and lent him their credibility, along with many of his American supporters. He announced that the Oman Ghana Trust Fund would spend eighty-six million dollars on development projects in the region. Blay-Miezah promised to build more than the British had in a century of colonization. "The Chinese say, every journey begins with the first step. Let us take the first step," Blay-Miezah said.

The promises gushed out of him. The Trust Fund would tar roads and build a bridge over the River Ankobra. There would be industrial farms and a fishing harbor at Bonyere to accommodate new deep-sea fishing vessels. The dusty machinery from West Conshohocken would be hired out to contractors working on the projects, and the Trust Fund would build a brick and tile factory at Nawule to supply them. They were hiring builders, engineers, architects, and management consultants, and were happy to take meetings. Blay-Miezah would spend four million dollars piping water to the villages, including the one he was born in. He promised that his investments would "make the average Ghanaian smile. How does a Ghanaian smile, and why does he smile? Because he is happy, morally, physically, spiritually, financially."

But the only donation Blay-Miezah actually made, at the time, was a hundred cedi, which he donated to the Ghana Muslim Council, to thank them for offering prayers in support of the "successful implementation of the $86 million projects." To placate Colonel Acheampong, Blay-Miezah "stressed that the Trust, as a private charitable organization, has no political aims and objectives, adding that its primary and overriding aim 'is to foster the

Blay-Miezah surrounded by the chiefs of the Western Region.

economic and social development of the Western Region.'" He made sure that his quote got into the *Times*. After the press conference, Blay-Miezah was photographed surrounded by the chiefs, President Nkrumah's former ministers, and his investors.

The announcement dominated the news, but it left few people convinced: Was Blay-Miezah really everything he claimed to be? More and more Ghanaians were growing quietly skeptical of his ostentatious claims. One newspaper editor who had been to the United States a couple of months earlier remembered seeing uncomplimentary headlines—something about Blay-Miezah and a bank in Philadelphia.

Accra's diplomats, too, were perplexed. Nobody at the American embassy had heard of Newman. So the Americans got in touch with the Belgian embassy—but no one there had heard of him either. The Swiss and the Germans were baffled, too, as were the Australians and the British. Geoffrey's was a real Belgian bank, but Arno Newman was a mystery.

DEBRAH WANTED THE world to know that Ghana was closed to con men. He was tired of his country's reputation being tarnished by one huckster after another. And he wanted Blay-Miezah out of the picture once and for all. By now, Debrah had done his research: he knew all about Blay-Miezah's Philadelphia operation and the scam he had tried to pull on Girard Bank. The ambassador saw to it that the news about the Girard Bank con was reported in every major newspaper in Ghana.

This sent Blay-Miezah into a mild panic. Desperate to bury the bad headlines, he called his favorite editor, Gyawu-Kyem at the *Times*. The editor wrote a column that, at least initially, seemed objective: "It is not so much the vastness of the money which Dr Miezah claims to hold in trust for Ghana that bothers people's minds. It is the mantle of secrecy which veils the source of the money and Dr Miezah's reluctance to disclose it." But the *Times* piece went on dismiss the American stories as a smear campaign. Blay-Miezah, the editorial said, was surrounded by crack politicians and big businessmen, the kind of "men who are not easy to be deceived or taken for a ride." He deserved the benefit of the doubt. "It might be wise to give Dr Blay Miezah a chance to prove true or false."

A few days later, the *Times* granted him that chance. The paper ran an exclusive interview with Blay-Miezah. His fortune, he said, was actually bequeathed to him by a friend he had made in Philadelphia in the 1950s, Daniel Wilbur Layman, a wealthy philanthropist who was moved by Blay-Miezah's plans for his home country and had donated millions to the cause. This was an entirely new origin story for the Oman Ghana Trust Fund. It was designed to appease Acheampong, who was wary of making Nkrumah seem like everything the Americans said he was. It let Blay-Miezah circumvent people like Debrah, who knew Nkrumah too well to believe his story for a second. It also sowed confusion: the more stories Blay-Miezah had, the harder it would be to prove that the money never existed. If pressed, he might reveal, in strict confidence, that Layman had actually been acting for President Nkrumah. (In Washington, the State Department promptly set to work researching this new angle: "Efforts by USG agencies to establish any connection between Layman and Nkrumah remain unsuccessful.")

Blay-Miezah said that he had received the funds on November 19. Amoako-Atta, Nkrumah's most trusted financial adviser, and Newman, from Geoffrey's Bank, were resolving some legal and financial issues so that he could transfer the money, with the help of "Matthew Coppolino, attorney at law and a member of the House of Representatives of the United States." The interview was a dizzying combination of half-truths and outright lies.

Debrah considered his next move. He and a few other government officials didn't just want Blay-Miezah jailed; they intended "this case to raise such a stink that you can smell it from London to Zaire." They wanted to "blow the whistle," Debrah told American diplomats, and take down Amoako-Atta and all the other politicians who had vouched for Blay-Miezah. It was a risky play. Blay-Miezah seemed to be able to talk his way out of anything. And several officials, including Colonel Acheampong, were still willing to wait and see if Blay-Miezah really did have any money. At this point, many were in too deep to admit that they might have thrown their support behind a con man.

Debrah considered charging Blay-Miezah with fraud: he had borrowed money from a number of banks in Accra using the Trust Fund as a guarantee. Those loans were about to come due. Most importantly, though, Debrah wanted him in jail. On December 19, Debrah gathered what little political capital he had left and had Blay-Miezah arrested for escaping police custody on the petty fraud case from 1969. Debrah planned to ensure that Blay-Miezah was charged with everything else he could think of. He would tie him up in legal proceedings long enough for the colonel to lose interest.

After his arrest, at police headquarters, Blay-Miezah was indignant. "The case is not true," he told reporters. "If I am a wanted person, the police should have arrested me long since. I think there is something fishy somewhere." He asked to be released on bail. "I am sick," he complained. The prosecutor, Deputy Superintendent E. K. Awuah, pointed out that the last time Blay-Miezah had been under arrest in Ghana, he had also complained about being unwell. Shortly afterward, on the way to the hospital in Cape Coast, he had escaped police custody. Blay-Miezah looked outraged. "This case is being raised only to soil my reputation," he said. Blay-Miezah's first court appearance was scheduled for December 20, just before Christmas, in Cape Coast.

The Americans seemed relieved. "We assume," wrote Temple Black, "Castle is now unanimous in wishing to prosecute Blay-Miezah at least on bail-jumping charge and through this charge to discredit him."

THE FIRST HINT that things were not going to plan came with the morning's papers. There was our man, on the front page of the *Ghanaian Times*, dressed in a white leisure suit and black loafers, grinning broadly. SABOTEURS CAN'T STOP ME, proclaimed the headline. Blay-Miezah told reporters that the police, American agents, and Ghana's detractors would not impede the work of his Trust Fund. He also "denied allegation[s] of his involvement in fraudulent checks in the US and claimed that the CIA and the FBI had colluded with other Ghanaians to discredit him."

Crowds gathered outside the court in Cape Coast where Blay-Miezah was due to appear. His lawyers were there. The prosecutors were there, led by Deputy Superintendent Awuah. Everybody was waiting on Blay-Miezah himself. Everyone wanted to "catch a glimpse of the first Ghanaian multimillionaire," to see what car he was in, who was in his entourage, and whether there was any truth to the rumors about his fortune. It was hot and very dry. The harmattan was about to start blowing. The light was intense, almost blinding. There was about to be a show.

Then, nothing happened. For hours, nothing kept happening. Slowly, the crowd started to thin.

Eventually, word came that the attorney general's office had dropped the case. Blay-Miezah had never even left Accra: he had been one step ahead of the prosecutors all along. Unlike them, he had known that the trial was not going to go ahead: his political capital now far outweighed Debrah's.

A few days later, Deputy Superintendent Awuah went to Blay-Miezah's mansion, cap in hand, to inform him that the case had been officially dropped. Blay-Miezah was magnanimous in victory; he even invited the officer to stay for a drink. In public, he vowed to get back to the work at hand. "I pledge again, if I am given a chance, and I am not disturbed, and I am not interrupted unnecessarily—within the shortest time, I will tell you, I will perform," Blay-Miezah said. "I will perform to the surprise of many. The doubting Thomases can still have their faith. It is not possible to have everybody believe in the existence of God."

Chapter 11

Hubris

1975

O n New Year's Eve, Blay-Miezah hosted a lavish dinner at the Continental Hotel in Accra. He sat at the head of the table, surrounded by friends both distinguished and infamous. On one side of him was Kwesi Amoako-Atta and his wife, Mary. Mary Lou Valinote, Blay-Miezah's secretary from Philadelphia, was on the other. Also at the dinner-dance was the Romanian businessman Noe Drevici, who was slumped in his chair, looking tipsy and smug in a shirt that was just a little too tight in the collar. He sat next to his wife, Ursula.

The Drevicis were friends of Krobo Edusei. Ostensibly, they were exactly the kind of people Blay-Miezah preferred to surround himself with: successful industrialists. They had arrived in Ghana in the 1960s and, with Edusei's help, quickly made friends in high places. "The Drevicis turned up in practically every ministry," wrote another European businessman vying for the same government contracts. "All the permanent secretaries felt themselves trampled over as Noe and Ursula went straight to the ministers." The Americans, at the time, called Drevici the "biggest con man yet" to stalk the halls of power. Almost none of the Drevicis' projects were ever completed. They would later claim that they had been granted fifty-six million dollars of promissory notes by Nkrumah's government. The couple had been expelled from Ghana repeatedly, most recently by Busia.

Noe Drevici had a habit of getting sloppily drunk and telling ghastly stories about paying off Nazis. "I had a big biscuit factory: I sold to the German army, I sold to the Russian army, I did good business. A German general came to me and demanded one million marks. I said to him: 'give me an order worth five million and tomorrow you can have a million.' He brought me the order for five million—I gave him the million." Ursula and Noe would get into competitive yelling matches about the atrocities committed by their respective nations. "We also paid our prisoners of war," Ursula, who was from Hamburg, would shout. "My dearest," Noe Drevici would yell, "you gassed them, you hanged them, and you let the wretches starve!"

That New Year's Eve, the Drevicis looked exceedingly pleased to be back in Ghana, and like they were about to be back in business. Blay-Miezah's desire for powerful friends was leading him further and further away from radical priests and economic liberation, and closer to people who delighted in committing—and profiting from—atrocities.

COLONEL ACHEAMPONG WAS getting impatient. Blay-Miezah had promised results in weeks, but months had gone by, and no money had arrived. And, despite the government dropping the court case against Blay-Miezah, questions about the money were getting more insistent by the day. J. K. Siaw, along with many of Blay-Miezah's other investors, wanted answers, or their money back.

Blay-Miezah, at this point, had two ways out: either run a con that made him enough money to pay everybody off and turn himself into a legitimate businessman, or attempt to keep his story going and—when the money failed to materialize—find someone to pin the blame on. At the beginning of 1975, Blay-Miezah was trying both.

Blay-Miezah accused everyone he could think of—from Debrah to the CIA and the Bank of Ghana—of standing in his way: of sabotaging the best thing to happen to the Western Region in hundreds of years. He called angry press conferences, gave outraged speeches, and did what he did best: put on a show. He hoped that pressure from the media, and from Acheampong, would make his critics fall back and fall into line. Meanwhile, he had a plan to steal enough money to buy his way out of the promises he had made.

For now, his scheme was—largely—going to plan. He had left Philadelphia as a bail jumper. He had been locked up in Ghana. Now, though, he was riding a wave: he had the mansion, the chauffeured cars, and the high life. He was so confident in his power that he could ignore his own court date. He could face down some of the most influential people in Ghana, like Debrah. He was acting as if he could not fail. It seemed like things could only get better.

But Blay-Miezah was rapidly collecting powerful adversaries. And he soon found that—even with friends in high places—there were lies he couldn't sell and enemies he couldn't make. Within weeks, Colonel Acheampong would bring the curtain down on Blay-Miezah's show.

BLAY-MIEZAH HAD NO way to make millions of dollars legitimately. But he did have a way to steal millions of dollars: the check scam, which had almost worked on Girard Bank in Philadelphia. Now, Blay-Miezah was trying to run it again. This time, he had the help of Arno Newman, an even friendlier banker than Gerald Smith. And this time, the scheme was even more elaborate. Unfortunately, for it to succeed, Blay-Miezah would have to scam Ghana's central bank, the Bank of Ghana, in the same way he had scammed Girard Bank. His plan was the equivalent of turning up at the United States Federal Reserve with an empty truck and expecting it to be filled with money. That was never going to happen.

In late 1974, Amoako-Atta had sent the Bank of Ghana a telex stating that he planned to open an account at a branch of Ghana Commercial Bank in London and make a deposit of ten million dollars. Staffers were nonplussed. It was an odd message to send.

Soon after, Amoako-Atta, Blay-Miezah, and Newman called at the offices of the governor of the Bank of Ghana to tell him, in person, about the deposit. The governor, Amon Nikoi, met them as a courtesy to Amoako-Atta, who had been deputy governor of the bank in the 1960s. Amoako-Atta must have known, thought Nikoi, that they did not need a central bank's permission to transfer their own money from one bank account to another. He wondered what they were really up to.

Nikoi was in fact being set up as a patsy for Blay-Miezah's next move. Blay-Miezah took the checkbooks he had picked up from five New York banks on his way out of the United States—Chemical Bank, Bankers Trust Company, Manufacturers Hanover Trust Company, Chase Manhattan, and American Bank and Trust—and wrote one check from each bank. Four checks were for thirty million dollars, and one was for twenty-one million dollars. He gave the five checks to Newman, who deposited them with Geoffrey's Bank.

Newman was supposed to see to it that, while they waited for the checks to clear, Geoffrey's Bank would extend a ten-million-dollar line of credit secured on the deposit. The millions would be transferred to the account Amoako-Atta planned to open at Ghana Commercial Bank in London. Blay-Miezah would then appear to be a legitimate multimillionaire.

WHILE HE WAITED for Geoffrey's Bank to open his line of credit, Blay-Miezah continued to act as if everything were proceeding as planned with the Trust Fund's development projects. On the first of January, looking fresh as ever despite the previous night's celebrations, he announced that he was setting up Oman Ghana Trust Holdings Limited. He chose the holiday not because it was convenient but because it was a slow news day. Kwame Gyawu-Kyem, the editor of the *Ghanaian Times*, could give him a front-page story, an editorial, and space on the photo pages. Everyone would see the news.

Blay-Miezah also staged a board meeting of the new company, for the benefit of the newspapers. His office was closed, so Amoako-Atta (in a loose collar, looking slightly worse for wear) and three chiefs from the Western Region—Awulae Kwesi Amakyi II, paramount chief of Western Nzema; Awulae Blay, paramount chief of Eastern Nzema; and Nana Ayebie Amihere, chief of Half-Assini—crowded around his dining table.

Blay-Miezah announced yet another dizzying array of plans: "industrial complexes, the establishment and take-over of factories and the entering into any joint-ventures. Others are constructional works, such as building of roads, bridges, houses, harbors, clinics and hospitals, quarrying and mining. The rest are wood processing, transportation services, establishment of plant pool and the participation in fishing, fish processing, and cold storage businesses."

Any concerns about how the company was actually going to do all this should be allayed by the presence of Amoako-Atta, the *Times* said, who had "satisfied himself that all is well." The *Times* also ran an almost evangelical editorial: "Since the famous Dawn Broadcast by Osagyfo Dr Kwame Nkrumah in 1961, that wealthy Ghanaians should bring back their funds from abroad and invest them locally in viable projects to help solve some of the economic problems of the country, the response has not been encouraging. Dr Blay-Miezah's good intentions are worthy of emulation." Blay-Miezah, the editorial implied, was Nkrumah's truest disciple.

Blay-Miezah had also invited some American investors to Ghana to tour possible sites for their projects. Ben Bynum and two Philadelphia businessmen, Samuel Canale and Robert Brandon, all visited the Western Region, along with Father James Woodruff. They were photographed at the site of the planned harbor at Bonyere, wearing short-sleeved shirts and slacks with sharp creases ironed into them. The *Times* described the men as American engineers inspecting the sites for planned development projects. The Americans also visited New Town, "where an 18-mile road will be constructed to break the old system of transportation along the sea shore."

The investors were in Ghana for a week. They didn't see much of Blay-Miezah himself: he was—they were told—very busy. He had maybe six hours to spare the entire time. That didn't stop them from visiting the U.S. embassy and lobbying on his behalf. Staffers at the embassy weren't sure what to think: "Aside from wanting to see the Ambassador (they did not), the only apparent reason for their visit was to 'inform' the Embassy of their presence and to inquire what the Embassy currently thought of Blay-Miezah (answer was non-committal, except to note that he had indictment to answer in the U.S.). All four gave the impression that they continued to have full faith in Blay-Miezah."

Blay-Miezah assured everyone that work on the projects would start soon—but only if he got everything he wanted. "Work starts on Oman Ghana projects this week," reported the *Times*, somewhat breathlessly. "Dr Blay-Miezah disclosed that about 10 million dollars was to be transferred to Ghana Commercial Bank's London branch by the Trust's bankers in Belgium," the paper said: "Mr Arno Newman, president of Geoffrey's Bank, Brussels,

*Blay-Miezah's investors, including Ben Bynum, Samuel Canale,
and Robert Brandon, inspecting a site near Half Assini.*

flew in on Sunday to hold discussions with Dr Blay-Miezah, he flies back
today to effect the transfer."

But, Blay-Miezah said, there were already signs that powerful Ghanaians
were trying to stop him bringing his fortune home. "Dr Blay-Miezah lamented
that he was not receiving the co-operation he expected from some quarters.
He said for example, a telex message sent to the Bank of Ghana last November
by his bankers seeking approval for the transfer of $10 million to Ghana on
his behalf has not been replied to up to yesterday." The *Times* didn't question
why Blay-Miezah would need approval to transfer his own money between
his own bank accounts. Or why Ghana's central bank was involved in the first
place.

What multi-multi-multi-multi-multimillionaire did not know how his
money was managed? More and more people were beginning to question
Blay-Miezah's stories. What began as dinner party gossip was growing louder
and more insistent. Ambassador Debrah had been saying—for months now—
that Blay-Miezah was a liar and a con man. Now people listened in earnest.

On January 11, Blay-Miezah held a press conference at his home in Airport
Residential. He offered anyone who doubted him an all-expenses-paid trip
to Brussels, courtesy of the Trust Fund, to meet with Arno Newman and
inspect Blay-Miezah's bank accounts. The *Times* dutifully reported that "he
said it was painful to see that Ghanaians in positions of responsibility are
trying hard to use their offices to destroy his image at home and abroad."

Once his bona fides had been established, Blay-Miezah promised, he would sue any remaining detractors for defamation of character. "Very soon, they will all be ashamed of themselves," he said.

Other papers started to line up behind Blay-Miezah. The editor of the *Palaver*, Chris Asher, ran an editorial suggesting that Debrah was slandering him, and claiming the ambassador was colluding with the Americans. In the end, the editorial said, it didn't matter where the money came from: even if Blay-Miezah had somehow pulled off a colossal heist and stolen millions upon millions of dollars from America, that was Ghanaian money now.

At the same time, Blay-Miezah's skeptics were growing more confident. The publisher of the *Daily Graphic*, Kofi Badu, pondered sending a reporter to Philadelphia or hiring someone in the city to dig up dirt on him. "Topic is currently most talked about in Accra circles," wrote Temple Black. "We assume chickens will soon be home to roost."

NEWMAN WAS SUPPOSED to make sure Blay-Miezah got his $10 million line of credit from Geoffrey's Bank. Five checks—totaling $141 million—were deposited in Blay-Miezah's account at the bank. But staffers at Geoffrey's decided to confirm that the checks were valid before extending the line of credit to him. The State Department, which was still watching him closely, cabled the American embassy in Accra with the news that Blay-Miezah's checks were arriving in America and bouncing sky-high. Chemical Bank received a letter "from Geoffrey's Bank enclosing photocopy of front and back of check for $30 million. Letter inquired as to legitimacy of check and indicated if check is bona fide, the original would be presented on December 24 in New York City." Chemical Bank replied that the check was worthless. So Geoffrey's Bank investigated the other checks, which were all likewise refused. There were no funds in the account at Manufacturers Hanover Trust Company, and there were no accounts at all at Bankers Trust Company, Chase Manhattan Bank, or American Bank and Trust.

At this point, Geoffrey's Bank wrote an indignant letter to the Oman Ghana Trust Fund, accusing Blay-Miezah of stealing bank letterhead to forge documents and telling him never to use the name of Geoffrey's Bank again.

The bank was, diplomats noted, "rather small to be engaged in any large international activities." No one could work out why the bank was involved. In fact, the reason was simple: Arno Newman was a crook.

Geoffrey's Bank was not all it appeared to be. Newman owned almost all its shares but held no official position at the bank, despite his habit of introducing himself as the president: his wife was the president, and his son—Geoffrey, the company's namesake—held a vaguely defined junior role. This left Newman free to do deals around the world, out of sight of the Belgian banking regulators. This arrangement proved very profitable for the Newmans: there would soon be a painting by Peter Paul Rubens hanging in their living room. In 1975, officials still thought Geoffrey's Bank was "clean"; they had no idea what the Newmans were up to.

Arno Newman had, however, been up to his neck in dubious deals for years. He was a friend of the notorious American political operative Roy Cohn, the former chief counsel to Senator Joseph McCarthy during the Red Scare, who now wielded power as a Republican Party fixer (and mentor to the young Donald Trump). Cohn and Newman had "certain business dealings" together, which included an incident in 1966, when "Geoffrey's Bank transmitted $100,000 to Cohn who deposited this sum in his personal bank account." The transaction "aroused the suspicions of the Securities and Exchange Commission," and Cohn was forced to explain himself in federal court. By 1975, Newman had racked up two convictions for fraud and had been refused entry to the United States.

When Blay-Miezah realized that no help would be coming from Geoffrey's Bank, and no ten million dollars would be arriving at the Trust Fund's account in London, he knew that his back was against the wall. But he had seen this possibility coming. He went on the offensive and offered up his preplanned scapegoat.

THE *GHANAIAN TIMES* ran a massive double-page spread, attacking the Bank of Ghana. The article was littered with typographical and grammatical errors, as if written in haste by someone not bound by editorial standards. Under a two-page banner headline that read BANK OF GHANA VERSUS DR. MIEZAH, it accused the governor of the Bank of Ghana, Amon Nikoi, of sabotage. Blay-Miezah told the paper that he had been trying to move his money into the country for months, but had not been able to secure permission from the Bank of Ghana to make the transfer. The *Times* even published a telex that Blay-Miezah claimed Geoffrey's Bank had sent to the Bank of Ghana on October 23, 1974: "Would you please advise us by telex if we could establish an external account with the Bank of Ghana in USA dollars. Thanking you."

"The facts here speak for themselves," the article fumed. "Up to yesterday, the Bank of Ghana had not acknowledged receipt of that telex message nor given the permission sought. That 'indifference' has deprived Ghana of an investment capital which the country needs so badly." Despite not receiving a response, Amoako-Atta had tried to transfer the money anyway, Blay-Miezah said. But the transaction didn't go through because of the Bank of Ghana. That was the holdup: that was why work had not yet started on the Trust Fund's projects. Colonel Acheampong and all the investors should

The two-page BANK OF GHANA VERSUS DR. MIEZAH *spread in the* Ghanaian Times.

talk to the governor of the Bank of Ghana if they had a problem with the delays.

But the governor of the Bank of Ghana was a terrible choice for a patsy. Blay-Miezah should have known that a central bank would have enough sway with a state-owned paper like the *Times* for someone at the bank to be asked to comment. The bank's blistering response took up a third of the spread.

"The provisions of the Exchange Control Act 1961 *do not and I repeat do not* place any restrictions on transfer of funds of any amount into the country by any persons or organizations," the statement read. "It is ABSOLUTELY NOT TRUE that the President of Geoffrey's Bank in Brussels, Belgium, has in a telex message to the Bank of Ghana requested the latter's approval to transfer an amount of $10 million to Ghana for investment."

The furor dominated the headlines for days. The National Redemption Council put out a statement the next day: "The integrity of certain top officials of these two national banks were seriously attacked in the papers. As a result government felt compelled to investigate the circumstances under which the two national banks came to obstruct Mr Blay Miezah."

Debrah was now not the only government official looking into Blay-Miezah. Special Branch had kept him under surveillance since he returned to Ghana. Now, they decided it was time to question him. His old schoolmaster Kofi Bentum Quantson—who had known him for decades—was assigned the task.

Quantson had been watching his former pupil closely. Blay-Miezah seemed to have acquired a new name and was telling a new variation of the story he told Quantson back in 1971, about the fortune he had acquired overseas. Quantson wondered how Blay-Miezah had "wormed his way into the top circles of the government and of the National Redemption Council." He brought Blay-Miezah in for questioning.

At first, Blay-Miezah was evasive. He wouldn't say how much money he had or how he came by it. But Quantson knew how to warm him up. Eventually, Blay-Miezah swore him to secrecy, then spilled. He said that soon, he would be running Ghana. He would appoint all the ministers and would choose who ran the Bank of Ghana.

Quantson would later write that he was horrified. This was the second time that Blay-Miezah had tried to drag him into plotting a coup. He realized

Blay-Miezah was obsessed with gaining power for himself and would do anything to make that happen. After the interview, Quantson immediately briefed his boss, who took it to a meeting of the National Redemption Council. But Blay-Miezah had friends in high places, and within hours, somebody had told him exactly what was said at the council meeting: he was a one-man national security breach.

Soon afterward, Blay-Miezah burst into Quantson's office and demanded to know why he had told the military about his plans. It had jeopardized everything. Quantson tried every trick he could think of to persuade Blay-Miezah that he wasn't the one who had told the government. He reminded him about the time they had met at the Star Hotel back in 1971, when he told an entire hotel bar that he was about to launch a coup, and almost got Quantson thrown in jail for treason in the process. "I pressed it down on him that, I was sure—in his big talks—he had told somebody else about his grand political schemes. He grudgingly gave me the benefit of the doubt."

NOW BLAY-MIEZAH HAD some explaining to do. The commissioner of economic planning, Colonel Roger Felli, wrote him a very public letter and gave him a week to explain himself. Blay-Miezah still had powerful allies, notably Acheampong, so he could not be dismissed: no matter how ridiculous his claims were, officials had to give him a hearing.

His lawyers offered up a reply that explained nothing—Blay-Miezah "merely invited the people of Ghana to accept his words on trust." Newman, he said, "was due in Ghana in a few days and would be in a position to make certain new facts available to the government."

In early February, Blay-Miezah was called before Colonel Felli. Everybody involved with the affair was there: the attorney general, the inspector general of police, the governor of the Bank of Ghana, the managing director of the Ghana Commercial Bank. Blay-Miezah's supporters were there as well: Siaw, the owner of Tata Brewery; Gyawu-Kyem, the editor of the *Ghanaian Times*; Edusei; and Newman; as well as Blay-Miezah's secretary from Philadelphia, Valinote. Blay-Miezah had also hired two distinguished lawyers: Alfred Augustus Akainyah, who had been a Supreme Court judge under Nkrumah; and Bashiru Kwaw-Swanzy, the former attorney general who had jailed

Blay-Miezah back in 1964 but who was now at work on behalf of the Oman Ghana Trust Fund.

Colonel Felli asked Blay-Miezah to explain himself: Why had he tried to embroil the government of Ghana in massive check fraud? And who, exactly, was Arno Newman? Newman offered some explanations. He said that while he no longer ran Geoffrey's Bank, he owned "99% of the share capital." The threatening letter from Geoffrey's Bank, Newman said, would be withdrawn once the checks were successfully deposited.

Blay-Miezah had no way of knowing that his five checks would bounce, Newman insisted. An American financial institution had been instructed to deposit his funds into the five banks on December 24, 1974, Newman said, and the payment failed through no fault of Blay-Miezah's. Newman claimed that "he was personally convinced that Blay-Miezah had funds with a certain institution in America. He [Newman] declined to disclose the name of this institution."

Newman said that "it was his belief that certain forces were operating to take advantage of Mr Blay-Miezah, and in his capacity as a friend of Mr Blay-Miezah he was prepared to do everything to counteract those forces." He just needed ten days, he told everyone at the meeting. He was planning to go to America and transfer the money himself. Blay-Miezah, he said, had even given him power of attorney.

Felli wanted to make it clear to Acheampong, and to Blay-Miezah's other influential supporters, that, had Blay-Miezah needed any help, he would have offered it. So "the Commissioner asked the representatives of the Oman Ghana Trust Fund whether they wanted the Government to assist them in any form with respect to the release of the funds from U.S.A. to Ghana. After some hesitation the representatives of the Oman Ghana Trust Fund replied that no such assistance would be necessary." Most of the people in the room knew that they were engaged in a farce—but Colonel Acheampong had thrown too much behind Blay-Miezah to back down just yet.

Newman flew out of Accra. For two weeks, investors waited by their phones. Then: nothing happened. Acheampong had seen to it that the government had given Blay-Miezah everything he asked for, but no money had materialized. Day by day, everyone involved was looking increasingly foolish. Newman asked for an extension. But Acheampong had lost patience: there would be no more extensions. Blay-Miezah could feel the atmosphere cooling around him. Just as he had before, he got his suitcase out. Soon, Newman cabled that Blay-Miezah had to leave Ghana immediately: he had to be on the next flight to Zurich to handle the matter. He tried to leave and was caught with a large sum of cash in his possession. The government seized both his personal passport and the diplomatic passport that Acheampong had given him.

Blay-Miezah, who always had a scapegoat ready, would later claim that the real reason the checks didn't clear was because Newman was a crook who had exploited him: "Under Belgian law he was not allowed to endorse or operate the bank, because of his outside business interests. For that reason, the banks rejected the checks, and did not pay." He—and the people of Ghana—had been duped by a confidence man. But, Blay-Miezah said, Newman's bungling could not conceal one simple fact: the money was real. Otherwise, he said, if it was a case of fraud, why didn't the five American banks file charges against him? "Even though Newman committed a blunder, they knew very well that the checks were not forged, that someone was taking advantage of me."

Colonel Acheampong had had enough of Blay-Miezah. He distanced himself from the whole embarrassing mess. To put an end to the matter, on February 20, the government of Ghana issued an eight-page statement about Blay-Miezah and the Oman Ghana Trust Fund. The attorney general looked into pressing charges.

The editor of the *Times*, Gyawu-Kyem, was in the "doghouse for his paper's support of Blay-Miezah and its attack on Bank of Ghana," American diplomats in Accra reported to the State Department. Gyawu-Kyem apologized to officials at the Bank of Ghana and printed the government's statement in full, under the headline GOVERNMENT NOT INVOLVED IN BLAY-MIEZAH AFFAIR. The government's report on Blay-Miezah, an editorial in the *Times* said, "should rightly relegate the whole episode of his Oman Ghana Trust Fund to the realm of mythology." Other papers published enraged letters, asking why the government had given Blay-Miezah a passport, and why a man like Amoako-Atta was even involved in a grubby little attempt at fraud. Siaw, who had invested at least a quarter million cedi with Blay-Miezah, demanded his money back. And at the worst time possible, back in

Philadelphia, Gerald Smith was sentenced to a year and a day in prison for his part in the attempt to defraud Girard Bank. Federal authorities in America asked the State Department to begin proceedings to extradite Blay-Miezah from Ghana, where he was, the *Philadelphia Daily News* said, "living like a king."

Blay-Miezah disappeared from public view.

Meanwhile, Nkrumah's wife, Fathia, and her children quietly moved back to Ghana, at the invitation of Acheampong. When Nkrumah's daughter, Samia, started at a prestigious secondary school, she found that her father's legacy still hung over her head. During an economics class, a teacher casually explained Ghana's recession by stating that President Kwame Nkrumah had taken all the gold.

Chapter 12

Silk

1975–1978

In Accra, the Castle started to hope that everyone would forget about the Blay-Miezah affair. He had caused a stink, and a number of wealthy, connected Ghanaians—the kind who had influential friends and political capital—had lost money.

Several officials, including Debrah, wanted Blay-Miezah arrested and charged. But he still had wealthy allies and expensive lawyers. Furthermore, it wasn't entirely clear what he could be charged with. A fraud trial would mean some of Ghana's most powerful people testifying in court about how they had been conned. Nobody was willing to publicly admit that, least of all Acheampong. "He has taken a number of local businessmen for presumably substantial funds, but none wishes publicly to admit they have been so taken," diplomats at the American embassy remarked. Testifying would mean revealing that, in a recession, instead of increasing the salaries of their employees or donating money, they had basically thrown millions of cedi into the sea. It would also mean admitting they had paid for lawyers and called in chips and bent the law in favor of a man they now wanted prosecuted. It would mean revealing how much the Castle had, despite several warnings, supported a man who was wanted in at least one other country.

There was also, many people thought, the possibility that Blay-Miezah did have the money. However he got it—and by now, there were several stories floating around—money didn't smell. And if it was even a fraction of what he claimed, people wanted in.

American diplomats speculated that the Castle would simply allow Blay-Miezah to make another miraculous escape from the country. It didn't matter where to.

Blay-Miezah bided his time and planned his next move. Everyone else was hoping he would stay out of the headlines and work on quietly bringing home the money. He was trying to figure out how to stay in the headlines, get more money, more investors, and, most important, more power. But first, he needed to reassure his investors—and stay ahead of law enforcement.

IN PHILADELPHIA, ROBERT Ellis's past was catching up with him.

Back in the early 1970s, Ellis's company, Industrial Dynamics, seemed to be on a roll. Contractors were invited to apply for work, and a representative of the company named Herb Burstein was soliciting undeveloped tracts of land. Industrial Dynamics even announced a development of town houses in Bensalem. "Construction would not disturb 'one tree, nor disturb the Neshaminy Creek,'" the company's vice president told the *Philadelphia Inquirer*. The company had even hired the architect Howard Krasnoff, who would design many of the new parts of Temple University.

In January 1972, Industrial Dynamics was registered with the Pennsylvania Securities Commission as a stock brokerage—a strange move for a real estate company. But the only stock Industrial Dynamics appears to have traded was its own. A grand total of 3,450 shares was sold to investors who thought that they were buying into the fastest-growing construction company in Pennsylvania.

After a year, however, the company did not renew its securities license and was suspended. Then things went quiet. Shareholders wanted to know what was going on, but the office stopped returning calls. Then the office stopped answering the phone. Then the phone line got cut off. By 1974, shareholders were contacting the press, asking what had become of the company and whether they could write off their losses. "Start deducting. Industrial Dynamics

Inc, is no longer a, how shall we put it, viable commercial venture," wrote a business columnist for the *Inquirer*. In early 1975, the Pennsylvania Securities Commission started looking into Ellis and Industrial Dynamics.

In April, Blay-Miezah once again became a wanted man. The U.S. attorney in charge of prosecuting the Girard Bank case, Greg Magarity, issued a warrant for his arrest. "National Crime Information Center and Interpol have been informed that Blay-Miezah is again considered a fugitive from justice," Henry Kissinger wrote.

But stopping Blay-Miezah and Ellis would be much harder than any of the investigators could have imagined.

Both of them had learned to look like open, honest people while being anything but. They became experts in doling out tiny details to their investors while ruthlessly controlling information about the inner workings of their organizations. They would leave seemingly important papers unsecured and their briefcases unlocked, then deliberately leave them unattended. They would encourage gossip and speculation. Few of the people around them— their employees, business partners, investors, friends, and family—were aware of how little they knew.

In the years to come, investigators who posed as investors, investors who became informants, and police officers instructed to monitor their every move could not see through the fog. Consequently, it would take officials and investigators across the world an extraordinarily long time to put the pieces together on the Oman Ghana Trust Fund.

Both Blay-Miezah and Ellis were so convincing that even people sent to investigate them genuinely didn't know what to believe, apart from one thing: a huge number of people had staked everything they had on the conviction that the two men would make them very, very rich.

Blay-Miezah and Ellis had recognized something important: their lie, the story of Nkrumah's gold, had power. No matter what happened, many of their supporters refused to turn on them. Instead, they backed the Oman Ghana Trust Fund more fiercely than ever before, with an almost religious fervor. Blay-Miezah, to them, was not a confidence man. He was, like Nkrumah before him, a martyr to his country's cause, and theirs.

Over the course of 1975, Blay-Miezah and Ellis realized their con had taken on a momentum all its own. Despite everything, their investors' faith was getting stronger. People were still standing behind them and giving them money. And so Blay-Miezah and Ellis stepped into their roles with redoubled confidence. If people insisted on believing that Blay-Miezah was the richest man in the world, then Blay-Miezah was going to be the richest man in the world, no matter what it took. For that, he would need more than a few businessmen in Philadelphia and some politicians in Accra. He would need to swindle the world.

Blay-Miezah realized that he did not actually need to give his investors any returns to keep them hanging on. He did not even need a real account with millions of dollars in it. He just needed seemingly incontrovertible proof that such an account—and Nkrumah's fortune—existed.

BLAY-MIEZAH LET IT be known that the Oman Ghana Trust Fund was almost ready to pay out. He asked his friends to intercede on his behalf again. He needed his passport—and, if the Castle were so inclined, his diplomatic passport as well—to draw the matter to a close. Then he could finally meet with the bankers and make arrangements to bring his fortune home. Quietly, Blay-Miezah was hoping for his passports back so that he could leave Ghana in a hurry, if Acheampong finally lost patience with him. Fortunately for him, the Castle also wanted him out of the country. His passports were returned. But this time there were stricter conditions.

Blay-Miezah would have to post a bond to guarantee that he would return to Ghana. His diplomatic passport would be returned, but he would never be allowed to have it in his possession. Instead, a police officer was assigned to travel with him. The officer would hold the passport and present it when necessary; he would also keep Blay-Miezah under surveillance. The officer assigned to the task knew him well. Deputy Superintendent E. K. Awuah had been instructed first to prosecute him at Cape Coast—then to go to his mansion and apologize to him for the prosecution. Blay-Miezah was thrilled. The two had become quite close since the Cape Coast incident.

On May 8, Blay-Miezah left Accra. But it was not in the quiet, stealthy way the Castle had tried to arrange. Blay-Miezah departed in the loudest way possible. He held a press conference at the airport and announced that he was bound for Zurich on what he described as a "journey of truth." He promised that he would be back in Ghana soon and would bring evidence of his fortune—which now amounted to $186 million—with him. The sun beat down, and Blay-Miezah inflated with wounded pride. Everyone who had written him off would eat their words. And anyone who claimed that he was a wanted con man, or was under indictment in the United States, was lying. Then he marched across the tarmac and up the stairs to his plane, his entourage in tow.

Blay-Miezah traveled with nine people, including Krobo Edusei and the former attorney general Kwaw-Swanzy. The newspapers mockingly pointed out that some of Blay-Miezah's biggest supporters were absent, particularly Kwesi Amoako-Atta and J. K. Siaw, "who has reportedly funded much of Blay-Miezah's Ghana activities and is said to be as much as half a million cedis in hole as result."

Ambassador Shirley Temple Black noted with relief that the U.S. government was no longer being accused of sabotaging him: "Some diehards may still use USG interference tactic [sic] to explain Blay-Miezah's lack of money," she wrote. "It is doubtful such a ploy will wash." She also noted that Blay-Miezah's money was now said to have left the United States and to be waiting for him in Switzerland: "Apparently the latest stop on its peregrinations from Philadelphia."

"It could be assumed that [the Ghanaian government] has permitted departure in hope that he will simply disappear," Temple Black wrote. "But he more likely will prove to be proverbial bad penny, less, of course, 186 million dollars."

ON JUNE 2, 1975, Blay-Miezah and his entourage walked into the headquarters of the Union Bank of Switzerland, at Bahnhofstrasse 45 in Zurich. They were there to meet with a manager named Georges Mayer. Another member of Blay-Miezah's entourage knew Mayer well and made the introduction.

Blay-Miezah told Mayer that he needed a bank to distribute $150 million to the Trust Fund's beneficiaries. He wanted to know if Union Bank of Switzerland was interested. Mayer said the bank was very interested, and they negotiated the terms. Perhaps overawed by Blay-Miezah's entourage, Mayer did not, at this point, ask any other questions.

Then Mayer made a decision he would regret for decades. Blay-Miezah asked for a letter outlining their agreement, and Mayer provided him with one that suggested the Union Bank of Switzerland could vouch for Blay-Miezah's fortune: "I wish to inform you," wrote Mayer, "that we retain your diplomatic passport no. 000065 issued at Accra 13th of February 1974 and valid until 12th of February 1979, until finalization of the pending financial transaction. The amount involved for the Oman Ghana Trust Fund of which you are the Beneficiary and Trustee is approx. US$150 millions (United States Currency one hundred and fifty millions). For the handling of the matter we need time and we assume that we shall be able to give back to you said passport at the end of July 1975."

It was addressed to "Dr John Ackah Blay-Miezah, Beneficiary and Trustee of Oman Ghana Trust Fund," and it was everything Blay-Miezah needed. The letter, not the money, was what he had really flown to Zurich for. For the next decade, he and Ellis, and many of their investors, would brandish the letter as proof that it was all true: a nation's fortune in gold really was hidden away in a Swiss bank, and Blay-Miezah really did control it.

It was years before Mayer realized what had happened. When he did, he started hyperventilating. All he could say was, "Oh, my God, oh my God, oh my God." When he got his breath back, he said, "I think I made a mistake." "There never was a hundred and fifty million dollars on deposit for the Fund, or for Blay-Miezah, or any account relating to the Fund of Blay-Miezah," Mayer would later tell investigators. "In fact, there never was any money whatsoever on deposit in a Fund account or in a Blay-Miezah account."

But at the time, Blay-Miezah was able to fly back to Accra in triumph, wielding Mayer's letter. The state-owned press was ordered to ignore him, so instead, ads in all the major newspapers announced his return and invited those who had wished him well to his home for drinks and small chops.

Rumors about the letter caused a furor. Ambassador Debrah refused to believe it existed, but soon enough, people who had seen it were telling everyone who would listen that a banker named Georges Mayer had confirmed everything Blay-Miezah had said. He was the real thing. Blay-Miezah now claimed that the money would be transferred to Ghana in the first week of July.

On July 4, 1975, the *People's Evening News* reported that several European businessmen—said to represent "SAI S.A. Lugano of Switzerland and Eromco of West Germany"—had signed contracts worth $160 million with the Oman Ghana Trust Fund. They were photographed with Amoako-Atta and Edusei. But this failed to distract people from the fact that there was, still, no money. Bankers all over Accra called one another and joked about the lack of any unusually large new deposits. Every time people laughed at him, Blay-Miezah became more convinced that he needed to be bigger, and he needed more power.

Later that year, Colonel Acheampong replaced the National Redemption Council with the Supreme Military Council. He remained very much in charge: he appointed himself chairman and, at the same time, gave himself a promotion to general. Among the congratulatory messages that poured into General Acheampong's office was one from Blay-Miezah, who "dispatched his sincere and warmest congratulations to the Head of State on his enviable promotion and wished him every success in the future."

GLADYS BLAY-MIEZAH WAS, initially, awed by her husband. "I had never seen anybody who was as interesting, as impressive. He was an enigma," she said. He was kind and generous, but it was increasingly clear he had a unique sense of morality that made him a less-than-perfect husband. "The ethical thing was really bad," she said. "There were too many women."

Gladys was a realist; she knew that her husband had a wandering eye. Blay-Miezah always claimed that his adultery didn't affect their marriage: "He would say all the looking around had nothing to do with the person you're in love with. He didn't even know their names," she remembered. Gladys, however, did. Over the years she made it her business to find out everything she could about her husband's girlfriends. It took some investigating. Her friends started calling her Columbo. And her husband started treading very carefully: while Blay-Miezah could control what his investors knew about the Oman Ghana Trust Fund, he quickly realized that the same tricks would not work on his wife.

One night, Blay-Miezah didn't come home for dinner. Gladys sat in the living room, waiting for him. He finally burst into the house, sweaty and agitated: one of his car's tires had blown, right outside the Continental Hotel. Blay-Miezah said that the driver had forgotten to keep the spare tire ready to go, so he had been kept waiting for hours. He could not apologize enough. He promised his wife that he was going to fire the driver, that very night. "I was so sympathetic," Gladys Blay-Miezah remembered. "I was begging for the driver." But her husband was not to be persuaded: the driver, he said, had to go.

Then, later that evening, she overheard voices from the living room. Blay-Miezah and the driver were laughing like co-conspirators. Blay-Miezah handed the driver a thick wad of cash and told him to pick him up at the usual time tomorrow. The whole thing had been a piece of theater. Gladys was so angry that she strode straight into the living room and confronted her husband.

At one point, Gladys decided to leave him. She moved back to her parents' house. Blay-Miezah tried to get her back. First, he asked her mother and aunt to intercede. When that didn't work, he bought her a gift. "He wanted to appease me," Gladys said. "At the time, nobody had a Mercedes Benz 450, so he gave me the keys in my mother's house. I threw the car keys back at him and said, 'I'm interested in love and loyalty, not bribery.'" Eventually, she agreed to give Blay-Miezah another chance.

IN 1976, THE Pennsylvania Securities Commission charged Ellis with securities fraud, over the dealings of Industrial Dynamics. He was also charged with making false statements on a loan. In 1977 Ellis was convicted of federal bank fraud, put on probation, and banned from trading in securities in Pennsylvania for three years.

Neither the FBI, nor the district attorney's office, nor the Philadelphia police saw what was right under their noses. While they were threatening Ellis over his paperwork on a four-thousand-dollar loan, one of the biggest scams of the twentieth century—the Oman Ghana Trust Fund—was in full swing, raking in an absolute fortune. None of the legal proceedings stopped Ellis from collecting investments in the Trust Fund. Nor did his conviction stop people wanting to invest their money with him.

Indeed, the Oman Ghana Trust Fund seemed to be unstoppable. In 1976, Ellis urged investors to act quickly, lest they lose their "golden opportunity." The payoff, he told them, was just days away.

The effect was intoxicating. "Silk. That's what John Ackah Blay-Miezah and Robert Ellis were as smooth as," the Philadelphia journalist Claude Lewis later wrote. "They operated the Oman Ghana Trust Fund so well that wallets practically flew open and the money—said to be more than $100 million—went into their coffers for lavish living and opulence most of us never dream of."

IN 1977, BLAY-MIEZAH founded Oman Ghana Trust Fund Holdings, which had twenty wholly owned subsidiaries, each with an almost identical board of directors. The companies were to invest in virtually every product and service available in the Western Region: rubber, palm oil, coconuts, sugar, fruit, root crops, castor seed and annatto, livestock, fisheries, timber, construction machinery, mining and quarrying, engineering and shipbuilding, chemicals and fertilizers, general contracting, mortgage finance, wholesaling, import/export, properties, housing estates, hotels, sports complexes, and transport. Each one of these subsidiaries represented a promise to an investor. To the investors, this looked like progress.

Oman Ghana Trust Fund Holdings claimed exemption from exchange control regulations in Ghana. This meant that the company and its subsidiaries could move money into and out of the country without reporting it. The arrangement, investigators later noted, was perfect for money laundering.

Blay-Miezah realized that he couldn't just surround himself with powerful people. He had to be one. And not just any powerful person—the most powerful one in the country. Blay-Miezah needed to be president of Ghana. It was the only sure way out of the maze he had built. With a whole country behind him, no one could touch him. The Americans would have to stop coming after him. If he controlled the state and the treasury, he could pay his investors back and give them the juicy government contracts he had been promising. Pretty soon, Blay-Miezah began to mention that the Oman Ghana Trust Fund had one extra, previously unmentioned condition: he had to be elected president.

GENERAL ACHEAMPONG'S HOLD on power was looking more precarious every day. Food prices were soaring, and the government responded with price control laws: traders who sold goods above the price set by the government were thrown in jail. Acheampong's Special Squad descended on Accra's hotels and nightclubs. In January 1978, the proprietors of the "Panama Hotel, Napoleon, Moustache, Penthouse, and Pussy Cat" clubs, along with the "Play Boy, Diamond, Supermarket, Adonten, C'est Si Bon, Black Cat, and Chez Marie Lou Restaurant," were charged with "the sale of beer above the control price." They got off easy. The *Daily Graphic* reported that a woman named Effua Afriba was jailed for three months "with hard labor for selling above the control price." Her crime? She sold "14 cubes of sugar for 40p instead of 10p."

"The pressure is now on," the newspaper wrote. "They will be chased unrelentlessly [*sic*] until they decide to quit or conform and sell at control price. The success of the exercise, of course, will depend on all of us."

In response, many traders simply closed their shops, which meant that instead of goods getting expensive, there were simply none to be had. Many Ghanaians spent hours every day waiting in lines to buy the most basic items. When a supermarket got a shipment of butter, the news would spread instantly, from house to house, friends would call one another, and people would race to the shop to grab some before it ran out again.

As circumstances became dire for most people, Blay-Miezah "led such a lifestyle as to make the public believe he was one of the richest, if not the richest, person then in Ghana." He still rode around town in a convoy of cars. He kept throwing wild parties. He had affairs. He was Ghana's most famous playboy millionaire. At night, the music drifted out over the city from his house. You could hear it from a mile away.

Acheampong tried vainly to persuade people that the struggling economy was a blessing. "General Kutu Acheampong has urged Ghanaians to refrain from the mad rush for money," reported the *Daily Graphic*. "Ghana will be a great and happy country to live in," Acheampong declared, "the day we stop making fetish of money."

It was clear to almost everyone that Acheampong's time was up. In 1978, he was deposed by his chief of defense staff, Lieutenant General Fred Akuffo. A lean, energetic soldier with fat cheeks and a bushy moustache, Akuffo had been Acheampong's de facto second-in-command. He accused his predecessor of corruption and "running a one-man show." Acheampong was stripped of his military rank and placed under house arrest in his hometown in the Ashanti region. Akuffo kept the Supreme Military Council in place, but brought a handful of civilians into government and released some political prisoners.

Blay-Miezah began to position himself as a man of principle: a man above petty power struggles, a man who held Kwame Nkrumah's legacy close to his heart, a man who could be trusted to call out corruption. He needed a story to dull memories of the last few scandals he had been wrapped up in. He needed to make sure that the new military government did not come after him. He needed to seem statesmanlike—but most of all, he once again needed a scapegoat. So Blay-Miezah went on the radio to announce that, four years earlier, he had been forced to pay a Special Branch officer named Abraham Sackey a substantial bribe. Sackey had stationed police officers in Blay-Miezah's home, he claimed, then presented himself and demanded forty-three thousand cedi to get them to leave. To many listeners, it sounded like an entirely plausible story. After his radio broadcast, Blay-Miezah issued a press release, emphasizing just how shocked he had been by the officer's behavior. Ghana deserved better.

Blay-Miezah had seen his opening. Our man would ride an anti-corruption platform all the way to the presidency.

Chapter 13

President Blay-Miezah

1979

Blay-Miezah stood behind a podium in front of a massive crowd at Accra's Arts Centre, a low-slung concrete complex next to the sea, just down the coast from Osu Castle. He had an announcement to make: he was running for president. It was the beginning of a campaign that people would talk about for decades.

The original plan had been to hold the rally at Accra Sports Stadium, which could accommodate thousands, but the venue was booked—many of the city's venues, in fact, were taken. It was an extremely busy time for anywhere that could hold a crowd, because after almost seven years of military rule, on New Year's Day 1979, Lieutenant General Akuffo had lifted the ban on party politics. There were to be free and fair elections, and the Supreme Military Council would not interfere, except "in the maintenance of law and order." Elections were planned for June 18, 1979.

People were ready. In the days following Akuffo's announcement, dozens of political parties appeared, as if from thin air: the United National Convention, the Reformed People's Party, the Third Force Party. There were launches and manifestos and rallies and conferences all over town. By the end of the month, twenty-three political parties had been formed. Among them was the

People's Vanguard Party, with Blay-Miezah as its chairman and presidential candidate. It, too, appeared seemingly overnight, on January 8, with manifesto, logo, slogan, bankers, accountants, auditors, lawyers, and a complex web of allied political, charitable, and business interests.

There was, however, a catch. Lieutenant General Akuffo announced that anyone who had been found guilty of fraud "as a result of adverse findings made against them by the various assets commissions and committees of enquiry set up by governments following the overthrow of the Nkrumah and Busia regimes in 1966 and 1972 respectively" had been disqualified and could not run for office. One hundred and four people were named, including almost every influential man who was standing behind Blay-Miezah: Krobo Edusei, his lawyer Bashiru Kwaw-Swanzy, and Ebenezer Ako-Adjei, the former minister for foreign affairs whose room had been opposite Nkrumah's at Lincoln University. The government's report also recommended Kwesi Amoako-Atta be prevented from holding public office. Almost everyone in Blay-Miezah's firm was banished from power. The web of influence he had spent years building was in danger of being torn down. His plans, and his carefully constructed credibility, were suddenly in jeopardy.

At the Arts Centre rally, Blay-Miezah was dressed from head to toe in white finery. He addressed the widest swathe of the population he could think of: "the youth in all walks of life, workers, farmers, fishermen, dedicated intellectuals, militant and dedicated youth in age, the militant and dedicated women, old age pensioners or retired men and women with the nation's rapid and balanced economic and cultural development at heart," he said. Oh: "and the unemployed."

A welfare state, Blay-Miezah said, was not enough. Without economic justice, without the major means of production in the hands of all people, Ghana could not abolish once and for all poverty, ignorance, and disease. Everyone who desired to use their skills to build a modern, stable nation without a power cut, a water shortage, or a coup every other week, a Ghana free from stop-and-go, was invited to join the party. A party "dedicated to Continental African Political Unity as inspired by the highest ideals and socialist teachings of the late Kwame Nkrumah."

Blay-Miezah did everything in his power to sound like the reincarnation of Ghana's first leader. He was flanked by all the Nkrumah-era ministers in his retinue. Amoako-Atta spoke briefly, telling the crowd the Vanguard Party would "enable as many people as possible to benefit from the national cake." Some of the audience wondered how much of that cake Amoako-Atta had personally eaten during his years in power.

As a sign of his commitment to his ideals, Blay-Miezah said, he would be funding the campaign himself. "No member would ever be called upon to make any financial contributions towards the upkeep of the party." None of the ministers in his government would get anything more than their basic salaries, he said: "As an antidote for careerism in political life and in the interest of probity in public life, the party's members in Government would be expected to surrender their emoluments or allowances to the state."

Besides, he had his own money—a fortune, as everyone already knew. And that fortune was how he was going to transform Ghana. Blay-Miezah would clean up politics by paying for everything himself. An organizer for the party, Memuna Al-Hassan, promised an immediate end to food shortages and price gouging. "The People's Vanguard would eradicate 'kalabule' in the society because the party's leader would be in a position to flood the market with consumer items." (Back in Philadelphia, Blay-Miezah's investors were attempting to arrange shipments of meat, fish, and rice, of questionable quality and freshness, from America to Ghana.)

In the weeks that followed, Blay-Miezah and other members of the Vanguard Party made even more commitments, promising everything under the sun to every Ghanaian who would listen. A job for every single person from the Western Region who wanted one. A review of Ghana's oil contracts, and invitations to foreign investors and farmers to "assist the country in its development programme." (Blay-Miezah knew just the investors too.) A resolution to centuries-old land disputes in the Dagomba Kingdom in northern Ghana.

If anyone asked Blay-Miezah about the many people who had bad things to say about him, he was apt to grow reflective. "I must say I have enjoyed the trials and tribulations which I have undergone," he was fond of saying. "A few of my pioneer friends and associates have fallen by the wayside or deserted the camp, mainly because the adverse forces were too powerful." But, he always said: "History is my final arbiter."

WHILE BLAY-MIEZAH MADE promises he had no intention of keeping, Ghana lurched from one emergency to the next. Accra was in the midst of a severe water shortage. There had been no rains for months, and the pumps at the Weija Dam, Kpong Water Works, and the Tema booster station had broken down, so pipes were running dry, even in the toniest parts of Accra. "This is about the sixth time the *Daily Graphic* is writing on the water situation this year alone," an exasperated 1979 editorial complained. "Since this time around the 'important' parts of the capital—Airport, Cantonments, Dzorwulu, Abelekpe, Labone, Roman Ridge and other such exotic areas—are involved, we hope that something concrete will be done now." Hundreds of people were driving, walking, or taking the tro tro several miles in search of water every day, first thing in the morning, before going to work. Some people were going all the way to the boreholes and wells near 37 Military Hospital, and even those were starting to run dry. At Labadi, a little girl trying to get just a bucketful was run over by a water tanker. Despite years of bluster and promises, almost nothing had been done to grow Ghana's economy since Nkrumah was deposed. Now, even relatively new infrastructure was falling apart. Instead of bringing Ghana's money home, a succession of ineffective governments had brought corruption and ruin.

As the economic crisis deepened, some of Blay-Miezah's biggest backers were starting to face the consequences of supporting him. J. K. Siaw's investment had decimated his brewery. With revenues at a low, Siaw had little to fall back on. He stopped paying suppliers. He stopped paying for maintenance. He stopped paying taxes. Without the cash to import fresh supplies, his workers resorted to brewing beer from old shipments of malt that had started to rot. In the ensuing scandal, the brewery was shut down.

In such difficult times, it was galling that an entire brewery was just sitting empty, already starting to look decrepit. The employees, many with years of specialist training and families to support, were struggling. "Considering the general hardship around," read an editorial in the *Daily Graphic*, "it is plain callous for everybody to sit around and watch while things deteriorate." No one could say when the brewery would be allowed to open again. Rumor had it that the government was demanding "huge taxes" from Siaw before production would be allowed to restart. After years of funding Blay-Miezah's lifestyle, Siaw now had no one to fund him.

THE VANGUARD PARTY was, initially, greeted with amusement. This was largely because Blay-Miezah wouldn't stop talking about the Oman Ghana Trust Fund. His campaign was ostensibly a "war over hunger," but at rallies, the most prominent signs often read: "Allow Dr Blay-Miezah to bring his millions."

The country already had all the money it needed to turn the economy around, Blay-Miezah would tell the crowds. "The People's Vanguard believe that certain individual Ghanaians have funds abroad which can be placed at the disposal of mother Ghana in its hour of need. We of the People's Vanguard are prepared to lead the way. We are appealing to our fellow countrymen to join us in this venture. Let's put our resources together to bail mother Ghana out of its present difficulty."

On closer inspection, the entire campaign seemed to be about the Oman Ghana Trust Fund. A *Daily Graphic* columnist pointed out that even before the ban on party politics was lifted, Blay-Miezah had talked about taking over, to stabilize the country. It was also, Blay-Miezah said, in the best interests of the Trust Fund. "Since 1971 I have been telling the people of this country I'm worth some $150 million in American and European Banks which will be judiciously used to develop the country. There have been problems with its repatriation. I have made all the documents available to the governments. As soon as my party comes into power, most of the impediments would hopefully be removed."

Very few people in government took Blay-Miezah's pronouncements—or his chances in the election—seriously. After all, if he really had $150 million to his name, why would he go into politics and risk being assassinated in a coup or executed by the military?

Once again, Blay-Miezah had been underestimated. It turned out that nobody knew what bright, hungry, ambitious young people wanted to hear better than he did. He had a very simple campaign strategy: give the people what they want. Blay-Miezah started giving them cash.

Before long, the People's Vanguard was drawing enough support to cause concern.

DURING THE CAMPAIGN, the government held a reception at Osu Castle for all the presidential candidates, including Blay-Miezah, who brought his wife, Gladys. While her husband worked the room—enjoying being back in the Castle, and not under arrest—Gladys surveyed the crowd with Amoako-Atta's wife, Mary. At one point a tall, young, and strikingly beautiful woman seemed to float into the room. Mary nudged Gladys and said, "This is Blay's latest." The young woman made the rounds, chatting with ambassadors and ministers.

Gladys was perhaps the only person in the world who knew how Blay-Miezah thought, and she knew how to rattle him. She was thinking about becoming a fashion designer and was courting as many beautiful, wealthy, and well-connected people as she could. So when the woman walked by, Gladys grabbed her by the hand and made her acquaintance. "Oh my God, what a beauty," she said, turning to Mary. "This one is a beauty over all beauties."

All the while, in the corner of her eye, Gladys was watching her husband. She could see that he had noticed her, and he was looking increasingly uncomfortable. He was actually shaking. So she insisted on walking her new friend over to meet her husband. The woman left the party five minutes later—but not before Gladys, without Blay-Miezah knowing, invited her to tea.

By then, the Blay-Miezahs had moved to McCarthy Hill, a neighborhood named for one of the British empire's more dimwitted servants, Sir Charles McCarthy, a former governor of the Gold Coast. McCarthy and a small British force under his command were annihilated by an Ashanti army in 1824. The Ashanti kept McCarthy's skull, covered it with gold, and used it as a royal drinking cup.

The house itself was number 45 McCarthy Hill. (Blay-Miezah said that he had chosen it because it had the same number as the Trust Fund's branch of the Union Bank of Switzerland in Zurich.) It was quite a place: a bright, modernist edifice, a midcentury fever dream of concrete and glass, with panoramic views to the west of Accra, all the way out to the salt flats and toward the Western Region. Blay-Miezah had painted parts of the house green, the color of the Oman Ghana Trust Fund's logo. There were quarters for guests and servants. There were shag-pile rugs and heavy curtains and low-slung mahogany furniture. There was a small library. Blay-Miezah named the house Ewusiwado.

The day after the reception at the Castle, Gladys welcomed her new friend to her home with tea and biscuits, and kept her talking until she heard Blay-Miezah's car pulling up to the house. He came in, saw the young woman, and instantly turned and fled. "All you could hear was the fat man running," Gladys recalled.

Blay-Miezah bolted out of the house and back into his car. Unfortunately for him, his driver had stepped away, so he just sat in the back seat, staring into space, until the driver returned. Gladys could see her husband through the window. As he drove off, she went on serving tea and biscuits as if nothing had happened.

When Blay-Miezah finally came home that night, he was all flattery. "Do you look at yourself in the mirror?" he said to his wife. "Do you know how beautiful you are? How can you tell this Humpty-Dumpty-looking girl that she's the most beautiful?" That night, he couldn't sleep: every hour, he would wake up and heave a huge sigh.

OUTSIDE HIS HOME, Blay-Miezah's popularity was growing. It was time, he decided, to hold a press conference at the Continental Hotel in Accra and inform the world that he was ready to prove he had $150 million in the bank.

Blay-Miezah arrived in a convoy of cars—all emblazoned with the People's Vanguard logo, a butterfly. Many had loudspeakers mounted on their roofs. Blay-Miezah himself was in a pristine silver-blue Mercedes. He stepped out of the back seat, clutching his cigar and waving cheerfully at his supporters. He was dressed in a denim jacket and a powder-blue shirt with a colossal collar and a pattern of magenta daisies.

Blay-Miezah led the crowd through the hotel lobby to a ballroom. There, hundreds of chairs were laid out, and a long table was covered with flowers.

Party dignitaries, including Ebenezer Ako-Adjei, awaited him. There were muttonchop whiskers and giant moustaches and indoor sunglasses everywhere. Young men in PEOPLE'S VANGUARD and BLAY-MIEZAH POWER T-shirts milled around. The ballroom was hung with posters proclaiming the FIVE REASONS WHY YOU SHOULD JOIN THE PEOPLE'S VANGUARD.

Blay-Miezah waited for the excited crowd to settle. His hand clutched the microphone tightly. He was wearing a gold ring on every finger. He told the audience that he needed only one thing: for the government to give him a new diplomatic passport and to allow him to leave the country. Then he would return to Ghana in just a month, he said, bringing with him everything the country needed: tons of rice, tinned milk, sugar, fish, and machinery—like functional water pumps—worth fifty million dollars. A small group of American investors stood in a corner. One, dressed in a batik shirt with an embroidered collar, waved as Blay-Miezah mentioned his foreign business partners.

Blay-Miezah assured the crowd that he would keep his promises. He was a politician they could trust. If he didn't return with the money, or the goods, he said, he would step down as the leader of the People's Vanguard, give himself up to the government, and face the consequences. Blay-Miezah was a stirring speaker: he paused for laughter, raised his fist for emphasis, and got emotional. The crowd applauded, but the press, gathered at the front of the room, looked considerably more skeptical.

Blay-Miezah claimed that he was asking for a diplomatic passport because he feared for his safety if he left Ghana without one. "I would not have asked for the renewal of the passport, but because I want to be safe when I travel to the U.S., I need protection to bring such a colossal sum," he said. The world, after all, was full of thieves. It had all been so hard for him.

At this point, Blay-Miezah broke down crying, his entire body quaking. It was not his intention to deceive Ghanaians, he said. All he wanted was to feed the hungry and give water to those who needed it. All he wanted was for Ghanaians to enjoy his legacy.

Blay-Miezah collapsed back into his seat, still weeping. He put his head in his hands. The people on either side of him leaned over to comfort him. He heaved a huge sigh and wiped his face with a silky white handkerchief.

Then, as the next speaker rose to address the crowd, Blay-Miezah lit up another cigar.

As the campaign event finished, his driver was dusting off the Mercedes outside the hotel. Someone had paid a waakye seller to provide lunch for all the young men in BLAY-MIEZAH POWER T-shirts. Blay-Miezah strode back to the car, smoking another cigar, surrounded by adoring crowds. He rested the hand clutching his cigar on the car and waved goodbye to his supporters with the other. The cigar stayed in place as he lowered himself into the Mercedes and swung his legs in. Only then, finally, did the cigar follow him in.

IT LOOKED LIKE John Ackah Blay-Miezah could be Ghana's next president. For many officials in the military government, this was unacceptable. Numerous other people watched in horror as Blay-Miezah campaigned and handed out food and envelopes of cash. If this was what he was prepared to do on campaign, what might he have planned for election day? Even a remote possibility that he might become president moved several people, who had held off from confronting Blay-Miezah for years, to go to the police. Blay-Miezah no longer had Acheampong's protection, so their reports were taken seriously.

Investigators dusted off old case files and started digging up everything they could about Blay-Miezah's past. In the run-up to his campaign, he had gone on the radio and admitted paying off a Special Branch officer. This gave authorities at least one thing to charge Blay-Miezah with: bribery. But they would still need to prove that he was at fault—not, as he had claimed, the victim of extortion. And to put Blay-Miezah away for good, they would need more: proof of several of his rumored crimes. Any trial would have to destroy his credibility entirely. Government officials knew from experience that Blay-Miezah could turn almost everything to his advantage. He had been discredited, disavowed, and locked up before—and each time, he had bounced back, more jovial, more powerful, and smoking a bigger, more expensive cigar. Anyone he couldn't bribe, he intimidated. He seemed to be untouchable. But the victims whom Blay-Miezah had left in his wake were about to catch up to him, in spectacular fashion.

Chapter 14

House of Cards

1979

In November 1978, the police had raided the offices of the Oman Ghana Trust Fund. Blay-Miezah had been arrested and charged with bribery, perjury, and forgery. At the time, he had brushed the charges off. He posted bail—fifty thousand cedi—and went right back to work. As Blay-Miezah campaigned, he never seemed to give the charges a second thought. The prosecutors, however, were determined to bring him down where everyone else had failed. Behind the scenes, they lined up witnesses who would reveal that almost everything he had said was a lie. The trial was set to begin on March 1, 1979, right in the middle of the presidential election campaign.

The lead prosecutor was President Kwame Nkrumah's old friend Joe Appiah. He had been a special adviser to General Acheampong, but had incurred the general's ire. During the final days of Acheampong's regime he was "eased out of his former duties as commissioner and special adviser to head of state" and sent to the United Nations as Ghana's ambassador. When Acheampong was deposed, Appiah was recalled to Accra.

Appiah was not accustomed to spending his days hanging around Accra's circuit courts, prosecuting forgery cases, but this was personal. Blay-Miezah made his living making claims Appiah knew to be false, claims that one of his oldest friends had been outlandishly corrupt and stolen an unthinkable

Joe Appiah.

fortune. During the Nkrumah administration, when Appiah was an opposition MP, he had made sure Krobo Edusei never escaped the shadow of his dalliance with the con man Emil Savundra. Under Acheampong, Appiah had led an anti-corruption investigation that embarrassed many of the country's most powerful men. If anyone had the tenacity to prosecute Blay-Miezah, it was going to be Appiah. He hoped to lock him up for twenty-five years.

Blay-Miezah's defense was led by his lawyer Bashiru Kwaw-Swanzy, Nkrumah's disgraced attorney general. Kwaw-Swanzy had a plan. Under no circumstances would Blay-Miezah be taking the stand. Instead, Kwaw-Swanzy was going to stall. He would object, ask for adjournments, give improbably lengthy speeches, arrive late to court, and demand original copies of every exhibit. He would do whatever he could to discredit every piece of evidence and run out the clock in the process. If the trial ran through the elections and Blay-Miezah was voted president before he could be convicted, it was over. He would be untouchable.

The circuit courts were airy white concrete buildings, wedged between the sprawl of Makola Market and a broad avenue that ran parallel to the shore. Every day of Blay-Miezah's case, the court was crowded with spectators. There were still more people outside, listening to the trial unfold through the open louver blades.

The courtroom itself was tiny, about twenty by twenty-five feet, with mahogany benches for Appiah's modest prosecution team. Blay-Miezah's seven distinguished lawyers were seated at tables in front of the bench, in a flurry of black gowns and somber wool three-piece suits. Journalists stood against the white walls, ready to dash out to file copy.

The judge, Stephen A. Brobbey, sat on the bench resplendent in a black gown, white tie, and judicial wig. There was no court stenographer. There had been a plan to start recording court proceedings, but the tape machines kept breaking and had to be sent abroad for repairs. Instead the judge took copious notes.

The prosecution's first witness was a puzzle to most of the spectators. Ghana's former ambassador to Liberia, Augustina Obetsebi-Lamptey, took the stand. There was palpable confusion in the courtroom as the ambassador was sworn in. She recounted what happened in Monrovia in 1971, when Dr. John Kolorah Blay appeared at her embassy and told her he had just graduated from the University of Pennsylvania, and was the elder son of R. S. Blay.

Spectators murmured as the ambassador gave evidence. Newspapers reported that she spoke of when she had learned that the Ducor Hotel expected the embassy to pay Dr. Blay's colossal bill. "The manager, she said, then showed her a letter purported to have been written by her and she discovered that her signature had been forged. The letter had the embassy's letterhead."

Then Appiah performed the great reveal. He asked Ambassador Obetsebi-Lamptey if Dr. John Kolorah Blay was in the courtroom. The ambassador pointed out Blay-Miezah. "He looks familiar," she said archly.

The next witness to testify was the ambassador's secretary, Nii Ashrifi Nunoo. Nunoo was the man who had, for much of September 1971, been under the impression that he was a close personal friend of John Kolorah Blay. Nunoo glared at Blay-Miezah from the witness stand. The embassy clerk said that he had not seen Blay-Miezah since 1971, but, like everyone else, he had read about his exploits in the papers. Nunoo told the court about Blay-Miezah's solicitous visit to the embassy, and about vouching for Blay-Miezah at the Ducor Hotel.

When it was Kwaw-Swanzy's turn to cross-examine, he took his time, making a show of trying to establish doubt about Nunoo's testimony. Perhaps, Kwaw-Swanzy suggested, this was a case of mistaken identity: "Have a look at Dr Blay-Miezah. Does he look exactly like the Mr Kolorah-Blay you saw in Monrovia?" Nunoo was adamant: "He looks exactly like him."

AS SOON AS the judge wrapped up proceedings for the day, Blay-Miezah went right back to politics. With General Acheampong gone, tinned food that had been hidden away to avoid his price control laws flooded the market, at extortionate prices. Tinned milk was two cedi and forty peswa per tin, sardines were six cedi a tin, and Exeter brand corned beef was an exorbitant twenty cedi a tin. Blay-Miezah started turning up at rallies with provisions for the crowds.

At a rally in Victoria Park in Cape Coast, he promised to end hunger in Ghana once and for all. The *Daily Graphic* reported that "the party regarded the struggle as the continuation of what was started 22 years ago by the late President Nkrumah." To some, Blay-Miezah began to look like a hero. Others joked that the Vanguard Party's acronym—PV—stood for the words *Pay Voucher*.

There was, however, more to a campaign than handouts. The Vanguard Party was required by law to submit reams of paperwork to the registrar of political parties. The party submitted just enough to get registered and kept asking for extensions on the deadlines to submit the rest. On March 9, the registrar wrote to the party, requesting some basic details, including the address of the party's head office. While Blay-Miezah could cobble together a political party convincing enough for a press release or a rally, he was sloppy with the details. The letter went unanswered.

BACK AT THE circuit courts, Appiah's next surprise was an old affidavit, dated January 3, 1968. It was borne into the courtroom and tendered into evidence by the commissioner for oaths, Dickson Abu Tetteh. The affidavit stated that a man named Jacob Badu wanted to change his name to John Kolorah Blay. Tetteh could not remember who had arrived at his office to sign the affidavit—it had happened eleven years ago. But the document was signed John Kolorah Blay.

Nobody could tell where Appiah was going with this. Kwaw-Swanzy was amused by it. "The person who changed the name of Jacob Badu to John Kolorah Blay knowing that the documents were not his had committed a crime" and was guilty of forgery. But of course, the prosecution had no proof that that person was Blay-Miezah; all Appiah had was the affidavit itself. And even if he was able to tie Blay-Miezah to the document, why would it matter? Appiah seemed to be wasting time. And that suited Kwaw-Swanzy just fine.

*The affidavit of name change introduced into evidence by Joe Appiah,
from the archives of the University of Pennsylvania.*

At this point, the prosecution could not even establish that John Kolorah Blay
was the same person as Dr. John Ackah Blay-Miezah.

Appiah had seen this problem coming, and he had a solution. A credible
witness who could prove that they were the same man, and undermine
Kwaw-Swanzy in the process. Benjamin Forjoe had been the director of

Special Branch during the early 1960s. He was in court to testify that in late 1963, he had met John Kolorah Blay, and that in January 1964, Blay was detained for harassing President Nkrumah. Anticipating Kwaw-Swanzy, Appiah asked the witness if John Kolorah Blay was present in court. Without missing a beat, Forjoe pointed out Blay-Miezah.

How had Forjoe met him? At Flagstaff House. The president himself had introduced them. They were countrymen, President Nkrumah reportedly said. Forjoe took this to mean that he should take care of Blay. "He therefore provided Kolorah-Blay with an accommodation and gave him a car and a driver, provided him with food and everything until he heard that Kolorah-Blay had been detained at the Ussher Fort prisons." Appiah's message was clear: Kolorah Blay and Blay-Miezah were the same man. He and Nkrumah had never been close. And Blay-Miezah had been causing trouble for decades.

When it was the defense's turn to cross-examine the witness, Kwaw-Swanzy asked who gave the order to have Blay-Miezah detained in 1964.

"The lawyer will be in the best position to tell," Forjoe said.

Kwaw-Swanzy feigned confusion: Which lawyer did he mean?

Forjoe looked straight at Blay-Miezah's lawyer. "Alhaji Kwaw Swanzy, because you were then the Attorney-General," Forjoe replied.

There was an absolute ruckus in court. Kwaw-Swanzy paused, then tried to imply that at the time, he had no control over the police. "I protested at the time that you policemen were detaining people indiscriminately," he said.

Forjoe immediately snapped back: "You were the mouthpiece of the government from whom the police received instructions."

THE TRIAL WAS getting uncomfortable for Kwaw-Swanzy, but beyond that it was not going poorly, as far as the lawyer was concerned. The prosecution still hadn't proved Blay-Miezah was guilty of forgery or perjury. But Kwaw-Swanzy and Blay-Miezah did not fully appreciate Appiah's flair for the theatrical.

Back in the 1950s, when Appiah was living in London, he would go to Speakers' Corner, in Hyde Park, dressed in Kente. Speakers' Corner was the most famously unruly part of London: at the northeast corner of Hyde Park, in the shadow of Marble Arch, politicians and freedom fighters, conspiracy theorists and cult members would gather to speak freely and lecture passersby. Everyone from Kwame Nkrumah to Karl Marx to George Orwell had spoken there. In the gray-blue London light, Appiah would stand above the throngs of bowler-hatted men and "harangue Britain for its unwillingness to grant independence to its African colonies."

One afternoon, midway through one of his addresses, a reporter and photographer from the *Daily Express*, "the most empire-promoting newspaper of its day," arrived. Appiah was shocked to see himself in the next day's *Express*, under a banner headline that read BLANKET-CLAD ZULU CHIEF BERATES EMPIRE. Appiah rolled his eyes at the lazy racism of it all and planned a little production.

At the time, Appiah was dating Peggy Cripps, daughter of the former British chancellor of the exchequer, Sir Stafford Cripps. Their romance is said to have inspired the 1967 movie *Guess Who's Coming to Dinner*. (Joe and Peggy would wed in 1953, in a ceremony that caused the leaders of the disintegrating British empire to collectively choke on their cornflakes.) After the *Express* published its hit piece, Appiah asked Sir Stafford to invite the editor to dinner. Appiah joined the party, dressed in an impeccable suit from Moss Bros. of Covent Garden. To the editor, he was unrecognizable.

Appiah led the editor into a long, learned debate about British libel law. Then, with a twinkle in his eye, he produced the offending article. To the raucous laughter of everyone else in the room, a guest asked the editor: "I say, doesn't that Zulu Chief bear an uncanny resemblance to someone in this room?" Years later, Appiah still relished the moment when the editor looked down at the article and up at him, and down at the article again, and "the penny dropped." "When the editor realized it was me," he remembered, "he blushed like red ink."

Now, in 1979, Appiah had a dramatic surprise lined up for Blay-Miezah and his defense team. On March 11, the surprise was in an airport in Paris, about to begin the journey to Accra.

APPIAH'S NEXT MOVE was made possible by a well-timed discovery. Through contacts in the Ghana Police Service, he had found information that illuminated how John Kolorah Blay, small-time hustler, had become Dr. John Ackah Blay-Miezah, Ghana's richest man.

After Blay-Miezah left Nsawam Prison in 1966, he had worked briefly at a marriage bureau. It wasn't particularly lucrative, but he did get an education in official documents, how they were made, and, consequently, how they could be forged. In 1968, Blay-Miezah wrote to the dean of students at the University of Pennsylvania. The letter appeared to be from his former roommate in Philadelphia, Jacob Badu. It stated that he had graduated in 1960, had lost his degree certificates, and needed copies for a job interview in just a few days. He also stated that his family had had his name changed, and he wanted the degrees issued in his new name: John Kolorah-Blay. He attached an affidavit of name change.

The letter contained several inconsistencies: For a start, the date of the job interview was more than a year in the past. Blay-Miezah also wasn't sure which degrees Badu had, so he asked for copies of a "BACHELORS DEGREE IN ECONOMICS" and "MASTERS DEGREE IN INTERNATIONAL RELATIONSHIP." The affidavit of name change was signed by an official at the Ministry of Education who didn't exist.

Still, a response came quickly. The chief clerk at the University of Pennsylvania was happy to send another diploma for Badu's master's degree in international relations, in the name of John Kolorah Blay, on receipt of a fee of five dollars. "The Graduate School of Arts & Sciences does not give a Bachelor of Science in Commerce. I suppose this was received through the Wharton School. Therefore, I am forwarding a copy of your letter to the Wharton School so that they can take action." For a few bucks and postage Blay-Miezah had stolen his old roommate's identity and his degrees.

It would be a while before Badu realized what had happened. Badu's uncle—his forwarding address in the United States—eventually got a postcard from the University of Pennsylvania addressed to John Kolorah Blay, and called his nephew. Badu wrote to the university, demanding an explanation: "Mr John Kolorah Blay, who has contrived to get his name on my records at the university, is well known in Philadelphia in some circles and to Ghanaian authorities. Your office can check on both of us through the Ghanaian Embassy in Washington." In 1978, Badu finally filed a police complaint in Ghana.

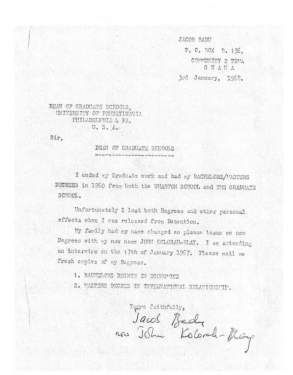

Blay-Miezah's letter to the University of Pennsylvania,
requesting that Jacob Badu's degrees be reissued in his name.

This allowed prosecutors to unravel, at last, what Blay-Miezah had been up to. Diplomats at the U.S. embassy in Accra were only too happy to help. Ambassador Shirley Temple Black had left to take up a position in Washington, but Blay-Miezah was still a priority for the embassy. Diplomats cabled the State Department to report that the "University of Pennsylvania kindly furnished copies of certain documents needed by police in pending criminal case against John Blay-Miezah, a.k.a. John Kolorah-Blay."

But Appiah didn't just want the documents. Blay-Miezah's defense team would try to discredit them, like they had with everything else. So Appiah worked his contacts at the embassy to ask whether a representative "of the University of Pennsylvania could bring to Ghana the originals" and also "exhibit them to the trial judge and certify that they are indeed part of the university's official files." That representative was now on a plane somewhere over the Sahara Desert. His name was Steven Burbank; he was a young

American lawyer who looked as if he had been born in a sweater-vest and khakis, clutching a yellow legal pad. He was the general counsel for the University of Pennsylvania. And he had no idea what he was getting himself into.

Burbank flew into Lome, Togo, on March 11. Accra's airport was closed, so Appiah had arranged for him to spend the night in Lome and then be transferred to Accra the next day. Two official cars, along with a diplomat and a serious-looking government minder, picked Burbank up from his hotel and drove him to the border with Ghana. Appiah was there, waiting for him. "I was a surprise witness, which is a good thing," Burbank remembered. But then people started talking about Blay-Miezah's ability to make his problems disappear. "I was young," Burbank said, "and I didn't have an appreciation for the potential risk to my life."

On the way to Accra, Appiah filled Burbank in on Blay-Miezah. "He'd managed to bribe everybody, apparently—not everybody—but a lot of people." Burbank also realized that Blay-Miezah's "political ambitions were taken more seriously than at first it appeared, if only because he [was] spending quite a bit of other people's money promoting himself."

That evening, in Accra, Burbank was taken out on the town and treated to dinner at a casino. Then, he was put up for the night in Government House, a former residence for British colonial administrators that was now looking decidedly the worse for wear. As Burbank was drifting off to sleep, he heard a hissing noise. Then a fine mist started seeping in through his window. Burbank jumped out of bed and backed up against the door. Just as he was entertaining the possibility that he was being poisoned, there was a massive bang: the air conditioner had exploded. The staff came running. Burbank "took a blanket and a pillow to the couch" and "managed another hour of sleep, but only after convincing the men that repair of the bedroom air conditioner could wait until the morning."

The next morning was blazing hot. A clerk from the attorney general's office met Burbank outside the courts in downtown Accra. Burbank also met the real Jacob Badu, who was now an executive with Sun Oil and was "relieved that his records [would] finally be straightened out." Then Burbank was hustled into the courtroom, where Blay-Miezah's massive legal team sat awaiting their client. Blay-Miezah himself did not show up for hours; he was finally "tracked down between eleven fifteen and eleven thirty in his office holding a political meeting."

A huge crowd was there to see him. Every seat in the courtroom was full. Bailiffs had to clear one side of the room to free the witness stand, and then proceedings started around noon. "I was called and sworn immediately," Burbank recalled. When he took the stand and explained who he was, the faces of Blay-Miezah's entire legal team dropped simultaneously. There was a tense silence in the courtroom as Burbank took Appiah through the details of Blay-Miezah's fraud: John Kolorah Blay's letter to the university, the claim that he had once been Jacob Badu, the request to "please re-issue his diplomas—his beloved diplomas—in the new name."

In one fell swoop, Appiah had connected John Kolorah Blay to the Blay-Miezah sitting in the courtroom, provided evidence that he was responsible for the affidavit of name change stealing Badu's identity, and established that Blay-Miezah was not in fact a doctor. Blay-Miezah was, however, a perjurer and a forger.

After Appiah had finished, Kwaw-Swanzy got reluctantly to his feet. Kwaw-Swanzy had not been expecting Burbank's testimony, so he had no cross-examination prepared. He knew, though, that he had to find a way to cast doubt on the authenticity of Burbank's documents. Blay-Miezah's letters, and the forged affidavit of name change, were in a battered manila folder from the university archives.

There was a strange mark on the cover of the folder—as if something had once been stuck to it. Kwaw-Swanzy lobbed a few bland questions at Burbank, then he picked up the manila folder, and said: "Mr Burbank, it looks as if there was something on this folder."

"It does," Burbank replied.

"Do you know what it was?" Kwaw-Swanzy asked.

"I don't know on personal knowledge, but I've been told what it was, but I'm sure you don't want hearsay," Burbank replied.

Kwaw-Swanzy created another line of questioning, then circled back to the manila folder, as if to catch Burbank off guard: "I want to know what you were told was on that folder," he said.

Burbank replied: it was a picture of Jacob Badu, from his Wharton record card. Police officers had pulled it off Badu's file—which had been reclassified in the name of John Kolorah Blay—when they were hunting for Blay-Miezah in Philadelphia, in 1972. The Philadelphia police had not realized that it was a picture of Jacob Badu.

That was not what Kwaw-Swanzy wanted to hear, Burbank remembered: "He immediately objected on the grounds of hearsay." The judge had no sympathy. Kwaw-Swanzy, the judge dryly remarked, had made an "invited error."

Burbank was soon on his way back to Philadelphia. He timed his exit well: by the time he left, someone was spreading rumors in Accra that he had been sent by the U.S. government to prevent Blay-Miezah "from getting his hands on his legacy."

Blay-Miezah would later try to explain it all away. He told his investors that he needed the degrees for reasons he could not divulge until the complicated business of the Trust Fund was over. And as for his title: "The 'doctor' is a name I chose myself," he shrugged.

FINALLY, ABRAHAM SACKEY TOOK the stand. Sackey was the police officer Blay-Miezah had accused of extorting forty-three thousand cedi from him. Before Sackey could begin, Kwaw-Swanzy tried to get the case thrown out of court. He argued that "the evidence so far adduced before the court showed lack of any substantive evidence which proves the guilt of his client." It was clear that Blay-Miezah's legal team was worried about Sackey's testimony. The judge was deeply amused: Blay-Miezah himself had gone on the radio and issued a press release, stating that he had bribed a police officer. He had confessed—voluntarily—and in the most public way possible to paying off Sackey. The case would continue.

Appiah was thrilled to be able to use Blay-Miezah's words against him: "Dr Blay-Miezah gave the money to Sackey at a time when the Special Branch was keeping surveillance on him," the prosecutor said. Blay-Miezah "explained that as he wanted peace, he parted with the money." Bribing a police officer was illegal; whether the police officer had asked for the bribe or not was irrelevant.

On the stand, Sackey said that he had not extorted money from Blay-Miezah. Instead, Blay-Miezah had been courting him for years. They had first met at Blay-Miezah's old haunt, the Star Hotel, back in 1971. Blay-Miezah wanted to be friends. Sackey—presenting himself to the court as naive—said that he had no idea he was being used. He admitted to taking the money—he could hardly have denied it, since Blay-Miezah paid him by check, and then announced it on the radio. But, Sackey insisted, the money was a loan, not a gift.

This claim put Appiah's whole case in danger. If Sackey had always believed the payment was a loan, Blay-Miezah could easily claim the whole affair was a simple misunderstanding and walk away from the most high-profile charge against him.

Appiah pressed Sackey for more details. After his first meeting with Blay-Miezah, Sackey said, they had stayed in touch. In December 1974, Blay-Miezah told him about his newly acquired wealth. "It was at this juncture that Dr Blay-Miezah asked him whether he could 'do something' for him as a friend." Sackey was trying to finish a building on a plot of land he had out in the suburbs in Madina. He said that Blay-Miezah offered him a loan to complete construction. Sackey insisted that the money had always been a loan—and he had paid back every pesewa.

But then, cracks began appearing in Sackey's story. He admitted that Blay-Miezah had also helped his uncle take a business trip to the United States, and sent his brother-in-law money to buy a car. Sackey maintained that, even though he had been head of counterespionage at Special Branch, he'd had no idea at the time that Blay-Miezah was being investigated—a claim that seemed highly unlikely. Finally, under Appiah's examination, Sackey's story fell apart entirely. The building he had borrowed money for? It had "not yet been completed." His superiors had discovered the payment from Blay-Miezah and had censured Sackey. "You were not subjected to any disciplinary action for taking the money?" Appiah asked Sackey. "I suffered a lot," Sackey answered, morosely. He thought that he would have been the head of Special Branch by now, if he hadn't met Blay-Miezah.

Sackey insisted that he had paid back every cedi he took from Blay-Miezah. He could no longer be seen to be involved with Blay-Miezah, he said, so he made the payments to J. K. Siaw at the Tata Brewery in Achimota. He had kept receipts for every repayment, and they were tendered into evidence. "How much," Appiah asked Sackey, "did you pay?"

"43,000 cedis," answered Sackey.

"Are you sure?" Appiah asked.

"Yes," replied Sackey.

Appiah was asking because Sackey's receipts actually added up to forty-eight thousand cedi.

IN EARLY APRIL, Blay-Miezah's lawyers were due to open his defense in the bribery case. While Kwaw-Swanzy had managed to cast doubt on much of the documentary evidence, it was harder to refute the messy, incriminating accounts of witnesses like Sackey. All that was left was to flat-out delay the trial.

So on the day of the next hearing, Kwaw-Swanzy simply did not turn up. He was nowhere to be found.

The next day, and the day after that, Kwaw-Swanzy was still missing. Blay-Miezah's other six lawyers all looked very contrite: they explained that Kwaw-Swanzy might be traveling—or perhaps he was simply "indisposed"—either way, he was quite unreachable. Would the judge mind granting a lengthy adjournment while they located him?

Judge Brobbey could see exactly what was going on. He was disgusted, but he decided to give the distinguished lawyer the benefit of the doubt.

On April 4, the judge's patience ran out. He revoked Blay-Miezah's bail and remanded him to custody. Blay-Miezah would stay there, Judge Brobbey told the remaining six lawyers, until Kwaw-Swanzy reappeared.

Kwaw-Swanzy was back in court first thing the next morning. He spent most of the hearing apologizing. He "told the court that his absence was not a deliberate attempt to retard the progress of work on the court." It was, he said, all due to "miscommunications" by his client.

For the remainder of the hearing, Kwaw-Swanzy tried, again, to have the case dismissed. The prosecution, he said, "had not been able to establish a prima facie case against his client on all eight charges including perjury and forgery of official document[s] or prove Blay-Miezah was guilty." Kwaw-Swanzy's requests to end the hearings were denied, but his reappearance did get his client released on bail. That night, Blay-Miezah was back at his mansion on McCarthy Hill, looking out over the city. It had been a close call. Imprisonment was now a real possibility. But he would do whatever it took to avoid it. He still had seven excellent lawyers and a decent shot—he thought—at becoming president. And every day the trial went on brought him closer to the election.

AS THE TRIAL drew to a close, it was clear that the evidence against Blay-Miezah was substantial. The defense team decided on a new direction. So Blay-Miezah sat in court, looking increasingly perturbed, projecting an almost youthful innocence. The defense team's new approach turned out to be very simple: Blay-Miezah would convince the court that he had been conned.

He said that he had been the victim of an unscrupulous, money-hungry policeman. Sackey had allegedly claimed the bribe was meant for his superior, the commissioner for National Redemption Council Affairs, E. K. Buckman. Blay-Miezah told the court that after he had handed Sackey forty-three thousand cedi in checks, the police officer had come back and asked for another bribe. It was then, Blay-Miezah explained, his voice tinged with regret, that he had decided to make sure the bribe had reached its intended recipient.

Alas, Blay-Miezah said, when he went down to Special Branch headquarters to confront Buckman, "he (Buckman) smiled and told him to leave the office, he would get in touch with him later." Blay-Miezah said that he "never heard from Buckman again."

He was, of course, horrified to learn that he had been the victim of a con. Truly, kalabule was everywhere: If respectable businessmen like him could not go about their work without falling victim, what hope was there for the country?

It was an impassioned statement, but one thing stood out about it, for everyone in court: Blay-Miezah refused to give evidence under oath. He was not going to do anything that jeopardized the remainder of his campaign, especially after watching Appiah's surprise witnesses dominate the headlines for weeks. Sackey's counsel protested. Making accusations in an unsworn statement, he said, was "wrong and dangerous," especially because Blay-Miezah had been shown to be "an untruthful person."

★

JUST IN CASE the trial did not go as planned, and Blay-Miezah walked free, the government had to ensure that he could not win the presidency. Even if he was jailed, he would remain dangerous: plenty of elections had been won by candidates behind bars. His campaign, and his party, had to be stopped.

The next morning, Blay-Miezah received news that the People's Vanguard been outlawed. The party had missed the deadline to file its paperwork. The registrar of political parties immediately took the party off the ballot for the summer's elections. The People's Vanguard was ordered to disband.

Without a place on the ballot, Blay-Miezah had no chance at power. And without power, his house of cards could come crashing down within weeks. The press had already stopped calling him "Dr Blay-Miezah"; now they started referring to his political party as "the defunct People's Vanguard."

Just as he always did when he was losing control of a situation, Blay-Miezah called a press conference. He bristled with indignation. "The proscription of his party was arbitrary and clear indication of a deliberate action aimed at nullifying the existence of the party, come what may," he said. "This together with other impediments" were "clear indications of deliberate attempts designed to thwart the efforts of the People's Vanguard." To add insult to injury, Blay-Miezah said his latest consignment of BLAY-MIEZAH POWER T-shirts had been stopped at customs "and sent to the Castle."

Blay-Miezah announced that the party would "institute court action against the electoral commissioner for 'illegally proscribing the party.'" Kwaw-Swanzy had yet more work to do.

SOON AFTER, THE People's Vanguard held a gigantic rally at Bukom Square in Jamestown, the heart of the old city. It was a fragile, beautiful part of town, all old whitewashed houses, sea air, and boxing gyms, with the high walls of Ussher Fort looming up to the east, and the blue-green sweep of the Korle Lagoon, winding toward the sea, in the west.

Blay-Miezah "urged the gathering not to judge the party through unfounded allegations levelled against him in person since there was not an iota of truth" in them. "We stand for truth," Blay-Miezah bellowed.

Kwesi Amoako-Atta, who stood beside Blay-Miezah, spoke next to explain that the court case, and the ban on the party, showed that powerful men were afraid of the People's Vanguard. "The road to political freedom is noted for its roughness and Ghanaians should note that recent developments in the country, notably against the party, are signs of big things to happen—success for the People's Vanguard in the forthcoming elections."

BLAY-MIEZAH'S TRIAL WAS almost over. It had been front-page news for weeks. Now, the country held its breath in anticipation.

In his summation, Appiah cut calmly through the bluster and braggadocio of the trial. "It was essential for the court to focus its mind on the prosecution's evidence and not to allow itself at this stage to be influenced by a multiplicity of issues which were not relevant," he said. "Dr Blay-Miezah could not be exonerated because his evidence were admissions and confessions made by himself."

The American ambassador composed a lengthy cable to the State Department, reporting that Blay-Miezah seemed—at last—to be done for.

On April 19, Blay-Miezah and Sackey were both found guilty and sentenced to four years in prison for bribery. On the charge of perjury, Blay-Miezah received an additional five-year sentence.

SHORTLY AFTERWARD, KWAW-SWANZY strode wearily into the High Court to try to get the People's Vanguard back on the ballot. He won a token victory: the People's Vanguard was allowed to keep its certificate of registration, but the party's registration was still canceled. No one would be voting for Blay-Miezah for president.

Blay-Miezah had bribed a high-ranking police officer, he'd forged documents, he'd stolen someone else's degrees, he'd skipped out on hotel bills. He'd lied, cheated, and stolen his way across the world, from Accra to Monrovia to Philadelphia. Now, he was going to be in prison for years, long enough for people to forget why they had ever had faith in him to begin with.

But once again, Blay-Miezah's luck would change quickly. Ghana was about to experience a reckoning that would mark the dawning of a terrible new era. And as usual, the devastation of his people was Blay-Miezah's good fortune. Both Ghana and Blay-Miezah were about to descend into darkness.

Chapter 15

Deal with the Devil

1979–1980

B lay-Miezah was sent to Nsawam Prison. He immediately had a convenient medical episode and got himself transferred from a shared cell to
the prison infirmary. The infirmary itself was considerably more pleasant
once he had someone put up mosquito netting and ordered in a refrigerator.
"Once a big man always a big man," said a fellow inmate. "Even in prison he
was a big man."

The big men at Nsawam could afford to have other inmates wait on them.
Someone else fetched Blay-Miezah's water, sometimes by paying off whoever
was manning the trailer that supplied the prison kitchens, or—when there was
a shortage during the dry season—walking as much as six miles to find water.
Other inmates cooked for Blay-Miezah. Instead of the prison food—which
was notoriously awful—wealthier prisoners and political detainees got
uncooked rations. Some days there would be a hundred prisoners cooking
together behind the cell blocks, many for other inmates.

At Nsawam, Blay-Miezah did everything in his power to make sure he was
well liked. He restarted the prison football league and bought enough equipment for everyone in the entire prison to play.

Once, Blay-Miezah paid for every prisoner to get a shape-up. His new
friends, he decided, were looking a little too scruffy, so he had the guards call

in barbers. "Shieee, Blay-Miezah," another man who was resident at Nsawam Prison remembered: "He paid five cedis on a haircut for each prisoner. At the time there were about 1,300 prisoners, so you can imagine how much it cost him. The prisoners always remember him."

As soon as Blay-Miezah had been sentenced, his lawyers filed an appeal. But the judge refused bail. It was going to be a long stay in prison, so Blay-Miezah settled in and got ready to see someone else be elected president. Whatever happened, he was determined to find a way to turn it to his advantage.

FIVE WEEKS BEFORE the presidential election, a group of low-ranking members of the armed forces hijacked a Ferret armored car and its driver at gunpoint and drove to the Fifth Battalion Barracks in Accra. It was the beginning of one of the most hapless coup attempts in Ghanaian history. But it also marked a turning point for the country. For the next decade, Ghana would be run—and overrun—by people more concerned with settling scores and making themselves wildly wealthy than governing the country. The first of these men was a flight lieutenant named Jerry John Rawlings.

Rawlings's military career was thoroughly undistinguished. He had tried, several times, to get promoted, but he was not well liked by his superiors and kept failing the exams. He had just been put on notice that, in July 1979, he would be sacked from the Ghana Armed Forces. Money was tight, and Rawlings was getting desperate. Because of his personal difficulties, Rawlings would trigger a chain of events that would plunge Ghana into a decade of death and destruction.

The officers who hijacked the armored car were armed with Heckler & Koch G3 rifles. They were going in search of Major Kwadwo Boakye-Djan, who was the commander of the Delta Company of the Fifth Battalion, as well as one of Rawlings's oldest friends and the best man at his wedding.

Boakye-Djan knew they were looking for him. He had been drinking with Rawlings at the Continental Hotel the night before the attempted coup. A good number of drinks in, Rawlings abruptly said that he was planning to stage a coup d'état.

"You and who?" Boakye-Djan asked. A lot of the boys, Rawlings said, were with him. They were ready to go—tomorrow—and Rawlings wanted

Boakye-Djan to join them. Boakye-Djan tried to warn Rawlings off. He told Rawlings he would be a sitting duck, but the man was hardheaded and did not listen. So Boakye-Djan decided not to show up at his post the next morning.

When Rawlings rolled up in the armored car, Boakye-Djan was nowhere to be found. Rawlings was livid, throwing down his rifle in frustration. This was a poor idea. He had left the safety off. The rifle started firing the moment it hit the ground. People scattered in every direction.

In the mayhem, one of the soldiers in the armored car tried to peel off, driving it straight into an open gutter. Rawlings panicked and fled the chaos he had caused. "He was now cannon fodder, as I had forecast," Boakye-Djan remembered. "I warned him, but he wouldn't listen."

A detachment of soldiers from the Fifth Battalion eventually found Rawlings hiding at the Air Force Station with only his service pistol for protection. The major who arrested him, Siedu Mahama, reportedly took the weapon and smacked Rawlings over the head with it, saying "You don't stage coups with a pistol."

THE SECOND MAN to publicly settle a score—and inadvertently trigger a series of events that would almost destroy his country—was George Aikins, the director of public prosecutions. One of Aikins's cases had been stifled, and he had it on good authority that General Fred Akuffo and the Supreme Military Council were responsible. Aikins had heard that between them, Akuffo and the council had taken two million dollars in bribes and a Mercedes Benz to subvert justice. Aikins was livid.

Now, the Supreme Military Council wanted Rawlings and his co-conspirators punished. Mutiny was a capital offense, and Aikins was expected to prosecute the officers involved accordingly. When it was time for the court-martial, Aikins decided he was done taking orders. He made Rawlings and his men idols. At the court at Burma Camp, the sprawling military base in the middle of Accra, Aikins "went out of his way to defend" Rawlings and his co-conspirators. They were freedom fighters, Aikins said. They had seen a corrupt, broken society and decided to do something about it. Joe Appiah—who had prosecuted Blay-Miezah—heard reports of the trial from his home in Kumasi. "Never in my long experience at the criminal bar had the case against an accused been so sympathetically presented," he wrote.

Decades later, Ghana's National Reconciliation Commission—which was set up to investigate human rights violations—would conclude that this was a disastrous decision: "By that singular act of indiscretion, Aikins unwittingly set in motion a chain of events leading to the deaths, not only of those he accused of corruption, but also of many innocent persons."

Rawlings himself was allowed to give a lengthy speech. The mutiny, Rawlings said, was not about imposing himself on Ghanaians but about fighting military commanders, politicians, businessmen, and "foreign criminals who have used our blood, sweat and tears—the tools of our laboring—to enrich themselves, to drown in wine and women, while you and I—while the majority of us—are daily struggling for survival." In Ghana, he said, "a vast majority of hungry people" were pitted "against a very tiny minority of greedy, inhumane, selfish" people and their bank managers.

He didn't believe a word he was saying, but he was intensely charismatic and talked with such conviction that audiences listening on the radio were instantly moved.

This was no trial, and Rawlings knew it. This was his chance to gin up support. "Let me tell you today that God will not help you," he said, ignoring the court and speaking directly to the public. Big men would not help, he said: their stomachs were full and their children were fed. It was only Ghanaians who had the power to help themselves. The sentiment traveled from the court to barracks, cities, towns, and villages all over the country.

"Overnight," the National Reconciliation Commission later concluded, "the band of conspirators became heroes."

EARLY ON JUNE 4, shortly before the presidential election was due to occur, a mob of young officers and soldiers (including Rawlings's best man, Boakye-Djan) broke Rawlings out of military jail. The conspirators then stormed the offices of Radio Ghana and took over. At seven thirty in the morning, Rawlings announced that they had overthrown the government. He was gasping for breath and fumbling with the microphone. He sounded shrill, almost hysterical: "The ranks have just taken over the destiny of this country . . . If you have any reason to fear them, you may run. If you have no reason to feel guilty, do not move . . . You are either part of the problem, or part of the solution. There is no middle way."

The junta named itself the Armed Forces Revolutionary Council and appointed Rawlings the chairman. The election, Rawlings said, would now be held on his terms. As the National Reconciliation Commission report noted: "The entire nation was looking forward to the dawn of a new era on 1st July. But that date was to pass without so much as a whimper."

Initially, the coup attracted support from idealistic students, working-class people, and left-wing activists who hoped that Ghana could be transformed for the better. They campaigned for free education, for ordinary Ghanaians "to take control of the processes of decision-making on matters affecting their lives," and for workers to "have the right to enjoy the full benefits of their labour." Hundreds of young people, students and workers, were caught up in a powerful wave of hope and went out into the country to ready Ghana for this new era. They helped women in remote villages prepare to run for office; they helped small farmers organize themselves into united groups so they could lobby the government. Change was coming, and everybody would need to know how to best use their power. Honoring the date of coup, they called themselves the June Fourth Movement. Such earnest revolutionaries had little in common with most of the men who now ruled Ghana.

Rawlings would later say that "a bloodbath was necessary to cleanse the country." Military officers went everywhere armed to the teeth: "rifles with double magazines taped together, pistols on both hips, bayonets, bandoliers with 7.62 mm bullets," even rocket-propelled grenades. Entire families were hounded into exile. Many people simply disappeared and were never found by their families. For those who remained, as the National Reconciliation Commission put it, "life became a shadow of its former self." Countless people were brutalized: some in public, with the pretense of justice, others quietly murdered.

On June 4, the day of the coup, Colonel Joseph Enninful, the president of Rawlings's court-martial, was attacked by soldiers at his home in Burma Camp. He and his wife, Josephine, were killed. Soon after, General Acheampong, deposed years earlier and now confined to his village, was dragged from his home and summarily executed.

Powerful people were not the only ones targeted. As the commission later reported, no one was safe. Gifty Adom sold fish in the market in Mampong, Ashanti. She was nine months pregnant when a soldier ordered her to sell the fish in smaller portions. "As she bent down to comply with the order, the soldier removed his belt and began to beat her with it. The iron hook of the belt hit Gifty on the stomach. Gifty delivered eleven days later. The impact of the belt on her stomach affected the child, Ibrahim Afrifa, who was born blind." Comfort Mensah sold sugar cane at Tema. She and her eight-year-old daughter, Kalibi, were returning home one evening when a stray bullet struck Kalibi in her abdomen. The girl was rushed to Tema General Hospital, "where it was found that the bullet had damaged her spine. As a result Kalibi became partially paralyzed." Afua Serwaa was married to a police officer in Tamale and owned two successful shops. On June 17, she and her husband were arrested by soldiers. Their hair was shaved off. Then they were "taken to the Tamale taxi rank and publicly flogged with a fan belt on their bare backs. At the time, Serwaa was nursing a newly-born baby."

Initially, people who heard the news thought that these were isolated incidents. People who were untouched by the atrocities did not realize how grave the situation had become. To many, Rawlings and the Armed Forces Revolutionary Council were heroes who would transform the country and right wrongs. Jerry John Rawlings—J. J., the chairman—was the nation's savior. He cultivated the nickname "Junior Jesus," and this coup was his Second Coming.

IN REALITY, THE National Reconciliation Commission concluded that Rawlings and the soldiers did not stage a coup because of their "desire to see democracy restored in the country; rather, it was to afford them an opportunity to punish those they held responsible" for their own woes and to enrich themselves. The soldiers looted everything in sight. The Armed Forces Revolutionary Council was a kleptocracy. Anything that could be carried was taken away. Everything else was claimed by the council or destroyed. The soldiers said they were reclaiming ill-gotten gains, but decades later, the National Reconciliation Commission would conclude that they had simply been stealing. They filled military bases with so many stolen automobiles, a reporter noted, that the "5th Battalion parade grounds looked like Heathrow Airport car park."

In the frenzy, countless families lost their homes and their livelihoods. Entire businesses—from small hawker stalls to factory complexes—disappeared into the maw of the Armed Forces Revolutionary Council. Baiden Amissah returned to Ghana after many years in Germany, just as the soldiers took power. He had shipped back a whole container-load of furniture and consumer goods—enough to furnish his home in Ghana and start a business. He had put every penny he had saved into brand-new construction machinery. Amissah cleared everything at the port and loaded the containers onto trucks. On his way home from the port, the soldiers stopped him. They took everything: his cooker, his television, his stereo, even his clothes. Then they came back for his tractor, his bulldozer, and his truck. Grace Tetteh and her husband, a diplomat, had recently returned from the United States. They lived above a shop in Accra. Soldiers descended on their apartment and stripped it bare—taking everything down to the cooking utensils and their children's clothes.

J. K. Siaw, Blay-Miezah's backer, lost everything. His assets and bank accounts were frozen, as were those of his relatives. Then the Armed Forces Revolutionary Council enacted a decree specifically designed to steal his business: "the Transfer of Shares & Other Proprietary Interests (Tata Brewery Limited) Decree, 1979 (AFRCD 9) transferring all the shares of the company to the State." Soldiers raided Siaw's home and carried away "goods, cash and vehicles said to be worth over £100,000."

Years later, Siaw's heirs were still fighting to regain their property. "It is our sweat and blood," his son, Joseph Apeadu Siaw, said. He had built the brewery with his father: he remembered carrying head pans of concrete during school holidays. In 1979, J. K. Siaw fled to Liberia. He left for London a few years later and died in exile in 1986.

AS WELL AS stealing, Rawlings's junta arrested people without cause and imprisoned people without trial. People would hear, over the radio, that they were under investigation, and either hand themselves in or flee the country. Joe Appiah soon heard his own name: he was one of a group of people ordered to "report to the guard room, Air Force Station, Burma Camp, Accra, immediately in their own interest."

Appiah packed a toothbrush, dressed in full cloth, and asked his driver to take him straight to Burma Camp, which was now the Armed Forces Revolutionary Council's base. He was there for a few chaotic days. He spent most of his time shadowboxing in the yard, to avoid thinking too much about what he was hearing: "the constant and merciless beatings of new captives" and the shouts of "Kill them!" that echoed around the barracks every night. Then he was transferred to Nsawam Prison.

A few weeks after sending Blay-Miezah to Nsawam, Appiah walked through the prison gates himself, to join the man he had convicted. It was not his first visit: Appiah had, of course, been sent there by Nkrumah's government and was greeted like an old friend by the prison officers. Back again? they asked. "Yes, not as I would wish; it's always at the wish of others," he replied.

Appiah moved into his favorite cell—number 12, next to the toilet and the showers "and the most airy of the cells." He was soon joined by the former head of state, Lieutenant General Akwasi Afrifa, who had been one of the leading plotters against President Nkrumah. Appiah and Afrifa played ludo, cards, and draughts and tried to make the best of things.

On Afrifa's second day at Nsawam, he was told to pack up and move to the block reserved for condemned men. "The General walked up to me," remembered Appiah, "asked for a few cigarettes, and bade me 'goodbye.'" As he left, he said to Appiah: "Uncle Joe, these boys want to finish me."

SOON AFTERWARD, JOSS Aryee, a reporter with the Ghana News Agency, was called to a press conference at a military firing range on the shore in Teshie, a few miles from the center of Accra.

"Little did I know then that this short, cryptic message was a hint of one of the most blood-curdling and traumatic political events ever to happen in the short history of this peace-loving nation since her birth in 1957," he later wrote.

Aryee's beat was the Armed Forces Revolutionary Council. Later, he would remember that the tension around Burma Camp at the time "was as thick as a two-day old palmnut soup." Outside the military base, all over Accra, "sullen-faced soldiers, itchy-fingered, trigger-happy and armed to the teeth, were everywhere, beating up men and women, old and young, so-called nation wreckers, traders, hoarders, 'kalabule' people, foreigners and God knows whom. And they did this without mercy; it was as if we were at war!" Aryee would start every day not knowing if he was going to make it home alive. "You could smell death in the air."

On the day of Aryee's trip to Teshie, the council had announced that every high-ranking member of the military who had led Ghana astray or taken power for their own ends—from the men who had deposed President Nkrumah on—would pay for what they had done. A massive crowd from all over Accra had gathered at the Teshie Military Range by seven in the morning. "This was a once-in-a-lifetime experience nobody wanted to miss," Aryee wrote. "People had climbed trees, electric and telephone poles, any available thing that could give them a good view of this pornography of violence." The scene was set: "There were six stakes, each with a rope dangling about it. Sandbags were piled behind each stake up to the shoulder level. Some twenty-five or so feet in front of the stakes were open ended tents for the firing squad."

Hours went by, and the early-morning crowd grew restless. Some of the students started singing the Bob Marley song written by Lee "Scratch" Perry—"If you are the big tree, we are the small axe, ready to cut you down"—and chanting "Wake up, J. J., the devil is coming to spoil the country and your children."

Finally, at nine in the morning, the crowd heard sirens screaming, coming from the direction of the La Trade Fair, a few miles down the coast. Minutes later, a convoy arrived: "an anti-aircraft gun vehicle with four soldiers on board, followed by two ambulances and, at the rear, a Pinzgauer with presumably the firing squad." The crowd went deathly quiet.

The condemned stepped out of the first ambulance: General Akuffo, who had just been deposed; Lieutenant General Afrifa from Nsawam Prison; General Robert Kotei, the former chief of defense staff; Colonel Roger Felli, who had once confronted Blay-Miezah as Acheampong's commissioner for economic planning; Air Vice-Marshal Yaw Boakye; and Rear Admiral Joy Amedume. They were blindfolded and led over the sand and tied to the stakes. Rear Admiral Amedume, Aryee remembered, was facing the sea.

Time sped up. "Hardly anyone saw the firing squad enter the tents, all attention was on the condemned officers. And there was no audible order to fire. Just a sudden: 'ko. ko. . . . ko.ko.ko.'" Aryee saw the bullet holes and the blood soaking through the men's clothes. Bullets tore through the ropes binding Colonel Felli, and he collapsed.

Then the firing stopped. Everything was quiet for a minute. Then Lieutenant General Afrifa stirred, and slowly rose. "Blood was streaming from his shoulders down his arm. He screamed, 'I am not dead . . . I am not dead . . .'" His expression was pure agony. The crowd was suddenly horrified. They had been promised quick, clean executions. Satisfying retribution. The pain, the blood, the look in the general's eyes were all unexpected.

Everybody immediately concluded that the soldiers had missed on purpose. The general was being tortured. A soldier standing next to Aryee was disgusted: "Why dey for punish the man so, eh? Say wetin at all 'e do?"

The commander of the firing squad took out his pistol with a flourish and strode toward Lieutenant General Afrifa, shooting. The dramatic performance impeded his aim: the first shot hit the sandbags. He fired again and the pistol jammed. The officer looked deeply embarrassed and stopped to fumble with his gun. Another officer, in a rush to save the moment, handed the assassin another pistol. The head of the firing squad tried again, this time firing six shots at point-blank range. Lieutenant General Afrifa collapsed. It was over.

As the crowd quietly dispersed, a fighter jet flew over the Teshie range and dipped its wings. It was Rawlings, everybody thought, taking a victory lap. Aryee rushed to file his story at the military training academy where he had parked his car. The nearest phone was at the guard post. When he got there, he overheard the officer on duty on a call: "Yes Sir . . . Yes . . ." the officer said. "Yes, they have just finished slaughtering the cows."

THE ELECTIONS WERE eventually held on June 18, under the close supervision of Rawlings. There was no clear winner in the presidential race, so there was a runoff election the next month, on July 10. The eventual winner, to general surprise, was a career diplomat named Hilla Limann, leader of the People's National Party.

On September 24, Rawlings "gave up his place in the huge state chair in parliament to President Hilla Limann." (The presidential seat, an enormous carved wooden chair, inlaid with gold and embossed with a black star, was first used by President Nkrumah. The diminutive Rawlings had always been dwarfed by it.) As he swore Limann in, Rawlings warned that Ghanaians would "resist and unseat" the new president if he disappointed them.

"It is," remarked one American diplomat, "very difficult to say if Limann will be in office six months from now."

Behind the scenes, Blay-Miezah's old business partner, Krobo Edusei, was pulling the strings of the People's National Party. Edusei, who called himself "the acting father of the PNP," was soon up to his old tricks. Shortly before Limann's inauguration, Edusei had obtained a loan of a million dollars from an Italian industrialist, which was "paid into a newly opened PNP bank account in London," the newspapers reported. Britain's bankers were, as always, happy to be of service. As soon as the money was in the bank, Edusei "demanded 70,000 US dollars as his share."

WITH HIS OLD ally back in power, Blay-Miezah suddenly had a way out of Nsawam. In February 1980, his lawyers announced that he had developed what the newspapers called a "galaxy of diseases." They arranged for him to be examined by a board of doctors at Korle-Bu Teaching Hospital.

Blay-Miezah's lawyers later told the papers that their client had "diabetes mellitus, hypertension, obesity and blindness in the left eye. An x-ray of the skull further revealed an abnormal bone formation in the brain, which in the view of the Board, needed further investigations." The lawyers argued that because many of the tests required were not immediately available in Ghana, their client should "be sent to Europe for further necessary medical care."

Supportive editorials began to appear in the newspapers, urging that Blay-Miezah be released, so that he could tend to his "remarkable galazy [sic] of diseases." The state-run Daily Graphic ran an oddly defensive piece, arguing that "the Blay-Miezah hospital business got out of hand, into absurdities. There is [sic] a whole lot of people in Ghana who have become cynical that such reports, instead of drawing sympathy, infuriate them."

Meanwhile, Blay-Miezah's legal team had been busy filing appeals and had finally met with some success. Bashiru Kwaw-Swanzy had managed to have the charge of bribery thrown out on a technicality. The new chief state attorney, J. K. Kaleo Bio, said the evidence that the money Blay-Miezah gave Abraham Sackey had been intended as a loan went uncontested during the trial. Therefore, the charge of bribery was clearly groundless. Kaleo Bio conveniently skirted the fact that Blay-Miezah himself had stated—on the radio, at a press conference, and in open court—that the money he had given the police officer was a bribe, and that he had gone to the officer's boss to check that the bribe had been received.

Kaleo Bio said he no longer supported Blay-Miezah's conviction. The judge at the appeal—who appeared to be as selectively forgetful as the state attorney—agreed. Blay-Miezah was released, and he was free to leave the country.

Chapter 16

Our Man in London

1981

B lay-Miezah landed in London. But instead of admitting himself to a hospital, as the board of doctors at Korle-Bu had recommended, he moved into the penthouse suite of the Montcalm Hotel, near Marble Arch. The hotel was converted from a series of Georgian houses originally built toward the end of the eighteenth century. "Encased in an elegant Georgian crescent and centrally placed," the Montcalm was, a guidebook gushed, "an extremely civilized house, admirably suited to those of sybaritic tastes." Inside, it was the height of eighties elegance: black leather sofas, duplex suites, and a wood-paneled club bar in the basement.

London was Blay-Miezah's kind of town. In 1979, after Prime Minister Margaret Thatcher came to power, criminal organizations from all over the world flocked to the British capital. Scammers and money launderers descended on London: it was a barely regulated paradise. There was so much dirty money passing through the city that Blay-Miezah's operation would be relatively insignificant.

London would also give Blay-Miezah a new hunting ground: a place where he could expand the Oman Ghana Trust Fund without the shadow of his recent prosecution hanging over him, and without as many people watching him. He could smooth over relations with his existing investors, who had been growing increasingly anxious over the last few years. And he could raise the money he needed to keep his con going: his protracted legal battles, and his time in prison, had been expensive. In London, there were new investors to charm, new associates to conspire with, and plans to make.

Ultimately, though, Blay-Miezah needed to find a way back to Accra and a way to get close to whoever was in power, when he got there. Accra was the heart of his scam, and without connections there, he would not be able to keep up the facade of the Oman Ghana Trust Fund for long. Blay-Miezah was more willing than ever to make himself useful to anyone who could help him get closer to power.

PETER RIGBY RAN a video studio in Muswell Hill in north London. His company also set up projectors and screens for conferences and banquets. In January 1981, he was the subject of a tabloid smear by the *News of the World*, which alleged that Rigby's company sold "highly-profitable parlour pornography" imported from Amsterdam, as part of a "boom in tapes which viewers can just plug into their own TV screens." A chief inspector at Scotland Yard insinuated, bizarrely, that Rigby was connected to American organized crime, telling the *News of the World* that he was "deeply disturbed about the American Mafia interest in London."

Soon afterward, Rigby was called to visit a client in the penthouse suite of the Montcalm. He was happy to oblige: clients at West End hotels paid a premium. Rigby would tip the concierges, so they would keep him in mind for the best gigs.

At the Montcalm Hotel, Rigby took in the client, in the flesh. Blay-Miezah was sitting on one of the three sofas in the lounge of his suite. He was naked above the waist, apart from a large gold Star of David—a gift from an investor—hanging from a gold chain around his neck. He was smoking an expensive cigar. Blay-Miezah said that his company needed to rent several pieces of video equipment and would pay handsomely. Rigby did not realize it at the time, but that meeting was about to change his life forever.

Rigby was fascinated by Blay-Miezah. "I had absolutely zero knowledge of him, his history, his country nor his ambitions." For now, though, Rigby was focused on "pandering to a very lucrative client." Soon Blay-Miezah's business became vital to his company. Rigby found himself spending more and more time at the Montcalm. He would arrive in the early evening, dine at the hotel restaurant at Blay-Miezah's expense, then provide Blay-Miezah with an audience. "Later I viewed his tactic as a carrot to a donkey," he wrote. "My association with this man developed into being at his beck-and-call at any time."

During the first few months of their business relationship, Rigby later realized, Blay-Miezah was molding him. Some of the conditioning was fairly simple: "He was a stickler for punctuality and I was the world's worst," Rigby wrote. "If I turned up more than three minutes late, he would punish me, making me wait fruitlessly outside his suite for what seemed hours." Then Rigby would be dismissed. It happened again and again "until I turned up exactly on time, day or night. I was totally aware of my predicament but became unwilling to resist. I wanted to be told."

Rigby learned more about Blay-Miezah from his associates, who had begun to filter into London in Blay-Miezah's wake. Rigby would drive them around town and chat. Kwesi Amoako-Atta said Blay-Miezah was in exile and was planning a return to Ghana. The way Amoako-Atta told it, Blay-Miezah ran for president, "was embroiled in accusations and counter claims against certain powerful people," and when Hilla Limann won the election, Blay-Miezah was jailed in retribution. His powerful friends managed to convince the Limann government to let Blay-Miezah out of jail, and he left for London immediately. Once again, history was being rewritten.

Rigby had an appetite for risk and a strong sense of adventure, but he had no idea who he was dealing with. Eventually, Rigby learned what his best customer had planned. Blay-Miezah was going to run for president again soon, and he was going to win. Rigby once asked him how he could be sure that he would be elected. He laughed and said: "It's a foregone conclusion." Then, Blay-Miezah said, he would have access to a fantastic windfall. That was when Rigby learned the story of the Oman Ghana Trust Fund. Immediately, he decided he wanted to come along for the ride.

In exchange, Blay-Miezah offered Rigby an opportunity. Rigby did not want to profit from a small, struggling country. Instead, when all this was over and Blay-Miezah was president, he promised that Rigby would help build the country by founding Ghana's first commercial television network. That was how Rigby was going to get rich.

Altogether, Rigby would spend over a decade at Blay-Miezah's side. One day, he would be shooting video in London and the next, Rigby said, he would be running cash and weapons into Ghana. His faith was unwavering. "Most people seem to think Blay-Miezah was the world's biggest con man," Rigby later said. "He wasn't. He was a patriot."

WHILE BLAY-MIEZAH WAS lining up investors in London, he also began to look further afield. The Oman Ghana Trust Fund had supporters on three continents. Now, he added a fourth.

The Trust Fund had begun to attract interest in South Korea. Blay-Miezah flew to Seoul to meet with potential investors. They took him to Yonsei University to see a spring festival called Akaraka. The campus was a sea of royal-blue flags and T-shirts. Students packed the stands of an open-air amphitheater, chanting. Blay-Miezah, who always had an ear for a good fight song, fastened onto one cheer that sounded just like his name, Ackah: "Akaraka! Akaraka, Ching Akaraka Cho!" the Yonsei students shouted. "Akaraka, ChingChing Chochocho . . . Hey Yonsei Yeah!" Blay-Miezah was superstitious, and it seemed like a sign: loosely translated, *akaraka* also meant "destiny" in Igbo and was the subject of many a high-life song.

Blay-Miezah's trip was a success, with several South Korean investors making contributions to the Oman Ghana Trust Fund. Meanwhile, back in Philadelphia, Robert Ellis was also hard at work scouting new prospects. He was a natural salesman. Business was booming. Word of the Trust Fund had spread through the Pennsylvania suburbs like a fever. In the back booths of restaurants, in law offices, and at parties, investors told their friends and families about the amazing opportunity they had stumbled onto. For most of the people handing over money, the "decision to invest was based on the reputation, financial status and the business successes of some of the other individuals involved in the Trust." It helped that Ellis made the Oman Ghana Trust Fund sound like a sure thing, almost like a government bond. The "investment was to be fulfilled through the government of the Republic of

Ghana, in West Africa," one investor from New Jersey later told the Federal Bureau of Investigation. "Whatever amount was invested was to be returned tenfold to the investor." And, Ellis told everyone, the deal was about to close: if they wanted in, there was no time to waste.

An investor in Brooklyn was told that he would get his return in just six weeks. When the time came, however, someone "would always make excuses as to why his investment was delayed, such as Blay-Miezah reinvested the money without anybody knowing about it." Some of the investors had been waiting for their returns for years now. They were getting restless and needed to be soothed. So Ellis arranged for them to visit Blay-Miezah in London. The trip was also an opportunity to share some good news with the investors. The Oman Ghana Trust Fund was close to being unlocked. Things were about to change in Ghana, in a big way—and Blay-Miezah needed an infusion of cash for the last push.

IN LONDON, GLADYS Blay-Miezah still thought her husband was a legitimate businessman. "If he had not had the money, why did all those Swiss bankers roll out the red carpet?" she said. "I felt like there was a gram of truth in the money thing." But she could see how the people around him were being changed by the Oman Ghana Trust Fund. Everybody was convinced that they were—or were about to become—very wealthy. It affected some of his children deeply. She could see that it was taking a toll on Blay-Miezah too. "He always said, 'The kind of life I'm leading, I won't live to 50.'"

Blay-Miezah had flown one of his former girlfriends from Philadelphia— we'll call her Kathleen—to London. They both insisted it was strictly business: Kathleen was there to work on setting up a London office for the Trust Fund.

Blay-Miezah would give Gladys five thousand pounds, tell her to spend it all at Harrods, and not bring a penny back. So she would. A few weeks later, she would always wish that she had spent one thousand pounds and saved the rest. Blay-Miezah would often run out of money entirely, she said: "Then I'm right by his side, broke until more money comes."

Gladys decided that if she wasn't going to become a lawyer, she would work for herself. She started a fashion company called Lady Butterfly. She had a boutique in Accra, as well as a factory under the overpass at Circle. "My slant was African fabrics, with the tie dye and batik," she said. "I just wanted peace, to design clothes." She held fashion shows in Liberia and Nigeria to raise money for UNICEF.

In London, everyone stayed in the same hotel: there was Gladys, Blay-Miezah, and their two toddlers; there was Robert Ellis and his wife, Faye; Amoako-Atta and his wife, Mary; Krobo Edusei and his wife; and Kathleen. "The ladies were like one big happy family," Gladys said. They were helping her plan a second wedding in London.

Then they got word from Philadelphia: there was a family emergency, and Kathleen had to go home. Everyone took up a collection to help, and Kathleen left. She would call every day to let them know everything was okay, but somehow, she always called when they were out.

Gladys was convinced that Kathleen was somewhere in London: she must have recognized that if Gladys picked up the phone and heard the perfectly clear line, she'd instantly know Kathleen wasn't back in Philadelphia.

So Gladys got hold of a telephone directory, made a list of all the first-class hotels in London—Blay-Miezah wouldn't have his girlfriend staying anywhere else—and called each one, asking for Kathleen. Faye Ellis watched in awe. "Oh God, Columbo," she said, "what are you investigating now?"

It didn't take Gladys long to strike gold. The Hilton on Park Lane had no Kathleen, but the Intercontinental, right next door, offered to put Gladys through to her room. Gladys put down the telephone. "I called the driver, sat in my Rolls Royce, and drove over to Park Lane."

The Intercontinental—a vast white stone edifice, built on the site of Queen Elizabeth II's former childhood home—loomed over Hyde Park Corner, with sweeping views of the park's greenery. As the Rolls-Royce pulled up, the hotel doormen scrambled to welcome Gladys. She swept past them to the reception desk and said that she was there to see Kathleen. The hotel kept its room keys in individual wooden pigeonholes behind the reception desk. Gladys watched the receptionist closely; she saw him glance at the bank of keys behind him, and watched his eyes settle on four pigeonholes, 140, 141, 142, and 143. Only one key was missing. He turned back to say that Kathleen was there, and Gladys said: "And her room number is 14 . . ." "142," the receptionist confirmed.

Outside room 142, Gladys put her thumb over the spyhole, so Kathleen would think it was Blay-Miezah being cute, and knocked on the door. "When she opened the door, she nearly dropped," Gladys remembered.

Once she had recovered, Kathleen apologized: "Sorry, I'm going to leave, I'm all packed." Gladys was not there for an argument. After she had checked that Kathleen really had packed her bags, she said: "Let's just sit down and wait for our husband."

Fifteen minutes later there was another knock at the door.

Blay-Miezah walked in, with a large Davidoff cigar in his mouth. He caught sight of his wife. His jaw dropped; the cigar fell and started to singe the carpet.

Without missing a beat, he turned to Kathleen and said, "You know I'm married. When you go, don't come back, we can't do this anymore."

Gladys went back to the Montcalm, packed her things, and moved herself and her children to the Cumberland Hotel without telling anybody. When Blay-Miezah finally tracked her down with the help of the driver, he promised, over and over again, to behave. Gladys believed him. He even bought her a ring similar to Princess Diana's—diamonds arranged around a sapphire. Gladys agreed to marry him again: "You know how stupid young girls are," she said, thinking back. And yet, she continued to be one of the few people who could outwit him.

The two renewed their vows and were married for the second time in London. It was a grand, white wedding. Gladys Blay-Miezah had her doubts, but her husband made so many promises that, eventually, she agreed to give him another chance. "Every time I would try to leave, he'd come with a cock-and-bull story—that there was something wrong with him, that we'd have to pray together." They honeymooned on a yacht and visited Amsterdam, before returning to London. Blay-Miezah had to get back to work.

INVESTORS STARTED ARRIVING in London in the spring of 1981. They would gather at the Montcalm Hotel to wait for an audience with Blay-Miezah. One recalled him slowly emerging from a chauffeur-driven gray Rolls-Royce, wearing a tailored suit and smoking a large cigar. "That day he was in a particularly jovial mood as he regaled the investors gathered in his penthouse

John Ackah Blay-Miezah

Robert Ellis

Kwame Nkrumah, first president of Ghana, wearing a PG or "prison graduate" cap, kicking a football at Owusu Memorial Park in Fadama, Accra, 1952. Photographed by James Barnor.

E. T. Mensah and His Tempos Band, playing at a birthday celebration in Adabraka, Accra, early 1950s. Photographed by James Barnor.

President Kwame Nkrumah addresses the United Nations General Assembly in 1960.

A fallen statue of President Kwame Nkrumah in 1966.

Ghana's head of state Colonel Ignatius Kutu Acheampong (left) in the 1970s.

Party at Quentin Quartey's house, Accra, 1970s. Photographed by James Barnor.

Two friends dressed for a church celebration in Accra, 1970s. Photographed by James Barnor.

Blay-Miezah on the front page of the Ghanaian Times *in 1974.*

Justice Annie Ruth Jiagge, the first woman to become a judge in Ghana, with U.S. ambassador Shirley Temple Black in Accra, 1970s.

E. T. Mensah and His Tempos Band at Battersea Town Hall, London, 1960s. Photographed by James Barnor.

A performance at a night club in Trade Fair, Accra, 1978. Photographed by James Barnor.

Portrait of a woman (Margaret Obiri-Yeboah) taken in Accra, 1970s. Photographed by James Barnor.

Military leader Jerry John Rawlings in January 1982.

Burial of the soldiers killed during the 1979 coup led by J. J. Rawlings. Photographed by James Barnor.

A swarm of soldiers brandish weapons during Rawlings's second coup d'état, January 1982.

A diplomatic passport issued to Blay-Miezah by Rawlings's government, 1980s.

Blay-Miezah (second from right) and Ebenezer Ako-Adjei (far left), one of Ghana's founding fathers, with associates in the London office of the Oman Ghana Trust Fund, 1980s.

Investors and associates gathered at the London office of the Oman Ghana Trust Fund, 1980s.

A staff designed for the Okyeame (the member of the royal court who speaks for the chief), thought to have been made for an Ashanti court.

suite with tales of his student days at the University of Pennsylvania. At one point he burst into a lusty version of the Penn fight song, every inch the loyal Ivy League grad."

Among the investors was Herb Burstein. In the early 1970s, he had been a sales representative working with Ellis's firm, Industrial Dynamics. Burstein lost track of Ellis after the company went quiet, then ran into him again at the Horn & Hardart automat on City Avenue in Philadelphia. When he heard about Ellis's new line of business, he was intrigued.

By 1981, Burstein had sold some property in order to invest several hundred thousand dollars in the Oman Ghana Trust Fund. He was hoping for a return of several million. The Trust Fund sounded like an escapade and a good bet: "I saw myself as an intelligent, perceptive businessman," he later told *Philadelphia* magazine. "Yet I got hooked." Soon, like Rigby, he was "hopscotching the globe as Blay-Miezah's emissary and messenger." Burstein had spent "weeks alone in cheap hotel rooms with nothing to do at night but write poetry" and get lost in increasingly elaborate fantasies. His children worried about his mental health, and a relationship he was in fell apart, but he persisted. "I wouldn't have traded one day of this spiritual journey," Burstein later said.

That year, a Philadelphia attorney named Barry Ginsberg also traveled to London to meet with Blay-Miezah. He had learned about the Oman Ghana Trust Fund from another lawyer he shared an office with. Earlier in 1981, Ginsberg and a friend had met with Ellis and heard the full pitch, about Kwame Nkrumah leaving a fortune to his nephew, Blay-Miezah (or his cousin, Ginsberg was not sure which—but he was convinced). "It looked like it might involve some travel," he later told a reporter. "It was the greed and the adventure." Ginsberg originally invested five thousand dollars, and he was expecting a return of fifty thousand in a month, maybe sooner. The promised fifty thousand dollars did not materialize, but Ginsberg, far from being disheartened, invested even more money. He convinced eleven other associates, friends, and family members, including his father, to invest too. "I said to my father, it's so outrageous, it's gotta be true," he recalled. "How can you concoct a story like this?"

Once Ginsberg got to London, he had to wait ten days for a meeting: he was told Blay-Miezah had a cold. When the day finally came, Ginsberg went to the Montcalm Hotel. He was escorted to the floor that Blay-Miezah and his entourage had taken over, and ushered into a darkened sitting room. Incense was burning, and there was classical music playing quietly in the background.

Blay-Miezah was in a silk robe, smoking a cigar, which he would remove periodically to speak. He had a quiet, low voice, and spoke of the wonderful things they would achieve together and the intrigue they would have to navigate along the way. Ginsberg was captivated. He finally asked when his payday would be coming. Blay-Miezah leaned in conspiratorially, put his arm around Ginsberg, and told him: "Soon, brother Ginsberg. Very soon."

For the next few years Ginsberg helped pay for the Trust Fund's offices and Blay-Miezah's penthouse suites. When Ginsberg got worried about how much money he was putting in, he reminded himself that the costs would pale in comparison to the windfall. "It's hard to describe," he would eventually explain. "I lost touch with reality."

BLAY-MIEZAH'S SUITE AT the Montcalm was a hive of activity. Many of Blay-Miezah's old investors from Philadelphia—like Ben Bynum, the nightclub owner—dropped in frequently. There were new faces, like Dr. J. F. Lopez from Singapore and Young-Joon Pei from the Kogha Development Company in Seoul. Father James Woodruff, the radical priest from Philadelphia, arrived with another priest and Sister Mary Andrew, of the Little Sisters of the Poor. The investors wanted to stay on Blay-Miezah's good side: one of them handed him seventy-five thousand dollars in cash.

Arno Newman, who had played the part of the president of Geoffrey's Bank for Blay-Miezah, also repeatedly visited the Montcalm. Both Newman and Geoffrey's Bank had recently found themselves subject to some unwelcome scrutiny. On September 20, 1978, "a crate at London Heathrow airport bound for Mogadishu and marked 'agricultural equipment' fell accidentally and split open to reveal the butts of guns. When the whole consignment was inspected, it was found to contain 500 machine guns together with hundreds of ammunition clips." The discovery led to the arrest of several executives from a French gun manufacturer that did business with Geoffrey's Bank. It turned out that the bank was favored by the seedier sort of arms dealer. The further investigators dug into Geoffrey's Bank, the more arms dealers they found: Jean Bernard Lasnaud, a.k.a. Bernard Lasnosky, "fond of bullshit, good tailors and grand hotels," who "set up his office on the bank's premises for a while, and abused its telex," and Jacques Monsieur, a.k.a. Monsieur Monsieur. After the "agricultural equipment" was discovered at Heathrow, Lasnaud moved his operation out of the offices of Geoffrey's Bank.

In the aftermath of the Heathrow incident, "the Liège police, together with a French investigative team, searched the bank and then the Newmans' home, where the policemen were very impressed by the Rubens in the salon . . . The Paris and Liège police blamed each other for not charging the Newmans. But what exactly the Newmans were up to was never fully established." Nevertheless, Arno Newman had been forced to surrender his interest in Geoffrey's Bank by the Belgian banking regulators. The official report concluded that "Arno Newman was not a competent bank manager." Newman did not, however, seem to be ready to retire to spend more time with his Rubens.

BACK IN ACCRA, President Limann was struggling. A career diplomat, he took to making verbose, almost impenetrable speeches at every possible opportunity. He blamed the "intransigent disputes of disloyal and intriguing followers and other sad events perpetrated by short-sighted, jealous, ambitious and power-hungry self-seekers."

Corruption was everywhere. In October 1981, many of the top officials of the Ghana Commercial Bank were dismissed for "misusing the bank to enrich their families or gain personal and private advantage." Shortages, too, were getting worse. Even bread was hard to come by. "Where have all the flour gone?" demanded the *Daily Graphic* plaintively. Meanwhile, almost a million cedi of meat, "imported with hard earned foreign currency," was found rotting in the cold-store rooms of the State Fishing Corporation.

For those with money, life in Accra was still good. The Funky Town Discotheque—"We build America Right Here in Ghana"—had just thrown open its doors. More than thirty Ghanaian DJs were preparing to compete for the title of "Mr Funky Town Disc Jockey." But ostentatious displays of wealth were starting to seem callous. The *Daily Graphic* ran a long, sarcastic piece by the columnist Elizabeth Ohene, under the headline PITY THE POOR BIG MAN.

In lean times, she wrote, members of Parliament still took home four thousand cedi, drove Peugeot cars, had new clothes, and had visibly put on weight—but things were tough for them too: "You just try being a big man for a day, and you might come to even sympathize with them."

Faced with a wrecked economy, Limann looked for people to blame. Headlines castigated "lazy employees." Tutors who boycotted an Independence Day celebration were arrested and charged with "gross disrespect to the nation." The president held a campaign to "examine the causes that have wrecked the moral foundation of the society, thus consequently bringing Ghanaians back to the right moral track."

Limann even interrupted celebrations at an Odwira festival in Kyebi to lecture the crowds about "disciplined and honest use of the country's rich human and natural resources and potentialities through hard work." He told everyone that "discipline and honesty in both private and public lives were among the most important pre-conditions for success in the crusade for moral recognition, economic recovery and national reconstruction."

Limann's authority was slipping away. Officials would be dismissed, their firings would be reported in the newspapers, then they would pop up in the following day's editions, to announce that they were still in their posts. Limann implored Ghanaians to resist "self-proclaimed redeemers and crazy adventurers," but that did nothing to reduce the popularity of Jerry Rawlings.

After handing over power to Limann, Rawlings had returned to the air force and become a walking circus. He was sent to Osu Castle as the leader of the Guard of Honor and regularly drew attention away from the president. "The government did not need any further urging to conclude that its interests were best served by retiring Jerry," wrote the journalist Mike Adjei.

This, however, did not solve the government's Rawlings problem. After his retirement, he was surrounded, almost all the time, by soldiers who had also been retired or dishonorably discharged. They hung out of his car—a Peugeot 505, a gift from the government to keep him happy—and hung around his home. "At one time they even pitched a tent on the grounds of the block of flats where he lived and kept an armored car there."

On December 17, a group of soldiers was arrested for planning a coup. They named Rawlings as the mastermind. Under questioning by the attorney general, Rawlings denied all knowledge and was released. But the incident underscored how little the government could do to stop Rawlings from attempting to seize power. His main obstacle, in fact, was that as an ex-member of the military, he had limited access to weapons.

Within weeks, the Rawlings problem would engulf Ghana.

ON DECEMBER 24, 1981, Rigby was throwing a Christmas party at his flat in Hoxton. He was a few drinks in when, close to midnight, he got a call from Blay-Miezah himself. Rigby was to be at the Montcalm Hotel at four in the morning, on Christmas Day, to accompany Blay-Miezah to Accra. He was to bring his camera. "It was a shock but I felt excited," Rigby said.

The next morning, a very hungover and sleep-deprived Rigby went to Heathrow Airport with Blay-Miezah, Gladys, and an elderly American he had never met before named Charles Lowenthal. On the flight, they all sat in first class, Rigby next to Lowenthal. They arrived in Accra in the evening on Christmas Day. Kotoka Airport, Rigby remembered, was virtually empty. He wondered about the mad dash to get there: "I felt very tired and had no idea what it was all about." Rigby spent the next few days being driven around Accra, visiting Kaneshie Market and the pristine beach near Jamestown Harbor, then back up McCarthy Hill to Blay-Miezah's mansion. From the high point of the hill, he could look over the rest of Accra as it twinkled with lights and glowed with kerosene lamps. The week passed, but Rigby was no closer to understanding the purpose of this trip.

ON DECEMBER 30, five thousand miles away, in New Jersey, at ten thirty A.M., a middle-aged man contacted the Federal Bureau of Investigation. He said that he had invested in the Oman Ghana Trust Fund in June that year. He had been told to expect a tenfold return on his investment almost immediately, but there was no sign of a payout.

According to the FBI's report, the man said "that funds invested with subjects were to go to purchase weapons and other equipment for the Republic of Ghana in West Africa." The money, he understood, was sent to Dr. John Ackah Blay-Miezah, "who handled the arrangements for obtaining and transporting materials from Germany to the Republic of Ghana." Another person who spoke with the FBI said that they were told their money was going to be invested in a new government in an unnamed African country. Both sources were under the impression that after this new government came into power, they would receive a return on their investments.

ON THE SAME day, Rigby and Lowenthal sat in the restaurant of the Ringway Hotel on Ring Road Central, in the heart of Accra. It was Bronya, so not much was happening; the restaurant was empty. They had just had breakfast, and they chatted as they waited for the car Blay-Miezah usually sent to take them to his house. Lowenthal had told Rigby that he was the head of the Bar Association of Philadelphia. All the judges were members, he informed Rigby grandly, so whenever he entered court, they always bowed to him.

Lowenthal was not, and had never been, the chancellor of the Philadelphia Bar. Far from being a respected member of the legal profession, he was a lawyer joke made flesh. After the Second World War, when money from the GI Bill was flooding into schools and colleges, Lowenthal took part in a byzantine bribery scheme involving new trade schools in Philadelphia: a city official would encourage the founders of these schools to approach Lowenthal for help dealing with local authorities, and Lowenthal, in turn, would promise to straighten things out—for a price. Lowenthal demanded that one school hand over "50 percent of the school's net profits to clear red tape." But first, the school would need to sign a contract with him. "He brought a copy of the contract round, and we read it, and it was ridiculous," recalled one of the people Lowenthal had tried to shake down. They showed a copy of the contract to a law firm, "and they just laughed. They said it was the most beautiful piece of legal fraud they had ever seen." In 1951, Lowenthal's license to practice law was suspended for a year after he was called before Congress to testify about these activities.

In 1966, Lowenthal became a bagman for Milton Shapp, in his first, unsuccessful run for governor of Pennsylvania. (Shapp would go on to be elected and serve as governor from 1971 to 1979.) Lowenthal paid ministers and athletes to support Shapp. It all fell apart when Lowenthal and Shapp were caught paying the National Association for the Advancement of White People for mailing lists. In court, Shapp insisted that he was "shocked" to discover that this organization was racist. After this second public humiliation, Lowenthal's mental health became increasingly fragile and his behavior erratic. During one 1976 trial, he simply failed to appear in court to defend his client; the judge ordered Lowenthal to be fined one thousand dollars a day until he showed up. Lowenthal's blundering sent many innocent people to prison. Edward Ryder, a jazz singer, was convicted of murder in 1973 and sentenced to "life without parole at Graterford Prison." Ryder's sentence was reversed decades later: Lowenthal's representation of Ryder was judged to have been "absolutely incompetent," and Lowenthal himself was said to have "had serious emotional problems."

Rigby, needless to say, had no idea about any of this. To him, Lowenthal looked exactly like the distinguished American lawyer he claimed to be: indeed, this was exactly why Lowenthal would prove so useful to Blay-Miezah in the years to come.

As the two men waited for Blay-Miezah's car, at around one o'clock in the afternoon, the double doors leading to the restaurant swung open. A short, lean man strode in and walked past them, sitting at a table behind Lowenthal. After he sat down, Lowenthal leaned toward Rigby and asked if he had gotten a good look at the man. Rigby looked past Lowenthal to the man again, and the man caught Rigby's look. It seemed to pique his curiosity. He leaned over and cordially asked why they were in Ghana.

Rigby automatically said something innocuous about visiting friends. Lowenthal made a face at him, turned to the man, and, in a booming voice, said, "We're here selling guns."

Rigby was horrified. He tried to distance himself from Lowenthal: "He might be here for whatever reason he's here, but I'm here visiting friends."

Finally, Blay-Miezah's driver came through the double doors. Rigby left immediately, but Lowenthal stayed behind. He said he would be right out. Rigby was more than happy to leave him there with the man. It was twenty minutes before Lowenthal joined him in the car.

It was a quiet drive to McCarthy Hill. At one point, Lowenthal leaned in and said, in a conspiratorial tone, that he was going to leave Accra that night. If Rigby had any sense, he would join him. Rigby wondered what on earth had happened in those twenty minutes. When they got to McCarthy Hill, Lowenthal disappeared into a meeting with Blay-Miezah that lasted an hour.

There was a KLM flight to Amsterdam that evening. Rigby had a business partner in the city, so he could see in the new year there. Besides, he was running out of clothes and cash; he had not planned to stay in Accra so long. New Year's Eve with friends in Amsterdam sounded like a better bet than more waiting around in hotel restaurants.

Blay-Miezah didn't want Rigby to go. It seemed like he needed him for something. Lowenthal disagreed. Somehow, they won Blay-Miezah over. As Rigby and Lowenthal were leaving Blay-Miezah's house at about seven that evening, a truck arrived loaded with what looked like freshly printed leaflets. It seemed that someone was making a big announcement.

As Rigby settled into his seat on the KLM flight, he didn't know that it would be the last one to leave Kotoka International Airport for weeks.

AS RIGBY'S FLIGHT was taking off, President Limann was at a party at the Ministry of Defense, in Burma Camp. Two miles south, at Labadi Beach, ten soldiers had gathered. They were armed with a motley collection of weapons: one pistol, one G3 rifle, and one AK-47. In the middle of the night, around two A.M. on New Year's Eve, they made their move.

The soldiers crept through the bush around the Teshie Military Range toward the Recce Cookhouse. They snipped the barbed wire around the barracks of the Recce Squadron, where two armored personnel carriers were parked. The guards were asleep—except for one, who was urinating against a wall. The soldiers waited for the man to finish pissing and fall asleep again. They stole the two armored cars without firing a shot.

A few minutes later, the two armored cars careened at full speed through the barrier of the army's Fifth Battalion camp, where several soldiers who had been implicated in the most recent coup attempt were being held under guard. None of the soldiers knew how to drive an armored personnel carrier, so the two vehicles were barely under control.

As day was breaking, the coup d'état appeared to have failed. The soldiers had engaged in a brief shootout with the chief of defense staff and driven their armored cars across the runway at Kotoka Airport, but they had not captured any buildings or people of importance. Journalists later reported that the coup leader was "flapping beside his armored car gunner who had doubled up as the driver." He "told his co-conspirators that it was all over and that they should make a dash for dear life, through the Republic of Togo, to the Republic of Benin where, he said, some Libyans would be expecting him."

The other soldiers thought staying and fighting was safer than driving stolen armored cars across two whole countries. They agreed that one of them would "keep watch over" the coup leader, and "if he made any attempt to run away he should shoot him." The leader had created a monster and immediately lost control of it.

By midmorning, firefights were erupting at army bases all over Accra. The plotters realized that they had to take Broadcasting House, which was guarded by the police. After a short standoff, they succeeded. "Having captured Broadcasting House, they now had to make an announcement. But all the workers had fled. A watchman was perhaps the only person around and offered to take them to the house of a technician who could come and operate the studio for them." By the time they found the technician, it was eleven A.M.

All over Accra, people had woken up ready to celebrate New Year's Eve. But one after another, they heard the sound of gunfire echoing across the city. Rumors began to spread that another coup was in progress. Then, a familiar voice came over the radio: Rawlings.

"Fellow citizens of Ghana, as you would have noticed we are not playing the National Anthem. In other words this is not a coup. I ask for nothing less than a revolution, something that would transform the social and economic order of this country . . . There is no justice in this society, and so long as there is no justice, I would dare say: let there be no peace."

AS THE NEWS spread through Accra, Rigby and Lowenthal were landing at Schiphol Airport. Lowenthal got on a flight to London. Rigby went to his friend's houseboat on Prinsengracht and settled in to sleep off the red-eye. Rigby's friend had been a merchant sailor, and he kept a radio in the houseboat tuned to the BBC World Service.

As Rigby dozed off, he heard a news report. In the early hours of the morning, there had been a military coup d'état in Ghana. Later that day, as Rigby was watching Dutch television, the screen filled with a picture of a man Rigby instantly recognized. It was the short, lean, slightly stern-looking man who had strode into the restaurant of the Ringway Hotel the day before. He was Flight Lieutenant Jerry John Rawlings, the news reporter said. He had just overthrown the democratically elected government of Ghana.

The borders were closed, Rawlings announced. If any other nation tried to interfere, he said, "West Africa would burn."

Chapter 17

Glory and Folly

1982

Rawlings said his coup—or rather, his revolution—was not "another opportunity for some soldiers and their allies in trade and the bureaucracy to come to power for their own ends." Instead, it was "an opening for real democracy, government of the people, by the people and for the people." Every last person in Ghana, the coup leaders promised, would have a say in how the country was run. Their voices would be heard, and their concerns addressed.

Rawlings, however, had always had other plans. He gathered some soldiers and established a military junta. He named it the Provisional National Defense Council and appointed himself chair. He installed himself at the increasingly run-down Castle to work on his real agenda: staying in power.

Power was all that mattered to Rawlings—and power, for him, was an end in itself. He knew nothing about building an economy or running a country. He had no real interest in doing either. Rawlings was there to get revenge and get rich. He didn't care what happened to Ghana along the way.

The members of the Provisional National Defense Council claimed that they wanted to eradicate graft and theft and kalabule. But justice, under the junta, became something dark and grotesque. Right and wrong lost all meaning: the result was a vacuum, not a society. Brutal punishments were meted out to market traders and kenkey sellers for making a few pesewas of profit, while corrupt businessmen and politicians who had stolen millions were actively courted. To mask the obvious hypocrisy, Rawlings and the junta repeatedly rewrote history. When one of their atrocities backfired and stirred up public outrage, they would immediately disown it or insist that it had never happened.

It was a regime after Blay-Miezah's own heart. And it was no coincidence that, over the next decade, Rawlings became his most powerful supporter. Blay-Miezah, meanwhile, would find ways to make himself extremely useful to Rawlings. He had begun his career as a petty crook. But now his ambitions and his tastes had become insatiable. Now, in order to keep his Rolls-Royces and his hotel suites, in order to keep himself safe and keep the Oman Ghana Trust Fund going, Blay-Miezah plunged into the darkness. Soon, he would be presiding over one of the century's most extensive criminal enterprises, awash with dirty money. He would dedicate himself to enabling mass murderers, and it would leave blood on his hands.

ON JANUARY 1, 1982, investors in the Oman Ghana Trust Fund all over the world woke up to some deeply unwelcome news. Toward the end of the previous year, Robert Ellis had told them the conditions required by the Trust Fund would be met that Christmas. Investors were instructed to stay by their phones: "There'd be important news any day." And so, they had waited by their phones all the way through Christmas, anticipating news that the Trust Fund, at long last, was ready to pay out. Instead, on New Year's Day, the investors' telephones finally rang, but it wasn't about money. There had been another coup d'état. All of Blay-Miezah's negotiations with the previous government—and all the money they had spent—had been wasted. "They'd have to start all over again."

In Philadelphia, agents at the FBI's field office opened their morning papers. Just days before, their informant had told them that the money he had invested in the Oman Ghana Trust Fund was going to buy "weapons" for Ghana. Now, in the *Washington Post*, the FBI agents saw the news staring back at them: "Jerry Rawlings, Ghana's last military ruler, took power once again this morning in a violent, military-supported overthrow of the

2-year-old civilian government he had shepherded into office." There Rawlings was on page 13 of the *Philadelphia Inquirer*, too, in a rumpled flight suit, peaked cap, and patchy beard, posed like a scruffy catalog model.

Overnight, the Oman Ghana Trust Fund became a top priority. The director of the FBI, William H. Webster, authorized the Philadelphia field office to send in an undercover agent.

Two years before, the FBI's Long Island field office had orchestrated the most successful undercover operation in the bureau's history—Abscam—which secured convictions against Philadelphia City Council president George X. Schwartz and two other councilmen. The Long Island office had sent in a petty con man who pretended to be an Arab sheikh with millions to invest, in return for the right favors. The FBI's Philadelphia office had been left embarrassed and sidelined, and now it needed a headline-grabbing case of its own. Soon, the telephone was ringing at the Oman Ghana Trust Fund—and an FBI agent was put through to Ellis.

The agent told Ellis that "he was interested in investing in the deal." Ellis "indicated the deal was about to close," but, he told the agent, there was still some time for him to invest, if he moved quickly. The two agreed to meet at the Roy Rogers restaurant on Route 130 in Pennsauken, New Jersey, on January 4.

The FBI arrived early. The parking lot of the Roy Rogers was staked out by agents with cameras and long lenses. The undercover agent had a Nagra tape recorder—the same model that the FBI had used for the Abscam stings—strapped to his body.

"Say howdy to fresh food at Roy Rogers!" urged the restaurant's commercials. "Howdy, roast beef sandwich!" said a man in a business suit, with a big smile. At ten fifty-seven A.M., Ellis took a seat and—unbeknownst to him—said "Howdy" to an FBI agent.

That morning, Ellis was in an expansive mood. He talked to the potential investor about the history of Ghana, "its various political leaders, and the recent military coup." He had brought along a large file of newspaper clippings, which he set on the table. Ellis also showed the agent a brochure about the Oman Ghana Trust Fund, which stated that it was a charity registered in the Cayman Islands and that Blay-Miezah was both the sole beneficiary and the sole trustee. "There were also listed numerous names and addresses of individuals" who were said to be "early investors and 'group leaders.' These 'group leaders' were responsible for attracting new investors and paying them off."

The agent asked for a copy of the brochure, but Ellis declined to let him keep it—he said he was running short because all the other brochures were in London. But, Ellis said, he could offer something better: a road trip.

Ellis and the undercover agent drove down Route 130 to H & H Industries Incorporated (with the other FBI agents following as discreetly as they could). They were there to see an investor named Walter Hajduk, whose metal fabrication business had made him a fortune. Hajduk looked every bit the portly industrialist. He had a gruff, familiar manner that made him a great pitch man for the Trust Fund. He would tell potential investors that there were boundless opportunities in Ghana—he had seen it for himself: "That country is so friggin' rich." Hajduk himself planned to get into hydroelectricity and wind power, in Ghana's Western Region, and in Florida.

Hajduk later said that he invested several million dollars in the Trust Fund, and he spent months camped in Blay-Miezah's London office, calling other investors, trying to figure out what was holding up the deal, and waiting for news it had all paid off. In the end, his devotion to the deal almost destroyed H & H Industries.

That day in January, he told the undercover FBI agent that he had "invested a substantial amount in this deal" and was currently "in the process of setting up the transportation of 25 tons of rice from a neighboring country into Ghana." When the agent asked about the delays the Trust Fund had encountered, Hajduk "advised that he was not worried, and an end was in sight."

On the drive back to the Roy Rogers, the FBI agent said that he wanted to invest. And, the agent told him, he just wanted to check that the money "he was about to give" Ellis "was being considered an investment." This was significant, as Ellis was not authorized to sell investments. He "responded that it was so considered" and that the special agent would receive "a return of 10 to 1." Repayment, he said, "would be from mid to late April 1982." Ellis wrote out a receipt, and the agent handed over the cash.

Soon, Ellis had good news. He told the agent that a supporter of the Oman Ghana Trust Fund had "been appointed to a position of financial responsibility in the new government." Rawlings's government, Ellis added, "was cooperating fully with his group." Ellis told other investors that Blay-Miezah was meeting regularly with Rawlings and they should be ready to travel "to consummate the investment deal" soon.

The FBI was beginning to realize that it had stumbled onto a major operation. The Philadelphia field office sent out a circular to every FBI office nationwide, asking them "to expeditiously cover leads and report results to Philadelphia as undercover agent currently meeting with subject." Agents across the country soon tracked down other investors in the Oman Ghana Trust Fund, in "Camden, New Jersey, Opa Locka, Florida and Brooklyn, New York."

IN GHANA, RAWLINGS landed on a novel approach to solving the country's problems: theater. When it rained, Accra flooded, and the gutters filled with raw sewage. The city was low lying, flood-prone, and surrounded by wetlands and the Gulf of Guinea. Despite this, it had few sewers and no real system of drains, because sewers and drainage were complex and expensive. Empty gestures, on the other hand, were free. So during the rainy season, Rawlings would make a show of getting a crew together and jumping into the gutters to clean them out. Soldiers would encourage citizens around the country to do the same, often at gunpoint.

Once Rawlings was done with the photo opportunity, he would leave for Osu Castle—or, over the years, a series of palatial homes, all with running water—to bathe. Almost everyone else knew that they would have to fetch or buy clean water. Even worse, people knew that no running water meant no indoor plumbing, which meant more shit in the gutters for Rawlings to pose with.

Beyond putting on a show, Rawlings showed little interest in the work of government. When he did attend cabinet meetings—his many bodyguards crowding into the room behind him—he would often fall asleep.

Many suspected that the person really running the country was Captain Kojo Tsikata, Rawlings's national security adviser. He was also the person above all else whom Blay-Miezah needed on his side. Tsikata had been trained at the British Military Academy at Sandhurst and had worked under both Nkrumah and Acheampong. His uniform was always crisp, and his accent was plummily British, but he lived in the shadows. In 1964, President

Nkrumah had ordered an officer named Major Sam Acquah to open an investigation into Tsikata after the captain was arrested attempting to cross the Congo River into Kinshasa. Tsikata did not have permission to leave Ghana at the time, let alone sneak into what was then an active war zone. There were rumors he had been trying to smuggle diamonds. Acquah's investigation led to Tsikata's dismissal from the military. In 1965, Tsikata was in southern Africa, working with the Popular Movement for the Liberation of Angola and calling himself Carlos Silva Gomes. Tsikata tried to visit Nkrumah in exile in Guinea, and on his deathbed in Romania, but the president refused to see him.

In 1976, Acheampong had Tsikata arrested for plotting a coup d'état. Tsikata smuggled a letter out of prison, in which he described being tortured: "I have been brutalized several times. My hearing is seriously affected. Every time you go for a session you are stripped naked and then beaten up by about four people. Result—swollen face, bleeding eyes, ears, mouth and nose." In Britain, left-wing politicians lined up to sing his praises in the newspapers—so much so that the Ghanaian high commissioner was forced to retort that his arrest was "necessary . . . in order to protect the sovereignty of the State of Ghana."

By the early 1980s, Tsikata was a highly respected intelligence operative with ties all over Africa, including to Libyan leader Colonel Muammar Gaddafi. In April 1982, Rawlings's right-hand man was the subject of an adoring profile in the *Guardian* by a journalist named Victoria Brittain. Brittain called Tsikata "a symbol of political alternatives." She didn't question his assertion that "reports of current ill-discipline [i.e., atrocities committed by soldiers] are grossly exaggerated by opponents of the regime."

Tsikata was keeping a very close eye on Blay-Miezah and the Oman Ghana Trust Fund. For the first time, Blay-Miezah had a bona fide spymaster looking over his shoulder: someone scarier, shadier, and better connected than anyone he had dealt with before. Tsikata had been involved in international intrigue for decades: he was almost impossible to manipulate. And he made it clear to Blay-Miezah that our man would be safe only as long as he remained useful.

MANY OF RAWLINGS'S ministers were members of the June Fourth Movement who had been appointed to government positions. Suddenly, students and writers were running government departments with shoestring budgets and instituting radical changes. There were signs of progress, but they would not last.

When the young ministers asked Rawlings to keep his promises and restore democracy to the citizens of the country, Rawlings got belligerent. He would "harangue, insult, and intimidate certain members of the Cabinet," wrote Zaya Yeebo, the minister for youth and sport at the time. "During such unnecessary haranguing," one government secretary, "with his hands behind his back like an obedient schoolboy before a tyrannical headmaster, shivered like a leaf in a rainy day and responded 'Yes-Sir' to everything Rawlings said."

When members of the June Fourth Movement met with Rawlings and Tsikata to discuss the Provisional National Defense Council's lack of economic policy, or even a plan to make economic policy, Rawlings was conciliatory and seemed willing to talk. But Tsikata turned aggressive and arrogant. He said the ministers running the government had "no business raising queries about the lack of an economic policy," and neither the June Fourth Movement nor anybody in Ghana "had the right to complain about the economy."

Soon, Rawlings and Tsikata started eliminating members of the cabinet. By the end of the year, many of the people involved in the June Fourth Movement had been imprisoned, forced into exile, or assassinated.

Tsikata's approach to economic planning further devastated the country. So much of Accra's infrastructure was wrecked that the city was repeatedly plunged into darkness, and no water could be piped in for long periods. By the end of 1982, inflation had reached 117 percent. The country spent less than 1 percent of its gross domestic product on education: "Teachers fled or did not work; schools became dilapidated, textbooks and paper rare." Two thirds of all vehicles registered in Ghana were off the road because there were no spare parts for repairs. Cocoa production plunged to a fifth of what it had been under Nkrumah.

Food became almost impossible to produce. Selling something as simple as kenkey was a daunting calculus. The corn to make it was suddenly expensive and rare, but the junta had set arbitrary food prices, with no regard to how much the seller's costs had increased. By the junta's calculations, food materialized, fully formed, from thin air, and selling it at any price would produce sufficient profit. If the kenkey seller actually charged what the kenkey cost to produce, she would be attacked, maybe even killed by soldiers for "exploitation," and accused of kalabule. When it became clear that the council's edicts were creating widespread shortages, it doubled down on attacking food hawkers and market traders.

TO THE MILITARY, it was clear that Rawlings had sanctioned plunder and revenge as state policy. So soldiers followed his lead, looting and killing their way through the country. There were countless stories, all "marked by a callousness and brute force that is not Ghanaian," a report in *West Africa* magazine noted. "Why was Nii Ayi shot in the leg? For being five minutes late for the 10 p.m. curfew; or because a trigger-happy soldier shot first and asked whether he had a curfew pass later?" A woman was shot at Palm Wine Junction on the Trade Fair Road; nobody knew why. Down the road in Labadi, a dozen people were gathered around a person who had been shot, when a soldier in a vehicle ploughed through the crowd, killing them all. This was just the beginning of what Rawlings had unleashed.

The maelstrom of violence broke over three days of chaos in Kumasi. On Sunday, February 7, 1982, Major Joe Darko stormed into The Lord Is My Shepherd Church waving a pistol and ordered the congregation out onto the street to fill potholes. The leader of the church, Prophet Odiyifo Asare, asked if he could complete Sunday service. The major agreed and said he would be back. Asare then sent a delegation from the church to the barracks to complain to Darko's superiors. The major heard about this and told his driver to take him back to the church. This time he went in shooting.

Corporal Joanna Essien, a police officer who was attending the service, tackled the major to disarm him. His gun went off, and a bullet grazed her jaw. Other members of the congregation tried to get the gun, there was a tussle, and it went off again. This time the major was shot. His driver saw the scramble and went back to the barracks to tell everyone. This was bad. Asare told the congregation to take Corporal Essien to hospital and then go into hiding. The next morning, on the radio, officials announced the church was closed and ordered all members of the congregation to report to police stations and military barracks "for their own safety."

The Provisional National Defense Council held a rally at Kejetia Market. "At the beginning of any revolution, it is very hard for everybody," declared Warrant Officer Adjei Boadi. "But eventually all will enjoy." He ordered traders to cut their prices and Ghanaians to eat just two meals a day. "Those who do not want to make sacrifices are enemies of the revolution and will not survive." An example, Boadi said, would be made very soon. That example was The Lord Is My Shepherd Church.

For the next two days, soldiers tore through Kumasi, searching for members of the church. "They fired their guns indiscriminately killing or wounding passers-by, including football fans, who were leaving the nearby Kumasi Sports Stadium."

Soldiers ultimately rounded up, tortured, and murdered seventy-eight members of the congregation and looted the church; they even ransacked the homes around it for good measure. Anything they could not carry away they set on fire.

Asare turned himself in to the police. Officers took him to the barracks nearby, where he was tied to the back of a military vehicle and dragged through the streets of Kumasi, all the way to Kejetia Market. He somehow survived, his wife, Hannah Asare, told the media: "When they got tired, they told him he could walk away, then shot him in the back, right there at the roundabout" at one end of the market. Then they set his body on fire, she later said, and made a proclamation: "Come and see, Odiyifo Asare is on fire."

The soldiers weren't done. They went to Komfo Anokye Teaching Hospital to find Corporal Essien. She had been in surgery, and when the army stormed the hospital, doctors were giving her a blood transfusion. As the soldiers entered, guns drawn, patients fled. The soldiers found Corporal Essien and shot her dead in her hospital bed. The doctor who had operated on her fled the city, still dressed in his surgical gown. Soon after, he left the country.

For days after the siege, people were forced to walk through Kejetia Market with their arms raised, as if in surrender. By the end of the month, members of the church's congregation—which had been ten thousand people strong—had fled the country for Nigeria. "The refugees said that anarchy now reigned in Ghana with troops ignoring all orders and pillaging and extorting money."

IN THE PAST, the judiciary had been able to stop Ghana's military regimes and their dictators from spiraling into this kind of endless, senseless violence. But Rawlings was determined not to be held to account. He also needed to cover up the mass killing spree he and the Provisional National Defense Council were on. So Rawlings instituted mob justice. The council set up People's Tribunals and Citizens' Vetting Committees throughout the country.

These tribunals did not even have the pretense of justice. People would turn up, make wild allegations, and if they fit the military's agenda, they were rubber-stamped. Trials lasted just a few minutes. There was no way to appeal, and punishments were outlandish. Officials were forced to make staged confessions, admitting that they had "opened the floodgate for kalabule." But while his regime was torturing and murdering ordinary people, Rawlings was quietly negotiating with kalabule's most prominent practitioner. Blay-Miezah was prepared to be very useful to the junta—and Rawlings needed allies.

On May 19, the junta issued our man a diplomatic passport, made to Blay-Miezah's exact specifications. It was a handsome red document: both a genuine passport and a piece of fiction. Blay-Miezah's profession was listed as "Government Official." His date of birth was given as 1924, rather than 1941. In his photograph, he posed in front of some flock wallpaper, wearing a checked suit, striped tie, and a look of ineffable delight. It was impossible to give him a passport numbered 000065, as he had asked, because numbers came pre-embossed on every passport. Instead, there was a stamp reading "the holder of this passport previously travelled on passport 000065 which has been cancelled." Blay-Miezah's new passport expired in exactly a year. That, Rawlings thought, would give Blay-Miezah plenty of time to fulfill his promises.

PETER RIGBY WAS getting nervous. His flight had just landed in Accra. "On exit, we the passengers were required to walk across the tarmac between two lines of armed soldiers and into the terminal building." On the plane, Rigby had been catching up on the news from Ghana. He had noticed a headline in the *Daily Graphic*, a warning that currency smugglers would be shot. That, Rigby realized, meant him.

Nobody was allowed to bring foreign currency into Ghana without the permission of the government: it was Rawlings's way of controlling the exchange rate and propping up the value of the cedi. So, whenever Blay-Miezah needed money, Rigby hopped on a flight from London to Accra. "I was his bagman," Rigby later wrote. "His runner. His errand boy and his confidante. I smuggled (inasmuch as it was never declared, otherwise they would have taken it) large sums of US dollars and British pounds into Ghana, at a time when Rawlings had a viselike grip over everything." Rigby was exhausted. He had been living on planes, shuttling back and forth between London and Accra every couple of weeks: "The flow of cash did not stop."

Inside the airport, the arriving passengers were lined up in front of more heavily armed soldiers, to be searched. "The Ghanaian man in front of me was caught with some foreign currency rolled up in his necktie. The soldier viciously beat him to the ground right in front of me, declaring him to be scum, kicked him and had him dragged off. He then turned to me to start his search."

Rigby was terrified. He had thousands of dollars stuffed in his underwear. The soldier started patting him down: checking his shoes and then making his way up the inside leg of Rigby's trousers. "As his hand made motions to touch my crotch, I jumped back, not deliberately, involuntarily and in panic." Rigby stared straight at the border guard. He thought his face—wearing an expression of guilt and alarm—made it obvious that he, too, was carrying cash.

"I stared wide-eyed, fully expecting some kind of backlash involving pain. He presumed I was defensive because of the sensitive parts in question, but in reality, I was freaking in fear he would feel the large roll of notes wrapped in cling film, clenched between my now sweating legs. He looked me straight in the eyes, smiled and waved me through to baggage claim."

Blay-Miezah's men were waiting for Rigby. He swore to himself that next time, he would find a better hiding place for the money.

When he got back to London, before the next trip, Rigby hollowed out a Sony Betamax player and packed it with cash: "I took out the large circuit board and some of the mechanics. The ventilation slots in the underside of the plastic casing now allowed 'the enclosed stash' to be seen if it was to be inspected, so it was lined with black paper." He did the same with an IBM Selectric typewriter, which "had a fair space inside already." Whenever he brought the machine into Ghana, he would say it had been repaired abroad and was being returned. Whenever he was leaving, with the hollowed-out machines, he would say that they needed repairs.

Rigby tried not to think about how much money he had brought Blay-Miezah over the last few months. "I did not keep an account, not even mentally, lest I should at some time be questioned. That's the way I was thinking. What I didn't know I couldn't tell." Blay-Miezah seemed impressed by how much Rigby could bring in. "Every penny collected by me was delivered intact," Rigby said. "That's why he extolled my virtues."

It was a well-oiled operation. Every few days, a fax would arrive at Blay-Miezah's office in Accra. It would look like a standard communication about an upcoming business trip, but, at the end, there would be a cryptic line like: "I am weight laden to arrive in Ghana on Saturday." That meant cash was coming. Blay-Miezah would make sure that his people at the airport knew someone had to be waved through. Other people who smuggled money got sentenced to forced labor—digging trenches and carrying wawa boards—while his crew went on their merry way.

Once, a member of Blay-Miezah's crew had arrived at Kotoka Airport with his entire torso encased in a surgical cast. He said he was coming to Ghana to recover after major surgery. He had letters from his doctor to prove it. But immigration officers were suspicious. Under the plaster of paris cast, they discovered thousands of dollars in cash.

In June, a large delivery for Blay-Miezah arrived at the Montcalm Hotel from America. It was stored in the hotel's trunk room. Rigby was asked to take it to Ghana. He flew first class to Accra, then climbed into a Mercedes awaiting him on the tarmac. The car drove him out of the airport, bypassing customs and immigration, to a nearby military warehouse. There, a general was waiting for Rigby and the trunk. Before he was ushered back into the car and driven to his hotel, Rigby got a glimpse of the contents of the trunk, when the general cracked it open: "Guns," he later said. "A selection."

FOR MOST OF 1981, three High Court judges—Justice Cecilia Koranteng-Addow, Justice Kwadwo Agyei Agyepong, and Justice Fred Poku Sarkodee—had tried to hold Rawlings to account. They had freed people serving long prison terms after conviction by his sham courts.

A soldier named Joachim Amartey Quaye later testified that on June 30, Captain Tsikata took him for a drive. Tsikata pointed out the judges' houses, telling him to organize their "arrest and detention." Tsikata was not someone whose orders you questioned, Amartey Quaye said. "I did not doubt his integrity and complied."

On the evening of June 30, a man marched into the home of Justice Koranteng-Addow. The justice was nursing her child at the time. The man said that one of her colleagues was in a car outside and needed help. It was a poor ruse to get the justice out of the house. "She bought the story and came out to see the judge who we said was in his car outside the gate," one of the assassins later recalled. "Immediately she got out of the gate[,] we whisked her into the Jeep and drove away, while her husband was desperately flagging us to stop." The assassins then abducted the two other High Court judges.

The three judges were taken to a secluded military firing range at Bundase, between Tema and the Shai Hills, along with Major Acquah, who had run the investigation that led to Tsikata being thrown out of the army. They were shot multiple times.

The assassins attempted to burn the bodies. If they had succeeded, the judges and the major would have simply disappeared like so many others. But it rained hard that night, and the assassins eventually gave up before the harsh dawn light exposed their crimes.

Initially, no attempts were made to find the judges; there were no search parties or police investigations. But as the news of the judges' abduction spread, it was the last straw, for many people.

The junta had reason to be anxious: there had been at least thirteen coup attempts over the past few years. Each brought with it a small wave of havoc:

"One of those coup attempts resulted in the shelling of Gondar Barracks, and the resultant exposure of a large cache of arms and ammunition newly-imported into the country. This created a free-for-all scramble for the guns." Every new coup attempt made Rawlings and Tsikata more jumpy.

After the judges disappeared, suspicion immediately fell on Rawlings and Tsikata. Justice Koranteng-Addow was known to have made an enemy of Tsikata when, in 1981, she dismissed his attempt to halt government surveillance of him on the grounds that "his rights and liberties were being infringed upon." It was increasingly clear that the regime would murder anyone to settle a score.

John Dumoga, editor of the *Echo*, ran a gigantic banner headline across his next edition reading MURDER MOST FOUL! Rawlings's men immediately stormed the newspaper's office and destroyed the printing presses. Dumoga, "a very short man with the heart of a lion," hid from the soldiers in a garbage truck and escaped to Nigeria.

A few days after the judges' deaths, Rawlings addressed the nation, claiming that "a search party" had found the bodies of the judges. Some saw the speech as a cruel ruse: Rawlings had never sent out any search parties. "Being a good actor and a pathological liar, Rawlings took in those who could be taken in," the journalist Mike Adjei wrote, "but the majority of Ghanaians were not much impressed by his crocodile tears on television."

The assassins had been loud and sloppy, and were easy for witnesses to identify. Amartey Quaye was soon under arrest. He implicated Tsikata. A Special Investigations Board ruled that Tsikata should be tried among the "accomplices and co-conspirators." But the attorney general ruled that there was insufficient evidence against him, and Tsikata never stood trial. He denied any involvement in the murders, but "was so worried about the damage that the revelations had done to his image that he set up a secret 'image recovery' and rehabilitation committee in the Castle." He would attempt to disappear all evidence of the past year's atrocities and of the accusations against him.

The assassins were tried and sentenced to execution by firing squad. Before the sentence was carried out, Rawlings went to see Amartey Quaye. After Amartey Quaye had been killed, Rawlings called a press conference and brought out a tape recorder: on the tape, just before his death, Amartey Quaye retracted all his claims about Tsikata.

Chapter 18

Showboys All the Way

1982–1983

B lay-Miezah was working hard to convince the junta that he was indispensable. "I know you need me. Because I am the key," he said. "And I can perform. I have never doubted at any moment that I can perform." Rawlings and Tsikata were dangerous partners, repeatedly turning on, jailing, and executing enemies and former allies alike. They had thrown his mentor, Krobo Edusei, into prison. Edusei would only be released just before his death in 1984.

The past few years had made Blay-Miezah look less like a statesman and more like a criminal: the very public trial, and the revelations about his past, undermined his claims that he was a wealthy industrialist and the guardian of the country's fortune. Now, he needed to make himself wildly popular, and difficult for the junta to dispose of, without also making himself look like a threat. Above all, Blay-Miezah needed Rawlings to take him seriously. Seriously enough to keep renewing the diplomatic passport and let him travel the world. Blay-Miezah got to work laundering his reputation.

By the time he was done, he would look grander and more powerful than he ever had before. Crowds of thousands would cheer for him. Chiefs would pay their respects. Choirs would literally sing his praises. But the same old lie underpinned Blay-Miezah's world—and he knew it would take only one bad day, or one bad decision, to bring everything crashing down. The higher he rose, the further he had to fall.

BLAY-MIEZAH INTENDED TO buy his credibility. For his first purchase, he thought back to his time at Nsawam Prison, to the one thing the gentlemen resident there found most agreeable: football. So Blay-Miezah got himself appointed chairman of a small team in Sekondi called Eleven Wise.

Founded in 1919, the team was originally made up mostly of local railroad workers; now, they were a professional outfit nicknamed the Western Show-boys. Blay-Miezah hired a German coach and shelled out thirty thousand dollars on stadium renovations. He brought in some of the best players in the country; the captain also played on the immensely popular national team, the Black Stars.

Blay-Miezah even introduced a new cheer for the fans, a version of the one he had heard at Yonsei University in South Korea: "Akaraka! Akaraka, Ching Akaraka Cho." Now in Ghana, fans of Sekondi Eleven Wise were roaring their team's impossibly catchy new cheer: "Akaraka chi, akaraka cho, akaraka chi, cha, chi, cha, cho." Ebo Quansah, who was deputy secretary of the Sports-writers' Association of Ghana, recalled that "in the whole country everybody would shout 'Akaraka chi, akaraka cho.' As I sit here, I still don't understand what it means." With a jumpy junta in charge, this was the only way Blay-Miezah could get away with having a stadium full of people cheering for him. It was the closest he could get to a campaign rally. On match days, in front of the crowd, our man was in heaven.

Blay-Miezah had a straightforward approach to motivating his players. Ken Bediako, the former sports editor of the *Daily Graphic*, remembered him handing eighty thousand cedi in a polythene bag to the coaches at the start of a match. The bag sat prominently on the touchline for the entire game. When Eleven Wise won, the players got the bonus. During Blay-Miezah's first year in charge, Eleven Wise won the Ghanaian Football Association Cup, the country's top competition. Football was the country's favorite sport: if a match was happening, entire cities shut down to watch. The players were cheered everywhere they went.

Blay-Miezah also donated eighty-five thousand dollars to Ghana's Olympic Committee. Much to the committee's surprise—"We knew the stories about him," Bediako, who was also the committee's public relations officer, remembered—his check actually cleared. Blay-Miezah was named Ghana's "Sporting Personality of the Year." Never one to miss a chance to put on a show, he arrived halfway through the awards gala. The band struck up abruptly. Bediako realized that he must have arranged this in advance: "The whole room changed, people started cheering. There was pandemonium. And he came in dancing and smoking a cigar." Blay-Miezah went from a celebrity to a hero.

PETER RIGBY SOMETIMES traveled with Eleven Wise and shot video of their matches. During one trip, the players were waiting at a military airfield to fly north for a match. Blay-Miezah was giving the team a pep talk in the terminal building and Rigby pulled out his camera to film. Soldiers descended on Rigby and confiscated his camera. The team departed without him or Blay-Miezah.

Later that morning, the two men were having breakfast at the Atlantic Hotel in Takoradi. Rigby's seat gave him a view of the lobby, and he watched, with a sinking heart, as the main doors to the hotel burst open and five heavily armed soldiers marched in. Rigby and Blay-Miezah were arrested at gunpoint. Everyone else in the lobby stood stock-still, grateful that the soldiers had not come for them.

Blay-Miezah and Rigby were driven back to the airbase. They were separated, and Rigby was ordered to strip. His underpants were returned, and he was pushed into a dark cell. Rigby realized that he had been mistaken for a spy. There was a faint smell of urine.

Soon, Blay-Miezah was pushed into the cell too. He was also in his underpants. He was the picture of calm. Rigby started panicking and, for the first time, lost his temper with Blay-Miezah. He kicked a piece of furniture in a fit of frustration. "You got me into this mess, you get me out of it," Rigby shouted. Blay-Miezah narrowed his eyes, displeased. He told Rigby to calm down.

When it came time for the prisoners to eat, Rigby smelled the repulsive prison food and panicked again. But Blay-Miezah had a plan. "Yet again, I had underestimated my man," Rigby wrote. Blay-Miezah had a talent for negotiating, even in the most difficult circumstances.

A portable table and two chairs were set up in the cell. A waiter appeared, carrying a large silver tray, and laid out a tea service and a large plate covered with a cloche. Rigby realized that he was standing in his underpants in a jail cell, watching a waiter lay out silver service, and he started giggling. The waiter lifted the cloche to reveal chicken and chips.

For three days, Rigby and Blay-Miezah were locked up together, and for three days, breakfast, lunch, and dinner were brought in. Finally, they were sent to Accra, so that military officials could examine Rigby's film. Rigby played it to an air force officer, to prove that they were not spying, and they were freed.

Gladys Blay-Miezah picked them both up in a chauffeured car, and they were driven back to Blay-Miezah's house on McCarthy Hill. Rigby staggered up to his room and collapsed on the bed. Perhaps sensing that he needed help calming down, somebody sent up a small bag of marijuana.

ELEVEN WISE DID not always play great football, but the team always put on a great show. The players danced before their games, waving white handkerchiefs to the crowd. At a match in Kumasi in May 1983, Blay-Miezah was determined to put on an even bigger spectacle. He had his favorite band set up by the pitch: keyboards, a drum kit, a guitar player, a horn section, and the lead singer, Jewel Ackah, who was dressed in black flares and a blindingly white shirt, open to the chest.

Then the team rolled into the stadium, led by Blay-Miezah, dripping with gold jewelry, in a polka-dot shirt and white shoes. The players piled off the bus behind him, jumping up and down to warm up, drumming on the seats, and singing at the top of their voices: "Akaraka chi, akaraka cho." Blay-Miezah paused in the middle of the crowd to light a cigar and enjoy the moment: all eyes were on him. "I am certain," he told reporters, "that the Akaraka boys will do a good job."

After matches, Blay-Miezah would walk across the pitch, wave at the crowd, and bask in the adulation, a cigar clenched between his teeth. He often changed into his football manager outfit for the occasion: a white cap, an expensive watch, a short-sleeved track-suit jacket, and a white T-shirt emblazoned with the words AKARAKA CHI. Underneath was the team's logo: a large black spider perched in the center of a web.

Blay-Miezah at a Sekondi Eleven Wise match, in an AKARAKA CHI T-shirt.

AFTER THEIR MATCH in Kumasi, the Western Showboys went to the Manhyia Palace to visit the Asantehene. Opoku Ware the Second, the absolute ruler of the Ashanti Kingdom, was the wealthiest and most powerful of Ghana's chiefs. Before he became king, he was Barima Kwaku Adusei. He had studied law at the Middle Temple in London and worked as a barrister and politician. He was familiar with Blay-Miezah.

Blay-Miezah dressed down for the occasion: the gold was gone, replaced with pastel green lace and a walking stick. There was no point in trying to impress the Asantehene: this was a man who controlled actual gold mines and whose palace was full of the accumulated wealth of the Ashanti royal family, stretching back generations. Blay-Miezah and the team were led through the palace gardens, past the peacocks—said to have been a gift from the shah of Iran—into the presence of the Asantehene. Our man was sweating.

Inside the palace, the Asantehene sat in a gilded baroque armchair. Blay-Miezah perched on a notably smaller and less elaborate chair next to him. Blay-Miezah had met military dictators, politicians, and spies. But he had never been up close with Ghana's chief of chiefs before. He was visibly nervous—standing up to address the Asantehene, sitting down again, dabbing his face with a handkerchief. The Asantehene did absolutely nothing to put him at ease.

Opoku Ware the Second did, however, go out of his way to charm Blay-Miezah's team and his camera crew. He gossiped with the players, joked with the crew, and could not have been more gracious and obliging to every last person in the room, apart from the man sitting next to him. Finally, Blay-Miezah leaned far forward and held out his glass of Fanta for the Asantehene—who was drinking whiskey poured from a crystal decanter—to clink. Opoku Ware the Second touched Blay-Miezah's glass and went right back to ignoring him.

Minutes passed. Blay-Miezah tried every trick in the book to insert himself into the conversation. He nodded along. He laughed at the Asantehene's jokes. He stood up and sat down again. All the while, the discomfort was building on his face. As far as Blay-Miezah had come, it seemed like he could never escape his past. The Asantehene—someone who actually had access to Swiss banks and untold natural resources—had no intention of forgetting who Blay-Miezah was or what he had done.

Blay-Miezah held out his glass of Fanta again for the Asantehene to clink. The Asantehene ignored him, leaving Blay-Miezah's glass hanging there in midair.

By the end of the audience, Blay-Miezah's shoulders were hunched and he was shifting around nervously on his feet. His team spilled out of the palace, grinning and delighted. Blay-Miezah rubbed his hand across his face, humiliated. He lit up his cigar and inhaled deeply. The day had convinced him of one thing: he needed to be bigger.

BLAY-MIEZAH'S OLD SCHOOLMASTER Kofi Quantson now sat on a panel of officials who ran a secret court at Air Force Station Accra. Prisoners were brought in chained and bleeding: "People had been put in [a] thick type of shackles like the one they used to . . . chain Samson. Very, very big, big ones," an eyewitness later testified. Then they went before the panel of officials, including Quantson. After "about two minutes, three minutes, all of a sudden . . . you hear the bullets just crying," the witness said. "You see them going to kill human beings like fowls."

Tsikata was keen to keep a close eye on Blay-Miezah. So he put Quantson to work investigating his former student. He told Quantson to find out if

Blay-Miezah was for real—and if his diplomatic passport should be renewed. Our man's ability to travel freely depended on it.

Years earlier, Quantson had become director of Special Branch but was fired by Limann's government, along with the heads of all the country's security services, for their collective failure to prevent Rawlings's first two coup attempts. After Rawlings's third coup attempt, the Provisional National Defense Council brought Quantson back as director. Quantson quickly became one of many "accessories to the human rights abuses committed by the PNDC regime," as a government commission put it two decades later. He was no longer someone Blay-Miezah could casually manipulate.

Still, Quantson wasn't eager to investigate Blay-Miezah. After all, this was the man whose big talk at the Star Hotel in 1971 had gotten Quantson hauled before his superiors on suspicion of sedition and caused him no end of grief. The very mention of his former student's name gave Quantson homicidal thoughts. It took him quite a while to compose himself before he could imagine sitting "face to face with Blay without strangling him."

When Quantson finally pulled himself together and called Blay-Miezah in for questioning, the tension was thick. Blay-Miezah seemed horrified to be back in front of his old schoolmaster. Quantson got right to the point: "Blay, destiny has thrown us together once more. You are the last person I ever wanted to deal with." Quantson said that he was willing to work with Blay-Miezah on one condition. "On no account should any of us talk about the past." At this, Blay-Miezah looked relieved. "Master, I thank you very much."

Quantson was no more inclined to believe the stories about Blay-Miezah's fortune than he had been in the past. If Blay-Miezah did have the money, Quantson thought, why did it take so long to get it back to Ghana? It had been "donkey's years." But at the same time, Quantson found it impossible to dismiss Blay-Miezah. He lived like a very wealthy man, yet there was no sign he had worked for it.

Blay-Miezah also had many courtiers. "They kept coming," Quantson wrote, from across the world: America, Canada, Britain, Germany, and Japan. "If there was indeed no money, then Blay was the biggest con man, taking the whole world for a jolly ride."

Of Blay-Miezah's visitors, the one who fascinated Quantson most was John Mitchell, former attorney general of the United States in Richard Nixon's administration. Mitchell represented the new ugliness of the Oman Ghana Trust Fund. In the 1970s, Blay-Miezah's organization had been founded, in part, by people committed to Black liberation. Now, it was packed with people who locked up and terrorized activists committed to the same cause. Mitchell paid off American Nazis in order to influence an election. He did everything he could to suppress Black protest movements. He had spent his career working to deny Americans basic civil rights. The Philadelphia journalist Claude Lewis wrote that "Mitchell called for 'no-knock' entry, warrantless frisking and wiretapping, preventative detention, the deployment of federal troops to repress crime in the capital, a slowdown in school desegregation and what he called a 'restructured' Supreme Court."

In 1974, Mitchell was convicted on perjury and conspiracy charges for approving the $250,000 payment that funded the burglary at the Watergate Hotel. He served nineteen months in prison and was disbarred. He was widely seen as the man who took the fall for Nixon: the highest-ranking member of his administration to be convicted for Watergate. Like many disgraced American politicians before and after him, once he got out of prison, Mitchell started a consulting firm.

Blay-Miezah told everyone that he and Mitchell went way back: he told some people that they had met in the 1960s, at the Union League Club of Philadelphia. He told others that "he hung out with lots of GOP figures, he was a worker at the party headquarters," one associate remembered. "That's how Mitchell ended up in Ghana." Federal investigators in the United States later determined that Mitchell's consultancy firm was hired to advise the Oman Ghana Trust Fund "to add to the aura of legitimacy." Mitchell was promised $733 million from the Trust Fund.

In 1983, Mitchell flew into Accra and went to work for Blay-Miezah. At least one investor would recall that, when he began to have thoughts about pulling out of the Trust Fund, he got a phone call from Mitchell: here was the former attorney general of the United States, saying that the money was coming. The investor stayed in the game. On one occasion, Mitchell visited Blay-Miezah at the Oman Ghana Trust Fund's office in Accra, near the

American embassy. After the meeting, Quantson remembered, Mitchell strolled over to the embassy "'to see one of my boys.' That was the Ambassador."

Quantson was fed up with Blay-Miezah. But he began to convince himself that our man was for real. However, for Blay-Miezah to get his diplomatic passport renewed, the junta needed concrete proof that there was money behind his claims.

To prove that the Oman Ghana Trust Fund was real, Blay-Miezah first asked two bankers, one from Switzerland and one from the island of Guernsey, to fly into Accra "to confirm their involvement." Quantson was at home on leave, so Blay-Miezah had them driven straight from the airport to Quantson's house. The bankers were due to fly home later the same day. Quantson asked why the bankers didn't just stay overnight: Accra had many fine hotels. He found their answer "quite revealing." They claimed that if they were in the country for even twenty-four hours, "there would be serious speculations in the financial world as to what those two top bankers were doing in Ghana."

Of course, Blay-Miezah had a long history of flying in bankers who were not quite what they seemed. But the next day, when Quantson checked up on the two mysterious men, they appeared to be who they said they were. Quantson may have been—once again—entirely too credulous.

Then, in August 1983, to seal his partnership with the junta, Blay-Miezah arranged for United Mizrahi Bank of Switzerland to offer its "best services to arrange for an irrevocable credit line of $50 million to be extended to the government of the republic of Ghana through the Bank of Ghana/Ghana Commercial Bank London." For the junta, that was enough. This seemed like proof that there was cold hard cash behind Blay-Miezah's stories: How else would he be able to arrange for a Swiss bank to offer a fifty-million-dollar line of credit?

But, Blay-Miezah said, there was just one small issue: the line of credit was dependent on a parallel deposit of fifty million dollars from the Oman Ghana Trust into United Mizrahi Bank. Blay-Miezah needed to leave the country to arrange for that deposit to be made (and unlock the Trust Fund). It worked. His diplomatic passport was renewed until May 1984.

There was just one catch: Captain Tsikata, who popped up wherever the Oman Ghana Trust Fund took over a hotel suite, dressed in a perfectly tailored suit, carrying a bowler hat and cane, and watching closely.

IN THE SUMMER of 1983, the man formerly known as Kerosene Boy, a nobody from a tiny village, born into poverty, became a chief, albeit a minor one. Blay-Miezah was nominated Gyaasehene, treasurer of the Western Nzema Traditional Council.

Years earlier, Blay-Miezah had promised to bring modernity to his hometown. But almost a decade had passed, electricity was still spotty, and many of the roads were unpaved. One of the paramount chiefs of the region had summed up the exasperation in a speech. "The Nzemas have remained in dust, dust, dust and on bumpy roads, whenever they travelled they were begrimed with dust, and I wonder whether the Nzemas shall still remain in this era of Ghana's Revolution."

President Nkrumah had been diligent about not showing his home region any favor, almost to the point of neglect. After the coup that deposed Nkrumah, Ghana's military leaders went out of their way to add insult to injury. At one point, Lieutenant General Akwasi Afrifa, whom Rawlings would later execute on the shore, called Nzema chiefs to a durbar so he could demean them all at once. When the chiefs were assembled, instead of delivering the standard platitudes and promises, Afrifa impugned the entire Nzema nation. He told the chiefs that if they wanted the roads tarred, they'd have to do it themselves, because their countryman Nkrumah had stolen all the money. People would talk about this affront for decades.

The chiefs of the region were more than happy to nominate anyone who seemed like they could build roads and factories. Blay-Miezah promised to—finally—bring development to the Western Region: "I pledge to assist my paramount chief and his elders, all the chiefs, to start an unique development in the Western Nzema Traditional Area . . . I personally promise that as soon as I am part of the development, I will do all I can, financially, to assist my area," he told them.

Before the ceremony, Blay-Miezah traveled to his village, Alengenzure. It was a quiet, reflective moment, before the weeklong celebration. He sat outside his parents' house, bare-chested, with the golden Star of David gleaming on his chest, looking very much the village boy done good.

Before Blay-Miezah was enstooled, he was confined for seven days. Chiefs gathered from all over the country for the occasion. The Western Showboys had traveled down the coast to pay their respects. Even before Blay-Miezah emerged, a crowd had gathered, clapping and cheering: "Akaraka chi, akaraka cho."

Each chief in the region had an orator. On the morning of the enstoolment, dozens upon dozens of orators met in the courtyard of the traditional council building in Beyin to formally elect Blay-Miezah. Each orator held an elaborate, sometimes ancient mace. They were a sight to behold. Each ceremonial mace had been carved from wood and, for the wealthiest and most powerful chiefs, covered entirely in sheets of pure, bright gold, pounded flat.

As the chill of dawn wore off and the heat of the day started to descend, Blay-Miezah made his entrance. A stool bearer, dressed in white, led the procession, carrying his throne, which was also covered in white cloth. There were drummers and dancers, and elders to pour libations. Blay-Miezah wore a crown of purple velvet studded with large gold ingots. He was dressed in gold-colored cloth, and was covered from head to toe in gold jewelry: chains, rings, and a heavy gold bangle, gleaming like the sun. He was hoisted above the heads of the crowd, in a palanquin. Then, with a police escort and a brass band leading the way, he was carried through the streets, as tradition demanded.

By now, there were hundreds of people there. A full choir in robes followed Blay-Miezah's palanquin. Three yellow-and-red ceremonial canopies twirled overhead. People sang, danced, and waved cloth and fanned the new chief. The celebrations echoed through the coconut groves for miles around. Gladys Blay-Miezah, fashionably dressed all in white, with a Kente headband, smiled as she walked alongside the palanquin. Despite the heat, there was not a hair out of place on her Jheri-curled head.

Inside the palanquin, Blay-Miezah waved the biggest fly whisk that anyone could remember seeing. He could barely contain his delight: a big, sweet grin kept on breaking through his composure. People reached out to fan him from every side. The whole crowd broke out into a deafening chant of "Akaraka chi, akaraka cho." Blay-Miezah dabbed at his face with a white handkerchief. He raised his hands to the crowd, in greeting and in victory.

The enstoolment took place at Fort Apollonia in Beyin, seven miles from Alengenzure. Fort Apollonia was built by the British in the late eighteenth century. It had lain abandoned for much of the nineteenth century before becoming the focus of an anticolonial protest in 1873. The British were soon obliged to send a gunboat to bombard their own fortress.

Blay-Miezah had to bite his lip to stay solemn as the kingmakers, the regional elders, and a representative of the Omanhene completed the ceremony. He kept suppressing a smile as he took the oath of office, was suspended three times over the stool, and given the title Nana Ackah Nyanzu the Second. He sat next to Gladys, surrounded by his entourage: a royal court in miniature. Kerosene Boy was royalty now, and no one could ever take that away from him.

Rumor had it that it cost him $250,000, although Blay-Miezah was irritated by the suggestion that he had to pay. He had royal lineage, he insisted: his mother's brother had been a chief linguist at Beyin, Nana Ackah Nyanzu the First. "If one day, this is traced, they'll find that that line, actually, is an honest one," he would say.

As thrilled as he was, becoming treasurer was a consolation prize. He wanted to be a full chief, with the power that came with it. So Blay-Miezah tried to parlay his enstoolment, his highest high yet, into more. "Today, I have made a solemn oath to my paramount chief. This oath symbolizes a new world." He told the crowd: "If next year, by this time, my Omanhene and his chiefs are not satisfied with the developments I have started or completed in the Western Nzema Traditional Area, they must write me off. If on the other hand, the chiefs see development, I am asking that the Omanhene and his chiefs will think again, and will offer me a higher appointment than Gyasahene . . . This is a wager." In the interim, Blay-Miezah told the Oman Ghana Trust Fund's investors outside Ghana—people who did not know how these things really worked—that he had already been made a paramount chief, that the title made him a state official, and that when he traveled, it gave him diplomatic immunity. It did not.

The party that night was talked about for months afterward. Jewel Ackah and his band showed up—Blay-Miezah's personal pop star, his shirt open, his shoes polished, and his Afro perfect. The Western Showboys draped a handsome white steer in the Eleven Wise flag, a gift for Blay-Miezah. As it was led in, everyone erupted in his favorite song. There was drumming until dawn.

The next morning, in the purple haze of first light, Blay-Miezah emerged from his house, with Gladys and his daughter Mona-Lisa at his side. They walked down the road, and along the beach to a church, in a procession led by two long ranks of women in choir ruffs and followed by another choir. The choirs sang a song specially composed for the occasion, in praise of Blay-Miezah, as they went.

A group of his associates followed behind the procession, including a distinguished-looking Ebenezer Ako-Adjei, a living reminder of the Nkrumah era. The songs echoed through the tall palm trees and drifted out to sea.

BY THE AUTUMN of 1983, Blay-Miezah was a chief who owned a football club and had a diplomatic passport. He seemed to have the junta just where he wanted and—for insurance—had a former attorney general of the United States in his pocket. The Oman Ghana Trust Fund, as the *Philadelphia Inquirer* put it, "had the trappings of a successful enterprise—offices in London, Zurich, Amsterdam and Seoul, a booklet describing the companies that would develop Ghana after the trust was released and even a flag showing the locations of the offices around the world." Across the globe, businessmen, bankers, and lawyers waited to do the Trust Fund's bidding. Our man had rewritten history. Anansi's stories had come true.

Chapter 19

Fool's Gold

1983–1985

I t was time. Or maybe it was not.

The investors would be paid tomorrow. Or maybe they would be paid next week—next month at the latest. Next month was guaranteed—unless something came up.

Something always came up. Someone had died. There had been some unrest. The bankers had balked. The government of Ghana had withdrawn its support. A new company had to be incorporated. The Americans had interfered. But not to worry, the investors were told: next time, the money would be released. All they needed was one last push.

Blay-Miezah's investors were exhausted. Many of them had spent years waiting for the call that would change their lives. They had staked their futures on the Oman Ghana Trust Fund. By now, many were in too deep to stop. They had spent too much time, and they had invested too much money. Many sacrificed their fortunes, their homes, their families, their dignity, and their businesses—a brewery in Achimota, a factory in Pennsauken, a video studio in Muswell Hill, and countless others—to advance the Oman Ghana Trust Fund.

None of the investors wanted to go home without their money. For years, their friends and families had been calling them stupid, pointing out that they hadn't been paid yet, telling them to demand their investments back or cut their losses. But even if they had wanted to confront Blay-Miezah, many investors believed that they could not risk it: when people made threats, or got violent, Blay-Miezah made a big show of cutting them out of the deal.

In a 1950s study, *When Prophecy Fails*, three scholars monitored the members of a cult whose leader had predicted the end of the world—and how they coped when it didn't happen. To the observers' surprise, the cult members' belief did not disappear when the apocalypse failed to arrive. Instead their belief became stronger. As one put it: "I've had to go a long way. I've given up just about everything. I've cut every tie: I've burned every bridge. I've turned my back on the world. I can't afford to doubt. I have to believe. And there isn't any other truth . . . I can't afford to doubt. I won't doubt even if we have to make an announcement to the press tomorrow and admit we were wrong."

When the day of the apocalypse passed, and the world kept on spinning, the cult members were remarkably insouciant: "Well, all right. Suppose they gave us a wrong date," one said. "Let's suppose it happens next year or two years or three or four years from now . . . All I know is that the plan has never gone astray. We have never had a plan changed."

The more dependent the investors became on the promise of massive returns, the more power Blay-Miezah and Ellis had. They understood that power. And they put it to work. But Blay-Miezah and Ellis, too, were trapped. They couldn't shrug their shoulders and admit that there never had been an Oman Ghana Trust Fund. They couldn't repay their investors. Just like in the stories of Anansi, they had been too clever for their own good. The web they had woven so beautifully had trapped them too.

The story of Nkrumah's gold began, slowly, to take on a life of its own. Blay-Miezah and Ellis had been telling it for years. They had used it to gain enormous wealth and power—but along the way, the story had warped the world around it and rewritten history. Now, Blay-Miezah and Ellis found that the story had grown too powerful for them to control. Gradually, they realized that the Oman Ghana Trust Fund had begun to consume them.

FOR NOW, ALL everyone could do was wait. By the winter of 1983, the London office of the Oman Ghana Trust Fund had become a bullpen for investors. The office was on the fourth floor of a building called Devlin House, in Mayfair, a block away from the high-priced shops of New Bond Street, and a fifteen-minute stroll through Green Park to Buckingham Palace. It was run with great efficiency by an amiable man with muttonchops named Ben Hayford.

Hayford had not wanted to run the Trust Fund's London office. He had a good job working for the Ghana National Trading Corporation. But then Ebenezer Ako-Adjei himself had called, several times, and convinced him that they needed a professional to manage the operation and that the role would come with other opportunities. Hayford could not say no to one of Ghana's founding fathers.

Initially, few of the investors understood what was happening at the office. Peter Rigby tried to get a friend's secretary placed there: a mole, he thought, might provide some useful information about what was taking place behind the scenes. But even the secretary had no idea what was going on.

There was a simple reason for this. The office was just for show. It was a theater set, and the investors were, largely, the audience. Occasionally they were the players, as a Philadelphia judge named Lynne Abraham later observed: "They were asked to go to various locations, including London, where they were on the phone, calling people cold and saying, 'Hello, my name is Joe Blow. I am an investor in the Oman Ghana Trust. And I know you don't know what the Oman Ghana Trust is so let me explain. It's a 'no fail' investment apparatus . . .' They were soliciting! Blay-Miezah put them to work."

The office was perpetually full. Investors, hangers-on, and people who had been sent to London by other investors to monitor the Oman Ghana Trust Fund gossiped and smoked and played cards and waited for the biggest payday of their lives. There was Stanley Baron, "a Philadelphia stock promoter," who had been named in "an assortment of civil lawsuits filed in both state and Federal courts in at least three different states and the District of Columbia." Baron was dressed in a trench coat and was talking football—the American kind, of course—with a man from South Philadelphia. The Eagles were having a bad year. "Yeah, they still lost," Baron groused. "Boy, it would have really been something," the other man said. "Inspirational if they'd won." Walter Hajduk sat at a desk, wearing a baby-blue sweater, a white shirt, and slacks, shuffling a deck of cards, muttering, "Where's the deuce of spades. No deuce of spades. I need the deuce of spades. The lousy deuce of hearts, deuce of diamonds . . ."

He teased Rigby about his plans for the evening. "You're out Peter-ing again, aren't you? Out at the discotheque, out jumping around. Aren't you a little old for that, Peter?"

"Have you ever been too old for anything, Walter?"

"No," Hajduk growled.

"Neither have I."

One investor told Rigby he had got word that Blay-Miezah had not yet formulated his latest plan.

Rigby was skeptical: Blay-Miezah always had a plan. "Who said? Doc?"

"That was the word we got this morning," the investor replied.

"Of course he's formulated his plan," Rigby said. "He knows exactly what he's doing."

"He just hasn't revealed it," the investor agreed, with a conspiratorial smile.

"That's all," Rigby continued. "If he's doing something, then he'll tell you if he needs you."

The clock ticked away, counting down the hours.

Rigby had an explanation for everything: all was for the best, in the best of all possible worlds. Hajduk thought that none of his explanations made sense. "Peter, your predictions are not very good. You don't have a clear insight of the whole situation. You're a farce. Period," Hajduk said, emphasizing the insult with a nod of his head.

Rigby was used to this: "What's that other expression you use for my intuition, Walter? You use one quite regularly. Peter, you're full of . . ."

Hajduk glared at Rigby.

"Shit," someone else volunteered.

At five every day, the investors dispersed for the evening. "Nothing's happened yet," one said, "but we'll be back tomorrow."

GLADYS BLAY-MIEZAH WAS also trying to figure out what her husband was up to. He was being unusually solicitous, calling her multiple times a day. There was definitely something going on. She was increasingly exhausted by her husband's antics. As always, Gladys could read her husband better than anyone else.

Blay-Miezah was at a meeting in Bermuda and had asked her to join him, but she declined. She joked about her luck being bad. "If we pass through the Bermuda Triangle, my soul will just vanish," she'd said. Plus, her mother was visiting, and Gladys didn't want to leave her alone in London.

Gladys never knew exactly what Blay-Miezah was doing on his business trips. She did know that huge amounts of money were involved. Americans would sometimes hand her staggering sums of cash, up to one hundred thousand dollars, to give to Blay-Miezah, and she would keep it for him. Like it was nothing. Like it was ten cedi. Every time her husband's exploits made the news, she would ask him what was going on. Blay-Miezah always used to say, "Why are they calling me a crook? If I had this thing and I said I'd give people 10-fold returns, are they not the crooks? People can walk away if they don't like the deal." The investors, Blay-Miezah complained, were taking advantage of him.

Gladys had put her own ambitions aside to take on the role of Blay-Miezah's perfect wife. "I was just in love and none of it mattered," she said. But as she sat in her hotel suite in London, she started to think about the fact that Blay-Miezah always had an agenda. He was constantly on the phone, filling the calls with, sweet, mundane details about the trip, how he had taken a whole floor, including the three-room presidential suite, at the hotel. Blay-Miezah traveled with a cook, and he said the suite had a kitchen, and that his cook would be making groundnut soup. "The thing is, when you deal with intelligent people, you can never underestimate them," she said. This much attention could mean only one thing. Blay-Miezah was checking that she was still in London.

Blay-Miezah and his entourage were ensconced at the Southampton Hotel in Bermuda. On a hunch, Gladys called and asked which room Kathleen—her husband's old flame from Philadelphia—was staying in. The Southampton promised discretion to its guests, but the hotel front desk gave her a room number immediately. Gladys was going to Bermuda.

When she arrived, she checked in to a smaller hotel and took a taxi to the Southampton. The hotel lobby was full of security men, all dressed in white. She strode past them, as confidently as possible, and made it into the elevator and pressed the button for the floor, before a guard caught up with her and asked her where she was going. She just smiled brightly at him as the doors closed.

On the way up to room 168, Gladys realized that she was praying. She knocked on the door. It opened. Two children stood in the doorway looking up at her. She was confused: these were surely not Kathleen's children. Kathleen was Black, and these children were not.

Gladys asked the children where their mother was. They took her to the window and pointed her out in the hotel pool. There was, apparently, an entirely different Kathleen staying at the hotel.

"I nearly died. It was like God wanted to tell me: stop your foolishness." Her husband hadn't been cheating on her, after all. She had just crossed an ocean to confront the wrong woman. She felt a wave of love and embarrassment and relief wash over her. All of a sudden, she couldn't wait to see her husband again.

As soon as she stepped out of the elevator on Blay-Miezah's floor, Gladys could smell the aroma of groundnut soup. At least this time she was in the right place. She knocked on the door, it opened, and there stood the other Kathleen. She had a plate in one hand and a dish towel in the other. As soon as Kathleen saw Gladys, she dropped the plate to the floor. The crash echoed through the suite.

Gladys heard Blay-Miezah's voice trumpeting: "How many plates will you break before you go back to Philadelphia?" Gladys walked past Kathleen, who was still frozen in shock, and into the living room, where her husband was sitting with Kwesi Amoako-Atta. At the time, Blay-Miezah didn't really drink, but he always had a tiny bit of cognac in a snifter, to go with the cigar. As she walked in, Blay-Miezah said: "Oh, my God." Amoako-Atta looked from Gladys to Blay-Miezah and said: "At this juncture, I have to leave."

IN 1983, A British hops merchant named Ralph Kenber discovered that an employee of his working in Ghana, John Ryman, had misappropriated large sums of money. How much precisely, Ryman was reluctant to say, but he had used the money to strike a deal with Blay-Miezah. Kenber went to Barry Rider at the Commonwealth Commercial Crime Unit. Rider—a lawyer by trade—was the chief commonwealth fraud officer, and he was already investigating a large number of advance-fee fraud cases.

Advance-fee fraud had been around as long as anyone remembered—as far back as the Drake scam. But, Rider noticed, these old grifts were becoming professional. "It was when the 419 letters started taking off in Nigeria," he said, referring to the infamous "Nigerian Prince" scam, covered by section 419 of the Nigerian Criminal Code. Advance-fee fraud was also everywhere in the 1980s because some of the scammers weren't just making empty promises, Rider said. "Occasionally the money was there."

Some advance-fee fraudsters would actually come up with the loans or payouts they had promised their clients, because they were laundering money, often from the drug trade in the United States. The scammers went from targeting random members of the public with letters to targeting businessmen, politicians, and governments. Rider remembered telling the premier of an Australian state that the money funding a development project was dirty: the proceeds of drug trafficking in the United States. The Australians said that it was not their fault if the Americans could not sort out their problems: "Money doesn't smell."

When Rider looked into the Oman Ghana Trust Fund, he realized that "it had all the trappings of a classic advance fee fraud." Investors were promised high returns—a deal that was too good to be true—if they would agree to cover the costs up front. Police in London had been keeping a file on the Trust Fund, but had concluded that "the lack of any UK complaint, however, makes it difficult to commit resources to the pursuit of a full-blown investigation into the case." Rider, however, decided to look into Blay-Miezah.

When Rider and his colleagues called Ryman in for an interview, they were bewildered. Far from being contrite, Ryman said that he was a spy. He was keeping an eye on Blay-Miezah, he said, "for the British government." He showed Rider what he claimed were "communications with intelligence organizations in Britain." In the final years of the Cold War, espionage was a growth industry: spies were facing off across the world. In Ghana, American, British, and Soviet spies were thick on the ground. Rider, however, was inclined to take Ryman's claims "with a pinch of salt." Like many of the people who had been drawn into Blay-Miezah's orbit, Ryman seemed to be living in a fantasy world—a hapless hops salesman who wanted to be a secret agent.

Rider decided to give Ryman a chance to go undercover for real: he was going to be Rider's mole in Blay-Miezah's organization. "I was always a bit saddened that we had to threaten him with prosecutions and goodness knows what, because I think he was, in many ways, a fool," Rider said.

But then, Blay-Miezah was persuasive. "Personally, I was never taken in by him. And I don't think any of my colleagues were taken in by him. But one could see how somebody who wasn't familiar with the situation in Africa at that time would have been taken in."

FINALLY, IN FEBRUARY 1984, the news came. Everybody was about to get paid. And when Blay-Miezah said "paid," he did mean *paid*. Many of the investors were now expecting returns of twenty to one, fifty to one, or a hundred to one on their original investments: it was Blay-Miezah's way of keeping them happy, if they grew impatient. Many of the investors expected to be millionaires by Easter.

Spring came to London, and so did the investors. They flew in from all over the world: Ghana, Germany, South Korea, Japan. The office in Devlin House filled up with hopefuls by the dozen. Word spread that Blay-Miezah was on his way from Ghana and that the Trust Fund was ready to pay out. The investors went into a frenzy. Someone went out to get his favorite incense. Someone else went to get flowers. A lavish suite was organized at the Intercontinental Hotel.

By the time Blay-Miezah finally arrived, the flowers were dead, and the suite was not to his liking—so the whole group decamped to the Sheraton Park Tower, a few minutes' drive away. The Sheraton's penthouse was paneled in dark wood. Even the bathtub had a sweeping view of Hyde Park and the rooftops of London.

Blay-Miezah was accompanied in all his travels by a police officer named Ezra D. M. Stephens, who was with Ghana's Bureau of National Investigation. Stephens was the keeper of the diplomatic passport. Blay-Miezah was never supposed to have it in his possession. Instead, when it was required, Stephens would present it. He was also supposed to keep an eye on Blay-Miezah and report his every move back to Accra. The junta wanted to know if he was really doing as he promised. But Stephens was not prepared for

Blay-Miezah's ability to bend people to his will. Blay-Miezah was "a phenom-enal figure," Stephens later said. Within months, he had turned Stephens into an ally.

At the Sheraton, investors queued up to meet with Blay-Miezah. Everyone was clutching promissory notes and paperwork. They had been told that there was one more chance, before the Trust Fund paid out, to renegotiate the terms of their agreements.

The lawyer Barry Ginsberg had flown in from Philadelphia. Ginsberg said that he and his family, friends, and associates had invested more than a million dollars in the Trust Fund. Ginsberg was negotiating not just for himself but for the people he had personally roped into the deal. At the time, Ginsberg said their promissory notes came to a total of fifty-two million dollars. He had spent years waiting for the call that would make him rich. "Nothing else seemed to matter," he later told *Philadelphia* magazine. He was married and had a child, but he was "too engrossed with the fund to pay much attention to her." If Robert Ellis told him to stay by the phone, he would not leave his apartment for days. He was devoted. "On one occasion he waited in John Blay-Miezah's anteroom for the privilege of giving him twenty thou-sand dollars, waited three hours to give the good doctor that money."

When it was finally time to meet Blay-Miezah, Ginsberg was on tenter-hooks, and his palms were sweating. Blay-Miezah greeted him effusively. "American friend and brother," he said. "I am appreciative of all you've done. Your friends will see that you were right to support us. Your patience will be rewarded. I am going to write a figure on this paper. If you don't think it's a fair repayment, just tell me." By now, Ginsberg's shirt was soaked with sweat. Blay-Miezah handed over the piece of paper. When he saw the figure, Ginsberg had to grab the side of his chair to keep from fainting. The note, he said, read $150 million. His throat was so dry, he could barely croak out a "Thank you."

Ernest Milou owned GoldStar Meat Packers Incorporated. He was hooked in March 1984, when he was approached with "a business proposition that involved the sale of meat to the nation of Ghana." The next month, Milou visited Ghana and Togo to review the shipping facilities. Mostly, however, he was taken on carefully planned drives past Oman Ghana Trust Fund bill-boards. He left with the impression that there were "Oman Ghana Trust Fund

Offices throughout the country of Ghana." Then Milou flew to London and waited, with bated breath, for his meeting with Blay-Miezah.

When Milou was finally ushered into Blay-Miezah's office, he was invited to "draw up a meat contract to supply Ghana," paid for by the Oman Ghana Trust Fund. It was not clear what Milou would be supplying, or to whom he would be supplying it, or even how he would be supplying it: he had no way to ship his meat across the Atlantic, and had no cold stores or distribution in Ghana. Milou later told the FBI that he "was under the impression that this meat deal could become a reality. He was looking at making a large sum of money on this meat deal as well as collecting from the Fund."

When Milou returned to America, he wired $250,000 to Blay-Miezah. Blay-Miezah promised him that he would receive a meaty return of $30 million for his $250,000 investment in the Oman Ghana Trust Fund, plus the profits from the meat deal. Milou admitted "that his motive was greed."

After meeting with all the investors at the Sheraton, Blay-Miezah had his Louis Vuitton trunks packed up and flew to Zurich with his family—to take care of some final arrangements, he said. They arrived in Switzerland after midnight and stayed at a hotel near the airport. Famished, Gladys called room service, but the night shift bellhop taking her order couldn't speak a word of English. He didn't understand the word *chicken*, so Gladys and the children resorted to making chicken noises to get him to understand. Blay-Miezah just sat back and watched, looking increasingly amused. After some more miming, they gave up and sent the bellhop away. Only then did Blay-Miezah call him back and order, in perfect French, *poulet, pommes frites, crème caramel.* Gladys remembered: "He made us make fools of ourselves first."

BLAY-MIEZAH TOOK A suite at the Dolder Grand in Zurich, which cost around one thousand dollars a night. Investors followed, filling up the hotel. Blay-Miezah stayed for twelve weeks, looking out over Lake Zurich from the hotel's Gothic windows. Investors sat around the hotel, hoping to catch a glimpse of him, and dusting off their plans: all the houses, Porsches, boats, and helicopters they were going to buy, and the people they were going to prove wrong.

In his hotel room, Hajduk gloomily did the math: the trip cost the investors four hundred thousand dollars, he later claimed. Hajduk realized that, despite spending months in Zurich, none of the investors had managed to ask a single banker one simple question: Did the Oman Ghana Trust Fund actually exist? "This is Switzerland," one investor whispered. "You know the secrecy laws. Besides, would I ask a banker if there's money when I already knew the money was there?"

Then, in April 1984, the investors got some very bad news. Kwesi Amoako-Atta had died in London. Amoako-Atta had been there since the beginning, Blay-Miezah told friends: "He never quit the job. From 1972, to the 21st of April, 1984." Blay-Miezah also liked to remind people that the great man had been his employee. "This man didn't work—excuse me to say, with all respect: did not work with me as my superior. He worked under me." Blay-Miezah announced that he had stopped negotiations with the bankers, out of respect. He left Zurich to assist with funeral arrangements. To the investors, it looked like Amoako-Atta's death was a catastrophe, a setback that it might be difficult to recover from. For Blay-Miezah, it provided yet another excuse—and another reason to extract money from the investors.

Blay-Miezah took out a classified ad in the *Guardian* to tie Amoako-Atta's legacy to his own. It read: "First Deputy Governor of the Bank of Ghana, Minister of Finance in the First Republic and Financial Advisor/Director Secretary of Oman Ghana Trust Holdings Ltd."

There were funeral services in Accra; Amoako-Atta's hometown of Kibi, in the Eastern Region of Ghana; and in London, at St. George's Church in Hanover Square. Gigantic bouquets of flowers overwhelmed the sanctuary. Amoako-Atta lay at the altar in a white suit and a red bow tie. After the service, Jewel Ackah and his band played softly for the mourners. Investors stood around awkwardly. Some were told the ceremonies would cost $60,000. Others claimed they spent $250,000.

Blay-Miezah eulogized Amoako-Atta and his devotion to the Trust Fund. "The honesty of this man. The selflessness of this man. The sincerity of this man. The patriotic devotion of this man to serve his country. My beloved friend passed away in harness," hard at work for Blay-Miezah.

After the funeral, Blay-Miezah confirmed the investors' worst fears: Amoako-Atta had been crucial to releasing the Trust Fund. He was the only link between Blay-Miezah and the current government. His death meant that they would have to start all over again.

But some of the investors were growing increasingly suspicious. To them, Blay-Miezah's latest story seemed like a transparent lie. Quietly, they started making plans. Some cut their losses and stopped taking calls about the Trust Fund. Some wrote off their investments. Some sold their promissory notes. Some saw Gladys Blay-Miezah regularly outsmarting her husband and started to think about ways to get the better of Blay-Miezah too.

BY NOW, THE Oman Ghana Trust Fund was operating out of offices in Denman House, at 20 Piccadilly, above a store that sold tweed suits and shooting accessories. There was an elaborate art deco entrance that led to an elevator, which opened straight into the office. Blay-Miezah could occasionally be found behind his enormous desk, with a lit cigar, in front of a group of investors.

He felt safe working out of London. It was the one place where no one had ever tried to arrest him, where authorities seemed only mildly interested in his activities. This was a matter of some frustration to the fraud investigator Barry Rider. "Blay-Miezah had a bit of a field day," he said. "We didn't really have any financial regulators in the UK," and there was a perception around the world that "if you wanted to launder money you did it through London."

Rider's team had been looking into Blay-Miezah's accounts. "The only money that we were able to identify passing through was money that had been filched from other people," he said. "Blay-Miezah had a first-class money laundering operation." Rider realized that he had connections in very high places. His bodyguards "were mostly British ex-servicemen. And some of them were armed," which was very rare in London, where even the police did not routinely carry guns. To Rider, that "indicated that there were elements in the British establishment that, if not sympathetic to Blay-Miezah, were concerned that he had ins to people that mattered." The guards worked for a private security company called Special Training Services and were reportedly being paid for by the government of Ghana. STS was pure British establishment: the chairmen were Vice Admiral Sir Peter Austin and Colonel John

Slim, Second Viscount Slim. One guard claimed to have helped break the Iranian embassy siege in London in May 1980 by abseiling from the roof.

Rider eventually managed to meet and interview Blay-Miezah, who made his dislike of the investigator clear. "He did have an incredibly charismatic personality," Rider said. "He claimed to have the ability to put the evil eye on you. And on one occasion, he actually did, you know, go through this. And I must say that I don't really hold with any of that."

THE INVESTORS WERE under the impression that Blay-Miezah was hard at work in Accra, finding a replacement for Amoako-Atta: someone who could pull the right strings with the junta. But in fact, by late 1984, many of Blay-Miezah's powerful friends were losing patience with him. Rider had built an extensive file on him—thanks to the hapless hops salesman and the investigative team's financial research—that made it clear that Nkrumah's gold had no basis in reality. When Rider told Ghanaian authorities that they were supporting a fraudster, and the information got back to Captain Tsikata, Blay-Miezah was livid—and scared.

When Tsikata demanded an explanation, Blay-Miezah did not try to convince him with stories about intransigent Swiss bankers or arcane Trust Fund conditions. First, he told Tsikata it was Rider who couldn't be trusted. "Captain, Rider's statements in this country are really obnoxious. Rider is not being sincere." Then, he set about providing Tsikata with irrefutable proof that the Oman Ghana Trust Fund was real. For that, Blay-Miezah called Charles Lowenthal in Philadelphia.

Lowenthal, the disgraced lawyer, was now introducing himself as chief counsel to the Oman Ghana Trust Fund. Lowenthal sent Tsikata a closely typed, three-page letter. In it, he assured Tsikata that Blay-Miezah did indeed have a secret fortune. But the money had not come from Nkrumah. Instead—borrowing a story Blay-Miezah had told in Ghana, during Acheampong's rule—he claimed that it had come from an American millionaire. Lowenthal claimed to have served as counsel to Daniel Wilbur Layman, who started a foundation (which was not named in the letter) to "enhance world standards."

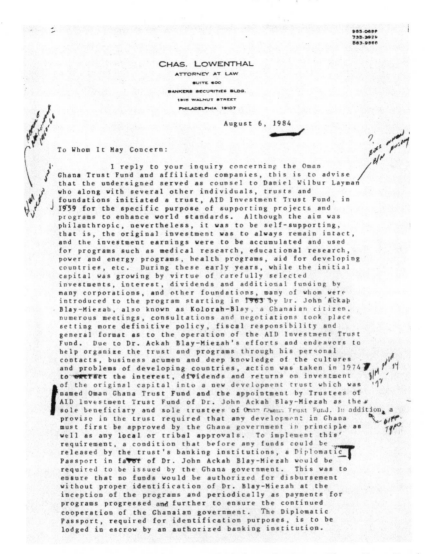

CHAS. LOWENTHAL
ATTORNEY AT LAW
SUITE 600
BANKERS SECURITIES BLDG.
1315 WALNUT STREET
PHILADELPHIA 19107

August 6, 1984

To Whom It May Concern:

I reply to your inquiry concerning the Oman
Ghana Trust Fund and affiliated companies, this is to advise
that the undersigned served as counsel to Daniel Wilbur Layman
who along with several other individuals, trusts and
foundations initiated a trust, AID Investment Trust Fund, in
1959 for the specific purpose of supporting projects and
programs to enhance world standards. Although the aim was
philanthropic, nevertheless, it was to be self-supporting,
that is, the original investment was to always remain intact,
and the investment earnings were to be accumulated and used
for programs such as medical research, educational research,
power and energy programs, health programs, aid for developing
countries, etc. During these early years, while the initial
capital was growing by virtue of carefully selected
investments, interest, dividends and additional funding by
many corporations, and other foundations, many of whom were
introduced to the program starting in 1963 by Dr. John Ackah
Blay-Miezah, also known as Kolorah-Blay, a Ghanaian citizen,
numerous meetings, consultations and negotiations took place
setting more definitive policy, fiscal responsibility and
general format as to the operation of the AID Investment Trust
Fund. Due to Dr. Ackah Blay-Miezah's efforts and endeavors to
help organize the trust and programs through his personal
contacts, business acumen and deep knowledge of the cultures
and problems of developing countries, action was taken in 1974
to extract the interest, dividends and returns on investment
of the original capital into a new development trust which was
named Oman Ghana Trust Fund and the appointment by Trustees of
AID Investment Trust Fund of Dr. John Ackah Blay-Miezah as the
sole beneficiary and sole trustees of Oman Ghana Trust Fund. In addition, a
proviso in the trust required that any development in Ghana
must first be approved by the Ghana government in principle as
well as any local or tribal approvals. To implement this
requirement, a condition that before any funds could be
released by the trust's banking institutions, a Diplomatic
Passport in favor of Dr. John Ackah Blay-Miezah would be
required to be issued by the Ghana government. This was to
ensure that no funds would be authorized for disbursement
without proper identification of Dr. Blay-Miezah at the
inception of the programs and periodically as payments for
programs progressed and further to ensure the continued
cooperation of the Ghanaian government. The Diplomatic
Passport, required for identification purposes, is to be
lodged in escrow by an authorized banking institution.

The letter composed by Charles Lowenthal about the Oman Ghana Trust Fund.

In 1963, the letter said, Blay-Miezah met Layman and, inspired by his generosity, convinced "many corporations and other foundations" (also unnamed) to donate to Layman's foundation. (There was no point in checking all this, Lowenthal wrote: all the banks involved were bound by nondisclosure agreements.) Layman, the letter said, was impressed by Blay-Miezah and "his personal contacts, business acumen and deep knowledge of the cultures and problems of developing countries," and donated the seed money of the Oman Ghana Trust Fund. This sum had, with a decade and some wise management, grown to more than two billion dollars. With that money, Lowenthal said, Ghana would take a quantum leap forward in infrastructure, in health, and in pride.

Tsikata may have found it suspect that Lowenthal did not elaborate on how Blay-Miezah had come to make Layman's acquaintance or "provide the government a copy of the complete instrument, nor did he indicate when the Fund was created or where any of the funds were held. Nor did he offer any explanation as to why this family was interested in Ghana's welfare."

In fact, Blay-Miezah only seems to have had a connection with one man called Layman: Daniel Layman, his former manager at the Union League of Philadelphia. Layman was astonished, years later, when asked if he was Blay-Miezah's benefactor, an investigator said: "No, he did not give Blay-Miezah a couple of hundred million dollars for the benefit of the Ghanaian people."

Lowenthal had gleefully boasted—to several different people—about making up almost everything in the letter. One, who watched him compose it, "heard Lowenthal talking about the phony 'Layman family trust' he had made up to fool officials in Ghana." Ginsberg told a reporter from *Philadelphia* magazine "that Lowenthal had bragged to him that the information sent to Ghana about the origin of the Trust was false and all made up." It was a ruse to get Captain Tsikata to renew Blay-Miezah's diplomatic passport yet again. It worked.

As Blay-Miezah was to discover, however, it was unwise to lie to someone as dangerous as Captain Tsikata.

Chapter 20

American Grifter

1985–1986

The Oman Ghana Trust Fund's offices in Philadelphia were in suite 702 of the Belgravia, a beaux arts building with bay windows at 1811 Chestnut Street. It was a grand edifice near Rittenhouse Square. Inside, the office was tastefully appointed in beige and peach.

In that office, Robert Ellis worked wonders. He could rely on a standard pitch. He would say that the Trust Fund had grown since the early 1970s because Blay-Miezah had placed the original funds in interest-bearing accounts all over Europe and North America. Most of the money was still "to be used to help the people in the Republic of Ghana, particularly in the Western region of Ghana, through purchases of food, medical supplies, farm equipment, trucks and other materials and merchandise necessary to the economic growth of Ghana." But, of course, your investment would be repaid first. Now, Ellis would inform prospective investors, the deal was finally closing. Blay-Miezah would be distributing returns in just a few months. For a modest investment, you could be a millionaire by Christmas.

Over the years, the alleged value of the Trust Fund oscillated wildly, depending on whom Blay-Miezah and Ellis were talking to and the promises they had made to investors. It was—initially—said to be worth about $150 million, but by now that was the size of the return a single investor had been promised. By the mid-1980s, the size of the Oman Ghana Trust Fund was said to be $160 billion. Blay-Miezah had, in other words, achieved a 100,000 percent return in a decade.

The pitch worked an astonishing number of times. Over fourteen years, Ellis got at least three hundred takers in Pennsylvania and New Jersey alone. In total, these investors allegedly put $15 million in the Oman Ghana Trust Fund. There were other investors in Maryland, New York, Washington, D.C., and California. Yoon Ok Kim of Massachusetts invested $2,000. Gregory Frazier of Detroit, Michigan, invested $250,000. Countless other people— including early investors like club owner Ben Bynum and Alija Dumas, the former member of the Pennsylvania House of Representatives—never spoke publicly about the sums they had given Ellis and Blay-Miezah. But they kept spending: not just on the Trust Fund but, over the years, on travel and living costs for Blay-Miezah and his entourage, and on flying all over the world themselves. The promissory notes stacked up in Ellis's office alone totaled a billion dollars. And that did not include investors whose names and stakes remained entirely secret.

One thing united most of the American investors: how little they understood about Ghana. Even those who made multiple visits knew remarkably little about the country or its history. They knew nothing about its laws or economy, despite signing on to build infrastructure and factories. They knew nothing about President Nkrumah, despite being under the impression that he was their benefactor. And they knew even less about his family.

This allowed Blay-Miezah to pretend that he—and his investors—were financially supporting President Nkrumah's widow. Fathia Nkrumah had publicly encouraged Ghanaians with money in other countries to invest in Ghana. Blay-Miezah openly courted her, meeting with her in Accra at least once. As soon as that happened, he made it appear that he had her full support. Blay-Miezah told investors that President Nkrumah's widow and nephew had "assigned any rights they had in the assets of the Trust and/or the assets of Nkrumah to Blay-Miezah."

The investors thought Blay-Miezah was funding an extravagant lifestyle for Fathia and for Nkrumah's children: the backers swapped stories of lavish shopping trips in Zurich and private schools in Britain. They were told Fathia Nkrumah had spent twelve thousand dollars in one shopping trip.

A secretary was told the sum was twenty thousand dollars. It was a far cry from the life Fathia and her children were actually living at the time—but the investors had no way of knowing that. In fact, Fathia Nkrumah had to sell her engagement ring in order to pay her children's school fees in Britain. Many investors didn't even know what she looked like.

Some of the investors would meet several prominent Ghanaians who worked with the Trust Fund, but never learn to pronounce their names, or even the word *Ghanaian*. (*ga-nay-NEE-an* was a popular choice.) Often, investors were not entirely sure whom they had met, or dined with, or bribed.

These details—on the whole—did not matter to the Trust Fund's newer investors. Unlike Father James Woodruff and many of the early supporters, they were not people seeking to improve the world with the Trust Fund. They were people who thought Blay-Miezah was offering them free money and didn't realize it: they thought he was an easy mark.

They were people who dismissed, out of hand, the fact that they would be stealing money from Ghana if Blay-Miezah's story were true. They were people who convinced themselves that they were better stewards of Ghana's wealth than those it belonged to. They were people who thought food, medical supplies, and trucks—furnished by them, at an enormous profit—would do more for economic growth than the hundreds of millions of dollars they planned to purloin.

Few of the new investors really cared if Blay-Miezah was President Nkrumah's adviser, or his cousin, or his nephew, or someone who had conned someone who had actually been close to Nkrumah out of millions of dollars. Few of them asked why the government of Ghana didn't simply sue Blay-Miezah, or the banks that allegedly held the Oman Ghana Trust Fund, and reclaim the money, or the gold bars, or the diamonds.

Instead, they saw Blay-Miezah, in his chief's finery, spinning a tale about darkest Africa, untold wealth, and a corrupt leader. And because the story—and the man—fit their preconceptions like a dovetail joint, they made up the rest of the story for themselves. They sold themselves on the Oman Ghana Trust Fund. As one of the investors later admitted to *Forbes*: "Everybody left the room believing a story he never told."

John Ackah Blay-Miezah had so thoroughly laundered his reputation that nothing stuck to him for very long. Barry Rider, from the Commonwealth

Commercial Crime Unit, had seen the same process at work plenty of times: the longer a scam or a con man was around, and surrounded by businessmen and elder statesmen and government officials, the more the whole enterprise seemed real. "Governments use legitimization as a means for dealing with criminals," Rider said. After a certain point, no one had anything to gain from pointing out that a captain of industry had committed a few crimes. It was the eighties: Hadn't they all? If there was indeed profit to be had, none of the people who had a stake in the Oman Ghana Trust Fund cared where it was really from. "The operation got to such a level," said Rider, "that to simply stigmatize it . . . would not be in anyone's interest."

The Oman Ghana Trust Fund seemed to be too big to fail.

The main reason for this was Rawlings, Rider said. "On the whole, the perception was, I think, internationally, that Rawlings was a good guy and a stabilizing influence." In London and in Washington, no one wanted to announce that Rawlings's regime was supporting criminals, or that it was propped up by criminals, especially if that was actually true.

On the surface, Blay-Miezah and Ellis appeared to be riding higher than ever before. But keeping the Oman Ghana Trust Fund afloat was taking every bit of imagination and money they had. The story of Nkrumah's gold was draining them, just as it was draining their investors. The risks Blay-Miezah and Ellis took, to keep the con going, led them into greater peril than ever before. Soon, Ellis would be in court and Blay-Miezah would be in direct conflict with Tsikata. They were both beginning to realize that the bigger they got, the further they had to fall.

ELLIS KEPT NO records, apart from copies of some of the promissory notes he drew up—typed up and signed, but not notarized, or witnessed. There were no books or ledgers of any kind.

Ellis insisted that all the money he raised—less the cost of running the Philadelphia office—was sent to Blay-Miezah. Blay-Miezah spent it fulfilling the objectives of the Oman Ghana Trust Fund, including his campaign for president. Ellis did not file taxes for the Trust Fund or on any of the money he used for his own expenses, because he had apparently been advised that there was "no tax on borrowed money." This meant—as some of the more unscrupulous investors quickly realized—that there was no way to check the stories they themselves told, either: how much money they put in, what they had spent on hotel bills and flights and chieftaincies and football teams and bribes.

Ellis claimed that he drew a salary of $150,000 a year—borrowed from the Trust Fund, so tax-free, of course. He used it to live well. He traveled in almost as much style as Blay-Miezah and—for a time—almost as frequently. During a trip to London, Ellis checked into the Dorchester Hotel on Hyde Park Corner, a monumental, blandly luxurious place favored by royalty and Hollywood stars. He cut quite the figure in navy pinstripes, and made friends and contacts wherever he went. His telephone at the Dorchester rang constantly. People wanted advice, updates, reassurance—any kind of news. Krobo Edusei's son needed to talk. A Philadelphia department store wrote to remind him that "long-overdue payment" for his account was outstanding. Ellis left the Dorchester with pockets full of business cards and countless invitations to lunch.

Ellis's home in Philadelphia was on Chancellor Street, in a three-story brown brick townhouse with smoked-glass bay windows, attached to Wanamaker House. He was a regular at the new Four Seasons Hotel on Logan Square, which had opened in 1983; there, he was known for "dropping heavy tips, flirting with female employees and attracting lots of attention as a big spender," according to *Philadelphia* magazine.

But behind the scenes, Ellis's finances were strained. At the Four Seasons, "a couple of checks for $1,200 and $2,500 had bounced but later been covered." Despite getting their money, the hotel called the police "to investigate a flashy guy," which, as it turned out, was not a criminal offense. Ellis also fell behind on his rent at Wanamaker House.

Ellis liked a well-tailored silk suit, but there were more prosaic reasons for his financial trouble. He had family to support: a wife and adopted child in Brooklyn, New York; an ex-wife and three children from a previous marriage in Philadelphia; and a girlfriend who often accompanied him on business trips. So he could not afford to stop selling the Oman Ghana Trust Fund. Even after things got tricky. Even after the law got involved.

BY 1985, ELLIS was not alone in feeling the financial strain. Several of the investors were grappling with the consequences of staking their futures on the Oman Ghana Trust Fund. Mortgages were in arrears and taxes went unpaid. Families were getting angry and desperate. There were rumors— unsubstantiated, but persistent—that some investors were facing other pressures: they had invested money belonging to, or laundered by, southern New Jersey–Philadelphia organized crime families, or perhaps the Detroit Mafia. And if the mob didn't get their money back soon, there would be a world of trouble.

When the investors called Ellis to find out when they would be paid, he would always tell them: soon. They could not live on "soon." Some of them had heard dozens, maybe hundreds of "soons."

One investor, an insurance broker named Robert Shulman, was getting frantic. As soon as he got involved with the Trust Fund, Shulman had become consumed by it. He convinced friends to invest as well, and started traveling to London and to Accra. Shulman spent time with John Mitchell and allegedly made secret tape recordings of him (in, it can be assumed, an ironic tribute to the tapes that tied Mitchell to the Watergate burglary). In Ghana, Shulman also met the chairman. In a photograph, Shulman sits next to Rawlings, with his legs crossed, dressed in a striped T-shirt and white slacks. He has a pipe clenched between his teeth. Shulman is playing the part of the international big shot, albeit unconvincingly. Rawlings wears aviator sunglasses, a khaki shirt, and flared jeans, and subtly obscures his face. Shulman leans toward Rawlings. Rawlings leans away from Schulman. Shulman looks like a mannequin at Macy's. Rawlings looks like a mercenary.

Over time, Shulman lost interest in his own business. He eventually sold his share to his partner so he could put more money—twenty-five thousand dollars—into the Oman Ghana Trust Fund. He always thought that he would be paid within months. It had been years. In the mid-1980s, he claimed that he was selling popcorn to make ends meet.

Shulman spent the last of his money flying to Ghana and tracked down Blay-Miezah in Accra. As soon as he saw him, Shulman immediately "had his hands around the fat man's throat," as an investigator later put it. After that, Blay-Miezah—understandably—declined to meet with Shulman a second time. So Shulman "took a car and tried to crash it through the gates housing John Blay-Miezah at the time," the investigator said. "He almost didn't get out of Ghana because you just don't do that in foreign countries."

Blay-Miezah and Ellis were gradually losing control of the Oman Ghana Trust Fund. The story was their reality now: they could not escape from it any more than Shulman could. The promises they had made were too numerous. Too many people were expecting entirely too much money from them. No matter how carefully they built their house of cards, it could not stay up forever. All they could do was keep the show on the road for as long as possible.

To keep the money coming in, Ellis began to pursue smaller investments. Joseph Bonaryo invested $7,500 with Ellis in 1985. David Ryland invested $1,000 that same year. Claude Lewis, the *Philadelphia Inquirer* columnist, reported: "A Philadelphia-area college student was wined, dined and romanced and forked over $800."

Sophia Stankus was sixty-seven when she invested. She heard about the fund from her son-in-law, Christopher Albertini, who worked at the offices of the Oman Ghana Trust Fund and had also invested. After her husband died of cancer, Stankus sold their home on Frankford Avenue. She told Lewis, the columnist, that she got seventy thousand dollars from the sale. "When I sold my home, for the first time in my life, I didn't have to worry about where next week's food would come from." Then Stankus met Ellis, "who fed her ego and imagination with promises of enormous wealth." She gave him sixty-five thousand dollars.

Diane Canter owned a ticket agency at the Marriott Hotel where Ellis often took meetings. Ellis would buy his theater tickets there. He was a good customer, and after a while, he opened a line of credit, running up a bill of several thousand dollars. This was when Ellis told Canter about the Trust Fund. He suggested that his bill could be converted to a stake in the Trust Fund. Canter also gave Ellis her credit card. In exchange, he offered her a return of $1.2 million. By April 1984, Ellis's bill had swelled to $50,000. Canter went out of business, and her husband left her alone to support their two children. Soon after, she went to Ellis's office, "sobbing hysterically, begging him: my kids can't eat, I am destitute, I lost my business." The best Ellis would do, she later said, was pay her for the theater tickets.

IN THE SUMMER of 1985, Kofi Quantson was passing through London. Blay-Miezah asked him to join him for a quick meeting. He told Quantson that "their journey to repatriate the millions" was almost at an end. Quantson was no longer investigating Blay-Miezah: it was Tsikata's case, and Quantson "did not want to intrude without his authorization." But he was still director of the Bureau of National Investigation, and his former student was keen to keep him friendly.

Quantson agreed to meet with Blay-Miezah, but he had one condition. Blay-Miezah liked things big, loud, and expensive, "in line with his millionaire fashion." Quantson did not want to be seen getting into a flashy car at the airport. It would look like he was just another powerful person in Blay-Miezah's pocket, and Blay-Miezah had gotten him in enough trouble already. When Quantson arrived at Heathrow, he was relieved to see a boxy sedan waiting for him: a Rover, rather than a Rolls-Royce.

London was warm and bright. The car pulled up at the Londonderry Hotel on Park Lane. Inside, there were bodyguards everywhere. Quantson changed into casual, breezy clothes and went up to Blay-Miezah's floor. He was welcomed into a meeting room. Inside were about eight men, all in three-piece suits. Quantson noticed that he was the shortest (he always noticed when he was the shortest) and most casually dressed of them all. Blay-Miezah introduced Quantson as his former schoolmaster. Faces fell around the table. Blay-Miezah's investors had expected "a rather big person as elaborately dressed as they were."

Blay-Miezah continued to thrive off the reputations of the people around him. The investors were probably told that Quantson was another important Ghanaian official, there to help them finish the business of bringing the cash home. They gathered to meet him, expecting a wool suit, a pocket watch, and gravitas.

Mitchell was at the Londonderry as well, and Quantson spent most of his time in London casually interrogating him about the Trust Fund. Why, he asked, would a man like Mitchell follow Blay-Miezah? Mitchell puffed on his pipe contemplatively and responded: "Kofi, let me put the question this way. Why would a man like me follow Dr Blay-Miezah if there is no money?"

That part was not a mystery for Quantson. "John, you are an ex-convict. You were jailed for telling lies in the Watergate scandal. Why would any decent person take you seriously?" Mitchell had had this conversation before.

"Kofi, I did no wrong," he said. "The Presidency of the United States must be protected."

If Blay-Miezah's story was true, Quantson said, what was taking so long? "The money is always there," Mitchell said. "It is the formula to reach the money that is the problem." Mitchell sounded confident, but there was no reason to believe that he had any idea what he was talking about. He had made a fortune packaging tax-exempt municipal housing bonds as a young lawyer in the 1950s, but those days were long gone. He was not versed in international finance.

Still, Mitchell's certainty was enough to convince Quantson—once again—that the Oman Ghana Trust Fund might actually exist.

Quantson had repeatedly vowed to have nothing more to do with Blay-Miezah. But like so many of the investors, he found it impossible to stay away from him. The Oman Ghana Trust Fund—the possibility that it might actually be real—was just too compelling. Without realizing it, by turning up to meetings, shaking hands with investors, hanging out with Mitchell, and being friendly with Blay-Miezah, Quantson was making the story of Nkrumah's gold seem real. While Mitchell was convincing Quantson of its veracity, Quantson was convincing Mitchell.

RAWLINGS AND TSIKATA had been lending the Oman Ghana Trust Fund their credibility for years. They had given Blay-Miezah a diplomatic passport. They had allowed him to launder huge sums of cash through Ghana. They had brushed off the phantom line of credit from United Mizrahi Bank.

They had even let Blay-Miezah build up his own little power base in the Western Region, with his football team and his minor chieftaincy. In Accra, diplomats gossiped about their "deep involvement in Blay-Miezah's affairs and activities." When Barry Rider and his investigators at the Commonwealth Commercial Crime Unit realized that the government of Ghana was protecting Blay-Miezah, they knew they had to tread carefully: they did not want to appear to be interfering in the business of a sovereign nation.

Rider understood that he had not been treading carefully enough when, in London, a car with diplomatic plates pulled up alongside one of his team running surveillance on Blay-Miezah. The officer was dragged "into the back of the car and beaten up." Rider couldn't get to the bottom of what had happened, "but that was supposed to be on the say so [of] Tsikata."

Rider was concerned about offending Rawlings, but the real problem was Captain Tsikata. That year, Tsikata had taken down a network of informants working for the United States Central Intelligence Agency in Ghana. He had used a classic piece of Cold War spycraft, an information-gathering technique known as "sexpionage." The target was a CIA clerk named Sharon Scranage who was stationed at the U.S. embassy in Accra. The honey trap was an aging playboy, and distant relative of Rawlings, named Michael Agbotui Soussoudis. The *New York Times* reported that Scranage had handed over "C.I.A. operational plans for Ghana, classified cable traffic, information about Central Intelligence Agency communications and radio equipment as well as an intelligence report on military equipment, which a Ghanaian group had requested from Libya." Scranage also told Soussoudis about Ghanaian dissident groups being funded by the Americans, and informants working with them. The CIA had no idea what was happening until Scranage failed a polygraph test. When Scranage was detained, Captain Tsikata immediately arrested and tried the CIA's entire network of Ghanaian informants: the man who tapped phones for the CIA got twenty-two years. One informant was reportedly murdered.

Tsikata wanted to be the one who decided if and when embarrassing facts about Blay-Miezah got out. Even though Ghana's ruling junta was still not sure whether the Trust Fund was real, the junta knew that Blay-Miezah was a crook. Ghana's rulers didn't mind that; after all, most of them were crooks too. But they wanted to be sure Blay-Miezah remembered that he was *their* crook. They were not to be conned. They were concerned that Blay-Miezah might be losing sight of this: he seemed to be more interested in building up his own power than in bringing home the money. Blay-Miezah was called back to Accra.

Once he landed in Accra, he convened a press conference. Everyone who knew Blay-Miezah knew what was going to happen next. When he felt trapped, he had only one move: attack and accuse. At the press conference, he solemnly charged Captain Tsikata with taking a fifty-thousand-dollar bribe.

Later that day, Blay-Miezah was detained and taken to the headquarters of the Bureau of National Investigation. Despite the junta's yen for imprisoning people in any old hole, he was not put in a cell. An office in an outbuilding was converted into an apartment especially for him.

Detention made Blay-Miezah contemplative, and contrite. He told Captain Tsikata he didn't need a reward for bringing Nkrumah's gold back to Ghana. He didn't even want credit. And he absolutely was not going to run for president again. "I don't want any post. I don't want any position from you, or from the government," he said. "If there's an award, or a medal, or even a citation, that is all that I'm after. I lie not. I'll never ask for any public office in this country." With Captain Tsikata's help, Blay-Miezah said, he could turn things around, finish this business for good, and finally transform Ghana for every single citizen. "Then, they are thankful to Captain Tsikata, who engineered this cause to come to realization," Blay-Miezah said. "History, indeed, will be our final arbiter."

He also quoted, at length, a hymn he had admired from his childhood, by James Russell Lowell:

Once to ev'ry man and nation
Comes the moment to decide,
In the strife of truth and falsehood,
For the good or evil side.
. . . .

Then to side with truth is noble
When we share her wretched crust,
Ere her cause bring fame and profit,
And 'tis prosperous to be just.

He emphasized the words again: "It is prosperous to be just." Then Blay-Miezah continued:

Then it is the brave man chooses
While the coward stands aside,
'Til the multitude make virtue
Of the faith they had denied.

Blay-Miezah wanted to make sure Tsikata heard the last part: "'Til the multitude make virtue of the faith they are denied," he said. "'Til the multitude make virtue of the fund that people thought never existed."

Several investors visited Blay-Miezah in detention and offered to act as intermediaries between him and Tsikata. When Herb Burstein visited, Blay-Miezah handed him a briefcase and told him, "Hold these for me, these are the Trust's most precious documents." Burstein, naturally, could not resist looking inside the briefcase, which Blay-Miezah had left conveniently unlocked. Inside was a diary said to belong to President Nkrumah, and a document that made Burstein catch his breath: a copy of the deed that had established the Oman Ghana Trust Fund, typed on government letterhead and signed by Nkrumah himself.

THE JUNTA WAS not alone in losing patience with Blay-Miezah. All over the world, people were looking for ways to force his hand and make him pay them. In 1985, a group of investors in Philadelphia thought that they had found their leverage. They began cooperating with the authorities in America and helped them build a case against Robert Ellis. The investors assumed that Ellis was so important to Blay-Miezah that, if Ellis was threatened with jail time, Blay-Miezah would immediately ensure that they got paid, to make the charges go away. They were wrong.

After another payout date came and went, Barry Ginsberg—who had promised his friends and family that they would soon be $150 million richer—called the FBI. Since launching its inquiry into Blay-Miezah in 1982, the FBI was said to have assembled "a stack nearly four-feet high about this operation." But several investigations had stalled or fizzled out because nobody wanted to testify: none of the investors wanted to lose their chance at a fortune.

After Ginsberg called the FBI, six months passed with no progress. So he called Philadelphia assistant district attorney William Wolf. "I'm going to tell you a story you won't believe," Ginsberg said.

Wolf and his investigators were concerned that Ellis would flee the country. So the prosecutor and two police officers spent a Sunday in January 1986 trying to get hold of a search warrant by any means they could think of. Wolf had to be discreet. Ellis was as well connected as Blay-Miezah—and Wolf knew that every piece of evidence in the Trust Fund's office could be destroyed within minutes of Ellis hearing that the authorities were closing in.

The next morning, the Philadelphia police raided the offices of the Oman Ghana Trust Fund. Officers carried out boxes and boxes of documents from Ellis's office, including "many exquisitely written letters and documents designed to 'prove' the existence of the Oman Ghana Trust Fund," an affidavit stating that Blay-Miezah was President Nkrumah's first cousin, and "several hundred photographs of him [Ellis] and an assortment of women performing various sexual acts." Each one was painstakingly logged into evidence.

Ellis was arrested on January 14, 1986. In his mugshot—in a light blazer and white shirt—he looks disheveled, as if brunch at the Four Seasons had turned into a bender. Over the next few weeks, prosecutors added charge after charge to the case against him: thirty separate counts of felonious theft and felony conspiracy, and six criminal violations of the Pennsylvania Securities Act.

"This is the biggest fraud in the history of Philadelphia," district attorney Ronald D. Castille told the press, as Ellis's charges mounted. Ellis and Blay-Miezah possessed "some of the greatest powers of persuasion known to mankind . . . There are people like that out there who can talk the fleas off a dog, as they say." In the complaint, Ginsberg said he and his immediate associates had invested two million dollars and not seen a cent in return.

Ellis was released on twenty-five-thousand-dollars bail. His passport was seized, to stop him fleeing to any of the exotic locales he had frequented over the past fourteen years. Ellis and Blay-Miezah continued to assure investors that everything was under control. "Distribution of the fund will occur in February of 1986." Then, when that date passed: March. Ellis kept selling investments in the Oman Ghana Trust Fund even while he was on bail.

When the news reached Accra, Captain Tsikata threatened Blay-Miezah with a charge of "economic sabotage," a capital offense. Blay-Miezah claimed that he was shocked—appalled—by the excesses Ellis had been accused of and the sums of money in question. Blay-Miezah also noted the charges against Ellis very carefully. The strongest part of the government's case didn't

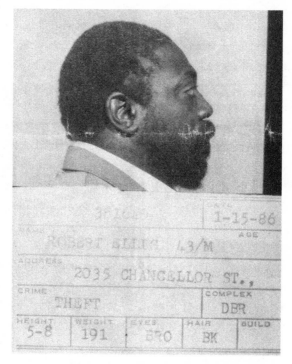

Arrest photograph of Robert Ellis, taken in Philadelphia in 1986.

appear to be the charges of theft or conspiracy but the charge that Ellis had been selling investments without being registered with the Pennsylvania Securities Commission. The prosecutors had proof that Ellis had been selling investments, but they did not have proof that the Oman Ghana Trust Fund itself was a fraud.

In June 1986, Blay-Miezah arranged for a letter to be sent to everyone involved with the Trust Fund. He said that he was horrified to learn that some people had been "telling others they are the largest 'investors' of the Oman Ghana Trust Fund." It had caused him "considerable pain and discomfort." There were no "investors" in the Oman Ghana Trust Fund: there were only "financial supporters."

AUTHORITIES HAD HOPED for a high-profile federal prosecution of Ellis, but almost immediately the U.S. Attorney's office announced that it would not be involved. The problem was the rushed search warrant, an assistant U.S. attorney said. It would not hold up in federal court—and that meant most of the evidence against Ellis would be inadmissible. Instead the case would be prosecuted by assistant district attorneys William Wolf and Joseph Casey, head of the Economic Crimes Unit.

Wolf and Casey could barely believe the scale of the operation Blay-Miezah and Ellis had built. "There just wasn't a limit to their imaginations," Casey marveled. And they had convinced so many people of a lie. "President Nkrumah is the George Washington of Ghana," Casey later said. "There's no evidence to suggest he took a nickel." The "investors were blinded by greed."

Ellis, who had helped mastermind a con that started in Philadelphia and spread to dozens of other cities, and eventually all over the world, would be tried in the Philadelphia Court of Common Pleas, in room 653 of City Hall, just up Broad Street from the Bellevue-Stratford Hotel.

BEN BYNUM WAS still a true believer. Over his years of involvement with the Oman Ghana Trust Fund, he had made several trips to Europe and to Ghana to help bring about the payout.

By 1986, Bynum had closed the Cadillac Club and turned it into a discotheque named Impulse. "This was the first Black-owned disco in Philadelphia. It catered to an older, thirty-plus, upscale clientele," wrote Michael Nutter, who went to the Wharton School with Bynum's son, Robert, and would eventually become mayor of Philadelphia. "The Impulse was one of the hottest clubs in its time," Nutter wrote, and it stayed hot for decades.

Nutter worked at Impulse the summer it opened. Located on the corner of Broad Street and Germantown Avenue in North Philadelphia, the disco was in a neighborhood full of iconic bars and restaurants: Prince's Total Experience Club, Chuck's Place, Dwight's Bar-B-Que, Sid Booker's Stinger La Pointe. "The Black owners of these bars and clubs employed mostly Black people and attracted a mostly Black clientele." Nutter's first few months at Impulse "coincided with a significant movement toward Black empowerment in Philadelphia's political structure . . . Many elected officials—Black and white, but primarily the Black establishment—had fundraisers, events and activities at the Impulse club."

In March 1986, investors gathered at Impulse. They had been hard at work using the threat of Ellis's conviction to force Blay-Miezah to finally pay them off.

Walter Hajduk—who, by now, owed $865,000 in back taxes—had recently flown "again to Ghana in the hope of convincing the government to let Blay-Miezah go to Switzerland one last time to get the money," and was back with good news. Blay-Miezah had told him to pass a message along to Captain Tsikata: if he was given just seven days, he could fly to Europe, talk to the banks, and straighten everything out. If he failed, the junta could just shoot him.

Hajduk told the investors that Captain Tsikata had taken him up on the offer. Blay-Miezah would be free soon. Then they would all fly to Europe and get paid. And if Blay-Miezah did turn out to be lying, Hajduk said, "I'll put the bullets in the chamber myself." (Soon after, Hajduk apparently got fifty thousand dollars of his investment back to help pay his taxes.)

Others had heard that Tsikata just wanted to establish, for good, whether or not Blay-Miezah had the Trust Fund, and "bring the matter to a final conclusion."

That day, Wolf, the assistant district attorney, had turned up to Impulse to try—unsuccessfully—to persuade the investors that they had been scammed. "What you had were some of the most successful and intelligent men and women in Philadelphia who bought a treasure map from con men," he said. The longer the investors listened to Wolf, the more uneasy and hostile they became: they had wanted the authorities to put pressure on Ellis and Blay-Miezah so that the investors would get paid. But Wolf wanted to put the Oman Ghana Trust Fund out of business. "They didn't want to hear what I had to tell them," Wolf said. He could not believe that the investors saw him as the bad guy: "I guess to take someone's money is one thing. But when you mess with their dream, they hate you."

Wolf was being willfully obtuse. Many of the investors—particularly people like Ben Bynum—had good reasons to distrust Philadelphia law enforcement. These reasons had been reinforced on May 13, 1985, when five hundred officers from the city's police department had launched an assault on a group of children and adults living in a house in a middle-class neighborhood near Cobbs Creek Park. The adult residents of the house were members of a radical group called the American Christian Movement for

Life, later abbreviated to MOVE. Officials began surveilling the group after its members started a campaign against police brutality. The mayor had announced plans to arrest members of the group, and the police had arrived to serve arrest warrants, equipped as if they were going to war. First they fired tens of thousands of bullets at the house; then they turned fire hoses into water cannons. Then the mayor, Wilson Goode, gave the police permission to fly a helicopter over the house and drop a bomb on it. The bomb started a rapidly spreading conflagration. The police commissioner, Gregore Sambore, initially refused to let anyone put it out. The fire destroyed sixty other homes, leaving 250 people homeless. Of the occupants of the MOVE house, just one child, Birdie Africa, and a woman named Ramona Africa would survive. Five children and six adults were killed. There was, for many people, no reasoning—in any matter—with officials who would bomb their own city, just to serve a few arrest warrants. Unsurprisingly, despite the many years and large sums of money they had invested in and spent on the Trust Fund, none of the Black investors in the Oman Ghana Trust Fund openly cooperated with Wolf's investigation.

IN THE AUTUMN of 1986, the investors' dreams seemed to be about to come true. They had all been summoned to the village of Schruns, in the Austrian Alps, to await the unlocking of the Oman Ghana Trust Fund. Blay-Miezah was ensconced in the Messmer Hotel, protected by the usual phalanx of grim-faced bodyguards.

He called Peter Rigby personally, to tell him the time had come. Rigby could barely contain his excitement. He flew to Zurich and hired a car for the drive to Schruns. When he arrived at the Messmer, it was late, and he had to talk his way past Blay-Miezah's security team before he could check in to the hotel.

The next morning, Rigby realized, for the first time, how many people were involved with the Oman Ghana Trust Fund: "I was surprised to learn 'we' were so numerous we occupied the whole hotel." Another cohort, mostly Americans, was staying at the Zurich Hotel, and a third group of people—everyone was quiet about who exactly was involved, "all this was cloak and dagger stuff," Rigby said—was quartered in another five-star hotel.

Blay-Miezah had hired a suite of offices in Schruns. There, he met with all the people who had invested time and money in the Oman Ghana Trust Fund, and authorized their promissory notes. There was another office in Zurich, where investors were to present their documents—contracts and promissory notes—to a panel after Blay-Miezah had authorized them. Ebenezer Ako-Adjei entered their names and details into a list of people and companies who would be paid. Then Kwesi Botchwey, Ghana's minister of finance, "authorized acknowledgement on each page of this list on behalf of the Government of Ghana."

Blay-Miezah seemed to have Botchwey's full support. Rider, from the Commonwealth Commercial Crime Unit, noticed that Botchwey helped Blay-Miezah on several occasions and had provided him with documents. "A lot of the documentation appeared preposterous," Rider said, "but it was very difficult to get anyone to really blow the whistle."

Botchwey had been appointed minister of finance and economic planning by Rawlings in 1982. He had been a stridently Marxist lecturer at the University of Ghana. Whenever anyone found fault with Marxist economics, Botchwey used to call their criticism "very worn-out." He stopped being a Marxist the minute he was appointed, and began courting the International Monetary Fund. Outside Rawlings's state-controlled media, Botchwey's about-face was greeted with incredulity. "Is it possible that Dr Botchwey has reached the stage where he cannot look himself in the face?" an article in *Talking Drums* asked. Botchwey's greatest expertise was, perhaps, in knowing which way the wind was blowing. Later in life, he would become a member of the "Commonwealth Expert Group on Good Governance and the Elimination of Corruption in Economic Management." But for now, he was signing documents for a con man.

AS SOON AS the administrative work was complete, Blay-Miezah told Rigby, he would ask Captain Tsikata to dispatch the final document he needed—his diplomatic passport—from the Ghanaian embassy in Vienna. Rigby was unaware—as were most of the others—that there was no Ghanaian embassy in Vienna.

The investors were giddy with excitement. "The constant theme was 'We can see light at the end of the tunnel,'" Rigby recalled. The investors gleefully opened Swiss bank accounts, to deposit their new riches. It was all going to be over, any day now.

Everyone waited. For months. Rigby spent the time driving people, documents, and letters back and forth between offices and hotels in Schruns and Zurich. Rumors, increasingly outlandish, circulated constantly: Rigby heard Captain Tsikata was in Switzerland—but never saw him; he heard Blay-Miezah had offered Rawlings fifteen billion dollars to step aside as leader of Ghana, so that Blay-Miezah himself could take over; he heard John Mitchell was trying to organize an enormous shipment of gold, which entailed his son being "required to remain in the Hotel Zurich as some kind of guarantee or hostage." Mitchell did not have a son.

CAPTAIN TSIKATA HAD quietly sent a group of intelligence officers, and a lawyer named Bright Akwetey, to Austria to monitor Blay-Miezah. Akwetey had, of course, heard of Blay-Miezah. "He took Ghana by storm: he funded Sekondi Eleven Wise . . . They excelled, that's what made him famous," he said. After that, all anyone could talk about was the Trust Fund. Akwetey said that he was amused to learn that the government had decided to call Blay-Miezah's bluff and release the diplomatic passport.

The team of investigators interviewed witnesses and bankers all over Europe. They fed Akwetey the information they found and wrote reports to Botchwey.

By now, Blay-Miezah had run out of lies about the origins of the Trust Fund. He told Captain Tsikata that he simply could not fully explain where the money had come from. "Captain, in confidence, some of this money," Blay-Miezah said, "it's a counterfeit." Some of the money came from "certificates" stolen from dead people and brokered through Arno Newman's bank in Brussels. Other funds, Blay-Miezah said, were bank drafts that John Ryman, the British hops dealer, and Kwesi Amoako-Atta had taken from Britain to the United States: "The drafts, which were valued in billions, were put at the back of the seam of Mr Ryman's coat," before Ryman got on the plane. "This money, the source, may be so filthy, that I am so embarrassed to sit and tell you the actual truth about it."

After a month, however, Akwetey's investigators could find no evidence for any of Blay-Miezah's claims. There was no Trust Fund, no bank accounts holding billions: the whole thing was a mirage. Rawlings and Tsikata had been taken by a con man. Everyone was called back to Accra. Captain Tsikata was pulling his support.

IN AUSTRIA AND Switzerland, investors slowly realized that everything had fallen apart again. First, "it was rumored Rawlings had withdrawn the requisite diplomatic passport 000065." Then Rigby heard Blay-Miezah had been given a diplomatic passport, but with a different serial number. The bankers would not accept it: the deal had been derailed.

Blay-Miezah mournfully explained that without the diplomatic passport numbered 000065, there was no way to unlock the Trust Fund. Not to worry, he said. It would all be straightened out very soon. His bankers in Guernsey had already been notified that they would now be in charge of the disbursal. Blay-Miezah was leaving for London immediately to make sure everything ran smoothly. In his suite, his valet, James Kaku Yanyani, hurriedly packed his Louis Vuitton trunks. Everyone went home, crushed, disappointed, livid.

After Schruns, the list of people willing to testify against Ellis grew. The charges against him were now up to sixty-four counts of theft and ninety violations of the Pennsylvania Securities Act.

ON DECEMBER 23, 1986, in room 653 of Philadelphia's City Hall, Judge Lynne Abraham eyed Ellis. Ellis's lawyer, Anthony DeFino, was petitioning to get his client's passport back and permission for him to leave the country. Ellis wanted to fly to London, then on to Guernsey, and perhaps to a third place, to help Blay-Miezah release the Oman Ghana Trust Fund. The courtroom was packed.

Abraham carried a gun, drank three cups of coffee a day, and was a vociferous supporter of the death penalty. She could barely walk a block in Philadelphia without being recognized. "Bus drivers, they honk at me, cabdrivers, construction workers, and they all yell, 'Yo, Abraham!' " She became a judge in 1977 and would later serve as Philadelphia's first female district attorney.

Many of the investors who packed the courtroom that day were cooperating with the district attorney's office. But few were ready to turn their backs on Ellis and the Oman Ghana Trust Fund. They still hoped to get paid. Some investors had just flown in from London after meeting with Blay-Miezah at the Churchill Hotel. "They are here today in support of Mr Ellis getting permission from Your Honor to receive his passport," said DeFino.

Abraham greeted the request with skepticism. "What assurances does anybody have, especially the Court, that Mr. Ellis will return?" she said. "Even before that, you haven't established yet—maybe you will—today, that these monies and accounts and places really exist."

Ellis and DeFino responded that they had it on good authority that a branch of the Royal Bank of Canada in Guernsey held money from the Oman Ghana Trust Fund. Blay-Miezah was heading to Guernsey to retrieve the money—and he needed Ellis there to manage payments to the American investors.

Ellis explained that he knew all the American investors. "I have been dealing on a one-to-one basis mostly, with the people," he said. Blay-Miezah wanted to expedite the payments and resolve the nasty business with the court as soon as possible, and that couldn't be done over the phone.

Joe Casey, the prosecutor, was incredulous. "Mr. Ellis, to your knowledge, is there any reason that the funds couldn't be transferred from the Royal Bank of Canada at Guernsey to your hometown of Philadelphia where you could arrange all the distributions?"

"Yes, there is," Ellis replied.

"What is that?"

"Doctor Blay-Miezah has to pay it in a specific manner for his own private and personal business reasons, and it's his money," Ellis said.

"What are Doctor Blay-Miezah's private, personal business reasons?" asked Casey.

"They wouldn't be private and personal if I told you," Ellis said.

So, to be clear, said Judge Abraham, Ellis wanted to get his passport back to travel to countries he could not reveal; to visit banks he could not name; to distribute money that he could not prove existed.

She had heard enough. Ellis was not getting his passport back. And she was not prepared to have her courtroom turned into a circus.

Ellis's attorney wanted to reconvene on January 5, 1987. Judge Abraham was already dreading coming to court for the next hearing: "For the 5th you will need a chair and a whip," she said.

Chapter 21

Soon Parted

1986–1987

Ladies and gentlemen, welcome to Guernsey," said the flight attendant as the tiny plane descended over a patchwork of brown-green fields and coastline. The Oman Ghana Trust Fund had come to the Channel Islands.

The investors trooped across the tarmac into the airport, carrying suitcases and wrapped in trench coats, wearing looks of grim determination. Guernsey was cold, wet, and miserable, and so were they. They had been told that the Trust Fund would finally be paying out, but the small group of Ghanaian, South Korean, American, and British supporters was subdued. There was none of the excitement of Schruns.

The tiny island of Guernsey, marooned in the English Channel off the coast of France, had long been a center of offshore banking and a favored resort for American grifters. Phil Wilson, a con man from St. Louis, ran the Bank of Sark on Guernsey in the 1960s. The operation was, in its entirety, "a mail-drop and a Telex machine run by a barmaid." It made Wilson millions.

Blay-Miezah had flown in ahead of the investors and was situated in a suite at La Grande Mare, a relatively new hotel on the west coast. Mary Lou Valinote, Blay-Miezah's secretary from Philadelphia, had also landed earlier. Now, she ushered new arrivals through a set of white double doors and into the reception room of Blay-Miezah's suite, where they all settled in on overstuffed sofas. Walter Hajduk squabbled with Peter Rigby. E. D. M. Stephens, the police officer monitoring Blay-Miezah, drank milky tea. Kim Chung Han translated for the South Korean investors.

In a second, smaller sitting room, Blay-Miezah, dressed casually in a red-patterned shirt and light slacks (appropriate for a seaside golf resort), welcomed his guests—almost every one of them dressed in sober, dark wool suits. He gave them the Ghanaian national handshake: a shake then a click. "That's it," he showed Ian Reed, a British investor who owned a construction company. The investors would spend most of the brief trip in their suites gossiping, or wandering around the island in the rain, waiting for something to happen.

Although he spent a great deal of his time living in hotels, Blay-Miezah hated hotel food. (He made an exception for the cakes.) So he traveled with his chef, who brought ingredients straight from Ghana and often cooked only for him. This time the chef had brought garden eggs and akrantie. Stephens remembered the chef taking over the hotel kitchen in Guernsey to cook: sometimes he made rice, sometimes he made fufu and soup. One day the chef prepared the akrantie soup, keeping the wild game and spices at a rolling boil for almost an hour. "The staff freaked out," Stephens said. It was more aromatic than the food ordinarily found in a Channel Islands hotel kitchen. "They ended up opening all the windows," he said. "They didn't complain, though. Blay-Miezah was spending too much money. If they complained, there'd be trouble."

Soon—sooner than usual—the word came from Blay-Miezah: the money was still locked up. There would be another delay. Blay-Miezah had his Louis Vuitton trunks packed again and headed back to London. The investors straggled after him. "It's become very awkward," one complained.

Blay-Miezah, as usual, had not explained much about what had gone wrong. On the way back to London, the investors filled in the rest with wild speculation. Blay-Miezah was a financial wizard, they all agreed, so the fault must have lain with some arcane banking rule or other.

Reed was under the impression that the funds had been trapped in five banks for decades now. Actually, it used to be sixteen banks, Hajduk interjected, as they drove back into central London from Heathrow Airport. "Now these sixteen banks, if you take twenty-seven billion, eight hundred, that means that each of these banks had a billion and a half," he said. Then the money was transferred to five banks.

"The five banks that have it now, of which Butterworth is one, in Bermuda—and nobody even ever heard of Butterworth—that's the government's bank," he said, confusing an American brand of high-fructose corn syrup and the Bank of N.T. Butterfield & Son, based in Hamilton, Bermuda: "The banks also needed a sweetener." The banks that held the Trust Fund money had lent it out, he theorized, and were struggling to recover it. So the investors would have to wait. "Now it's fifty bank days, that's seventy-some days," counting weekends.

Reed was not sure he could wait that long. "We're in a lot of shit now," he said, his accent lapsing into full Cockney as he got more agitated. He was worried about making payroll. "We haven't got a credit card left that we can use."

"You do what you want to do," Hajduk replied. "I don't even care."

INVESTIGATORS ON THREE continents were looking into Blay-Miezah and Ellis. And investors were increasingly willing to talk to them. In a courtroom in Philadelphia, those investigations would come together and reveal the true scale of the Oman Ghana Trust Fund. It would be so deeply damaging that by the time the court hearing was over, Blay-Miezah would disavow Ellis. Years earlier, Ellis had gotten Blay-Miezah out of jail, and their friendship had powered one of the largest frauds of the twentieth century. Now, though, it was every con man for himself.

On April 8, 1987, Judge Lynne Abraham's courtroom was again packed. Ellis and his lawyer, Anthony DeFino, faced the two prosecutors, Joseph Casey and William Wolf. Behind them, investors filled almost every seat in the court. Judge Abraham had studied African history in college, and she knew enough about it to see right through Ellis's stories. "This case," said Judge Abraham, "is one of the most fascinating and complex legal matters that I have ever seen." Depending on whose version of Ghana's history you believed, the judge later wrote, "Nkrumah was either the greatest benefactor or the worst thief in the recorded history of that nation."

For the investors, it had started with a story: about President Kwame Nkrumah and Ghana's wealth, and John Ackah Blay-Miezah, the Trust Fund's sole beneficiary, and how "a lot of money was needed to maintain Dr Blay-Miezah" until the Trust Fund paid off. That story was about to fall apart.

OFFICE OF THE PRIME MINISTER

OSU CASTLE
ACCRA, GHANA

Telephone: 74937

Our ref: K N /G M /7 D

Your ref:

Date: 6/3/59

TRUST DEED

I, Osagyefo, Prime Minister of The First Republic of Ghana, hereby direct that all minerals and funds now deposited or to be deposited from East Africa, Central African Republic, Ethiopia and Ghana, our new independent country, currently in an account at the Union Bank of Switzerland named Kwame Nkrumah Trust Fund, I now direct that these minerals and funds be put into another account known as Oman Ghana Trust Fund. Purpose of these funds is to assist the under-developed countries in Africa and the rest of the third world. The Bureau of African Affairs, whose main office is in Accra, may be empowered by the undersigned to use the good funds to harness the organisation of African Unity.

All the funds under the various accounts of Kwame Nkrumah Trust Fund, Oman Ghana Trust Fund, and Guards Trust shall be used directly and specifically by my personal confidant, Dr. John Ackah Blay-Miezah, also known as Kolorah-Blay, a nephew of mine and of the same Province and Region. He must always be identified with a valid Diplomatic Ghanaian Passport bearing Number 000065.

That the said trust funds should first be used to develop our Region which is in the Western Region (NZIMA), including proper electrification in the area, good pipe-borne water, roads, bridges, hospitals, clinics, well-equipped schools, universities and technical laboratories, fishing industry, mining, harbours, airports and all that he, Dr. John Ackah Blay-Miezah, my nephew, shall see fit. That Dr. John Ackah Blay-Miezah shall also have the right of access to the

.../2

One of the forged deeds to the Oman Ghana Trust Fund, dated 1959.

Early in the proceedings, Casey and Wolf brought out their star exhibit: the deed to the Oman Ghana Trust Fund. When it was displayed in court, the investors were on the edges of their seats. Finally: the holy grail. Only a handful of investors had seen it before. Most had only heard rumors about it. One investor thought he saw it in the vault of a Swiss bank—but he only saw a locked box, which he had been told contained the deed. (Gladys Blay-Miezah saw it once, while she was going through her husband's briefcase, searching for proof of his most recent infidelity.) Blay-Miezah and Ellis always spoke of it in hushed tones. This was a document that would change world history and make them fabulously rich in the process. It was thought to be locked in a vault.

The prosecutors produced two different versions of the Trust deed, one on letterhead that read "Office of the President" and was dated "6/3/54." The second version was on letterhead reading "Office of the Prime Minister" and was dated "6/3/59."

At the very top of the deed to the Oman Ghana Trust Fund was Ghana's crest. The date was scrawled underneath in ballpoint pen. The deed directed that all the assets in an account at the Union Bank of Switzerland belonging to President Nkrumah should be placed in an account known as the Oman Ghana Trust Fund. Control of the Trust Fund should be passed to Nkrumah's personal confidant Dr. John Ackah Blay-Miezah. Blay-Miezah would be able to prove his identity to the Union Bank of Switzerland via a valid diplomatic passport, issued by Ghana, bearing the number 000065.

The assets of the Trust Fund—minerals, cash, and "gold bars from the various countries which are carried personally by Dr. John Ackah Blay-Miezah"—would be used to develop Ghana's Western Region. This would include "proper electrification in the area, good pipe-borne water, roads, bridges, hospitals, clinics, well-equipped schools, universities and technical laboratories, fishing industry, mining, harbors, airports," and anything else Blay-Miezah saw fit.

If the deed was real, then two short years after independence, Nkrumah—who was prime minister at the time—had been able to embezzle millions of dollars in cash, gold, and diamonds, transport them thousands of miles without anyone noticing, and then make an estate plan that transferred those assets to a teenager who in one version of the deed was his nephew, and in another, his cousin. At the time, of course, Dr. John Ackah Blay-Miezah was still John Kolorah Blay: he had not yet acquired his title.

And that was just the first page. On the second page, the document really began to fall apart. It stated "that Dr. John Ackah Blay-Miezah shall also have the right to use at his discretion the Trust funds to financially benefit my beloved wife, Madam Fathia, and my children Gorkeh, Somia, and Francis." Here, in a document allegedly authorized by President Nkrumah, his own daughter's name was misspelled. Moreover, Samia Nkrumah had not yet been born in either 1954 or 1959.

Many of Nkrumah's closest friends, colleagues, and peers were said to have contributed to the Trust Fund. But the author of the Trust deed egregiously misspelled—and sometimes outright forgot—some of their names. The document stated that the contributors to the Trust Fund—along with Nkrumah himself—included "Houphette Boingah of the Ivory Coast, Kasavubu of Congo, Lumumba of Central African, Dr. George Padmore and Dr. Horace Bond of the United States of America." The name of the president of the Ivory Coast, Félix Houphouët-Boigny, had been typed phonetically, as if by someone who had never seen it in print. At the time the document was purportedly written, Joseph Kasa-Vubu was a leader in the independence movement of what was then known as Belgian Congo, as was Patrice Lumumba, who was not actually from the Central African Republic. George Padmore, Nkrumah's old friend, was from Trinidad and knew Nkrumah in London, not the United States. Horace Mann Bond had become president of Lincoln University in 1945, long after Nkrumah left. It is not clear why any of the people named would have been inclined to donate millions in cash, gold, or diamonds to fund the development of Ghana's Western Region.

At the bottom of the document was a shaky signature that read "Kwame Nkrumah." Next to it, in a similar hand, was the rather more firm signature of Charles Lowenthal, Blay-Miezah's favorite forger.

Casey and Wolf, the prosecutors, had shown the Trust deed to Ghana's ambassador to the United States, Eric Otoo. When they asked him about the relationship between Nkrumah and Blay-Miezah, the ambassador burst out laughing. He said that "Nkrumah would have nothing to do with him." The prosecutors had asked Otoo if there had been any connection at all between Nkrumah and Blay-Miezah. "Well," the ambassador said, "Nkrumah put Blay-Miezah in jail." Ambassador Otoo had pointed out the telephone number listed on the first page of the "Office of the Prime Minister" Trust deed. This was for Osu Castle, he explained, in Accra. The area code, the ambassador said, was for another region of Ghana entirely. "And the Castle, of course, has always been in one spot."

The deeds to the Oman Ghana Trust Fund were blatant forgeries.

IN COURT, ONE after the other, the investors testified about how they had been promised wild returns and untold riches. One, Raymond Gold, invested fifteen thousand dollars "and was promised a twenty to one return." "Twenty to one?" Judge Abraham asked, incredulously. "Yes, twenty to one," said Casey.

Some had invested without telling their families. Maytor McKinley had invested without telling his wife, Loni. Loni McKinley had invested, from a separate account, without telling her husband, Maytor.

The prosecution had found only one person who had successfully gotten money back from Ellis. After one too many delays, Michael P. Morris "went down to the defendant's office and, in his own words, made a pain of himself, he was always there, and eventually the defendant gave him that money back."

A police officer named Aloysius Stoltz and his wife, Deborah, had invested after Ellis told them "about monorails that were going to be put into Ghana, hydroelectric plants and the like." They had tried to get their money back in May 1985, but were told that "an individual who was a finance minister in the Nkrumah regime working for the Fund, a man named Atta, had died, and that held up the distribution of the fund." The investment "caused quite a strain on the relationship between Deborah Stoltz and her husband, and she said she was constantly criticizing her husband for getting them into that." By the hearing, they had separated.

In response to all these tales of misfortune, Ellis's lawyer, DeFino, sought to present Ellis as a misunderstood businessman, rather than a con artist.

DeFino introduced witness after witness who did not want to see Ellis prosecuted. Clare Gallagher, who had invested along with her husband, protested against Ellis being charged in the first place. "My husband and I, when we talked to the detectives and the District Attorney's Office," she said, "we did not in any way wish to press any type of charges against Mr. Ellis. As a matter of fact, we told them we didn't want to be involved in any of that sort. Our wishes were not respected."

Judge Abraham was unmoved. "That's interesting," she replied, "but it doesn't mean a hill of beans, because that's not your decision to make."

Then there was the meat wholesaler Ernest Milou, who was certain that he would get his return later that month. He had invested $250,000 with Ellis, in the hope of a return of $4 million. He was confident that his investment was rock-solid: "I have seen the officials from Ghana, we have talked to them, they are giving their full cooperation to Dr. Blay-Miezah without a question of a doubt. This is not hearsay," Milou testified. His memory of the meeting, however, was notably hazy. He kept referring to a "Doctor Tsikata."

Many of the witnesses were under the impression that they were simply waiting for a complex business deal to close. Romeo Bruno had just returned from meeting with Blay-Miezah in London. Bruno was running an unsuccessful import-export business, bringing in vehicles from Brazil. But no one in America wanted to buy them, because Bruno imported only the cheapest and flimsiest buses and trucks. Bruno was hoping Blay-Miezah would help him offload his stock in Ghana. "I was interested because the Brazilian products are very similar to the African needs, they are not so sophisticated," said Bruno, who had—thus far—failed to find anyone in Ghana interested in buying one of his cars. Just a month before the hearing, however, he had signed a four-hundred-million-dollar agreement with Blay-Miezah.

In court, Judge Abraham was shocked by how many people had fallen for the tale of the Trust Fund. It just didn't make sense. Nobody could explain how Nkrumah had arranged for everything to be smuggled from Ghana to Switzerland in the first place. "How could he haul all that gold?" Judge Abraham later said: "Did he have a train?" And then this money appeared to have toured the world. Witnesses claimed that it was in Romania, then the United States, then Switzerland, and now: the Channel Islands. All the while, apparently, "it kept growing exponentially at huge rates." But, the judge said, she was not there to decide if the Trust Fund was fake. She was there to determine if Ellis was part of a conspiracy to rip people off with the promise of a huge payoff, and if he had committed securities fraud.

MICHAEL LENET'S TESTIMONY started out promisingly for Ellis. Lenet was a CB radio enthusiast who called himself the Silver Shadow. He turned his hobby into a business supplying traffic reports to local radio stations, the Shadow Traffic Radio Network, which he eventually sold. At the time of the hearing, he was running Delaware Valley Auto Spring, a truck repair shop. He, his brother, and his father had invested hundreds of thousands of dollars of family money in the Trust Fund. Lenet had just come back from London; DeFino asked him to explain what he had been doing there.

"Well, the purpose of us being there was to receive our monies, and at the same time, bring to a conclusion the receipt of all of these monies that are probably still scattered all over the place on their way to London."

The judge asked for clarification: "When you say scattered all over the place?"

There were "several, many, many, billions and billions of dollars," Lenet said. The Trust Fund was proving hard to reassemble because "the banks lent these monies out to people," he said. "To retrieve all of this money," then disburse it to hundreds of people, "is a mammoth task and takes [a] considerable amount of time."

The judge pointed out that banks didn't actually work that way. "Mr. Lenet, today is an age of electronic banking. Banks don't go out and go to somebody they put a loan out with and say, 'Charlie, you know that two million dollars I loaned you last week? You have to give it back to me, because I have to give it back to the guy we owe it to.'"

Then the judge asked if, while he was in London, Lenet had met anybody who actually knew what was going on with the Trust Fund. Lenet said he had. He had spoken to John Mitchell, and to Ghana's minister of finance, and even to the leader of Ghana. "I met and said hello to Mr. Tsikata, who, I believe, is the head of state of the Ghanaian government." Nobody in the courtroom corrected him.

Once, Lenet added, he was in the Churchill Hotel, when "in came a rush of people. And I was talking to some of the other investors, and it was related to me that these were all bankers coming in to meet with Dr Blay-Miezah. But as far as physically seeing funds or anything, I did not."

Lenet started to sound like he was having doubts. He admitted that the business of the Oman Ghana Trust Fund was far larger anything he had dealt with before. "The deal is beyond my comprehension," he said.

Judge Abraham could see that: "From Delaware Valley Auto Spring to many billions of dollars, it's a quantum leap." But she was curious. Lenet had spent thousands of dollars "to support the lifestyle of all the people, to fly people around, to put them up in hotels, to pay for car rentals, bar bills." Was all this money considered an investment too? Or was it just the cost of doing business with the Trust Fund? "Are you willing to go the freight [cover the cost] of supporting all these people in their lifestyle so you can get your ten to one investment?" Abraham asked.

Yes, Lenet said. But, he acknowledged, it was a punt. "We have always viewed this deal as highly speculative. Any time the return is enormous in relation to the investment . . ." he said, trailing off, perhaps realizing how it all looked from the outside. "I guess we took a shot."

THE EVIDENCE AGAINST Ellis was mounting, and even some of the investors there to support him were wavering. Even worse: word had come from London that Blay-Miezah was shocked to hear about Ellis's actions. He had, he claimed, not been aware of what Ellis had been up to—and had never received a penny from Ellis.

Ellis and DeFino were reeling: they had not expected the prosecution's case to be this strong. Wolf and Casey knew far more about the Oman Ghana Trust Fund than they should have been able to discover from raiding Ellis's office.

This was because investigators in Accra, who did not understand why the Ghanaian government was backing Blay-Miezah, had quietly passed on information about his 1979 trial. The American prosecutors had also worked with the investigators at the Commonwealth Secretariat in London. Rider and his team provided so much of the investigative material that was used in Ellis's case that they would receive commendations from the Commonwealth of Pennsylvania.

Ellis felt the walls starting to close in around him. Among the charges he faced were twenty-four counts of third-degree theft, each of which came with a potential maximum sentence of 7 years—a possible 168-year prison term. He had no desire to spend the rest of his life behind bars. He and DeFino started negotiating a plea bargain with the district attorney's office.

The lawyers took some time to deliberate with the judge. Once they were done, Abraham turned to Ellis. "This is your decision, what do you want to do?" For once in his life, Ellis had no wish to risk it all. He was terse, defeated: "Continue."

A court official addressed Ellis: "Robert Ellis, on Bill of Information Number 2087, April Term, 1987, charging you with violation of Pennsylvania Securities Act 1972, 201, 301, and 401, how do you plead, guilty or not guilty?"

"Guilty," said Ellis.

After his plea, Ellis addressed the court. "I have worked very hard for fifteen years in something I sincerely, truly believed in," he said. "Very shortly it should all prove out I was right. I just want to go on record I had no intentions ever to take someone's money and they not receive back whatever I said they were going to get back."

ELLIS WAS HOPING for probation. But in their sentencing memorandum, the prosecutors argued that he should receive substantial jail time and pay restitution. Ellis, they argued, "took, and took, and took some more."

He left a "path littered with broken promises and traumatized and injured victims . . . For 15 years, the defendant has lived a decidedly opulent life-style of Zimmers and townhouses, of hundred-dollar ties and $3.50 English muffins at the Four Seasons, of glitter and glitz in London and Zurich." The prosecutors ended, with a flourish, by quoting Gilbert and Sullivan:

My object all sublime
I shall achieve in time
to let the punishment fit the crime.

The judge was unimpressed: "I am not really interested in three-fifty muffins, Mr. Casey, with all due regard."

Judge Abraham found the facts of the case, and the statements that many of the witnesses had made, extraordinary. But, she said, "it is not my job to keep people from being stupid." Ellis, she said, "is either the best con man in the whole world or Robin Hood hoping to save Ghana and the investors in the Oman Ghana Trust."

The judge hoped, somehow, that everyone involved would get their money, "in which case we are all going to look very foolish." But this seemed unlikely, despite Ellis being "so persistent and persuasive in his beliefs."

Ellis was sentenced to "not less than five nor more than fifteen years in the State Correctional Institution."

Soon after, the FBI quietly reopened its investigation into the Oman Ghana Trust Fund.

Chapter 22

The Throne and the Chain

1987–1989

For Blay-Miezah, life continued much as it had before. The white Rolls-Royce was as polished as ever. The hotel suites were just as large and just as lavish. The cigars were undiminished. The suits were perfectly tailored. He bought his daughter Mona-Lisa a sapphire and diamond necklace for her tenth birthday.

Wherever Blay-Miezah went—whether it was to the office, or to visit his children at their schools, or to take them to get hamburgers at Wimpy—there was a routine. His Rolls-Royce would pull up, and his security team would fan out: former Special Forces soldiers, dressed in blue blazers and gray trousers, sporting bushy 1980s moustaches. (When they all lined up, it was like a Tom Selleck look-alike contest, but pale and British.) Then Blay-Miezah himself would emerge, in leisurely fashion.

All, on the outside, seemed well.

But Blay-Miezah's position was more precarious than it appeared. And his instinct for getting out of trouble, once so sharp, was fading. Soon, a series of misjudgments and investor revolts would leave him looking dangerously vulnerable—and more alone than he had been for decades.

The investors' questions were becoming more pointed: they wanted to get to the bottom of the wild stories. And it had finally occurred to someone that the money belonged to Ghana, and the government might consider simply suing the banks involved, bypassing Blay-Miezah entirely.

To forestall these concerns, he sent investors like Ben Bynum letters, written on official letterhead, and apparently signed by Kwesi Botchwey, Ghana's minister of finance. One stated that "the Oman Ghana Fund originated partly from Ghana and partly from contributions by financial institutions in Europe and North America," was kept in banks in Europe and North America, and had no connection with illicit drugs or illicit transactions. Another letter assured investors that the government of Ghana would not stop them from getting their payments.

Investigators in Philadelphia discovered that, in an attempt to smooth things over with Jerry Rawlings and Kojo Tsikata, Blay-Miezah had instructed an accountant to "create a document falsely stating that he had examined the books of the Oman Ghana Trust Fund, confirming that the fund controlled huge sums of money," and forged "correspondence purporting to be from banks all over the world supposedly verifying the existence of huge sums of money and the transfer of portions of the fund."

Blay-Miezah was proud of his ability to coax anyone around to his way of thinking. People who had been enemies, he liked to say, were now his friends. He had curried favor, built friendships, and even hired people who had thrown him in jail, like his lawyer Bashiru Kwaw-Swanzy. Blay-Miezah claimed that he had already made amends with Ambassador Eric Otoo, who had told American investigators he was a nuisance and a con man. There was no one, Blay-Miezah thought, that he could not charm, or manipulate. "I forgive and forget," he said.

Even E. D. M. Stephens, the Special Branch officer who had been assigned to keep an eye on Blay-Miezah, was now fiercely loyal to him. Stephens introduced himself as Blay-Miezah's head of security and publicly defended him at every opportunity: "Dr Blay-Miezah has been the subject of these stories and allegations for years. All that you have heard is basically untrue," he told reporters. The American prosecution had nothing to do with Blay-Miezah. "There is a fund and there are some genuine investors, and others who thought they were investors, but were duped and the money did not go to Dr Blay-Miezah," he said, disavowing Ellis on behalf of Blay-Miezah. He was an innocent man. "This individual has suffered more than any individual that I

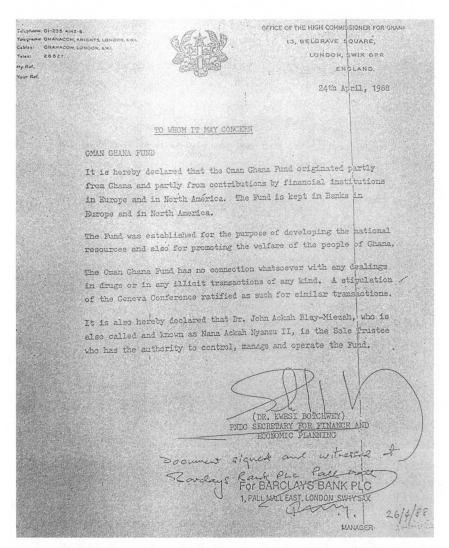

*Letter allegedly written by Kwesi Botchwey, Ghana's minister of finance,
regarding the Oman Ghana Trust Fund.*

know. Do you think the Ghana government would issue a diplomatic passport to someone who was not respectable?"

Blay-Miezah could not afford to collect any more enemies, in Accra or
elsewhere. His credibility—his entire enterprise—was built on the good

names of other people. He needed as many good reputations at his disposal as possible. With Robert Ellis on his way to jail, and the investors making more demands, Blay-Miezah needed to keep his remaining allies happy.

Investors started to realize that he seemed entirely untroubled by Ellis's conviction. So they looked for other ways to put pressure on him. As the investors were to discover, however, his feelings toward them were far from benevolent. Their betrayal had not gone unnoticed. Blay-Miezah did not appreciate their attempt to use Ellis to manipulate him, nor where their play had landed Ellis. Now, he was determined to bring them back into line, by any means necessary. The investors were about to find out that trying to control Blay-Miezah was an even more costly business than supporting him.

EVEN BY BLAY-MIEZAH's standards, his new suite in London was a lavish one: it was at the top of the Carlton Tower Hotel, in Knightsbridge. There was a dining room with a bar, a kitchen—of course—and, Peter Rigby remembered, "an enormous lounge sporting floor to ceiling windows that curved over at the top to form a conservatory." The suite came with a butler and was going to cost the investors at least a thousand pounds a night.

A few days into Blay-Miezah's stay, a small group of investors staged a full-fledged revolt. They confronted him in his palatial suite and said that they would not be paying for any more opulent hotels or offices, or flights or funerals. They would not be wiring him the money for this very hotel until they themselves got paid.

Blay-Miezah told them he was deeply upset by this. He had sacrificed greatly for them and now he was being punished? He always insisted he had no money stashed away. "I tell you today," he said, "I have no property." Blay-Miezah told the investors that, if they could "establish that I have £50 hidden in any part of the world, in any bank, or kept by an individual elsewhere, call me and find me guilty that I've lied to you." Every penny they gave him had been spent fulfilling the conditions of the Trust Fund. The Trust Fund was "like a big chain over my shoulder, which I want to unlock," he said, never missing a chance to make a pitch. The investors, however, were unmoved. The hotel bill was coming due.

Then, Blay-Miezah had a heart attack.

A doctor was called in. He looked Blay-Miezah over and decided that he should be admitted to a private hospital nearby. An ambulance whisked him away from his substantial hotel bill.

The doctor, Gordon Kells, had a posh Harley Street practice. He was also fresh off a scandal involving Ronnie Kray, one of London's preeminent gangsters; Lord Boothby, a closeted aristocrat; and Boothby's lover, Leslie Holt. Kells had been accused—and cleared—of killing Holt with a "massive overdose of a fast-acting anesthetic drug, which the doctor mistakenly thought was the tranquilizer Valium." In court, the prosecutor held up a small brown phial of Valium and the large jar of white powder containing the anesthetic, which had to be mixed into a solution before being administered, and said "there could be no question of confusing the two drugs." One of his Harley Street colleagues called Kells "an obsessive psychopath." Summoning Kells, rather than an ambulance, was not a choice that most people suspecting a heart attack would have made.

With Blay-Miezah hospitalized, the investors panicked. If he died, their promissory notes would be worthless: "People have been afraid that if anything happened to him, we'd all go down the tubes," one investor said. They immediately went out of their way to seem remorseful, paying the hotel bill and offering to cover Blay-Miezah's medical costs and hire Kells as his personal physician.

A group of investors gathered all the cash they could find and went to the Harley Street Clinic. Blay-Miezah was lying on the hospital bed with his eyes closed. His close friends, and his valet, James Kaku Yanyani—who rarely left his side—were seated in a semicircle around his bed, in absolute silence.

There were "multiple cords, cables and tubes attached to his partially exposed torso with an oxygen mask covering his mouth and nose." A heart monitor beeped. Kaku whispered in his ear, and Blay-Miezah opened his eyes to greet his visitors. One investor proffered the wad of cash to him. He remained stock-still, apart from his right hand, which emerged slowly from under the sheet, clutched the cash, and disappeared back under the sheet again.

Blay-Miezah's health soon improved markedly. He was even referred by Kells to his brother's fashionable West End gym to try a gentle martial art that was all the rage in London for the wealthy and heart-disease prone. For years after, Blay-Miezah would talk incessantly about his morning tai chi chuan.

Now, whenever investors got upset, or people started to ask awkward questions, Blay-Miezah's health would worsen again, and Kells would be called in. "Every time it was a suspected heart attack and every time a different hospital," Rigby said. He remembered Blay-Miezah had a fondness for Emil Savundra, the con man who had so enraptured Krobo Edusei. Savundra had frequently faked heart attacks to get out of awkward situations and criminal proceedings. Rigby thought that perhaps Blay-Miezah, too, "had mastered the art of a phantom seizure."

But by 1988, he was truly unwell. It was likely that he had hereditary heart disease, and he was staggering under the weight of the Oman Ghana Trust Fund. The devil's bargain he had made with Kells—to rush him to hospital, whenever he needed it—sat uneasily with Blay-Miezah: it kept the investors at bay for a little while longer, but it also came at a cost. The people around Blay-Miezah were becoming grubbier and more predatory: Kells, from the first, saw him as a mark to be fleeced. With Ellis out of the picture, Blay-Miezah was now more isolated than he had been since he got out of prison at Graterford in 1973. "I am a tragic figure," he later said. He knew that he could not sustain his story for much longer.

During one of Blay-Miezah's episodes of ill health, Kells admitted him to another private clinic, the Wellington Hospital near Green Park. It cost $1,015 a night. Kaku kept Blay-Miezah's favorite incense burning. Bodyguards surrounded his hospital bed. The investors again trooped into the hospital to see Blay-Miezah, who lay back in his bed and complained bitterly about how ungrateful they all were. All he did was give, give, give, and still people questioned his motives. "I have no property, I have no personal accounts. I have to beg to get my medical bills paid," said Blay-Miezah, ruefully stroking his gold-and-diamond Patek Philippe watch. The investors quickly realized that paying for hospitals would be even pricier than paying for luxury suites. They fell back in line.

BACK IN PHILADELPHIA, in May 1987, the time came for Ellis to begin his sentence. The investors turned out in force to wave him off. William Wolf, the prosecutor, was incredulous. "I couldn't believe it," he said. "It looked like he was about to take a cruise on the QE2 rather than be taken to prison. I just stood there."

In the harsh light of the courtroom, the mystery and awe of the Oman Ghana Trust Fund, built up over so many years, should have been shattered. But the Trust Fund was still standing. Nobody had their money, but the investors who saw Ellis off to Graterford Correctional Institute looked as if they had just come from a cocktail party: they were clearly still hoping to get paid. Observers were baffled. The *Philadelphia Daily News* called them "suckers."

After Ellis pled guilty, Barry Rider's investigators used his conviction to shut down the Trust Fund's attempts to court new bankers. "As soon as we heard that Blay-Miezah or anyone related to him was operating," Rider said, "we just sent the indictment and the judge's sentencing memorandum." Rider's investigation—and his surveillance of Blay-Miezah—wound down.

CAPTAIN TSIKATA, HOWEVER, was still watching Blay-Miezah closely. And his patience was at an end. Rawlings and the junta had propped up Blay-Miezah for years. But the Oman Ghana Trust Fund was looking less and less useful. Millions of dollars of loans from the International Monetary Fund had been pouring into Ghana since 1984. Rawlings could now get colossal sums of money, while Blay-Miezah could not. But the loans—part of the IMF's "structural adjustment" program—did little to turn Ghana's economy around. The national debt ballooned, more than doubling over the course of the 1980s, and per capita GDP was stagnant. Rawlings and Tsikata were now feverishly building bridges with the United States: they wanted Washington on their side when they were negotiating with the IMF and the World Bank. Blay-Miezah—a flashy con man who drew headlines and stares wherever he went—was looking more like a liability every day.

Blay-Miezah's back was against the wall. In early 1988, under pressure from the junta, he sent faxes to investors around the world telling them to "assemble for disbursement in the Cayman Islands." Blay-Miezah promised Rawlings and Tsikata more than $12 billion, almost twenty times the $638 million in loans the junta had so far received from the IMF, and a sum that dwarfed the country's national debt of $3.1 billion. He had nothing to offer them, and no plan. But that had never stopped him before.

Rigby and Kim Chung Han were summoned to Grand Cayman in March. Nobody really explained why. "Of course we eagerly set off, fully expectant of being paid, again," Rigby wrote. "We were not privy to exactly what he was doing in Grand Cayman." There were rumors that Blay-Miezah was going to cut a deal to sell the Oman Ghana Trust Fund to a bank in the Cayman Islands, and pay everyone.

Rigby found himself booked into a five-star hotel, in the room next to John Mitchell. Blay-Miezah had already been there for a while. He was staying nearby, in an apartment complex with a private beach. "Kim and I were summoned to attend the next morning," Rigby remembered. "We had no function. There was nothing for us to do. We only had to wait in this luxury until he 'dealt' the Oman Ghana Trust Fund." Though Rigby didn't know it, Blay-Miezah, too, was waiting.

Days turned into weeks, and Rigby and Kim were moved out of the hotel and into a chalet on a beach five miles out of town, with other investors. Most of them spent their days on the phone chasing down money to pay all the expenses being incurred.

Rigby and Kim amused themselves. Kim caught a lobster, which was illegal, as it was breeding season. He gifted it to Blay-Miezah. Rigby gossiped with Walter Hajduk and experimented with time-lapse photography. More investors and officials kept arriving. Kwesi Botchwey and Tsikata were rumored to have flown out for the occasion.

The atmosphere was tense. Blay-Miezah attempted to explain away the years of delays. "The very fact that this job is delayed does not mean that it does not exist," he told Tsikata, soothingly. "The funds are such," he said, "that you cannot pin them down. They keep skipping from bank to bank."

Yet another final list of investors was drawn up. Ghanaian supporters were owed almost four hundred million dollars. There were two different groups of American supporters, who were owed a total of almost five billion dollars. European supporters would get another two billion dollars. Three different companies, representing other groups of investors, were promised a total of ten billion dollars for agricultural products, infrastructure, fisheries, hospitals, and industrial projects. Two whole pages of the ledger were secret and represented around four billion dollars of promissory notes. In total, Blay-Miezah's promises came to almost sixty-two billion dollars.

One day, Blay-Miezah just disappeared. He didn't tell anyone he was leaving. There was no excuse, no elaborate reason why the Trust Fund could not be accessed or sold. Blay-Miezah and his entire entourage simply left. Captain Tsikata was, everyone said, humiliated and furious. The investors were devastated. One investor, Roy Simpson, reportedly confronted Botchwey in his hotel. "We've paid so many bills," Simpson said. "We've spent so much money. We are losing our homes. We are losing our families. We are losing our properties. All our money has gone to the Oman Ghana Fund."

Months later, Blay-Miezah would claim that everything in Grand Cayman fell apart because an investor was trying to do a side deal to steal the fund from Ghana. John Mitchell had told him what was going on. Blay-Miezah made a big show of canceling the investor's promissory note. Mitchell had a heart attack and died in November 1988, so he was not in a position to corroborate the story.

Blay-Miezah insisted that the problems they had encountered in getting hold of the money were insignificant in the grand scheme of things. "I still say," he declared, "I am the sole beneficiary of the Oman Ghana Fund, and I can produce the funds, I can surface the funds. The delay in time is immaterial, if you are looking into the issues properly."

Some of the investors began to wonder: Could they bypass Blay-Miezah and deliver the Oman Ghana Trust Fund to the people of Ghana without him? Why not, after all? He had had his chance and had failed. It was time for someone else to take over from him—it was what President Nkrumah would have wanted.

Blay-Miezah arrived back in London and checked into decidedly unglamorous lodgings at a Holiday Inn near Marble Arch. Even he knew the investors would be too angry to cover another lavish suite. And, he thought, it was time for a change. He had a plan to turn things around. But first, our man wanted a house.

BLAY-MIEZAH LOOKED AT, and dismissed, a "very luxurious country house with a glassed enclosure covering a large swimming pool" and chose

60 Avenue Road, a redbrick Georgian mansion, in St. John's Wood, at the very top of Primrose Hill. There were massive wrought-iron gates and a grand front door, and in the back there was a rose garden, a huge stone fountain, and a gazebo.

None of those things impressed Blay-Miezah as much as a single piece of furniture, Peter Rigby remembered. "His eyes lit up when we reported, 'This one comes complete with a throne,'" Rigby said, "as though every house should have one, just in case." It was a gold-upholstered Louis Quinze–style chair, reminiscent of the one the Asantehene sat in when Blay-Miezah met him. It was in keeping with the opulent décor in the rest of the house, which was a mishmash of art deco, art nouveau, and maximalist French design. There were white-and-gold flocked walls, brocade sofas, and mock-Tiffany windows. Once Blay-Miezah moved in, he added some carved Ghanaian sculptures. It was the picture of 1980s excess.

Blay-Miezah had big plans for his new home. It was almost time for Kundum. The Nzema Association of Britain held a big celebration for the end of the harvest back home every year and invited regional chiefs from Ghana to preside. In 1988, Blay-Miezah offered to host. He had an agenda. (He always had an agenda.) He was going to use the festival—and his lavish house and his legendary generosity—to assuage his investors: to remind them of the wealth and mystery of Ghana. At the same time, he could ingratiate himself with the paramount chief of Western Nzema and see if he could finally convince the Omanhene to make him a full chief too. He had not delivered a fraction of the developments in the Western Nzema Traditional Area he had promised in the speech he made when he was enstooled, but he could certainly make it look as if he had. He could already see the Omanhene of Western Nzema sitting on the Louis Quinze chair, giving Blay-Miezah his blessing.

Blay-Miezah called his new home Butterfly House. A brass plaque was erected on the gatepost, with the Oman Ghana Trust Fund's butterfly fluttering above the name.

Behind the wrought-iron gates of Butterfly House, everything looked picture-perfect. A photographer came to take portraits of Blay-Miezah's children. His son John Blay-Miezah Jr. was a natural. He was dressed in a beautiful little gray suit, and he struck a pose: hands in his pockets, legs in midstride, the picture of nonchalance. He looked like a corporate raider in miniature.

But inside his mansion, Blay-Miezah was isolated. Once, he flew Jewel Ackah's band, his longtime favorite, over to London to play for him on the terrace outside the house. But when they arrived, he wasn't there—just a cameraman. The band dutifully struck up. Blay-Miezah watched the video feed from his bedroom.

An unbridgeable rift was opening up, not just between him and the world but also between him and his wife. He told Gladys that he wanted their children to stay with him in London, and used his giant security team to keep them from her. Gladys decided that she wanted her children back in Ghana.

In classic Gladys Blay-Miezah fashion, she flew to London, arrived at 60 Avenue Road unannounced, and proceeded to outwit both the building's security system and Blay-Miezah's team of former Special Forces soldiers. First, she disabled part of the security system, and then she scaled an exterior wall, jumped down into the front garden, and was at the front door before anyone realized what had happened. The butlers and security team, wordlessly admitting defeat, went upstairs, en masse, to fetch the children.

The children were stunned. "Mr. Martin, one of my favorite drivers, gave her an 'A' for maneuvering herself over the walls," Mona-Lisa Blay-Miezah remembered, "and he said that my mum sounded pretty upset with my dad. She announced that Johnny and I would be traveling back to Ghana with her against my father's wishes."

IN THE EARLY 1970s, Richard Butera had been working as an attorney at a law firm in Norristown, Pennsylvania. He also owned WIOQ radio. Robert Ellis offered to buy the radio station. The money for the acquisition, Ellis said, would be coming from the Oman Ghana Trust Fund.

Dick Butera came from a high-profile family. His brother, Bob, was a politician, and Dick's business partners included Billie Jean King. Ellis invited Butera to Switzerland to meet the Trust Fund's bankers. In 1977, he and several other investors attended a meeting in Switzerland, where he spoke with Blay-Miezah and learned the true scale of the Trust Fund. Butera was one of the fortunate few who also saw the Trust deed. The paper looked old and weathered, and every correction was initialed: to Butera, it looked like a real legal document.

"Blay-Miezah told Butera the trust had been written by Nkrumah at the University of Pennsylvania with the help of numerous black professionals from the Philadelphia area." Butera was convinced, even though in Switzerland, "at the last minute it was discovered that Blay-Miezah had submitted a forged document to a bank. Everyone went home without the promised payoff." Nevertheless Butera, along with his family, and friends, invested several hundred thousand dollars in the Oman Ghana Trust Fund.

When investigators later asked Butera why Nkrumah would hand all this money to a man he had once jailed, Butera told them that he was not at liberty to say. "The money is there, look at Marcos' money," Butera said. (At the time, Ferdinand Marcos—the president of the Philippines—and his wife, Imelda, had just fled into exile in Hawaii, taking with them two C-141 transport aircraft full of possessions. The Supreme Court of the Philippines later estimated that Marcos stole ten billion dollars from the country.)

As for the people who had lost money, Butera had always maintained that investing in the Oman Ghana Trust Fund was the same as the cash he'd sunk into oil wells that turned out not to have oil in them: it was highly speculative. "Don't feel sorry for these people," Butera said. "They knew what they were doing."

By the late 1980s, Butera had moved to Aspen, Colorado, and gone into real estate. He kept in touch with people from Philadelphia, including the journalist Ed Bradley, who liked to ski and had a house in Woody Creek, Colorado, about thirty minutes away. Bradley got his start at WDAS radio, next door to Butera's station, and the two became good friends. Since then Bradley had covered the Vietnam War, the fall of Saigon, and Jimmy Carter's presidential campaign. In 1981, Bradley became host of a news magazine show on the CBS network. He turned *60 Minutes* into one of the most-watched programs in U.S. television history. During the 1980s, it was always one of the top ten programs on television.

At the time, Bradley's specialty was crooks. As one of the program's journalists put it, "A crook doesn't believe he has made it as a crook until he has been on *60 Minutes*." When Butera told him about Oman Ghana Trust Fund, Bradley saw a story.

Blay-Miezah, initially, seemed reluctant to sit down with Bradley. But he allowed Butera to convince him; he wanted to keep one of his biggest investors happy. Blay-Miezah claimed that he had consulted the Ghana High Commission and his solicitors before agreeing to the interview. In fact, he had begun to think that Bradley—with his direct, unflappable manner and distinctive head of salt-and-pepper hair—looked like a perfect pitchman. On *60 Minutes*, he could sell the Oman Ghana Trust Fund to the world. Blay-Miezah thought that he could also use the interview to clear some things up. People were increasingly skeptical of his claims about the origins of the Trust Fund, and Captain Tsikata had told Blay-Miezah to stop telling tales about President Nkrumah. Blay-Miezah promised he would fix it. "I was advised by the captain, 'You will ruin this great man's name, the man you know and love, and that I know and love,'" he later said. "So we had to find another source."

Blay-Miezah was dangerously unaware of how fragile his position had become. He had been able to placate Rawlings, Tsikata, and his investors many times before. He had made excuses, invented roadblocks, and used everything from coups to deaths to keep his story going. He had been able to manipulate the media successfully for decades: from journalists in Philadelphia writing breathless articles about the Bureau of African Affairs to newspaper editors in Ghana who let him use their pages to denounce the Bank of Ghana. It didn't occur to him to see *60 Minutes* as a threat.

Blay-Miezah got both Butera and Bradley to promise that his interview would not air until the Trust Fund had been disbursed, in the new year. Then he invited CBS to film at the Kundum festival. It was to be Blay-Miezah's greatest show.

IN SEPTEMBER 1988, the Omanhene of Western Nzema and the chief of Half-Assini arrived in London, along with other officials Blay-Miezah had invited. They came through immigration at Gatwick Airport dressed in full cloth, preceded by their orators, bearing golden staffs. Then British Airways electric carts whisked them to the curb, to Blay-Miezah's fleet of cars.

That evening, Butterfly House was lit up for a reception. Investors, dressed up to greet the chiefs, hung around in clumps in the drawing room. The

French doors were open and the fountain on the patio was bubbling. The next day, before the main event, the paramount chief of Western Nzema sat on the Louis Quinze chair and poured libation.

The festival itself was held at Porchester Hall, in Bayswater. Hundreds of people filled the grand art deco ballroom; some sat at banquet tables set up on the periphery, some near the center of the ballroom, where drummers, heralding the end of the harvest back home in Nzema, had been playing for hours, surrounded by traditional dancers. There were families from across Britain and dignitaries invited by the association. There were American investors looking sharp and middle-aged British men looking sweaty.

The chiefs arrived, Blay-Miezah in tow. The security team—bumped up for the chiefs and their priceless finery—emerged. Outside the hall, the procession assembled, and for once, all that glittered was truly gold. The chiefs were enrobed in swathes of vintage Kente and brocade; the orators carried gold maces with gold finials. A huge red parasol twirled high as they made their way into Porchester Hall, through the waiting crowd and up to the dais. Blay-Miezah looked spectacular, draped in yards of shimmering burgundy and blue cloth. The investors in the crowd looked up at the dais in wonder. This was the Ghana they had been dreaming of, and dreaming of skimming hundred-to-one returns from.

The master of ceremonies introduced everyone at the high table to polite applause. Blay-Miezah sat next to his lawyer Bashiru Kwaw-Swanzy, who was introduced as the "Attorney-General of the First Republic of Ghana, under President Kwame Nkrumah." When the emcee introduced Blay-Miezah, the polite applause became raucous, and Blay-Miezah broke into an unrestrained grin. He stood up and bowed, and let the waves of cheering and drumming wash over him. He said a few words, then basked in the applause again.

As the night wore on, Jewel Ackah and his band started playing, and in the tradition of every Ghanaian function, for just one song, everybody in the building was pulled onto the dance floor. The paramount chief led the chain dance, with his orator, bearing a golden staff, in front of him, and his security detail behind him. Blay-Miezah followed, similarly surrounded. There were women in kaba with colossal puffy sleeves and form-fitting skirts, and men in three-piece suits. Walter Hajduk was in his shirt sleeves, red-faced and grinning, shuffling from one foot to the other.

SOME OF THE investors, however, remained in open revolt and were determined to recoup the money that they had sunk into the Oman Ghana Trust Fund. A group of American investors—most of them lawyers—filed a civil suit against Blay-Miezah, Robert Ellis, and the Union Bank of Switzerland. They claimed that Blay-Miezah, Ellis, and the bank had colluded to defraud them using the Oman Ghana Trust Fund. They wanted $1,795,000 and "treble damages." The suit alleged that the bank, in particular, had sent cables stating "that the requirements of the Trust had been met and that the funds would be released by Union Bank immediately," and that in 1982, a banker had visited Philadelphia and personally told investors that "the Trust would be distributed shortly."

Lawyers from the bank pointed out that the banker in question had "not been in Philadelphia since the early 1970s." Some of the investors, it seems, had once again been meeting imposters. The bank responded to the lawsuit with open contempt, calling for it to be dismissed and labeling the investors' case "an undefined, unsupported, barely pleaded conspiracy theory." The case was dismissed. But every time the inner workings of Blay-Miezah's operation—the endless promises, the fake bankers—were exposed in public, keeping his scam going got harder.

BRADLEY AND THE CBS crew visited Blay-Miezah on a Saturday afternoon. Blay-Miezah welcomed them ceremoniously to Butterfly House. Before they started filming, he insisted on pouring a libation for Bradley with Beefeater Gin. Then, Bradley said, Blay-Miezah asked "to carry out an old tribal custom—the vow to speak the truth, the whole truth, and nothing but the truth." He took a swig of gin, then sprayed it, three times, at his ceremonial sword. Neither the tribal custom nor the ceremonial sword had any basis in reality. Blay-Miezah was still selling the mystery of Africa—and Bradley was buying: he called the Louis Quinze chair a "tribal throne."

"Have you defrauded people?" Bradley asked Blay-Miezah.

"I have not," Blay-Miezah replied. "Mr. Bradley," he said, "my word is better than my bond. When I promise you that after giving me a hundred thousand dollars, I will give you a million dollars, I will never, never, never dishonor it."

Blay-Miezah was, however, artfully vague about the original source of the Oman Ghana Trust Fund. When pressed by Bradley, he denied ever telling the story of Nkrumah's gold: "Our former president has no involvement in the fund. These are mere suggestions by the public," he said. Instead, Blay-Miezah claimed that the money had been bequeathed by Ghana's ancestors. Then he smiled knowingly.

"I'm totally confused," said Bradley.

"You should be," answered Blay-Miezah.

When Bradley asked him about his 1979 conviction in Ghana, Blay-Miezah grew indignant: "It is not correct, Mr. Bradley. It is a frame-up."

A few days later, in the Oman Ghana Trust Fund's offices on Piccadilly, Blay-Miezah addressed Bradley, the investors, and—most important—the cameras. "Over the years," he told the assembled crowd, "I have been branded as a confidence man, a flimflam artist. I say, I have not defrauded anybody."

Blay-Miezah acknowledged that the Oman Ghana Trust Fund had taken a long time to pay out. But, he said, no one could have done more than he had to see it through. "How many people in this world, for eighteen years, can drive these transactions?" he asked Bradley. "There is not a single person. I'm the only one in the universe."

In fact, that week, Blay-Miezah told Bradley, the entire matter would be drawing to a close. He projected serene self-confidence. All would be well, he promised Bradley, the investors—and himself.

"It was really very annoying," Blay-Miezah said after the crew wrapped up. "The questions came out, they gushed out, and I answered them. I thought I was using that opportunity to clear the former president's name. Who has the right to ask me the source of my funds? Who has reported stolen money? Who has reported missing money?"

Chapter 23

The Ultimate Con Man

1989–1992

For decades, Blay-Miezah had been able to turn events to his advantage. He could always find a way to exploit whatever circumstances he found himself in—instability, military coups, imprisonment, bad headlines—and come out on top. Now, however, all over the world, the Oman Ghana Trust Fund was under attack. Blay-Miezah did not realize it, but he had massively overplayed his hand. Events were about to run him over.

Rumor had it *60 Minutes* was not going to be the glossy advertisement for the Oman Ghana Trust Fund that Blay-Miezah had hoped for. In London, his creditors started calling in his debts. In America, the FBI had begun issuing subpoenas to investors and other associates of Ellis and Blay-Miezah.

Worst of all, after the Cayman Islands fiasco, Jerry Rawlings and Kojo Tsikata were no longer interested in listening to Blay-Miezah's promises and excuses. Early in 1989, when word came that the *60 Minutes* segment was going to be bad, he was ordered to return to Accra. Rawlings withdrew his diplomatic passport and issued a one-way travel document. The junta had heard rumors that E. D. M. Stephens, the investigator monitoring him, had been compromised. Blay-Miezah had—it was said—bought him clothes and taken care of him. Stephens certainly seemed to be enjoying his time in London. Now, he, too, was recalled.

Behind the wrought-iron gates of Butterfly House, Blay-Miezah and his inner circle desperately tried to plan their next move. Nobody wanted him to go back to Accra.

One night, Blay-Miezah called Peter Rigby into the dining room at Butterfly House. Rigby was used to being at his beck and call and thought little of it. But then Blay-Miezah looked up from his meal and asked Rigby: "What do you think I should do?" It took Rigby a moment to recover from the shock of being asked for advice by Blay-Miezah.

He explained that he had to make a choice: if he flew back to Accra, he expected to be imprisoned and interrogated by Rawlings. Or, he said, he could escape and flee to Brazil.

Rigby was still a believer in the Oman Ghana Trust Fund. The only way to resolve things, he told Blay-Miezah, was for him to fly back to Ghana, face Rawlings and Tsikata, and prove them all wrong by finally honoring his promises and disbursing the Trust Fund.

Blay-Miezah flew to Accra on a Ghana Airways flight on Sunday, January 29, 1989. Rigby went to Heathrow to see him off. At the airport, Blay-Miezah seemed ebullient. He assured everyone that he would be back in just two weeks.

LATER THAT SAME day, in Philadelphia, Jeannine Blay-Miezah got a call. A friend told her to turn to CBS: her ex-husband was on *60 Minutes*. She turned on her television, and Blay-Miezah's face filled the screen. He was in London, sitting on his golden chair, living, as Ed Bradley put it, in "a style that wouldn't embarrass the Queen." He looked like he was still using people and still up to his old tricks. She was disgusted.

Sophia Stankus, the retired widow, watched *60 Minutes* from her daughter's basement, which she called a "rat hole." Her family, she said, never came down to see if she was dead or alive, and she got one hot meal a day, from a Senior Citizens Center. She still thought fondly of Robert Ellis—he had treated her like his own mother, she told the columnist Claude Lewis, weeping. But now, Bradley was calling the man she had staked her future on "the ultimate con man." She watched Blay-Miezah in his mansion and thought: "He lives like a king, and I don't have food."

In one shot, Bradley stood in a green, open cattle field and told the story almost all the investors had heard: about how President Kwame Nkrumah gave Blay-Miezah control of the Oman Ghana Trust Fund while he was on his deathbed, in 1972.

Then the camera panned to reveal high, concrete walls, stretching out as far as the eye could see: Graterford State Correctional Institute. Blay-Miezah, Bradley explained, could not have been with the president when he died, because he was imprisoned at Graterford at the time.

Within days, VHS and Betamax tapes of *60 Minutes* were with investors in Accra and London, and all over the world. Diplomats sent each other gossipy summaries of the show. For years, people would pick up recordings on their travels and take them back to Ghana.

WHEN BLAY-MIEZAH LANDED in Accra, he was immediately put under house arrest by Tsikata. There were no visitors, just a modest staff and Blay-Miezah's valet. The house was in Abelemkpe, a quiet neighborhood on the edge of the city.

For Gladys Blay-Miezah, her husband's latest arrest was the last straw. She told him she was leaving him. She and their children went back to the family home, which was in Labone. Blay-Miezah immediately started looking for a way out. His attempts sent Accra's diplomats into a flurry of furtive activity.

A few weeks later, Britain's high commissioner in Accra, Arthur Wyatt, was called in for an urgent meeting with Ghana's deputy foreign minister, Mohamed Ibn Chambas. Wyatt later wrote that "having dismissed all the advisers and note-takers who normally sit in on such occasions," Chambas told him "the Ghanaian authorities had information that Blay-Miezah would be applying shortly for a UK visa and they hoped it would be possible for us to stall over this."

A few days later, Blay-Miezah put in an application. Blay-Miezah's associates sent a deluge of supportive telexes to the High Commission. One claimed Blay-Miezah was "urgently required in London to conclude a very substantial contract which would involve an enormous amount of export business with Ghana." Another impatiently explained: "The financial negotiations in which we are involved with Dr Ackah Blay-Miezah are now reaching a critical point which require his personal presence in London and also in Geneva. We therefore request you to kindly supply Dr Ackah Blay-Miezah with a visa." Diplomats also reported that they "received a series of telephone calls and visits during the subsequent two days from one of Blay-Miezah's minions asking whether there was any news."

After a couple of days, Blay-Miezah deduced that the British were stalling, and "sent one of his men to say that he was withdrawing his visa application and wished to have his passport returned immediately." Blay-Miezah had successfully secured a Swiss visa and was trying to persuade Rawlings and Tsikata to let him travel to Geneva. "The story is," another British diplomat wrote, "that he will have five days to prove beyond doubt the existence of the Trust Fund and a further twenty-one days to transfer the money to the Ghanaian authorities." The British did not know that Blay-Miezah was under house arrest, and reported that he had been seen at the Novotel in Accra, while another source claimed that he was already in Switzerland. "I would not like to be in Blay-Miezah's shoes," one official wrote, "if and when he fails to provide the goods, as will almost certainly happen. But he has slipped out of tricky positions in the past and will doubtless make every effort to do so again."

In June, Blay-Miezah sat alone in the small office of the house in Abelemkpe and attempted to compose himself. He spoke into a tape recorder and, with hymns playing softly in the background, he told his story one last time: trying desperately to convince Tsikata to release him from house arrest so that he could deliver on his promises and bring home the Oman Ghana Trust Fund.

"You, and anyone who may be hearing this tape thereafter, may find it the same old story," Blay-Miezah began. "Why should it not be an old story? Because it is the truth."

He told Tsikata he needed one very last chance to release the money. If he didn't succeed, he would happily face the consequences. "Captain, if this time, I go to Geneva, and I am left fully to work alone, without any disturbance, and I come empty-handed again to your soil, Captain, I John Kolorah Blay, I will volunteer myself to you, and tell you, 'Captain, take me to the firing range, take me to the firing squad, and have me shot.' That is, if I fail."

The only reason the Oman Ghana Trust Fund was still locked away was *60 Minutes*, Blay-Miezah said. The banks had heard Bradley's wild allegations.

They had heard President Nkrumah was a fraud and that he had stolen gold bars—and now they wanted nothing to do with Blay-Miezah. "I cannot prove myself," he said. "No bank would work with me." It was all Dick Butera's fault. "Butera guaranteed that they would not show this program until the whole Oman Ghana Fund was over," he said. "Why couldn't they wait?"

But, Blay-Miezah said, he could fix it. He knew that he would be victorious. He had foreseen it. Months before he left London, he had a dream. "In my dream, I saw an officer, struggling with me over my diplomatic passport. I said, 'You can't take that from me, it was given to me by the captain.'" Blay-Miezah said that in his dream, he could not see his assailant. Whoever it was, they were working to turn Captain Tsikata against him. But in his dream, he prevailed. "There was triumph."

The most important thing in the world for him, Blay-Miezah said, was finishing the business of the Trust Fund. "The need to go out and finish the job is more important to me than even my health. Once I complete this job successfully, I will be so well, so youthful, so virile, and what else only God knows."

Then, Blay-Miezah made what sounded like a veiled proposal. "Captain, there is so much I would have done with the money I've got—or I had—if this was a fraud," he said. If the Oman Ghana Trust Fund was a con, he said, he would have admitted as much to Tsikata, and offered to split the proceeds with him. He would have told Tsikata that "the people are not paying monies anymore. So far, what I have gathered and hidden is about twenty million dollars. Please, take half of it, and hide me in this country. I leave you the rest to set up an industry, with which you can build this country. There is no Oman Ghana Fund. This is all the money that I have."

For a moment, his guard was down. Then he went right back to being Blay-Miezah again. "Captain, I would have told you that," he said. "But Captain, I say there is more than $31.15 billion available to this country." His tone was frank, confessional even. "Some part of me is rotten. Some part of me is false. But that part of truth is the Oman Ghana Fund."

It didn't work.

OUTSIDE THE HOUSE in Abelemkpe, Ghana slowly began to fight off the worst elements of the junta. Rawlings could not last forever. The attempts to remove him, however, could and did. "The firing squads and long prison terms had not been effective deterrents to the spate of coup attempts," wrote the journalist Mike Adjei. Rawlings could not imprison or summarily execute everyone in the country. Indeed, instead of cowing people, each new atrocity triggered another spate of attempts to remove him from office.

Even usually stony-faced judges were openly disgusted with the government. In 1991, a judge in Brong Ahafo was presiding over a grisly day's work. Justice D. K. Okyere had back-to-back hearings for murder, attempted murder, and manslaughter: thirteen defendants in all. Justice Okyere looked at the dockets and then looked out at his packed courtroom. It was all a farce. What separated these defendants from the soldiers wandering around town, who had murdered and maimed countless people with impunity?

All the defendants, Justice Okyere said, were charged based on laws stating that "whoever caused the death of another person would suffer the consequences of their actions." That law applied to every person in Ghana. So, he asked, "has justice been done to those who were murdered by soldiers?" There were audible gasps in the courtroom. Justice Okyere's statement made the news.

Rawlings was out of options. In May 1991, he announced that the government would hold elections in just over a year. He would resign from the military and, as a civilian, run for president. "The turnaround in Rawlings' attitude to elections did not come about because he had suddenly realized there was some merit in democracy," Adjei wrote. It came because the people of Ghana gave him no choice.

Overnight, Rawlings transformed himself from a military dictator into a charismatic politician, a charming rogue who happened to have committed some human rights abuses. The lies that had swept him to power, the atrocities that kept him there, and the crooks he had propped up, needed to be forgotten. Disappeared. Rawlings had no further use for Blay-Miezah.

BLAY-MIEZAH'S OLD SCHOOLMASTER Kofi Quantson was one of the few people allowed to visit him at the house in Abelemkpe. Blay-Miezah seemed exhausted, "weighed down with all the 'multifarious problems.'" His health was getting worse.

Blay-Miezah's doctor in London, Gordon Kells, had been sending him medicine, but it didn't seem to be working. "His condition kept deteriorating." Blay-Miezah was deeply agitated. He seemed to want—desperately—to prove everyone wrong. To prove that he was the person he said he was.

One day, when Blay-Miezah was talking with Quantson, he "broke down and wept bitterly like a boy who had been deprived of a cherished prize." Quantson "felt deeply sorry for him."

Then, months into house arrest, Blay-Miezah had a stroke.

He spent weeks recovering in one of the nicest rooms in 37 Military Hospital. The facility had been named—unimaginatively—by colonial authorities building hospitals during the Second World War. It was home to both some of the country's best army-trained doctors and a roost of about a million large fruit bats. Legend had it that the bats arrived with a chief from the Eastern Region who was gravely ill. When the chief died in the hospital, the bats began an endless wake. Every dusk, as the sun set red and gold over Accra, a million bats stirred in the trees on the grounds of 37 Military Hospital and rose to hunt, high above Accra, for hours.

While Blay-Miezah was in the hospital, a distant relative of his, a woman named Joyce Nyameke-Adjow Kolorah, went to see Gladys Blay-Miezah. Kolorah's husband was in the United States, and she thought that maybe her kindly uncle, with all his American connections, could help her get a visa. Gladys Blay-Miezah helped her petition Tsikata for permission to see Blay-Miezah.

Gladys was not entirely surprised to hear, shortly afterward, that Kolorah and Blay-Miezah were in a relationship. Gladys considered Kolorah much too young for him, not to mention that she was a relative. But perhaps, Gladys thought, she herself "had made a way for that kind of thing" by turning a blind eye to so many other affairs. In March 1992, Kolorah and Blay-Miezah—who were both still married to other people—had a traditional wedding.

BACK IN PHILADELPHIA, the columnist Claude Lewis was still getting calls from people who had invested in the Oman Ghana Trust Fund. Despite everything that had happened, some investors were expecting to officially become millionaires, any day now. "No one could create such a story," one told Lewis. "It simply has to be true."

Others—apparently under the impression that Blay-Miezah had the *Philadelphia Inquirer* delivered to Accra—made threats. "Listen, either I get the money I'm entitled to, or he goes," another investor told Lewis. "All somebody has to do is give the word, and the guy's gone."

BY THE SPRING of 1992, the FBI's investigation into the Oman Ghana Trust Fund was almost complete. Investors told agents about tenfold returns, and trips to Ghana, and endless expenses, and money wired across the world. The FBI was particularly interested in the telexes, faxes, and phone calls everyone had used to keep track of transactions and summon investors. In these messages, Blay-Miezah liked to speak in code. "Blay-Miezah used the word sugar to represent cash." But by sending those messages into and out of the United States, under the false pretense that the Oman Ghana Trust Fund was real, he had—investigators argued—committed wire fraud, a federal crime.

The American investigators were, however, still struggling to understand some basic details of Blay-Miezah's operation. Agents from the Criminal Investigation Division of the Internal Revenue Service repeatedly referred to a President "Nacuma."

Robert Ellis, who was still in Graterford, was indicted again, this time for tax fraud. He was accused of siphoning off investments in the Oman Ghana Trust Fund and concealing "this income from the IRS by not filing personal or corporate tax returns."

FBI investigators now had boxes and boxes of documents, surveillance photographs, and covert recordings, as well as interviews with people who had invested in and worked for the Oman Ghana Trust Fund, ready to present to a federal grand jury. The Ghanaian government seemed to be willing to extradite Blay-Miezah.

For three years, he had been under house arrest. He had tried everything he could think of to get back in favor with the government. Nothing had worked. It was starting to look like there was no way out. It was time for Blay-Miezah's last performance.

Chapter 24

Anansi's Last Tale

1992–2001

George Padmore, President Kwame Nkrumah's old friend, had died in 1959. His ashes were interred in the walls of Osu Castle, in a ceremony broadcast on NBC in the United States. "Who knows but from this very spot [Padmore's] ancestors were carried out across the ocean there, while the kinsmen stood weeping here as silent sentinel," President Nkrumah said. "We've brought his ashes home to rest." Then Nkrumah wept. In 1961, he established a library in Padmore's honor.

In the summer of 1992, with the election campaign in full swing, the junta organized a grotesque campaign stunt. They had Padmore's ashes disinterred from the Castle and reburied at the George Padmore Research Library in Accra. Captain Kojo Tsikata was the guest of honor at the ceremony, on June 27. Tsikata was desperate to launder his reputation. He wanted to associate himself with Padmore and with Padmore's ideas about African unity. That day, he wiped the blood off his hands with Padmore's ashes.

After Nkrumah was deposed, the Padmore Research Library had been looted and its books burned. "One would have thought that harmless institutions such as libraries dedicated to learning and scholarship would be protected from the excesses of that period," Tsikata said. "In the attempt to wipe out the memory of Kwame Nkrumah from our history, this library named after his friend did not escape attack." Now Tsikata—who had done so much to enable the destruction of Ghana's history and the lies of Blay-Miezah—urged the audience, with no hint of irony, "to face up to our history."

TWO DAYS LATER, a dozen reporters were called to Blay-Miezah's house in Abelemkpe. They were told that he was having heart trouble, and the government had refused to give him permission to leave the country for treatment.

At the house, every half hour, somebody would come out of Blay-Miezah's room and whisper details about his current state to the reporters. He was apparently "suffering from massive palpitations." The reporters kept watch for hours before leaving to file their stories.

The following morning, rumors about Blay-Miezah began to spread around Accra. Some people said that he had left the country. Some said he was dead. Gladys Blay-Miezah rushed to the house. The gates were locked. It seemed like there was no one inside. Something awful had happened. Eventually, Gladys got word that her husband was dead, that he died in bed with his new wife: "They were having sex when he died." The story spread around Accra; her grieving children were teased about it for months.

But the truth was, no one knew exactly what had happened to our man, Dr. John Ackah Blay-Miezah. None of the reporters who went to his house ever actually saw him. Nor did Gladys.

THE NEXT DAY, July 1, President Kwame Nkrumah was finally buried in Accra with full military honors. The timing was right only for the presidential campaign of Jerry Rawlings. He intended to exploit President Nkrumah's legacy to gain power and to launder his reputation—just as Blay-Miezah had.

To that end, the president's coffin had been exhumed from the modest concrete mausoleum in his hometown and taken to Parliament. There, he lay in state, twenty years after his death. On June 29, while the reporters gossiped outside Blay-Miezah's house, the line of people waiting to pay their respects to Nkrumah wound through the building, out the entrance, down the stairs, and into the parking lot.

On July 1, the president's coffin was draped in a flag. Nkrumah took one last ride through Accra, in a huge procession. The streets were filled with soldiers in dress uniforms and civilians in mourning cloth.

Countless dignitaries from all over the world flew to Ghana for the ceremony. Sam Nujoma, who was now president of Namibia, was there, and the South African freedom fighter Oliver Tambo, whom Nkrumah had supported; also in attendance were Julia Wright—Nkrumah's godchild and the daughter of the American author Richard Wright, who had moved to Ghana after independence—and Betty Shabazz, widow of Malcolm X.

A towering silver marble mausoleum had been built on the site where, more than three decades earlier, the president had declared independence in front of a crowd of thousands. "We are laying Dr. Nkrumah's remains to rest at the site of his greatest triumph," Rawlings said. "In the name of the people of Ghana, of Africa and the diaspora, and in the name of all those who truly seek freedom and justice, we dedicate this park to the memory of Dr. Kwame Nkrumah." "Rawlings urges all to continue Nkrumah's battle," reported the *Daily Graphic*.

"This will be a place of pilgrimage for all black Americans," said Shabazz. President Nkrumah, she said, "gave up ownership of himself to Ghana and to Africa." And Ghana shared him with millions. "He is the father of us all."

The ceremony was two decades too late, and it happened for all the wrong reasons, but President Nkrumah finally received the burial he deserved.

SOON AFTER NKRUMAH'S burial, Blay-Miezah's old schoolteacher Kofi Quantson got home from a trip and found several urgent messages from Blay-Miezah waiting for him. When Quantson called, Blay-Miezah's valet picked up the phone and hesitated. Quantson immediately knew that something bad had happened: he was sure that Blay-Miezah was dead, but his valet couldn't say so.

It took a while for the news of Blay-Miezah's death to reach the investors. Each group heard a different story: one investor insisted that Blay-Miezah had been allowed to travel to Germany for medical treatment and had died there. The investor claimed to have been at his bedside when he died.

Ed Bradley was told that Blay-Miezah's body had been flown—in secret—to Geneva. There, it was being kept in a cryogenic chamber, "to keep the fingerprints and everything intact," so that—at some point in the future—the Oman Ghana Trust Fund could be released.

A couple of months later, on September 8, a federal grand jury indicted Blay-Miezah on five counts of wire fraud. "If convicted of all counts, Blay Miezah could be sentenced to twenty-five years imprisonment, and a $1,250,000 fine," said Michael Baylson, the U.S. attorney for the Eastern District of Pennsylvania. Baylson said that he would request an extradition.

A week later, American officials were finally told that John Ackah Blay-Miezah had died. At first, no one believed it. The FBI sent an official request to the government of Ghana to fingerprint Blay-Miezah's body. The prints matched. Blay-Miezah was dead. The case was closed.

But not everyone was convinced.

Many people were sure Blay-Miezah's death was just another one of his stunts: a convenient exit. Years later, Kwesi Pratt Jnr, who had been one of the journalists at Blay-Miezah's house the night before his alleged death, noted that it had been a strange spectacle. "He chose to die in front of the media, without the media seeing him," said Pratt. "I have a sneaking suspicion that it is possible that he did not die, at least not at that time."

THE PRESIDENTIAL ELECTION was held on November 3, 1992. Just as he had promised, Rawlings permitted other candidates to run against him. But those other candidates quickly found that the odds were stacked against them: Rawlings deployed the full machinery of the junta, and its penchant for attacking civilians, in support of his campaign.

On the campaign trail, Rawlings wrapped himself in Nkrumah's legacy. "The Leader of the Revolution, Chairman Jerry John Rawlings," wrote the *Daily Graphic*, "said in Accra yesterday that the most meaningful monument that can be built to the memory of Dr Nkrumah is to continue the battle that he began."

Almost a million new voters appeared on the national electoral register. Rawlings won in a landslide.

A new constitution was drawn up. Rawlings made sure that he and the rest of the junta would never have to answer for everything they had looted and all the Ghanaians they had murdered. The constitution gave them "perpetual indemnity." "It is quite unthinkable that a man whose government has the worst human rights record in Ghana's history," the journalist Baffour Ankomah wrote, "should seek to escape the mark he himself has set for the country."

BLAY-MIEZAH'S FUNERAL WAS held in 1993. It was a modest affair by Ghanaian standards, especially for a man known for ostentatious displays of wealth. The wake keeping lasted five days. Each day his body was dressed in different cloth and different jewelry, and he was surrounded, always, by pink and white flowers. At his feet was a large gold butterfly. The body certainly looked like Blay-Miezah. But some people still refused to believe that he was actually dead.

Choirs sang hymns, bands played high-life, and mourners gathered. Crowds of onlookers and children from the neighborhood passed by, to see what a billionaire's funeral looked like. Blay-Miezah's family stood on a second-floor balcony and watched it all unfold. At one point, one of his relatives started throwing money to the children.

Jewel Ackah and his band played for Blay-Miezah one last time. He stood next to Blay-Miezah's body and sang his heart out, his voice breaking. The slow, sad songs went on far into the night. As everything was winding down, Ackah led the band in Blay-Miezah's favorite number: "Akaraka chi, akaraka cho, akaraka chi, cha, chi, cha, cho." Soon, the whole crowd—men and women, young and old, dressed in black—were on their feet and dancing, smiles breaking through their tears.

There were hundreds of people at the funeral service, although none of Blay-Miezah's prominent Ghanaian supporters attended. There was just one foreign supporter. Blay-Miezah's coffin sat at the altar, embossed with the Oman Ghana Trust Fund butterfly and lined with the purest white satin. His uncle introduced him, for a final time, as "Dr John Ackah Blay-Miezah, also known as Nana Ackah Nyanzu, also known as Butterfly Man, Akaraka Chi, Akaraka Cho." Blay-Miezah's eldest daughter, Roxanna Kim, spoke on behalf of all his children. "You were called by several names, some of which were rather uncomplimentary," she said. "But to us, you were simply 'Daddy.'" It must have been the will of God, she said, that their father left so suddenly, and without a word.

Blay-Miezah's eulogy was written in our man's own inimitable over-wrought prose and read by a relative. First there was a poem, the relative said, written by Blay-Miezah himself.

The leaves may fall,
The flowers may fade and pass away
They only wait, through wintry hours,
The warm sweet breath of May.

The poem was in fact written in Iowa, in 1863, by a man named John Luckey McCreery. It had been plagiarized. The rest of the eulogy was similarly immodest. It made Blay-Miezah sound superhuman.

Like all good legends, Blay-Miezah's began with a prophecy. Years before he was born, the eulogy explained, a roaming soothsayer arrived at his parents' house. The soothsayer proclaimed that "a potentate was going to be born in that town." The child would be "endowed with extraordinary powers of vision" and would be able to see into all the world's mysteries. He would return in triumph to his home village and be "the first citizen to land there in an aircraft."

In 1974, the prophecy was fulfilled when Blay-Miezah landed in his village in a helicopter. That was also the year he decided to share the news of his great fortune with the world—but the world was not ready to hear what he had to say. "In fact, Blay-Miezah's claim to funds abroad seemed to have caused the eruption of a social volcano, which gushed forth avalanches of acrimonious outpourings, misinterpretations and slander."

Then, the eulogy said, came the most exciting part of his life: "Eighteen long years, packed full with every conceivable kind of human experience." There was a detailed account of Blay-Miezah's kindnesses, many of which were news to the assembled crowd. "He donated $85,000 to the Olympic Committee." He was a patron of three different choral societies—"his residence always resounded with the choicest music"—and he spent his last days, sick in bed, arranging for friends to receive medical care at his expense.

"One thing remains," the eulogist said. "In spite of everything said about him, and despite the many troubling problems that he faced for long periods on end, Blay-Miezah did not relax in performing what he regarded as his mission, to do all he could to relieve the misfortunes and necessities of his fellow men."

"We pray," the eulogy ended, "that we may be blessed with his virtues."

Anansi himself could not have asked for better. Blay-Miezah's myth was made.

AFTER BLAY-MIEZAH'S DEATH, many former friends turned their back on his family—particularly on Gladys and her children, Mona-Lisa and John Jr. Gladys opened a little stall in front of their giant rented house in Labone, selling popcorn and ice water. John Jr. manned the stall. At school, it turned him into a pariah: none of his rich friends would be seen with him anymore. Even as a child, it struck him: none of the arrests, or the press coverage, or *60 Minutes* led to him being ostracized. It happened when the money ran out.

Eventually, the family had to move to a cheaper place in Kokomlemle. Gladys shut down her boutique. "The fashion thing was not going to help me pay school fees," she said. She came out of the marriage without a house, a car, or ten pounds to her name.

"It was the biggest transition that we had to go through as a family," Mona-Lisa Blay-Miezah said. The enormous staff of servants disappeared. "For the first time at age 18, I had to hurriedly learn how to cook, clean, and keep a home."

Gladys Blay-Miezah eventually left Ghana. "She had to leave us with our maternal grandmother and rush to make a living in Monrovia, Liberia, because no one was really being supportive of us in Ghana," Mona-Lisa remembered. "They either thought that she knew where my father's money was stashed, or she was not as impoverished as she seemed to portray."

BLAY-MIEZAH'S DEATH SET off an unholy scramble to claim his assets.

Over the years, he had had at least fourteen children—a few of them adults by this point—and had married at least three times on as many continents.

He seemed to have made several wills, including one that was held at the Union Bank of Switzerland.

The battle over Blay-Miezah's assets would last almost a decade. It would go all the way to Ghana's Supreme Court and set legal precedent. Many of the claimants valued his estate at around forty-three billion dollars. "As to whether he did indeed have all that," a judge stated, "is another matter."

Supporters of the Trust Fund splintered into competing factions, each claiming to be Blay-Miezah's rightful heirs, and each claiming to know the real way to get hold of the legendary Trust Fund. Each faction went to bizarre lengths to rally support: they tried to scam, lie, and cheat their way to control of another scam, the Oman Ghana Trust Fund.

Before the arguments over Blay-Miezah's estate could be settled, the Union Bank of Switzerland would cease to exist. After a flurry of bad financial bets, which were remarkable even by the standards of the day, the bank was forced into a hasty merger with Swiss Bank Corporation in 1998. The original plan was to call the new company United Bank of Switzerland, but that name was already taken, so it was simply called UBS. As one financial journalist put it, UBS now "officially stands for nothing." (The new bank didn't learn from Union Bank of Switzerland's mistakes. In 2008, it lost thirty-eight billion on credit derivatives alone—more than all but the wildest valuations of the Oman Ghana Trust Fund.)

The first claims on Blay-Miezah's estate came from investors and from Dr. Gordon Kells's brother John, Blay-Miezah's tai chi instructor. John Kells brandished a will typed up on Oman Ghana Trust Fund letterhead, which appeared to be signed by Blay-Miezah. When asked why Blay-Miezah would leave Ghana's inheritance to an Irish tai chi teacher in London, Kells said that he had been in on the Oman Ghana Trust Fund from the very beginning. He claimed that he had met Kwame Nkrumah in London in 1948 and had been a supporter of Blay-Miezah and the Trust Fund ever since. In 1948, John Kolorah Blay had been seven years old.

While the case was still in court, Kells started calling himself the sole executor and beneficiary of the Oman Ghana Trust Fund and began to send messages on Blay-Miezah's letterhead (complete with the butterfly logo) to investors. The letters stated that the case was over and Kells had won. Kells claimed that he had sent a cease-and-desist to another investor, Gregory

Frazier, in July 1998. "The High Chief Justice of Ghana" the letter claimed, "will no longer tolerate any further interference from those who opposed the awarding of Probate to Dr Kells." There was no high chief justice of Ghana.

Kells's lawyer, William Adumoah-Bossman, was a former president of the Ghana Bar Association and had represented Rawlings when he was put on trial in 1979 for his first failed coup attempt. After Rawlings took power, Adumoah-Bossman became "closely associated with the abuses perpetrated" by the regime, according to the National Reconciliation Commission. While Adumoah-Bossman was representing Kells, his son Emmanuel wrote hit pieces about rival investor Gregory Frazier under the name Calus Von Brazi. In one piece, he insisted that "only John Robert Kells can ever extract a single cent for anyone."

In the end, several judges found Kells's claims—and the will that he based them on—laughable. Ghana's Supreme Court pointed out that Blay-Miezah had handed out so many sheets of headed and signed paper that literally anyone associated with our man could have faked a will. In fact, many did. Kells's specimen was not even a particularly good forgery: it contained "some material misspellings" and obviously fake signatures. It was a document worthy of Blay-Miezah himself.

After several claims on Blay-Miezah's estate had been dismissed, his cousin Francis Kaku Mensah was named as his executor, along with Ebenezer Ako-Adjei. His relatives traveled to Switzerland, hired lawyers, and tried to track down any accounts that they could. Even if the Oman Ghana Trust Fund didn't exist, Blay-Miezah's operation had seemingly raised tens of millions from investors. But no one knew where the money was. David M. Howard, an assistant U.S. attorney, thought that there was no money left because Blay-Miezah and Ellis had spent it all. "It's gone. All our indications are that it was spent maintaining a very nice lifestyle."

And indeed, after the legal proceedings were concluded, nothing could be found of the Trust Fund's billions or Blay-Miezah's millions. The gold and diamonds, the grand houses and cars, the millions upon millions of dollars collected from investors all over the world, the Oman Ghana Trust Fund itself: everything had vanished into thin air.

That should have been the end of the story of the Oman Ghana Trust Fund. It was not.

Epilogue

The Rest Is History

The Oman Ghana Trust Fund was a cheap story. A small-time con man told it, one day in Pennsylvania, hoping to make a few dollars. Then he told it again, and again, in Accra and London and Seoul. The story turned out to be so compelling that the con man could not escape it, and many people who heard it could not forget it. No matter how many times it fell apart—no matter how many times the con man's tricks were exposed—the story kept growing. Soon, it outgrew the con man. Then, like the very greatest stories, it ceased to be a story. For people across the world—from schoolchildren in Ghana to investors in America—the legend of Kwame Nkrumah's gold simply became reality.

Once Anansi has told his story, he disappears. You are assured that things did not end well for him. But long after he is gone, his stories are still there. If he told you he was a king, you would keep a crown waiting for him. If he told you a story about buried treasure, you would keep searching for it. If he told you your country was founded by a thief, you would still believe him.

Blay-Miezah was not the first person to tell the story of President Nkrumah's gold, and he would not be the last. The lies began before Ghana's independence. They were told by corrupt politicians, unscrupulous business-people, and hostile intelligence agencies. But Blay-Miezah knew how to ride a wave. From the day President Nkrumah died in 1972—from the moment the president couldn't say a word—and for the next two decades, Blay-Miezah told his story: President Nkrumah stole Ghana's gold.

According to Blay-Miezah, Nkrumah stole more gold than everyone else put together. More than the Portuguese, or the Danes, or the Dutch, or the British. Suddenly, all of them were off the hook, because Ghanaians were the real thieves. Blay-Miezah told Ghanaians that their country was ruled by thieves, and it always would be. It was a racist lie.

Con men should not be able to change history. The only reason Blay-Miezah did was because of the people around him. He worked to surround himself with people who got rich stealing from Ghana, got caught, then claimed that their bank accounts and wealth actually belonged to Nkrumah. Blay-Miezah courted people who needed to launder their reputations as much as he did. Those people turned him from a petty crook into perhaps the greatest con man of the twentieth century. They helped him write his lie into history.

Many of the people with the power to stop Blay-Miezah chose to profit from him instead. He appeared to be wealthy and powerful—and perhaps somewhat exploitable. And that was enough for people all over the world, from military dictators to widows in Philadelphia, to suspend their disbelief, so long as there was profit to be had.

Blay-Miezah, with his cigars and his suits, was a perfect instrument of misdirection: as long as all eyes were on him, and everyone was paying attention to the tale of Nkrumah's gold, they were less likely to notice the ways in which Ghana was being robbed blind, sometimes by some of Blay-Miezah's most powerful supporters.

For decades, Ghana has been systematically looted in ways that make the crimes of Krobo Edusei seem modest by comparison. Lasting wealth, all over the world, has been built on that plunder. Plenty of people in Ghana today are exactly who Blay-Miezah said he was: wealthy industrialists with stolen money and Swiss bankers at their beck and call. But none of them has been subject to a fraction of the scrutiny trained on President Nkrumah. Blay-Miezah was a very convenient distraction. It's one reason why so many governments were happy to let him be, and let him keep scamming. As much as Blay-Miezah was using them, they were also using him. In the end, it's impossible to tell who had the last laugh.

If Blay-Miezah were just a fast-talking con man with a great lie, his story would not matter as much as it does. But the story of Dr. John Ackah Blay-Miezah is not just a story about a con man. It is a story about how the world works: about how lies change history, and about how so much of today's world is built on lies. Blay-Miezah matters because he was not the exception—he was the rule.

RIGHT NOW, SOMEWHERE in the world, someone is telling Blay-Miezah's lie about Nkrumah's gold, and someone is investing in it.

Ever since Blay-Miezah's death, people have kept telling his story. Mostly, they have done it to keep running his con, to extract more money from people who had already invested in the Oman Ghana Trust Fund, or to ensnare entirely new investors.

These con men carried on in much the same way as Blay-Miezah himself had. They said that they were raising money to recover the Trust Fund. Soon after Blay-Miezah's death, one of the investors, Gregory Frazier of Detroit, Michigan, bought a one-way ticket to Accra. Frazier said that Blay-Miezah had passed on the secret of Nkrumah's gold to him, and to him alone. He announced that he had formed the Friends of the Oman Ghana Trust Fund, and spent years trying to convince successive Ghanaian governments to help him claim the money.

For a while, Frazier was constantly on television, telling the story of the Trust Fund, which he said was started by President Nkrumah and W. E. B. Du Bois. "To use an analogy—these great men went out late at night, they took a gigantic mango seed, and planted it. They covered it up, they protected it so no one could see it while it got bigger and bigger," Frazier said in an interview. The Trust Fund was worth hundreds of billions of dollars now, he said. "Our external debt would be a peanut."

In 2009, the Friends of the Oman Ghana Trust Fund successfully petitioned the government of President John Atta Mills to look into the Trust Fund. A commission led by the president's brother, Cadman Mills, was formed to investigate it. This led to "a group of Americans" sending "a warning to the delegation, reminding them that they are the owners of the fund." They were not. The commission found no evidence that the Trust Fund existed. That didn't stop people asking the next government, and the next.

For a few years, Kobla Asamani was the spokesman for the Friends of the Oman Ghana Trust Fund. One evening, not too long ago, Asamani sat on the veranda in the lush grounds of a boarding school in Accra's industrial area. The school was an oasis of green amid a tangle of factories and smoke-stacks and paint wholesalers.

"The task of retrieving the money was originally given to John Ackah Blay-Miezah," Asamani said. "But he got corrupt, he conned people, he tarnished the whole process. Greg Frazier knew him personally, and was at his deathbed, and Blay-Miezah passed the secret on to him. And at the appointed time he will retrieve the money." Then slowly, hesitantly, as if he were trying to remember words that he had been told a long time ago, Asamani began to tell the story of Kwame Nkrumah and the Oman Ghana Trust Fund.

EVENTUALLY MOST OF the investors realized that not only were Nkrumah's billions not coming, but they also wouldn't be getting their money back. Others, though, never lost faith in the story.

E. D. M. Stephens, Blay-Miezah's former minder, retired from the police force and built a hotel in Tema. In a move that Blay-Miezah would have approved of, every room has a small kitchen. Stephens works out of a huge office, decorated with vacation photos from all over the world and pictures of his children and grandchildren. In one corner of his office, in front of a small globe, is a photograph of a smiling, boyish Blay-Miezah, framed in gold.

Some of the investors, even the ones who have long since stopped pouring money in, still believe. Ben Bynum's club defined Philadelphia nightlife for a generation. Well into his nineties, he could be found working the room at his sons' restaurants. Until he died, Bynum senior got calls from con men, asking for money for the Oman Ghana Trust Fund. Every time Bynum's family saw him whispering into a phone from his hospital bed, still wrapped up in Blay-Miezah's story, their hearts broke a little. Bynum's sons now run one of the city's iconic restaurant groups. Their restaurants have some of

A photograph of Blay-Miezah kept in the office of E. D. M. Stephens.

Philadelphia's best live music—inspired, in part, by the time one of the younger Bynums spent working in West Africa.

Peter Rigby is still a firm believer. He has lived in the same flat since his days with the Oman Ghana Trust Fund, when it seemed like everyone who passed through London stayed there. Until he died, Ben Hayford, the manager of the Trust Fund's London office, would stay with Rigby when he was in London. (Hayford and his family once had a home in London. But then he went to work for Blay-Miezah—and because Blay-Miezah never paid him the salary he promised, Hayford lost the home. He was estranged from his family for decades.) He and Rigby were like brothers, Hayford said. He didn't like talking about the time he spent with Blay-Miezah. Rigby still has the promissory note Blay-Miezah gave him. He knows that it's not really worth anything, but he's adamant that Blay-Miezah failed simply because the time wasn't right. The money is still out there, he said, and sometime in the future, Ghanaians will discover this.

Blay-Miezah constructed a beautiful lie that gave everyone what they wanted. He told Rigby that the Oman Ghana Trust Fund went back further than Nkrumah, back to Ghana's colonial days. Unthinkable quantities of gold had been taken from Ghana by the British. But they hadn't stolen it, just kept it safe, as a bond to be returned at independence. (In reality, the British never intended to return the wealth or the land that they stole, and still hold on to plenty of both.) Of course, the bit of the

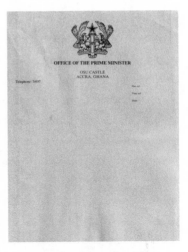

Letterhead found in Blay-Miezah's files by Peter Rigby.

beautiful lie that really pulled Rigby in was that he was going to be very, very rich: he was going to start a television network, help build a country, and make a fortune.

After Blay-Miezah left for Ghana for the last time, Rigby closed up the house in St. John's Wood and the office in Piccadilly. As he packed up brochures and documents, he found a single sheet of heavy bond paper embossed with the seal of the Office of the Prime Minister, Osu Castle. At the very top was Ghana's crest. Underneath was a five-digit phone number—just like on the deed for the Oman Ghana Trust Fund. Otherwise, the sheet of paper was blank, but dusty and smudged, as if it had been used several times.

ONE THING THAT Blay-Miezah said, back in Philadelphia in 1972, was true. Ghana is a young country. Countless kingdoms were destroyed by colonial wars and never rebuilt. British contributions to the country's infrastructure were insignificant. At independence, Accra, despite being the capital, had no real government buildings, just a wood-and-zinc town hall. For years after independence, this would be Ghana's first House of Parliament. In other countries, and in India in particular, the British built thousands of miles of railways, palatial government buildings, and cities that were meant to last forever. In Ghana they built almost nothing. The country was just a colossal mine to be hollowed out. When Takoradi Harbor was finally built in 1928, that modest-sized port was the biggest investment that the British made in an African colony in the entire decade.

After independence, almost everything had to be built or remade, including the story of Ghana itself. Since then, Ghana has been a land in search of its stories. And in Anansi's country, there is always someone ready to tell you a story.

The Oman Ghana Trust Fund lives on because, like the stories Anansi told—like all myths—it explains the world. For generations, people have wondered how a resource-rich country like Ghana could be so poor. The real answer—that for centuries it was a mine that other countries used to get rich—is abstract and hard to look straight at. Because if your country is just a colossal mine, what are you?

Blay-Miezah, and the people who enabled him, desecrated the story of a brand-new country for the sake of a few dollars. What happened to Ghana? Blay-Miezah had an easy answer: the man who founded the country hid its wealth away. Blay-Miezah also had a solution: trust him, and he would get Ghana's gold back, and kick something your way in the process. You could save the world and get rich along the way. Who would say no to that?

SOURCES AND REFERENCES

History is a fragile thing. Ghana's history is especially fragile, because so many people have worked hard to keep it that way. Massive personal archives have disappeared abroad. Even President Nkrumah's papers are held not in Ghana but in Washington, D.C., in a basement at Howard University. The archive is made up of papers donated from London by Nkrumah's former editor, and material gathered by a Howard student who moved to Accra to track down archives from the Nkrumah era.

Since I first heard the story of the Oman Ghana Trust Fund, I've been looking for sources: biographies of Acheampong and Rawlings, a book written by Nkrumah's secretary, a book written by a former CIA agent who claims to have evidence that the agency helped remove Nkrumah from power. Some of these sources simply don't exist: there are no authoritative biographies of Rawlings or Acheampong. Even the full report of Ghana's National Reconciliation Commission is difficult to find and has been removed from the government website. The rest of the books are out of print or almost impossible to get hold of outside of a few libraries. Much of an entire nation's rich history is almost out of reach.

The same is true of official records. Every single coup d'état in Ghana brought with it incredible destruction. Government ministries were ransacked and massive fires destroyed huge amounts of records. Archives at the original Ministry of Foreign Affairs building and the headquarters of the Ghana Broadcasting Corporation both went up in flames. After Nkrumah's death, the papers he left in Guinea were packed into boxes and stored. Then there was a coup in Conakry. Some boxes were destroyed, some were left to sit in

The office of President Nkrumah, ransacked during the first coup.

rainwater or became infested with mice and insects. In Accra, offices of numerous leaders have burned down or been ransacked.

Innumerable documents have been destroyed, by accident or on purpose. People tried very hard—and are still trying very hard—to cover up the less-than-honorable parts of their involvement in Ghana's recent history. Books go out of print or go missing entirely. Pages are torn out. Magazines go missing from folios. Documents are scrubbed from the internet. Many seem to be under the impression that facts, just like people, can be disappeared.

So when Blay-Miezah turned up with his story about Nkrumah's secret fortune, there was no way to verify his claims, but there was also no way to disprove them. That was not an accident. It was business as usual.

Ghana's history is manipulated in other ways too. In 1992, six people were charged with kidnapping and murdering the three High Court judges who were abducted in 1982. They were found guilty. The trial was briefly mentioned in a report by the *Independent* newspaper in London. Soon after, Captain Tsikata hired a prominent London law firm and filed defamation proceedings against the newspaper. The *Independent* eventually issued a correction to their article, apologizing for implicating Tsikata in the murders. To this day, if you try to google the assassinations, the most credible-looking result is that correction.

Years later, British intelligence were investigating the journalist Victoria Brittain, who had written a flattering *Guardian* profile of Tsikata in 1982. Large, unexplained sums of money were passing through her bank account. It turned out that Britain had funneled £250,000 from Libyan intelligence officers to London to pay for Tsikata's legal action against the *Independent*. Tsikata was doing what he did best: rewriting history.

While I was researching this book, many people who were part of it died. Each one took part of the story of Blay-Miezah with them. Claude Lewis, the pioneering Philadelphia journalist who spent years trying to put Blay-Miezah out of business, died soon after I tried to get a message to him. Jewel Ackah, the leader of the band Blay-Miezah flew out to London, and June Milne, Kwame Nkrumah's literary editor, soon after. Jerry Rawlings and Kojo Tsikata, before the victims of their rule could hold them accountable. Countless other figures, including Greg Frazier, Ben Hayford, Ben Bynum, and Kwesi Botchwey. Early on in my research, I got a text from Peter Rigby: "You've got to be quick Yeppi," he wrote. "We are all getting old and closer to oblivion."

History survives. Memories of this period—and the story of the Oman Ghana Trust Fund—live on, in unpublished memoirs, in family archives, in out-of-print books, in declassified reports, in heaps of photographs in grandparents' homes, in half-remembered stories and in notes scrawled on yellow legal pads. It takes much longer to disprove a lie than it does to tell it. Yet Ghana's history has been preserved, thanks to countless people devoting their lives to passing on knowledge of it, even in the most impossible circumstances—so that maybe the next time a fast-talking con artist turns up with a story about Ghana's past, fact can be sorted from fiction, and they can be stopped.

SELECTED BIBLIOGRAPHY

Accilien, Cécile, Jessica Adams, and Elmide Méléance. *Revolutionary Freedoms: A History of Survival, Strength, and Imagination in Haiti.* Coconut Creek, FL: Caribbean Studies Press, 2006.

Acheampong, I. K. *The Fifth Milestone: 13th January 1976–12th January 1977.* Accra: Ghana Publishing Corporation, 1978.

——. *Speeches and Interviews by Col. I. K. Acheampong.* Accra: Ministry of Information, 1973.

Adjei, Mike. *Death and Pain in Rawlings' Ghana: The Inside Story.* London: Black Line, 1994.

Akyeampong, Emmanuel Kwaku, and Henry Louis Gates. *Dictionary of African Biography.* Oxford: Oxford University Press, 2012.

Allen, Tony, and Michael E. Veal. *Tony Allen: An Autobiography of the Master Drummer of Afrobeat.* Durham, NC: Duke University Press, 2013.

Appiah, Joe. *Autobiography of an African Patriot.* New York: Praeger, 1990.

Bennion, F. A. R. *The Constitutional Law of Ghana.* London: Butterworths, 1962.

Blay, J. Benibengor. *The Story of Tata.* Aboso, Ghana: Benibengor Book Agency, 1976.

Botchwey, Kwesi, and Commonwealth Expert Group on Good Governance and the Elimination of Corruption. *Fighting Corruption, Promoting Good Governance.* London: Commonwealth Secretariat, 2000.

Burton, Richard. *To the Gold Coast for Gold*. London: Chatto and Windus, 1878.

Buser, Hans. *In Ghana at Independence: Stories of a Swiss Salesman*. Basel: Basler Afrika Bibliographien, 2011.

Countryman, Matthew. *Up South: Civil Rights and Black Power in Philadelphia*. Philadelphia: University of Pennsylvania Press, 2007.

Ellis, Alfred Burton. *A History of the Gold Coast of West Africa*. London: Chapman and Hall, 1893.

Fager, Jeff. *Fifty Years of 60 Minutes: The Inside Story of Television's Most Influential News Broadcast*. New York: Simon and Schuster, 2017.

Festinger, Leon, Henry W. Riecken, and Stanley Schachter. *When Prophecy Fails: A Social and Psychological Study of a Modern Group That Predicted the Destruction of the World*. New York: Harper, 1956.

Herbst, Jeffrey. *The Politics of Reform in Ghana, 1982–1991*. Berkeley: University of California Press, 1993.

[Hydrographic Office, London]. *The African Pilot, or Sailing Directions for the Western Coast of Africa from Cape Spartel to the River Cameroons*. London: Hydrographic Office, 1856.

Jackman, Ian. *Con Men: Fascinating Profiles of Swindlers and Rogues from the Files of the Most Successful Broadcast in Television History*. New York: Simon & Schuster, 2003.

Kandeh, Jimmy. *Coups from Below: Armed Subalterns and State Power in West Africa*. New York: Macmillan, 2004.

Kelsey, Harry. *Sir Francis Drake: The Queen's Pirate*. New Haven, CT: Yale University Press, 1998.

Kojo Addae, S. *The Gold Coast and Achimota in the Second World War*. Accra: Sedco, 2004.

Konings, Piet. *The State and Rural Class Formation in Ghana*. London: Routledge, 1986.

Logan, Rayford W., and Michael R. Winston, eds. *Dictionary of American Negro Biography*. New York: W. W. Norton, 1982.

Marais, Genoveva. *Kwame Nkrumah as I Knew Him*. Chichester, UK: Janay, 1972.

Milne, June. *Kwame Nkrumah: A Biography*. London: Panaf, 1999.

[Ministry of Information, Ghana]. *Report of the Fisheries Division, Ghana*. Accra: Ministry of Information, 1961.

Nash, Jay Robert. *Hustlers and Con Men: An Anecdotal History of the Confidence Man and His Games*. New York: Evans, 1976.

Nkrumah, Kwame. *The Autobiography of Kwame Nkrumah*. Edinburgh: Thomas Nelson and Sons, 1957.

——. *Dark Days in Ghana*. London: Panaf, 1973.

Nugent, Paul. *Big Men, Small Boys, and Politics in Ghana: Power, Ideology, and the Burden of History, 1982–1994*. London: Pinter, 1995.

Owusu-Ansah, David. *Historical Dictionary of Ghana*. Lanham, MD: Rowman & Littlefield, 2014.

Powell, Erica. *Private Secretary (Female) / Gold Coast*. London: C. Hurst, 1984.

Quantson, Kofi Bentum. *Ghana: Peace and Stability. Chapters from the Intelligence Sector*. Accra: NAPASCOM, 2000.

Rake, Alan. *Who's Who in Africa: Leaders for the 1990s*. Metuchen, NJ: Scarecrow, 1992.

Ralet, Olivier. *Illegale wapenhandel*. Berchem, Belgium: EPO, 1982.

Rayner, Richard. *Drake's Fortune: The Fabulous True Story of the World's Greatest Confidence Artist*. New York: Doubleday, 2002.

[United States Congress]. *House Select Committee to Investigate Educational and Training Program under GI Bill*. Washington, D.C.: United States Government Printing Office, 1951.

Versi, Anver. *Guinness Presents: Football in Africa*. London: Longman, 1987.

Vieta, Kojo T. *The Flagbearers of Ghana*. Accra: Ena Publications, 1999.

Yankah, Kojo. *The Trial of JJ Rawlings: Echoes of the 31st December Revolution*. Hampton, VA: U.B. & U.S. Communication Systems, 1992.

Yeebo, Zaya. *Ghana: The Struggle for Popular Power*. London: New Beacon Books, 1991.

IMAGE CREDITS

INTERIOR IMAGES

p. 10   British Museum, Af1914,1013.1. Copyright the Trustees of the British Museum.

p. 15   "Flag of Newest Nation Unfurled at Independence Hall," *Philadelphia Evening Bulletin*, March 6, 1957. Getty Images/Bettmann, 515026214.

p. 30   Getty Images/Popperfoto, 114953929

p. 44   Topfoto, IPU469288

p. 103   "Chiefs Informed of Big Plans," *Ghanaian Times*, December 9, 1974

p. 112   "Oman Trust Experts at Project Site," *Ghanaian Times*, January 14, 1975

p. 115   *Ghanaian Times*, January 18, 1975

p. 142   ANL/Shutterstock, 1351631a

PLATE SECTION

James Barnor, one of the greatest photographers of the twentieth century, opened his Ever Young photography studio in Accra in 1953 and has chronicled seven decades of Ghanaian history. Images from his archive are reproduced with his kind permission, and that of Galerie Clémentine de la Féronnière, Paris.

Page Two:

—Kwame Nkrumah: Courtesy Galerie Clémentine de la Féronnière.
  © James Barnor.

—E. T. Mensah and His Tempos Band: Courtesy Galerie Clémentine de la
  Féronnière. © James Barnor.

—President Kwame Nkrumah: Getty Images/Underwood Archives

Page Three:

—Ghana's head of state: Getty Images/Ullstein Bild

—A fallen statue: Getty Images/Bettmann Archive

—Party at Quentin Quartey's house: Courtesy Galerie Clémentine de la Féronnière.
  © James Barnor.

Page Four:

—Two friends: Courtesy Galerie Clémentine de la Féronnière. © James Barnor.

—Blay-Miezah on the front page: The *Ghanaian Times*.

Page Five:

—Courtesy Galerie Clémentine de la Féronnière. © James Barnor.

Page Six:

—Portrait of a woman: Courtesy Galerie Clémentine de la Féronnière.
  © James Barnor.

—Military leader Jerry John Rawlings: Getty Images/Popperfoto

—Burial of the soldiers: Courtesy Galerie Clémentine de la Féronnière.
  © James Barnor.

Page Seven:

—A swarm of soldiers: Getty Images/Jérome Chatin

Page Eight:

—A staff: Getty Images/Universal History Archive

NOTES

CHAPTER 1: OUR MAN

2   "a good home to live in": John Ackah Blay-Miezah, tape recording, June 17, 1989, private collection.

3   Blay-Miezah looked good: Kwesi Pratt Jnr, "Saboteurs Can't Stop Me," *Ghanaian Times*, December 20, 1974.

3   At the time, he had been commander: United States, Central Intelligence Agency, *Daily Report, Foreign Radio Broadcasts*, 1–10, January 3, 1972, 1.

3   "We have told those": I. K. Acheampong, *Speeches and Interviews by Col. I. K. Acheampong* (Accra: Ministry of Information, 1973), 1:36.

4   stories about the mysterious fortune: Office of the National Redemption Council, "Statement on John Ackah Blay-Miezah and the Oman Ghana Trust Fund," news release, February 19, 1975.

4   "back from Britain": *Daily Graphic*, April 29, 1978.

4   Her controversial appointment: Charles G. Hurst, "Shirley Shuffling to Africa," *Chicago Defender*, August 29, 1974.

4   Temple Black pointed it out to him: "Ghana's Love Affair with Shirley Temple Black," *Ebony*, March 1976, 114.

5   "Those who believe": U.S. Embassy Accra to Department of State, Washington, D.C., cable, 1975ACCRA00017, January 2, 1975, U.S. National Archives.

CHAPTER 2: KEROSENE BOY

8   They named him: Eulogy for John Ackah Blay-Miezah, video, private collection.

8   basks of Nile crocodiles: Matthew H. Shirley, William Oduro, and Hilaire Yaokokore Beibro, "Conservation Status of Crocodiles in Ghana and Côte-D'Ivoire, West Africa," *Oryx* 43, no. 1 (2009): 136–45.

8 If it rained hard enough: Fable, from my maternal grandmother.

8 never more than two canoes: Fisheries Division, Ministry of Information, *Report of the Fisheries Division, Ghana* (Accra: Ministry of Information, 1961), 30.

9 a ship called the *Great Apollo*: Richard Burton, *To the Gold Coast for Gold* (London: Chatto and Windus, 1878), 2:78; Alfred Burton Ellis, *A History of the Gold Coast of West Africa* (London: Chapman and Hall, 1893), 77.

9 the mightiest rulers: Pierluigi Valsecchi, "The Fall of Kaku Aka: Social and Political Change in the Mid-Nineteenth-Century Western Gold Coast," *Journal of West African History* 2, no. 1 (Spring 2016): 5.

9 a gold cannon: *United Service Magazine* (London: H. Hurst, 1850), 224.

9 entirely independent: Valsecchi, "Kaku Aka," 5.

9 I will reward you with gold: David Owusu-Ansah, *Historical Dictionary of Ghana* (Lanham, MD: Rowman & Littlefield, 2014), 337.

9 entirely unemployable: National Archives (UK), CO 96/10.

9 "to his bearings": *United Service Magazine*, 57.

10 "the Governor": *United Service Magazine*, 224.

10 "The king's treasure": *United Service Magazine*, 225.

11 suspected that Swanzy had stolen gold dust: National Archives (UK), CO 96/15.

11 anarchy, violence, and plunder: Valsecchi, "Kaku Aka," 14.

11 "That call": John Ackah Blay-Miezah, tape recording, June 17, 1989, private collection.

12 There were so few homes: F. A. R. Bennion, *The Constitutional Law of Ghana* (London: Butterworths, 1962), 79–81.

12 John Kolorah Blay enrolled: Kofi Bentum Quantson, *Ghana: Peace and Stability; Chapters from the Intelligence Sector* (Accra: NAPASCOM, 2000), 276.

12 "wielded the cane": Quantson, *Ghana*, 277.

12 "he did the right thing": Quantson, *Ghana*, 276.

12 "Once to ev'ry man": James Russell Lowell, "Once to every man and nation" (1845).

13 "gifted in more senses": Eulogy for John Ackah Blay-Miezah, video, private collection.

14 "clients": Quantson, *Ghana*, 277.

14 the *African Glade* steamed past: New York State, Passenger and Crew Lists, 1917–1967, A4115—New York, 1958–1967, 538.

14 4037 Locust Street: *Philadelphia Inquirer*, June 17, 1959.

14 Rudolph von Ballmoos: *Philadelphia Inquirer*, June 23, 1963.

14 more African students enrolled: *Philadelphia Inquirer*, June 27, 1954.

14   von Ballmoos, dressed in Kente: Dominic Pasquarella, "Flag of Newest Nation Unfurled at Independence Hall," Temple University Libraries, Philadelphia, PA, March 6, 1957.

15   "All these African princes": Oliver St. Clair Franklin, interview with author, 2019.

15   "pointed up the problems facing": "African Students Show and Dance," *Philadelphia Tribune*, June 16, 1959, 8.

16   "The bride wore": "Ghana and Liberia Unite in Impressive Ceremony," *Philadelphia Tribune*, July 11, 1959, 8.

16   Blay worked as a busboy: Blay-Miezah, tape recording, June 17, 1989.

16   Blay was fired: Carol Saline, "Out of Africa," *Philadelphia*, October 1986, 103, 166–82.

CHAPTER 3: LEGENDS AND LIES

18   the exact date of his birth: Erica Powell, *Private Secretary (Female) / Gold Coast* (London: C. Hurst, 1984), 88.

18   The first was his grandmother's death: Kwame Nkrumah, *The Autobiography of Kwame Nkrumah* (Edinburgh: Thomas Nelson and Sons, 1957), xviii.

20   "To sleep under the stars": Nkrumah, *Autobiography*, 39.

20   "Poverty and need": Nkrumah, *Autobiography*, 40.

20   baptized hundreds of people: During his sermons, the congregation would be spellbound as Father Divine randomly intoned, again and again, "Tens, hundreds, thousands, ten thousands, hundred thousands, millions" (Rayford W. Logan and Michael R. Winston, eds., *Dictionary of American Negro Biography* [New York: W. W. Norton, 1982], 179).

21   Nkrumah preached: Nkrumah, *Autobiography*, 41.

21   "A mist covered my eyes": Nkrumah, *Autobiography*, 48.

21   George Padmore picked him up: Joe Appiah, *Autobiography of an African Patriot* (New York: Praeger, 1990), 163.

22   cafés in Camden Town: Nkrumah, *Autobiography*, 60.

22   walking around London: Nkrumah, *Autobiography*, 55.

22   "the determination of colonial peoples": Nkrumah, *Autobiography*, 53.

22   "We went and reported": Appiah, *Autobiography*, 167.

22   Ako-Adjei studied at Columbia: Kojo T. Vieta, *The Flagbearers of Ghana* (Accra: Ena Publications, 1999), 57.

23   The authorities seemed thrilled: Nkrumah, *Autobiography*, 63.

23   He shook Nkrumah's hand: Nkrumah, *Autobiography*, 66.

24   "They defended": Ashley Jackson, *The British Empire* (Oxford: Oxford University Press, 2013), 171.

24 "underpaid": Adrienne M. Israel, "Measuring the War Experience: Ghanaian Soldiers in World War II," *Journal of Modern African Studies* 25, no. 1 (1987): 162.

24 "looked like hell": Israel, "Measuring the War," 163.

24 "We didn't like": Israel, "Measuring the War," 160.

25 The British had to move: Nkrumah, *Autobiography*, 79–83.

25 communist incitement: *Hansard*, HC Deb 01 March 1948, vol. 448, cc. 37–9.

25 "by fire": Richard Rathbone, "Police Intelligence in Ghana in the Late 1940s and 1950s," *Journal of Imperial and Commonwealth History* 21, no. 3 (1993): 110.

25 "At this period": Nkrumah, *Autobiography*, 120.

25 "I was too bewildered": Nkrumah, *Autobiography*, 135.

26 kept him fed: Nkrumah, *Autobiography*, 161.

26 "Nkrumah appeared at her home": "Nkrumah is a 'Doer' not a 'Talker,'" *Jet*, July 31, 1958.

26 Nkrumah thought about: Nkrumah, *Autobiography*, 159.

CHAPTER 4: ONE BIG COCKTAIL PARTY

27 Special Branch kept twenty-eight out of the thirty-seven: Rathbone, "Police Intelligence," 120.

27 "two whole pages": National Archives (UK), KV 2/1851.

27 "At long last": "Kwame Nkrumah—Independence Speech," Accra, March 6, 1957, https://www.youtube.com/watch?v=xf5CPacHt4Q.

28 "Nkrumah saw to it": June Milne, "Kwame Nkrumah: Life after the Coup and the Conakry Period," *New Directions* 14, no. 4 (1987): 38–40.

28 "I was alone": Genoveva Marais, *Kwame Nkrumah As I Knew Him* (Chichester, UK: Janay, 1972), 4.

28 "I am used to big cars": Hans Buser, *In Ghana at Independence: Stories of a Swiss Salesman* (Basel: Basler Afrika Bibliographien, 2011), 12–13.

29 "took care of Africa": Cameron Duodu, "Frantz Fanon," *Pambazuka News*, December 5, 2011.

29 "Stone tells me in confidence": National Archives (UK), DO 35/9426.

30 "I would like to go": "Celebration of the Life of the Late Madam Fathia Nkrumah," privately printed, private collection.

31 almost everybody she encountered: Powell, *Private Secretary*, 134.

32 "One of Chicago's most spectacular welcomes": *Chicago Defender*, July 31, 1958.

32 "Others stood as if stunned": Powell, *Private Secretary*, 135–36.

32 "should not be kept away": *Chicago Defender*, July 30, 1958.

32 Britain siphoned off: "Ghana's Flag Flies in Place of Union Jack," *Daily Telegraph*, March 6, 1957.

33 The British had mismanaged Ghana's funds: National Archives (UK), DO 35/9427.

33 "hard to refute": National Archives (UK), T 236/6604.

34 "Nothing new has come out": National Archives (UK), DO 35/9427.

34 "lacked competence": National Archives, UK, CAB 129/198/12.

34 "squandered by the United Kingdom": National Archives (UK), T 236/6604.

35 "Those who would judge us": Kwame Nkrumah, *Dark Days in Ghana* (London: Panaf, 1973), 76.

35 "discussing Africa's untapped wealth": Malcolm X and Alex Haley, *The Autobiography of Malcolm X* (New York: Ballantine Books, 1973), 358.

36 he had led the group of young rebels: Nkrumah, *Autobiography*, 79–83.

36 "Edusei was, for all these reasons": Marais, *Nkrumah*, 106.

36 "When I receive my salary": "Ghana: Talking Back," *TIME*, May 5, 1961.

36 "Krobo used to say": Marais, *Nkrumah*, 106.

36 "imprison, without trial": "Mr Edusei Seeks New Powers," *Guardian*, December 12, 1957.

36 "I love power": "Ghana Aide Vows to Jail Political Foes," *Washington Post*, September 28, 1957.

36 "King, life is great!": Powell, *Private Secretary*, 173–74.

37 Savundra appeared in Ghana: Richard Davenport-Hines, "Savundra, Emil [formerly Marion Emil Anacletus Pierre Savundranayagam] (1923–1976), Swindler," *Oxford Dictionary of National Biography*, September 23, 2004.

37 "Joe Appiah used to watch": Cameron Duodu, "Farewell to the 'Zulu Queen,'" *New African*, April 4, 2006, 44.

37 sent to Nsawam Prison: Cameron Duodu, "How I Wish Krobo Edusei Was Alive," *Daily Guide*, July 11, 2015, https://www.modernghana.com/news/629034 /how-i-wish-krobo-edusei-was-alive.html.

37 pictured in the society pages: Buser, *In Ghana*, 72.

37 "Every wife will know how I feel": "Ain't Ghana Give Up 8G Bed Despite Uproar," *Philadelphia Daily News*, March 31, 1962.

38 Nkrumah signed an order: "August 1, 1962: Nkrumah Is Injured by an Attempt on His Life from a Bomb in Kulungugu," Edward A. Ulzen Memorial Foundation, August 1, 2017, https://www.eaumf.org/ejm-blog/2017/8/1/august-1st-1962 -nkrumah-is-injured-by-an-attempt-on-his-life-from-a-bomb-in-kulungugu.

39 "My hatred for the regime": Appiah, *Autobiography*, 271.

CHAPTER 5: CROOKS AND HEROES

40 sent John Kolorah Blay to Nsawam Prison: "Blay-Miezah Was Detained in 1963," *Daily Graphic*, March 10, 1979.

41 Blay and Nkrumah never met: Blay-Miezah, tape recording, June 17, 1989.

41 "Intensive efforts": Susan Williams, *White Malice* (New York: Hurst, 2019), 489.

41 "Kingsway stores, their U.T.C.": "Outside Financial Control Strangled Ghana's Economy," *Gazette and Daily* (York, PA), March 18, 1966.

41 "the careless expenditure policy": Politisches Archiv des Auswärtiges Amt, PA AA B34 572, Schaad to Foreign Office, January 22, 1965.

41 Behind the scenes: Matteo E. Landricina, "From 'Our Experiment' to the 'Prisoner of the West': Ghana's Relations with Great Britain, the United States of America and West Germany during Kwame Nkrumah's Government (1957–1966)" (PhD diss., Universita Degli Studi Di Roma Tre, 2016), 276.

41 With the help of Krobo Edusei: Buser, *In Ghana*, 55.

41 "a flour mill": Kenneth L. Whiting, "Smart Operators Making Money in Ghana," Associated Press, September 12, 1965.

42 celebrated by German diplomats: Politisches Archiv des Auswärtiges Amt, PAAA B34 487, Steltzer to Foreign Office, September 2, 1964.

42 Amoako-Atta realized: Charles Torkornoo, "Vanguard's Man for Presidency," *Daily Graphic*, April 24, 1979.

42 sat in silence for fifteen minutes: Baffour Ankomah, "Mugabe—Beware Corruption," *New African*, April 1989, 41.

43 "All in all, looks good": Johnson Library, National Security File, Memos to the President, Robert W. Komer, vol. 21, 3/3/66–3/20/66, confidential. A handwritten *L* on the source text indicates that the memorandum was seen by the president.

43 imprisoned after being accused of involvement: *National Reconciliation Commission*, Ghana, October 2004, vol. 4, chap. 2, 2.5.5.

43 sat by her bedside: "Nkrumah Wept by My Bedside—Kulungugu Bombing Victim," *Daily Graphic*, April 16, 2015.

44 "the springs burst": Maya Angelou, *All God's Children Need Travelling Shoes* (London: Little, Brown, 2013), 86.

44 "locked up at Nsawam Prison": Commission of Enquiry into Ghana Prisons, and J. B. Danquah, *Dr. J.B. Danquah: Detention and Death in Nsawam Prison: Extracts from Evidence of Witnesses at the Commission of Enquiry into Ghana Prisons* (Accra: Ministry of Information, 1967), 111.

45 "Joe, Ghana is in pieces": Appiah, *Autobiography*, 253.

45 "Freedom for Africa Movement": National Archives (UK), FO 1110/2342.

45 "the straw that broke": Williams, *White Malice*, 491, 493.

45 "The plotters are keeping us briefed": Johnson Library, National Security File.

45 raiding the Chinese embassy in blackface: Seymour Hersh, "C.I.A. Said to Have Aided Plotters Who Overthrew Nkrumah in Ghana," *New York Times*, May 9, 1978.

46 "seemed fearless": "Celebration of the Life of the Late Madam Fathia Nkrumah."

46 "brutally shot": Nkrumah, *Dark Days*, 26–27.

46 "At Flagstaff House": Nkrumah, *Dark Days*, 25.

46 The home where Nkrumah had been born: Powell, *Private Secretary*, 221.

46 "When I was released": "Nkrumah's Mother Awaits Return of Son's Body," *New York Times*, July 5, 1972.

46 "into an ear-splitting grin": Williams, *White Malice*, 495.

46 "made no attempt to cover up": "Reason for Africa's Coups—To Preserve Financial Colonialism," *York Daily Record* (York, PA), July 11, 1966.

47 "almost pathetically pro-Western": Johnson Library, National Security File.

47 "Foreign multinationals": Williams, *White Malice*, 496.

47 "It may come as a shock": "Market Manipulation and Political Power in Ghana," *Gazette and Daily* (York, PA), November 14, 1966.

47 "on the brink of national bankruptcy": "Nkrumah's Ideas of Finance," *Tampa Tribune*, February 28, 1966.

48 bring home the fortune: "Nkrumah Wealth Reported by Aide," *New York Times*, March 4, 1966.

48 "accepted a bribe": *Guardian*, March 30, 1966.

48 "gold plated Cadillacs": John Yost, "U.S. Governor Transforms Samoa," *Capital Times* (Madison, WI), April 19, 1966.

48 "Nkrumah is estimated": "Ghana's Government Nabs Nkrumah's Loot," *Arizona Republic* (Phoenix), March 11, 1966; *Daily Independent Journal* (San Rafael, CA), April 22, 1966.

48 "would not take a bribe": National Archives (UK), DO 35/9427.6.

48 "24-hour campaign against Nkrumah": Charles P. Howard, "A Seaman Reports," *Gazette and Daily* (York, PA), June 26, 1968.

49 "shut up and was given books": "Nkrumah Wealth Reported by Aide."

49 Nkrumah actually had $132 million: "Charge Nkrumah Has $132 Million in Holdings," *Jet*, May 5, 1966, 21.

49 "Asked if Dr. Nkrumah were corrupt": *Daily Telegraph*, March 30, 1966.

49 "had conveyed 13 boxes containing gold bars": *Africa Report* 11, no. 5 (May 1, 1966): 29.

49 "maintained a villa": "Nkrumah Wealth Reported by Aide."

50 the Thunderbird was bought for her: *Life*, March 18, 1966.

50 "I am an international man": National Archives (UK), T 236/6604.

51 his story changed: Daily Report, Foreign Radio Broadcasts, United States Central Intelligence Agency, May 16, 1966.

51 why the president would need a trustee: Daily Report, Foreign Radio Broadcasts, United States Central Intelligence Agency, January 17, 1967.

51 in Ayeh-Kumi's own name: Daily Report, Foreign Radio Broadcasts, United States Central Intelligence Agency, May 16, 1966.

51   "uncalled for and unjustified": *West Africa*, issues 3242–3258 (1979): 1796.

52   "built on two levels": Milne, "Kwame Nkrumah."

52   "These visitors, freedom fighters": Nkrumah, *Dark Days*, 173.

52   "United States and Caribbean Black Power advocates": National Archives (UK), FCO 168/4280.

52   tinned sardines: Ama Biney, "The Development of Kwame Nkrumah's Political Thought in Exile, 1966–1972," *Journal of African History* 50, no. 1 (2009): 81–100.

52   "feared that they might be hijacked": Williams, *White Malice*, 499.

CHAPTER 6: THREE HOTELS

54   The government built it: *Sunday Mirror*, August 6, 1967.

54   chalets on the grounds: *Ghana Year Book*, *Daily Graphic*, 1966.

54   "fastest gentleman smoker": "Miss 'Star' Contest Tonight," *Daily Graphic*, June 28, 1969.

54   "Ghana was really swinging": Tony Allen and Michael E. Veal, *Tony Allen: An Autobiography of the Master Drummer of Afrobeat* (Durham, NC: Duke University Press Books, 2013), 59–60.

55   Quantson looked up from his beer: Quantson, *Ghana*, 277–78.

55   "because he liked him": Afua Serwah-Berkoh, "C 43,000 Wasn't Meant for a Bribe," *Daily Graphic*, March 24, 1979.

55   an executive with the African Development Bank: Quantson, *Ghana*, 278.

57   His uncle offered him the same salary: Quantson, *Ghana*, 88–89.

57   "What a question!": Quantson, *Ghana*, 279.

58   he miraculously disappeared: Pratt Jnr, "Saboteurs Can't Stop Me."

58   Blay had gone in: Kwesi Pratt Jnr, interview with author, 2018.

58   he said that he was the eldest son: "Witness: Kolorah Blay Said He Was a Graduate," *Daily Graphic*, March 2, 1979.

59   he planned to teach: Afua Serwah-Berkoh, "I Never Attended Varsity—Blay-Miezah," *Daily Graphic*, March 16, 1979.

59   gave the hotel manager his card: "Witness: Kolorah Blay Said He Was a Graduate."

59   a white modernist pile: "Ducor InterContinental Hotel Monrovia, Liberia (1962–1985)," InterContinental Hotel Corporation Digital Archives via The Neal Prince Trust, accessed June 9, 2020, https://nealprince-asid.com/id632.html.

60   a curious papaya pie: Rare Book Division, The New York Public Library, "Menu for a Dinner in Honour of the International Association of University Presidents, Ducor Intercontinental Hotel," New York Public Library Digital

Collections, accessed June 9, 2020, https://digitalcollections.nypl.org/items/ae2 f51ec-c00a-66c6-e040-e00a18066cf3.

60   frequently dined with him: "Witness: Kolorah Blay Said He Was a Graduate."

60   left Bergdorf Goodman: Steven Burbank, interview with author, 2017.

61   Philadelphia would lose 140,000 jobs: "Philadelphia Suffers in Manufacturing Jobs Exodus," *New York Times*, August 15, 1981.

61   The doctor also presented a letter: Saline, "Out of Africa."

62   He was said to be selling gold: Clark White, interview with author, 2018.

62   B.S.: "Bellevue-Stratford Hotel," Restaurant Ware Collectors Network IDwiki, May 18, 2020, https://rwcn-idwiki-2.restaurantwarecollectors.com/content/bell evue-stratford-hotel-2/.

63   there was no Ghanaian diplomat: "'Diplomatic Aide' Convicted in Hotel Fraud," *Philadelphia Evening Bulletin*, March 15, 1972.

CHAPTER 7: THE CREW

64   "defrauding an innkeeper": Act of June 12, 1913 (P.L.481, No.318), now repealed, titled "An act relating to inns and hotels; regulating certain rights and liabilities of hotelkeepers and innkeepers; and providing penalties for fraud against innkeepers and hotelkeepers."

64   "There has only been an adventure": "Overthrown Prime Minister Busia of Ghana Interviewed in London," AP Archive, January 13, 1972, https://www .youtube.com/watch?v=-n4ylDLuMdg.

64   frozen their assets: "Ex-Chief's Assets Frozen by Accra," *New York Times*, January 17, 1972.

66   "He's full of lies": Peter H. Binzen, "'Full of Lies'? Man of 'Integrity'? Or, Per his Lawyer, 'An Enigma'?" *Philadelphia Evening Bulletin*, November 1, 1973.

67   forced haircuts: Pamela Haynes, "Graterford Warden Is Sued by Inmates for 'Cruelty,'" *Philadelphia Tribune*, March 9, 1971.

67   the "glass cage": Dominick Codispott, "Imprisoned Citizens Union Started by Starving Prisoner in Solitary," *Philadelphia Tribune*, September 2, 1972.

67   Some tried protesting: "Inmates Save Lives during Disturbance at Graterford," *Philadelphia Tribune*, November 28, 1972.

67   started a union: Codispott, "Imprisoned Citizens Union."

67   "is it a crime of the first magnitude": *Philadelphia Tribune*, September 21, 1971.

67   "this man cannot distinguish reality": Saline, "Out of Africa."

67   sleeping beside Nkrumah's bed: June Milne, *Kwame Nkrumah: A Biography* (London: Panaf, 1999), 259.

67   "For two long days": "Celebration of the Life of the Late Madam Fathia Nkrumah."

68 flew President Nkrumah home: Appiah, *Autobiography*, 294.

68 "for the acquisition of wealth": Appiah, *Autobiography*, 322.

68 would not believe that her son was dead: "Celebration of the Life of the Late Madam Fathia Nkrumah."

68 "Many Philadelphians will remember": "Nkrumah Was a Great Builder of a New Africa," *Philadelphia Tribune*, May 2, 1972.

68 "the Malcolm X of the Episcopal Church": "Cab Heist Leaves Scholar Paralyzed," *Times Leader* (Wilkes-Barre, PA), December 28, 1995.

68 "marched with the Reverend Dr. Martin Luther King Jr.": "Obituary, Rev. James Woodruff," *Philadelphia Inquirer*, February 5, 2002.

69 "hate whitey": George Ingram, "Activist Priest Takes Rights Post," *Philadelphia Inquirer*, January 17, 1968, 9.

69 "persecuted, abandoned": "Cab Heist Leaves Scholar Paralyzed."

69 "a hateful and infidel pestilence": Anonymous, *Pastoral Letter from the Bishops of the Protestant Episcopal Church* (Augusta, GA, 1862), 12.

69 "confrontations with white people": Willard S. Randall, "Gracie and Woodruff Shake Up Old Order," *Philadelphia Evening Bulletin*, September 3, 1969.

69 "The American Dream is a nightmare": "Minister Discusses Race Relations," *Star-Gazette* (Elmira, NY), February 27, 1970.

69 "like a breath of fresh air": Acel Moore, "Fr. Woodruff, the Priest who became a Cabdriver," *Philadelphia Inquirer*, December 21, 1995.

69 "Woodruff quickly won the trust": "Cab Heist Leaves Scholar Paralyzed."

69 dressed in a long liturgical robe: Randall, "Gracie and Woodruff Shake Up Old Order."

69 The bishop refused: "DeWitt Refuses to Fire Gracie and Woodruff, Episcopal Bishop Rejects Demand of Oreland Vestry," unattributed newspaper clipping, May 14, 1969, Temple University Archives.

70 would rather see an entire parish die out: Matthew Countryman, *Up South: Civil Rights and Black Power in Philadelphia* (Philadelphia: University of Pennsylvania Press, 2007), 267–70; Michael E. George, "The Black Manifesto and the Churches: The Struggle for Black Power and Reparations in Philadelphia" (MA thesis, Temple University, 2013), https://scholarshare.temple.edu/bitstream/handle/20.500.12613/1285/George_temple_0225M_11477.pdf

70 "life and love": "D'Ortona's Statements on the Cookman Church Controversy Ludicrous," *Philadelphia Tribune*, July 15, 1969.

70 "the Idi Amin of Pennsylvania": "Democrats Urged by Black Leaders to Scratch Philly," *Times-Argus* (Barre, VA), June 9, 1979.

70 "placing a telephone book on a suspect's head": Jack W. Germond, "Philly Mayor Frank Rizzo 'Seems to Be Fading,'" *Town Talk* (Alexandria, LA), August 24, 1977.

70 thrown out and stepped on: "D'Ortona's Statements on the Cookman Church Controversy Ludicrous."

70 "This is a house of God": "8 Ministers Jailed as Church Seizure Ends at Cookman," *Philadelphia Tribune*, July 12, 1969.

70 "Father Woodruff dropped out of sight": Acel Moore, "Urban Perspective Column," *Philadelphia Inquirer*, December 21, 1995.

71 Stevie Wonder was the best man: "Stevie Wonder Best Man at Wedding of Songwriter," *Jet*, August 24, 1972, 59.

71 He held rap sessions: "Comedian to Speak," *Morning Call* (Allentown, PA), April 7, 1972.

71 "Nkrumah and I were more than brothers": Binzen, "'Full of Lies'?"

72 "establish a tradition of black heroes": "Minister Discusses Race Relations," *Star-Gazette* (Elmira, NY), February 27, 1970.

72 "Where do you find our precious metals": Blay-Miezah, tape recording, June 17, 1989.

72 "fair and equal distribution": Gay Boyd, "Philadelphia Speaks on Racial Problems," *Lincoln Journal Star* (Lincoln, NE), April 24, 1971.

72 "You always had the feeling with Bob": Saline, "Out of Africa."

73 town houses in South Philadelphia: "Townhouses Frankly Aim for Profits," *Philadelphia Inquirer*, March 19, 1972.

73 $1.5 million: "Black-Owned Building Firm Makes It Big in 10 Months," *Philadelphia Inquirer*, March 12, 1972.

73 the most successful minority-owned company: "Industrial Dynamics: Black Building and Land Development Firm Making It Big," *Black Business Digest*, 1971, 145–60.

73 they raised another $250,000: "Black-Owned Building Firm Makes It Big in 10 Months."

74 Bynum's first job: "Benjamin L. Bynum Sr.," *Tribute Archive*, accessed June 21, 2022, https://www.tributearchive.com/obituaries/22711623/benjamin-l-bynum-sr.

74 the Queen of Soul had her ears pierced: Gayle Ronan Sims, "Ruth Bynum, 80, Club Owner," *Philadelphia Inquirer*, July 6, 2005.

74 Blay-Miezah was out of prison: Binzen, "'Full of Lies'?"

75 none other than Emmanuel Ayeh-Kumi: Commonwealth of Pennsylvania, Department of State, Articles of Incorporation, Bureau of African Affairs and Industrial Development, Inc., 49406.

75 suite 455: *Philadelphia Tribune*, October 6, 1973.

75 seven hundred thousand tons of timber: "Area Firm to Import 700,000 Tons of Timber fron [*sic*] Ghana," *Philadelphia Tribune*, February 26, 1974.

75 promotional greeting cards: *Philadelphia Tribune*, October 6, 1973.

75   filed to copyright a notepaper folder: *Catalog of Copyright Entries: Third Series* (Washington, D.C.: Library of Congress, Copyright Office, 1974), 493.

75   "chief meeting site": Leslie James, *George Padmore and Decolonization from Below: Pan-Africanism, the Cold War, and the End of Empire* (New York: Palgrave Macmillan, 2014), 178.

75   sent out agents: Matteo Grilli, "Nkrumah, Nationalism, and Pan-Africanism: The Bureau of African Affairs Collection," *History in Africa*, January 30, 2017.

75   "assisting the State apparatus": Public Records and Archive Administration Department, RG/17/1/198 (ex SC/BAA/357), Barden to Nkrumah, May 20, 1964.

75   the Bureau of African Affairs was closed: James, *George Padmore*, 178.

76   "They thought I was telling lies": "African Businessman Has Status Cleared," *Philadelphia Tribune*, March 26, 1974.

76   his company had so many orders: Binzen, " 'Full of Lies'?"

76   The two were married: Marriage License Application, John Blay-Miezah and Jeannine West, April 18, 1973, Philadelphia County, Pennsylvania, A167478.

76   "I married him in April": Jeannine Blay-Miezah, interview with author, 2019.

76   "a close associate": "Local Firm Honors Memory of Kwame Nkrumah," *Philadelphia Tribune*, September 29, 1973.

77   distinctive tiki bar: Rachel Hildebrandt, "Dusting the Sand off of Philly's Tiki Heritage," *Hidden City*, May 21, 2014, https://hiddencityphila.org/2014/05 /phillys-tiki-heritage/.

77   The guests included: "Local Firm Honors Memory of Kwame Nkrumah," *Philadelphia Tribune*, September 29, 1973.

77   reportedly cost $1,200: Saline, "Out of Africa."

77   "Every day in New York": Blay-Miezah, tape recording, June 17, 1989.

78   "the mystery of Africa": Claude Lewis, "The Mystery Behind an Investment Scam," *Philadelphia Inquirer*, March 29, 1986.

CHAPTER 8: THE LONGEST CON

79   the king of Spain's treasure ships: Harry Kelsey, "Drake, Sir Francis (1540–1596), pirate, sea captain, and explorer," *Oxford Dictionary of National Biography* (Oxford: Oxford University Press, 2004).

79   put him on trial for witchcraft: Harry Kelsey, *Sir Francis Drake: The Queen's Pirate* (New Haven, CT: Yale University Press, 1998), 108–9.

80   making him a knight: Kelsey, "Drake, Sir Francis."

80   She brandished a sheaf of faded documents: Richard Rayner, *Drake's Fortune: The Fabulous True Story of the World's Greatest Confidence Artist* (New York: Doubleday, 2002), 37.

80   Iowa, Indiana, Missouri, Kentucky: Rayner, *Drake's Fortune*, 41.

80   tens of thousands of dollars: Rayner, *Drake's Fortune*, 45.

80   For $25, the Hartzells could buy a share: Rayner, *Drake's Fortune*, 38–39.

81   Hartzell caught up with the Drake scammers: Rayner, *Drake's Fortune*, 42–43.

81   a winning smile: Rayner, *Drake's Fortune*, 44.

81   "You took small pickings": Jay Robert Nash, *Hustlers and Con Men: An Anecdotal History of the Confidence Man and His Games* (New York: Evans, 1976), 79–80.

CHAPTER 9: GIRARD BANK

83   made some veiled threats: Department of State, Washington, D.C., to U.S. Embassy Accra, cable, 1974STATE041806, March 1, 1974, U.S. National Archives.

83   "several apparently fraudulent business transactions": Department of State, Washington, D.C., to U.S. Embassy Accra, cable, 1974STATE013766, January 22, 1974, U.S. National Archives.

84   "other influential Ghanaians": Department of State, Washington, D.C., to U.S. Embassy Accra, cable, 1974STATE041806.

84   He showed it to his investors: Department of State, Washington, D.C., to U.S. Embassy Accra, cable, 1974STATE041806.

84   This set off a scramble: Secretary of State, Washington, D.C., to U.S. Embassy Accra, cable, 1974STATE121107, June 7, 1974, U.S. National Archives.

84   Under the first deposit, they typed the date: Saline, "Out of Africa."

85   leaving his fingerprint: United States District Court, Eastern District of Pennsylvania, United States v. John Ackah Blay-Miezah and Gerald H. Smith, November 12, 1974, 74-660, complaint.

86   had enslaved people: Cécile Accilien, Jessica Adams, and Elmide Méléance, *Revolutionary Freedoms: A History of Survival, Strength, and Imagination in Haiti* (Coconut Creek, FL: Caribbean Studies Press, 2006), 126.

86   helped fund American raiders: Albert J. Gares, "Stephen Girard's West Indian Trade, 1789–1812," *Pennsylvania Magazine of History and Biography* 72, no. 4 (1948): 311–42.

86   "retaining all the valuables": "A Slave's Wealth," *Lewisburg Journal* (Lewisburg, PA), June 16, 1886, 4.

87   None of the other schools: *Jet*, May 20, 1965, 15.

87   Gerald Smith was arrested: William J. Storm, "Export Executive and Ex-Banker Indicted in Check Forging, Fraud," *Philadelphia Evening Bulletin*, October 9, 1974.

88   "could sell a Toyota to the president of General Motors": "Banker Gets a Year for Fraud," *Philadelphia Inquirer*, February 22, 1975.

CHAPTER 10: MULTI, MULTI, MULTI

90   He and Edusei knew: *Report of the Jiagge Commission Appointed under the Commissions of Enquiry Act, 1964 (Act 250) and N.L.C. (Investigation and Forfeiture of Assets) Decree 1966 (N.L.C.D. 72) to Enquire into the Assets of Specified Persons* (Ghana: Ministry of Information, 1969), 123.

90   slapdash and dragged-out: Piet Konings, *The State and Rural Class Formation in Ghana* (London: Routledge, 1986), ebook.

90   lent him several cars: Kwesi Pratt Jnr, interview with author, 2018.

91   promised them money: U.S. Embassy Accra to Department of State, Washington, D.C., cable, 1974ACCRA07033, December 18, 1974, U.S. National Archives.

91   "multi, multi, multi, multi, multimillionaire": Joseph Amamoo, interview with author, 2018.

91   he had been shielding the president: "Ghana Attaché Charges Nkrumah Misunderstood," *Baltimore Afro-American*, December 17, 1960.

92   one of the most popular diplomats: Ethel L. Payne, "A Portrait of an Aware Diplomat," *Chicago Defender*, October 10, 1970.

92   "others did not want to understand it": "Ghana Envoy Stresses Togetherness," *Baltimore Afro-American*, May 20, 1972.

92   "the authentic black power handshake": Payne, "Portrait of an Aware Diplomat."

92   compote Nsawam: "Ghana's Foreign Minister Honored," *Baltimore Afro-American*, October 17, 1970.

92   Washington's leading diplomat: *Jet*, January 21, 1971.

93   "Just put $150 million down": Blay-Miezah, tape recording, June 17, 1989.

93   "I am prepared to stick out my neck": "Is He Really a Crook?" *Ghanaian Times*, March 5, 1979.

93   looked like a legitimate businessman: Quantson, *Ghana*, 280.

94   Colonialism was about exploitation: Joshua Dwayne Settles, "The Impact of Colonialism on African Economic Development" (PhD diss., University of Tennessee, 1996), https://trace.tennessee.edu/utk_chanhonoproj/182.

94   "If African countries were permitted to industrialize": Charles P. Howard, "Reason for Africa's Coups," *York Daily Record* (York, PA), July 11, 1966.

95   Siaw named it Tata: J. Benibengor Blay, *The Story of Tata* (Aboso, Ghana: Benibengor Book Agency, 1976), 43.

95   forty thousand cartons of beer: Blay, *Story of Tata*, 20.

95   a thousand apartments: Blay, *Story of Tata*, 39.

95   Siaw invested: U.S. Embassy Accra to Department of State, Washington, D.C., cable, 1975ACCRA03020, May 13, 1975, U.S. National Archives.

96   "a truly qualified Black": Hurst, "Shirley Shuffling to Africa."

96 "fortitude, ingenuity and enterprising spirit": "U.S. Envoy at Makola," *Ghanaian Times*, January 9, 1975.

97 "bombarding [her] on this rotary phone": Gladys Blay-Hill, interview with author, 2018.

98 "is now considered a worthy citizen": Department of State, Washington, D.C., to U.S. Embassy Accra, cable, 1974STATE141433, June 29, 1974, U.S. National Archives.

98 transferring money from North Philadelphia to South Philadelphia: Secretary of State, Washington, D.C., to U.S. Embassy Accra, cable.

98 contacted the State Department: Department of State, Washington, D.C., to U.S. Embassy Accra, cable, 1974STATE141433.

99 "No luck to date": Secretary of State, Washington, D.C., to U.S. Embassy Accra, cable, 1974STATE121107.

99 Coppolino claimed: Secretary of State, Washington, D.C., to U.S. Embassy Accra, cable, 1974STATE121107.

99 went to Zurich: Department of State, Washington, D.C., to U.S. Embassy Accra, cable, 1974STATE145890, July 5, 1974, U.S. National Archives.

99 ran a detective agency: "Private Eye an Example of Tenacity," *Philadelphia Daily News*, July 5, 1972.

99 he could not believe how many zeroes: Secretary of State, Washington, D.C., to U.S. Embassy Accra, cable, 1974STATE195546, July 5, 1974, U.S. National Archives.

99 The State Department tried to find out: Department of State, Washington, D.C., to U.S. Embassy Accra, cable, 1974STATE141433.

99 one hundred thousand dollars in fees: U.S. Embassy Accra to Department of State, Washington, D.C., cable, 1974ACCRA07033.

100 "They might well be glad to get rid of him": U.S. Embassy Accra to Department of State, Washington, D.C., cable, 1974ACCRA05405, September 27, 1974, U.S. National Archives.

100 "Missions should NOT repeat NOT": "The Bank of Ghana versus Dr. Miezah," *Ghanaian Times*, January 18, 1975.

100 They had to catch a plane: Department of State, Washington, D.C., to U.S. Embassy Accra, cable, 1974STATE235849, October 25, 1974, U.S. National Archives.

101 "The Ministry of Economic Planning was careful": "Statement on John Ackah Blay-Miezah and the Oman Ghana Trust Fund," Office of the National Redemption Council, News Release, February 19, 1975.

101 Newman said he was: U.S. Embassy Accra to Department of State, Washington, D.C., cable, 1974ACCRA06795, December 6, 1974, U.S. National Archives.

102 "every journey begins": Blay-Miezah, tape recording, June 17, 1989.

102 four million dollars piping water: U.S. Embassy Accra to Department of State, Washington, D.C., cable, 1974ACCRA06795.

102 "make the average Ghanaian smile": Blay-Miezah, tape recording, June 17, 1989.

102 "successful implementation": "Chiefs Informed of Big Plans," *Ghanaian Times*, December 9, 1974.

102 "no political aims": "Trust to Invest $86m in Ghana," *Ghanaian Times*, December 5, 1974.

103 Blay-Miezah was photographed: "Chiefs Informed of Big Plans."

103 remembered seeing uncomplimentary headlines: U.S. Embassy Accra, to Department of State, Washington, D.C., cable, 1974ACCRA07033.

103 Arno Newman was a mystery: U.S. Embassy Accra to Department of State, Washington, D.C., cable, 1974ACCRA06795.

104 "the vastness of the money": "Come Out of Your Shell, Doctor Miezah," *Ghanaian Times*, December 14, 1974.

104 an exclusive interview: "Miezah Not Sent to Court," *Ghanaian Times*, December 21, 1974.

104 "establish any connection": Department of State, Washington, D.C., to U.S. Embassy Zurich, cable, 1974STATE141434, June 29, 1974, U.S. National Archives.

104 "such a stink that you can smell it from London to Zaire": U.S. Embassy Accra to Department of State, Washington, D.C., cable, 1974ACCRA07033.

105 many were in too deep: U.S. Embassy Accra to Department of State, Washington, D.C., cable, 1974ACCRA07033.

105 He would tie him up: U.S. Embassy Accra to Department of State, Washington, D.C., cable, 1974ACCRA07080, December 20, 1974, U.S. National Archives.

105 "there is something fishy": "Blay-Miezah in Court," *Daily Graphic*, December 20, 1974.

105 "Castle is now unanimous": U.S. Embassy Accra to Department of State, Washington, D.C., cable, 1974ACCRA07080.

105 SABOTEURS CAN'T STOP ME: Pratt Jnr, "Saboteurs Can't Stop Me."

106 "the CIA and the FBI had colluded": U.S. Embassy Accra to Department of State, Washington, D.C., cable, 1974ACCRA07080.

106 "catch a glimpse": "Miezah Not Sent to Court," *Ghanaian Times*.

106 went to Blay-Miezah's mansion: "Miezah's Case Withdrawn," *Ghanaian Times*, December 24, 1974.

106 "I pledge again": Blay-Miezah, tape recording, June 17, 1989.

CHAPTER 11: HUBRIS

107 a lavish dinner: "Holding Firm Formed," *Ghanaian Times*, January 2, 1975.

107 "The Drevicis turned up": Buser, *In Ghana*, 54.

107 "biggest con man yet": U.S. Embassy Accra to Department of State, Washington, D.C., cable, 1975ACCRA00017.

108 "you gassed them": Buser, *In Ghana*, 53.

111 "Since the famous Dawn Broadcast": "Holding Firm Formed."

111 "an 18-mile road will be constructed": "Oman Trust Experts at Project Site," *Ghanaian Times*, January 14, 1975.

111 "wanting to see the Ambassador (they did not)": U.S. Embassy Accra to Department of State, Washington, D.C., cable, 1975ACCRA00300, January 14, 1975, U.S. National Archives.

111 "Work starts": "Work Starts on Oman Ghana Trust Projects This Week," *Ghanaian Times*, January 7, 1975.

113 "they will all be ashamed": "Blay-Miezah Throws a Challenge," *Ghanaian Times*, January 11, 1975.

113 colluding with the Americans: U.S. Embassy Accra to Department of State, Washington, D.C., cable, 1974ACCRA07085, December 20, 1974, U.S. National Archives.

113 "chickens will soon be home": U.S. Embassy Accra to Department of State, Washington, D.C., cable, 1975ACCRA00300.

113 "Letter inquired as to legitimacy": Department of State, Washington, D.C., to U.S. Embassy Accra, cable, 1974STATE271110, December 11, 1974, U.S. National Archives.

113 "Geoffrey's Bank wrote an indignant letter": "Government Not Involved in Blay-Miezah Affair—Official Statement," *Ghanaian Times*, February 20, 1975.

114 "rather small to be engaged in any large international activities": U.S. Embassy Brussels to Department of State, Washington, D.C., cable, 1974BRUSSE09974, December 17, 1974, U.S. National Archives.

114 Rubens hanging in their living room: Olivier Ralet, *Illegale wapenhandel* (Berchem, Belgium: EPO, 1982), 171–72.

114 no idea what the Newmans were up to: U.S. Embassy Brussels to Department of State, Washington, D.C., cable, 1974BRUSSE09974.

114 "deposited this sum in his personal bank account": 289 F.Supp. 3 (1968), Securities and Exchange Commission v. Fifth Avenue Coach Lines, Inc., Victor Muscat, Edward Krock, Thomas A. Bolan, Roy M. Cohn, Defendants, No. 67 Civ. 4182, United States District Court S. D. New York, July 26, 1968.

114 two convictions for fraud: U.S. Embassy Brussels to Department of State, Washington, D.C., cable, 1974BRUSSE09974.

114 BANK OF GHANA VERSUS DR. MIEZAH: "The Bank of Ghana versus Dr. Miezah."

116 "It is ABSOLUTELY NOT TRUE": "Bank's Reply to Comment," *Ghanaian Times*, January 18, 1975.

116 "The integrity of certain top officials": Office of the National Redemption Council, "Statement on John Ackah Blay-Miezah and the Oman Ghana Trust Fund."

116 "wormed his way": Quantson, *Ghana*, 278.

117 "I pressed it down on him": Quantson, *Ghana*, 280–81.

117 "due in Ghana in a few days": "Government Not Involved in Blay-Miezah Affair—Official Statement."

118 "he was personally convinced": Office of the National Redemption Council, "Statement on John Ackah Blay-Miezah and the Oman Ghana Trust Fund."

119 caught with a large sum of cash: U.S. Embassy Accra to Department of State, Washington, D.C., cable, 1975ACCRA03020.

119 The government seized: U.S. Embassy Accra to Department of State, Washington, D.C., cable, 1975ACCRA00755, January 31, 1975, U.S. National Archives.

119 "the banks rejected the checks": Blay-Miezah, tape recording, June 17, 1989.

119 "doghouse for his paper's support": U.S. Embassy Accra to Department of State, Washington, D.C., cable, 1975ACCRA00755.

119 GOVERNMENT NOT INVOLVED IN BLAY-MIEZAH AFFAIR: "Government Not Involved in Blay-Miezah Affair—Official Statement."

119 published enraged letters: U.S. Embassy Accra to Department of State, Washington, D.C., cable, 1975ACCRA00802, February 4, 1975, U.S. National Archives.

120 Gerald Smith was sentenced: "Ex-Banker Sentenced," *Philadelphia Daily News*, February 22, 1975.

120 "living like a king": "Wanted," *Philadelphia Daily News*, January 23, 1975.

120 During an economics class: Samia Nkrumah, interview with author, 2018.

CHAPTER 12: SILK

121 "He has taken": U.S. Embassy Accra to Department of State, Washington, D.C., cable, 1976ACCRA01585, March 1, 1976, U.S. National Archives.

122 American diplomats speculated: U.S. Embassy Accra to Department of State, Washington, D.C., cable, 1975ACCRA01813, March 21, 1975, U.S. National Archives.

122 Contractors were invited: "Business Opportunities," *Philadelphia Inquirer*, September 22, 1971.

122 Herb Burstein was soliciting: "Ground Wanted," *Philadelphia Inquirer*, November 22, 1971.

122 "Construction would not disturb": "Townhouses Frankly Aim for Profits," *Philadelphia Inquirer*, March 19, 1972.

122 "Start deducting": "Action Line," *Philadelphia Inquirer*, February 21, 1974.

123 "considered a fugitive from justice": Department of State, Washington, D.C., to U.S. Embassy Accra, cable, 1975STATE088781, April 17, 1975, U.S. National Archives.

124 would have to post a bond: U.S. Embassy Accra to Department of State, Washington, D.C., cable, 1975ACCRA02537, April 21, 1975, U.S. National Archives.

124 "journey of truth": U.S. Embassy Accra to Department of State, Washington, D.C., cable, 1975ACCRA03020.

125 knew Mayer well: Commonwealth v. Robert Ellis, Court of Common Pleas, First Judicial District of Pennsylvania, Criminal Trial Division, April 8, 1987, 218–20.

126 "we retain your diplomatic passport": George Mayer to John Ackah Blay-Miezah, typescript letter, June 3, 1975, private collection.

126 "Oh, my God": Commonwealth v. Ellis, 220.

126 "there never was any money": Commonwealth v. Ellis, 219.

126 announced his return: U.S. Embassy Accra to Department of State, Washington, D.C., cable, 1975ACCRA03896, June 20, 1975, U.S. National Archives.

126 "SAI S.A. Lugano": U.S. Embassy Accra to Department of State, Washington, D.C., cable, 1975ACCRA04364, July 10, 1975, U.S. National Archives.

127 They were photographed: U.S. Embassy Accra to Department of State, Washington, D.C., cable, 1975ACCRA04364.

127 "sincere and warmest congratulations": I. K. Acheampong, *The Fifth Milestone: 13th January 1976–12th January 1977* (Accra: Ghana Publishing Corporation, 1978), 250.

127 "He was an enigma": Gladys Blay-Hill, interview with author, 2018.

128 convicted of federal bank fraud: Alix Freedman, "Philadelphia Orders Ghanaian's Arrest Over Alleged $100 Million Fund Scam," *Wall Street Journal*, March 20, 1986.

128 banned from trading in securities: Claude Lewis, "Ghana Man Accused in $15 Million Scam Here," *Philadelphia Inquirer*, March 20, 1986.

129 Blay-Miezah founded Oman Ghana Trust Fund Holdings: "Blay-Miezah: Leave Nkrumah out of It!" *New African*, July 1987, 17.

130 "Moustache, Penthouse, and Pussy Cat": *Daily Graphic*, January 7, 1978.

130 hours every day waiting in lines: James K. Matthews, "General Ignatius Kutu Acheampong," *Journal of Third World Studies* 5, no. 2 (Fall 1988): 109–11.

130 "led such a lifestyle": Supreme Court, Ghana, Dr John R. Kells and Joseph K. Whaja v. Dr E. Ako Adjei and 3 Others (2001), JELR 68294 (SC), 8/2000, October 24, 2001.

130 from a mile away: Ajoa Yeboah-Afari, via Akyaaba Addai-Sebo, interview with author, 2018.

130 "Ghana will be a great and happy country": *Daily Graphic*, February 20, 1978.

131 released some political prisoners: Emmanuel Kwaku Akyeampong and Henry Louis Gates, *Dictionary of African Biography* (Oxford: Oxford University Press, 2012), 1:153.

CHAPTER 13: PRESIDENT BLAY-MIEZAH

132   The original plan: "People's Vanguard Party Born," *Daily Graphic*, January 8, 1979.

132   lifted the ban on party politics: "Ban on Politics Lifted," *Daily Graphic*, January 1, 1979.

132   "maintenance of law and order": "S.M.C. Won't Interfere," *Daily Graphic*, January 1, 1979.

132   Elections were planned: "June 18th Fixed for Presidential, Parliamentary Polls," *Daily Graphic*, March 6, 1979.

132   twenty-three political parties had been formed: Kofi Akumanyi, "Armour of the Vanguard," *Daily Graphic*, January 30, 1979.

133   "adverse findings made against them": "104 People Disqualified," *Daily Graphic*, January 1, 1979.

133   "the youth in all walks of life": "People's Vanguard Party Born," *Daily Graphic*.

133   "inspired by the highest ideals": "People's Vanguard," *Daily Graphic*, January 16, 1979.

134   "the national cake": Nelson Duah, "People's Vanguard Will Pay Ministers' Salaries," *Daily Graphic*, January 15, 1979.

134   "an antidote for careerism": "People's Vanguard Launched," *Daily Graphic*, January 23, 1979.

134   "Vanguard would eradicate 'kalabule'": "Vanguard Will Settle Chieftancy Disputes," *Ghana News Agency*, March 3, 1979.

134   "assist the country": "Vanguard to Review Oil Pact," *Ghana News Agency*, February 15, 1979.

134   centuries-old land disputes: "Vanguard Will Settle Chieftancy Disputes," *Ghana News Agency*.

134   "I have enjoyed the trials and tribulations": Blay-Miezah, tape recording, June 17, 1989.

135   "This is about the sixth time": "And Not a Drop to Drink," *Daily Graphic*, March 1, 1979.

135   a little girl trying to get just a bucketful: "Water Situation Gets Worse," *Daily Graphic*, March 2, 1979.

135   "Considering the general hardship": "Government Must Act in Tata Brewery," *Daily Graphic*, February 7, 1979.

136   "war over hunger": Felix Amanufu, "Ours Is War over Hunger," *Daily Graphic*, February 27, 1979.

136   "Ghanaians have funds abroad": "I'll Bring in Foods Worth $50m," Nelson Duah, *Daily Graphic*, February 8, 1979.

136 in the best interests of the Trust Fund: Kofi Akumanyi, "Armour of the Vanguard," *Daily Graphic*, January 30, 1979.

137 "This is Blay's latest": Gladys Blay-Hill, interview with author, 2018.

137 The Ashanti kept McCarthy's skull: James Stuart Olson and Robert Shadle, *Historical Dictionary of the British Empire* (Westport, CT: Greenwood Books, 1996), 1:78.

138 "All you could hear was the fat man running": Gladys Blay-Hill, interview with author, 2018.

138 Blay-Miezah arrived in a convoy of cars: Film footage, private collection.

139 worth fifty million dollars: "Vanguard Can Lead Nation," *Daily Graphic*, February 3, 1979.

139 he paused for laughter: Film footage, private collection.

139 "I would not have asked for the renewal of the passport": Duah, "I'll Bring in Foods Worth $50m."

140 Blay-Miezah lit up another cigar: Film footage, private collection.

CHAPTER 14: HOUSE OF CARDS

141 "eased out of his former duties": U.S. Embassy Accra to Department of State, Washington, D.C., cable, 1977ACCRA05705, July 27, 1977, U.S. National Archives.

141 recalled to Accra: *Washington Star*, September 2, 1979.

142 an anti-corruption investigation: Appiah, *Autobiography*, 296.

142 He hoped to lock him up: Steven Burbank, interview with author, 2017.

143 "her signature had been forged": "Witness: Kolorah Blay Said He Was a Graduate," *Daily Graphic*, March 2, 1979.

144 twenty cedi a tin: "The Goods Are Back but Prices Are Prohibitive," *Daily Graphic*, February 15, 1979.

144 "the party regarded the struggle": Amanufu, "Ours Is War over Hunger."

144 *Pay Voucher*: *West Africa Magazine*, March 12, 1979.

144 the registrar wrote to the party: Republic v. Registrar of Political Parties; *ex parte* People's Vanguard Party (1979), JERL 65046, High Court, Accra, Ghana, May 23, 1979.

144 "The person who changed the name": "Blay-Miezah Is Guilty," *Daily Graphic*, April 10, 1979.

146 "The lawyer will be in the best position to tell": "Blay-Miezah Was Detained in 1963," *Daily Graphic*, March 10, 1979.

147 "harangue Britain": Duodu, "Farewell to the 'Zulu Queen.'"

147 choke on their cornflakes: "Peggy Appiah, 84, Author Who Bridged Two Cultures, Dies," *New York Times*, February 16, 2006.

147 "an uncanny resemblance": This story may be apocryphal. Duodu, "Farewell to the 'Zulu Queen.'"

148 he had worked briefly: Saline, "Out of Africa."

148 Blay-Miezah wrote to the dean: John Kolorah Blay to University of Pennsylvania, typescript letter, January 3, 1968, private collection.

148 "Your office can check": Steven Burbank, interview with author, 2017.

149 "University of Pennsylvania kindly furnished copies": U.S. Embassy Accra to Department of State, Washington, D.C., cable, 1979ACCRA01905, February 28, 1979, U.S. National Archives.

150 "I was young": Burbank, interview with author, 2017.

152 he needed the degrees: Saline, "Out of Africa."

152 "I chose myself": Blay-Miezah, tape recording, June 17, 1989.

152 "any substantive evidence": "Counsel: No Case Has Been Made against Blay-Miezah," *Daily Graphic*, March 8, 1979.

152 He had confessed: "Blay-Miezah, Sackey Have a Case to Answer—Judge," *Daily Graphic*, March 14, 1979.

152 "as he wanted peace, he parted with the money": "Court to Rule in Blay-Miezah's Case," *Daily Graphic*, March 9, 1979.

153 "Dr Blay-Miezah asked him": "C 43,000 Wasn't Meant for a Bribe."

153 money to buy a car: "C 43,000 Wasn't Meant For A Bribe."

153 "I suffered a lot": "I Refunded C43,000 Loan Through Siaw," *Daily Graphic*, March 27, 1979.

154 Kwaw-Swanzy reappeared: "Absence of Kwaw Swanzy . . . Blay-Miezah Custody," *Daily Graphic*, April 5, 1979.

154 "miscommunications": "Blay-Miezah Released," *Daily Graphic*, April 6, 1979.

154 "a prima facie case": "Free Blay-Miezah," *Daily Graphic*, April 6, 1979.

155 "never heard from Buckman again": "Blay-Miezah: Why I Gave 40,000 to Sackey," *Daily Graphic*, April 7, 1979.

155 "an untruthful person": "You've Not Been Fair, Say Counsel," *Daily Graphic*, April 14, 1979.

156 ordered to disband: Republic v. Registrar of Political Parties; *ex parte* People's Vanguard Party (1979), JERL 65046.

156 "thwart the efforts of the People's Vanguard": "People's Vanguard to Take Electoral Commissioner to Court," *Daily Graphic*, April 9, 1979.

156 "not an iota of truth": "We Stand for Truth—Blay-Miezah," *Daily Graphic*, April 17, 1979.

157 "confessions made by himself": "Court to Rule in Blay-Miezah's Case," *Daily Graphic*, March 9, 1979.

157 a lengthy cable to the State Department: U.S. Embassy Accra to Department of State, Washington, D.C., cable, 1979ACCRA03750, April 23, 1979, U.S. National Archives.

157 four years in prison: "Blay-Miezah Appeals," *Daily Graphic*, April 21, 1979.

157 an additional five-year sentence: "Blay-Miezah Is Freed," *Ghana News*, vol. 9, September 1980.

157 a token victory: Republic v. Registrar of Political Parties; *ex parte* People's Vanguard Party (1979), JERL 65046.

CHAPTER 15: DEAL WITH THE DEVIL

158 "Once a big man always a big man": Mike Adjei, *Death and Pain in Rawlings' Ghana: The Inside Story* (London: Black Line, 1994), 87.

158 fetched Blay-Miezah's water: Adjei, *Death and Pain*, 82.

159 "He paid five cedis on a haircut": Adjei, *Death and Pain*, 88.

159 the judge refused bail: "Blay-Miezah Appeals," *Daily Graphic*, April 21, 1979.

159 he would be sacked: *Africa Watch*, February 28, 2010, http://justiceghana.com/index.php/en/dine-a-wine/10-main?start=720.

159 "You and who?": "Why I Saved Rawlings—Boakye Djan," *New African*, January 21, 2003.

160 throwing down his rifle: *Africa Watch*, February 28, 2010.

160 "You don't stage coups with a pistol": "May 15, 1979: Flt. Lt. Jerry Rawlings Arrested After Failed Military Uprising," Edward A. Ulzen Memorial Foundation, https://www.eaumf.org/ejm-blog/2018/5/15/may-15-1979-flt-lt-jerry-rawlings-arrested-after-failed-military-uprising.

160 "went out of his way to defend": National Reconciliation Commission, Ghana, October 2004, vol. 2, chap. 6.

161 "Never in my long experience": Appiah, *Autobiography*, 303.

161 "unwittingly set in motion": National Reconciliation Commission, Ghana, October 2004, vol. 2, chap. 6.

161 "God will not help you": Kojo Yankah, *The Trial of J. J. Rawlings: Echoes of the 31st December Revolution* (Hampton, VA: U.B. & U.S. Communication Systems, 1992), 42–44.

161 broke Rawlings out: "Why I Saved Rawlings—Boakye Djan," *New African*.

162 "you may run": Yankah, *Trial*, 22.

162 "the dawn of a new era": National Reconciliation Commission, Ghana, October 2004, vol. 2, chap. 6.

162 "full benefits of their labour": *Ghana News* 8, no. 10 (November 1979).

162 "a bloodbath was necessary": "Dissident Officers Oust Ghana Ruler," *Washington Post*, June 5, 1979.

162 "life became a shadow": National Reconciliation Commission, Ghana, October 2004, vol. 2, chap. 6, 6.1.4.1.

162 Countless people: National Reconciliation Commission, Ghana, October 2004, vol. 2, chap. 6.

162 "summarily executed": National Reconciliation Commission, Ghana, October 2004, vol. 2, chap. 6, 6.1.4.

163 "The iron hook of the belt": National Reconciliation Commission, Ghana, October 2004, vol. 2, chap. 6, 6.5.5.

163 "the bullet had damaged her spine": National Reconciliation Commission, Ghana, October 2004, vol. 2, chap. 6, 6.5.16.

163 "flogged with a fan belt": National Reconciliation Commission, Ghana, October 2004, vol. 2, chap. 6, 6.6.3.

163 "Junior Jesus": Jimmy Kandeh, *Coups from Below: Armed Subalterns and State Power in West Africa* (New York: Macmillan, 2004), 61.

163 "to punish those": National Reconciliation Commission, Ghana, October 2004, vol. 2, chap. 6.

164 "Heathrow Airport car park": National Reconciliation Commission, Ghana, October 2004, vol. 2, chap. 6, 6.1.4.1.

164 soldiers stopped him: National Reconciliation Commission, Ghana, October 2004, vol. 2, chap. 6, 6.12.19.

164 Soldiers descended on their apartment: National Reconciliation Commission, Ghana, October 2004, vol. 2, chap. 6, 6.12.7.

164 "transferring all the shares of the company": National Reconciliation Commission, Ghana, October 2004, vol. 2, chap. 6, 6.12.4.

164 "goods, cash and vehicles": National Reconciliation Commission, Ghana, October 2004, vol. 2, chap. 6, 6.12.5.

164 "It is our sweat and blood": "We Want Our Brewery Back," GhanaWeb, June 3, 2002, https://www.ghanaweb.com/GhanaHomePage/NewsArchive/We-want-our-brewery-back-Tata-Brewery-owner-8217-s-son-24540.

164 imprisoned people without trial: National Reconciliation Commission, Ghana, October 2004, vol. 2, chap. 6.

165 "report to the guard room": Appiah, *Autobiography*, 305.

165 "merciless beatings": Appiah, *Autobiography*, 308.

165 "not as I would wish": Appiah, *Autobiography*, 311–12.

165 "these boys want to finish me": Appiah, *Autobiography*, 314.

166 "You could smell death in the air": National Reconciliation Commission, Ghana, October 2004, vol. 2, chap. 6, 6.1.4.1.

168 "the huge state chair": "Climbing into a Clean, Warm Seat," *Economist*, September 30, 1979.

168 first used by President Nkrumah: "The Intangible Heritage of Ghana's Presidential Seat," ParallelAfrica, August 25, 2016, https://parallelafrica.wordpress .com/2016/08/25/the-intangible-heritage-of-ghanas-presidential-seat/.

168 "resist and unseat": "Climbing into a Clean, Warm Seat," *Economist.*

168 "six months from now": "Ghana Looking to New Leader for Better Life," *New York Times*, October 10, 1979.

168 "demanded 70,000 US dollars": *Ghana News*, February 1982.

168 "galaxy of diseases": "Blay-Miezah's Galaxy of Diseases," *Daily Graphic*, February 16, 1980.

168 "such reports, instead of drawing sympathy": Nana Essilfie-Conduah, "The Blay-Miezah Hospital Business," *Daily Graphic*, February 16, 1980.

169 thrown out on a technicality: "Blay-Miezah Is Freed," *Ghana News*, vol. 9, September 1980.

169 to check that the bribe had been received: "Blay-Miezah, Sackey Have a Case to Answer—Judge," *Daily Graphic*, March 14, 1979.

CHAPTER 16: OUR MAN IN LONDON

170 a series of Georgian houses: "Our History," Montcalm Hotel, accessed April 16, 2021, https://www.montcalm.co.uk/our-history-527.html.

170 "suited to those of sybaritic tastes": Richard Moore, *Fodor's Great Britain 1984* (New York: Fodor's Travel Guides, 1983), 128.

170 wood-paneled club bar: "Montcalm Hotel, Marylebone, London: The Club Bar in the Basement," Royal Institute of British Architects, accessed April 16, 2021, https://www.architecture.com/image-library/ribapix/image-information /poster/montcalm-hotel-marylebone-london-the-club-bar-in-the-basement /posterid/RIBA79354.html.

170 money launderers descended on London: Association d'économie financière, *Money and Morals Worldwide: First Annual Report* (France: Association d'économie financière, 1995), 42.

171 a tabloid smear: "Mafia Muscles into Video Vice," *News of the World*, January 4, 1981.

171 Rigby took in the client: Peter Rigby, interview with author, 2018–2022.

171 "absolutely zero knowledge": Peter Rigby, unpublished memoirs, private collection.

173 Ghana's first commercial television network: Rigby, interview with author, 2018–2022.

173 "Akaraka, Ching Akaraka Cho!": "Yonsei Cheer," Yonsei University, accessed April 16, 2021, https://www.yonsei.ac.kr/en_sc/intro/symbol11.jsp.

173 Ellis was also hard at work: Commonwealth v. Ellis, Affidavit of Probable Cause to Arrest, 8.

174 "returned tenfold to the investor": Federal Bureau of Investigation, file of Dr. John Ackah Blay-Miezah, Memorandum of Interview, August 17, 1987, United States Attorney's office, Philadelphia, Pennsylvania.

174 "always make excuses": Federal Bureau of Investigation, file of Dr. John Ackah Blay-Miezah, Memorandum of Interview, August 17, 1987.

174 "there was a gram of truth": Gladys Blay-Hill, interview with author, 2018.

176 married for the second time: Register of Marriages, Greater London, Westminster (January–March 1981), 15:925.

176 "a cock-and-bull story": Gladys Blay-Hill, interview with author, 2018.

177 "a lusty version of the Penn fight song": Saline, "Out of Africa."

177 "It was the greed": "The Big Payoff: A Dream Born of Faith, Fed on Promises," *Philadelphia Inquirer*, March 26, 1986.

177 "including his father": Kit Konolige, "Blind Trust," *Philadelphia Inquirer*, March 20, 1986.

177 "it's so outrageous, it's gotta be true": "The Ultimate Con Man," *60 Minutes*, CBS, January 29, 1989.

178 "Soon, brother Ginsberg": Saline, "Out of Africa."

178 Ginsberg helped pay: "The Big Payoff."

178 "I lost touch with reality": "The Big Payoff."

178 a hive of activity: Visitor's Book, Oman Ghana Trust Fund offices, private collection.

178 Handed him seventy-five thousand dollars: Federal Bureau of Investigation, file of Dr. John Ackah Blay-Miezah, Memorandum of Interview, March 1, 1989.

178 "500 machine guns": *Quarterly Economic Review of Uganda, Ethiopia, Somalia, Djibouti* (1978): 20.

178 the arrest of several executives: Cour de cassation, France, Chambre criminelle, du 2 mai 1989, 86-93.152, Inédit; *Le Monde*, January 26, 1980, "Trois cadres de la S.F.M. sont inculpés d'infraction à la législation sur les armes."

179 "fond of bullshit": Ralet, *Illegale wapenhandel*, 138: "De Bernard houdt van bluf, goede kleermakers en grote hotels . . . Hij vestigt voor een poos zijn kantoor in de gebouwen van de bank en maakt gebruik en misbruik van haar telex."

179 Lasnaud moved his operation: Ralet, *Illegale wapenhandel*, 138.

179 Impressed by the Rubens: Ralet, *Illegale wapenhandel*, 171–2: "De Luikse gerechtelijke politie doorzoekt, samen met een Franse onderzoekskommissie, de bank en dan de woning van de Newmans, waar de politiemannen zeer onder de indruk is van de Rubens in de salon . . . De gerechtelijke politie van Parijs

en Luik stellen elkaar verantwoordelijk voor het niet in beschuldiging stellen van de Newmans. De rol van de Newmans wordt echter niet helemaal opgehelderd."

179 "Arno Newman was not a competent bank manager": J. Spreutels and A. Vandeplas, *RDC TBH: Revue de Droit commercial Belge*, no. 3 (1994): 264: "Arno Nejman [Newman], n'était pas un dirigeant de banque competent."

179 "disloyal and intriguing followers": "Resist Crazy Adventurers," *Daily Graphic*, March 9, 1981.

179 "misusing the bank": "Top Bank Men Sacked," *Daily Graphic*, October 31, 1981.

179 "Where have all the flour gone?": "Where have all the flour gone," *Daily Graphic*, January 19, 1981.

179 Rotting in the cold-store rooms: "4,000 Bags Maize Left to Rot," *Daily Graphic*, October 3, 1981.

179 "Mr Funky Town": "Funky Town Discotheque," *Daily Graphic*, November 25, 1981.

180 "try being a big man": Elizabeth Ohene, "Pity the Poor Big Man," *Daily Graphic*, November 10, 1981.

180 "lazy employees": "F.P.C. to Dismiss Lazy Employees," *Daily Graphic*, October 23, 1981.

180 "gross disrespect": "24 Tutors Interdicted," *Daily Graphic*, March 19, 1981.

180 "the right moral track": "Wanted: Right Moral Track," *Daily Graphic*, January 5, 1981.

180 their firings would be reported: "I've Not Resigned," *Daily Graphic*, October 7, 1981.

180 "best served by retiring Jerry": Adjei, *Death and Pain*, 177.

181 "I felt excited": Rigby, interview with author, 2018–2022.

181 "purchase weapons and other equipment": Federal Bureau of Investigation, file of Dr. John Ackah Blay-Miezah.

182 "50 percent of the school's net profits": "Year Suspension Given Lowenthal," *Philadelphia Inquirer*, December 22, 1956.

182 "the most beautiful piece of legal fraud": United States Congress, *House Select Committee to Investigate Educational and Training Program under GI Bill* (Washington, D.C.: United States Government Printing Office, 1951), 27.

182 Lowenthal's license to practice: "Year Suspension Given Lowenthal," *Philadelphia Inquirer*, December 22, 1956.

182 Lowenthal paid ministers: "Can You Trust a Certain Democratic Chap," *Indiana Gazette* (Indiana, PA), November 3, 1966.

182 paying the National Association for the Advancement of White People: *Intelligencer Journal* (Lancaster, PA), August 10, 1966.

183 fined one thousand dollars a day: "Rigler's Attorney Fined in Contempt," *Philadelphia Daily News,* July 30, 1976.

183 "absolutely incompetent": "Convicted Murderer Gets Chance for Freedom," *Philadelphia Inquirer,* March 25, 1993.

184 the last one to leave: Pranay Gupte, "Rawlings Tightens His Grip on Ghana after Coup," *New York Times,* January 16, 1982.

184 they made their move: Adjei, *Death and Pain,* 169–71.

185 "There is no justice": Paul Nugent, *Big Men, Small Boys and Politics in Ghana: Power, Ideology, and the Burden of History, 1982–1994* (London: Pinter, 1995), 15.

185 As Rigby dozed off: Rigby, interview with author, 2018–2022.

186 The borders were closed: "Civilian Government Overthrown in Ghana, Accra Radio Reports," *Philadelphia Inquirer,* January 1, 1982.

186 "West Africa would burn": "Jerry Rawlings Again Leads Military Seizure of Power in Ghana," *Washington Post,* January 1, 1982.

CHAPTER 17: GLORY AND FOLLY

187 "an opening for real democracy": *Daily Graphic,* January 2, 1982.

187 Every last person: Zaya Yeebo, *Ghana: The Struggle for Popular Power* (London: New Beacon Books, 1991), 116.

188 "start all over again": Saline, "Out of Africa."

188 "a violent, military-supported overthrow": "Jerry Rawlings Again Leads Military Seizure of Power in Ghana."

189 "he was interested in investing": Federal Bureau of Investigation, file of Dr. John Ackah Blay-Miezah.

189 "Say howdy": "Roy Rogers Restaurant 'Howdy!' Commercial (1978)," accessed April 16, 2021, https://www.youtube.com/watch?v=ml0fBy-1QEw.

189 At ten fifty-seven A.M., Ellis took a seat: Federal Bureau of Investigation, file of Dr. John Ackah Blay-Miezah.

190 metal fabrication business: "About Us," H&H Industrial, accessed April 16, 2021, http://www.hhindustrial.com/about-us/.

190 "That country is so friggin' rich": Saline, "Out of Africa."

190 "25 tons of rice": Federal Bureau of Investigation, file of Dr. John Ackah Blay-Miezah.

192 Tsikata's dismissal from the military: Adjei, *Death and Pain,* 121.

192 calling himself Carlos Silva Gomes: *Guardian,* August 4, 1976.

196 "I have been brutalized": "Fears for a Soldier Held in Torture Prison," *Observer,* April 11, 1976.

192 "protect the sovereignty of the State of Ghana": Colin Legum, "Five Lives May Start Rebellion," *Observer,* April 25, 1976.

192   an adoring profile: Victoria Brittain, "The Front Runners," *Guardian*, April 16, 1982.

193   Rawlings got belligerent: Mensah Adinkrah, "Political Coercion in Military-Dominated Regimes: A Subcultural Interpretation" (PhD diss., Washington University, 1988), 78, quoting *West Africa*, July 19, 1982, 1855–56.

193   "shivered like a leaf": Yeebo, *Popular Power*, 38.

193   "no business raising queries": Yeebo, *Popular Power*, 116.

193   "Teachers fled": Jon Kraus, "The Struggle over Structural Adjustment in Ghana," *Africa Today* 38, no. 4 (1991): 22.

193   Cocoa production plunged: Osman Al-Hassan, "Politicized Soldiers: Military Intervention in the Politics of Ghana, 1966–1993" (PhD diss., Washington State University, 2004), 269.

194   accused of kalabule: *West Africa*, September 9, 1985, 1888.

194   "a trigger-happy soldier": *West Africa*, July 19, 1982, 1855.

194   "he went in shooting": National Reconciliation Commission, Ghana, October 2004, vol. 4, chap. 1.

194   on the radio: "The Murder of Odiyifo Asare—His Wife's Testimony," Joy FM, December 17, 2019, https://www.facebook.com/silentyearsghana/videos/80572 5133223294/.

195   "for their own safety": "Church Closed; Members Asked to Report," Accra Domestic Service in English, via Foreign Broadcast Information Service, FBIS-MEA-82-026, February 8, 1982.

195   "enemies of the revolution": "PNDC's Boadi Warns Smugglers Will Be Shot," Accra Domestic Service in English, via Foreign Broadcast Information Service, FBIS-MEA-82-030, February 12, 1982.

195   "They fired their guns indiscriminately": "The Murder of Odiyifo Asare."

195   fled the city, still dressed in his surgical gown: National Reconciliation Commission, Ghana, October 2004, vol. 4, chap. 1.

196   "anarchy now reigned in Ghana": "Rampaging Troops Kill Religious Sect Members," *AFP* (Paris), February 23, 1982.

196   Trials lasted just a few minutes: Adinkrah, "Political Coercion," 78, quoting *West Africa*, July 19, 1982, 1855–56.

196   "opened the floodgate": *Daily Graphic*, March 24, 1982.

196   a handsome red document: John Ackah Blay-Miezah, diplomatic passport, private collection.

197   lines of armed soldiers: Rigby, interview with author, 2018–2022.

197   controlling the exchange rate: Jeffrey Herbst, *The Politics of Reform in Ghana, 1982–1991* (Berkeley: University of California Press, 1993), 53.

197   "I was his bagman": Rigby, interview with author, 2018–2022.

198   "weight laden to arrive": Quantson, *Ghana*, 284.

198 digging trenches: National Reconciliation Commission, Ghana, October 2004, vol. 2, chap. 7, 7.6.100.

198 Under the plaster of paris cast: Quantson, *Ghana*, 284.

199 "Guns": Rigby, interview with author, 2018–2022.

199 tried to hold Rawlings to account: National Reconciliation Commission, Ghana, October 2004, vol. 4, chap. 1, 1.25.8.1.

199 They had freed people: Adjei, *Death and Pain*, 121, quoting the Special Investigations Board report into the judges' deaths.

199 "arrest and detention": Quoted in Adjei, *Death and Pain*, 108.

199 "She bought the story": Quoted in Adjei, *Death and Pain*, 110.

199 the assassins eventually gave up: National Reconciliation Commission, Ghana, October 2004, vol. 4, chap. 1, 1.25.8.1.

199 at least thirteen coup attempts: Adinkrah, "Political Coercion," 78, quoting *West Africa*, July 19, 1982, 1855–56.

200 "scramble for the guns": National Reconciliation Commission, Ghana, October 2004, vol. 4, chap. 1, 1.25.9.1.

200 "his rights and liberties": Adjei, *Death and Pain*, 122.

200 MURDER MOST FOUL!: Adjei, *Death and Pain*, 116.

200 He implicated Tsikata: Yeebo, *Popular Power*, 135.

200 "accomplices and co-conspirators": Adjei, *Death and Pain*, 123.

200 "worried about the damage that the revelations had done": Yeebo, *Popular Power*, 136.

200 Quaye retracted all his claims: England and Wales Court of Appeal (Civil Division), Tsikata v. Newspaper Publishing Inc, September 30, 1996, 1996 EWCA Civ 618.

CHAPTER 18: SHOWBOYS ALL THE WAY

201 "I can perform": Blay-Miezah, tape recording, June 17, 1989.

201 just before his death: "Mr Krobo Edusei," *Times*, March 5, 1984.

202 hired a German coach: Anver Versi, *Guinness Presents: Football in Africa* (London: Longman, 1987), 80.

202 some of the best players: Rigby, interview with author, 2018–2022.

202 "Akaraka, Ching Akaraka Cho": "Yonsei Cheer."

202 "everybody would shout": Ebo Quansah, interview with author, 2022.

202 eighty thousand cedi in a polythene bag: Ken Bediako, interview with author, 2022.

203 "We knew the stories": Bediako, interview with author, 2022.

203 "You got me into this mess": Rigby, unpublished memoirs.

204 "the Akaraka boys will do a good job": Peter Rigby, video footage, private collection.

205 A large black spider: Versi, *Guinness Presents*, 72.

205 He had studied law: "Obituary: King Opoku Ware II of Ashanti," *Independent*, October 23, 2011.

205 He was visibly nervous: Rigby, video footage.

206 "you hear the bullets just crying": National Reconciliation Commission, Ghana, October 2004, 7.1.24, 463.

206 he put Quantson to work: Quantson, *Ghana*, 282.

207 "accessories to the human rights abuses": National Reconciliation Commission, Ghana, October 2004, vol. 1, chap. 5, 5.7.6.11: "By turning a blind eye on the tortures that went on under their very noses, not only Quantson and Nanfuri, but also Dr Koranteng who treated them of their injuries and made no protest, and Agyekum, who tried and convicted them, became accessories to the human rights abuses committed by the PNDC regime."

207 "without strangling him": Quantson, *Ghana*, 282–84.

208 "warrantless frisking and wiretapping, preventative detention": Claude Lewis, "No Sad Songs for John Mitchell," *Philadelphia Inquirer*, November 12, 1988.

208 the highest-ranking member: Tyree Johnson, "If He's Like Robin Hood, He's out of the Woods," *Philadelphia Daily News*, April 10, 1987.

208 "That's how Mitchell ended up in Ghana": E. D. M. Stephens, interview with author, 2018.

208 "the aura of legitimacy": United States District Court, Eastern District of Pennsylvania, United States of America v. John Ackah Blay-Miezah, September 8, 1992, count 14.

208 promised $733 million: Ian Jackman, *Con Men: Fascinating Profiles of Swindlers and Rogues from the Files of the Most Successful Broadcast in Television History* (New York: Simon & Schuster, 2003), 185.

209 "That was the Ambassador": Quantson, *Ghana*, 285.

209 "credit line of $50 million": "Blay-Miezah: Leave Nkrumah out of It!" *New African*, July 1987, 17.

209 passport was renewed: Blay-Miezah, diplomatic passport, private collection.

210 "The Nzemas have remained in dust": Beyin Stool Affairs, (file) [November 3, 1952–May 9, 1990], Fort Apollonia Museum of Nzema Culture and History, BL-EAP569/2/1/10, accessed April 17, 2021, https://eap.bl.uk/collection/EAP569-2-1.

211 Blay-Miezah made his entrance: Rigby, video footage.

212 It had lain abandoned: Hydrographic Office, *The African Pilot, or Sailing Directions for the Western Coast of Africa from Cape Spartel to the River Cameroons* (London: Hydrographic Office, 1856), 1:138.

212 Blay-Miezah had to bite his lip: Rigby, video footage.

212 he had already been made a paramount chief: Barry Rider, interview with author, 2019.

212 diplomatic immunity: Rigby, unpublished memoirs.

213 The songs echoed through the tall palm trees: Rigby, video footage.

213 "a flag showing the locations": *Philadelphia Inquirer*, March 26, 1986.

CHAPTER 19: FOOL'S GOLD

215 "I've had to go a long way": Leon Festinger, Henry W. Riecken, and Stanley Schachter, *When Prophecy Fails: A Social and Psychological Study of a Modern Group That Predicted the Destruction of the World* (New York: Harper, 1956), 168.

215 "We have never had a plan changed": Festinger, Riecken, and Schachter, *When Prophecy Fails*, 166.

216 "Blay-Miezah put them to work": Lynne Abraham, interview with author, 2017.

216 "a Philadelphia stock promoter": *Philadelphia Inquirer*, April 19, 1974.

216 "Yeah, they still lost": Rigby, video footage.

218 "Why are they calling me a crook?": Gladys Blay-Hill, interview with author, 2018.

220 he was already investigating: "Prompter," *International Legal Practitioner* 10, no. 2 (June 1985): 71.

220 "Occasionally the money was there": Rider, interview with author, 2019.

220 "the lack of any UK complaint": National Archives (UK), FCO 65/4851.

221 "Personally, I was never taken in": Rider, interview with author, 2019.

221 a hundred to one: Commonwealth v. Robert Ellis, Court of Common Pleas, December 23, 1986, 2017–93.

222 "a phenomenal figure": Stephens, interview with author, 2018.

222 their promissory notes: Saline, "Out of Africa."

222 "the privilege of giving him twenty thousand dollars": Commonwealth v. Ellis, Court of Common Pleas, April 8, 1987, 210.

222 "American friend and brother": Saline, "Out of Africa."

222 GoldStar Meat Packers: *Urner Barry's Meat & Poultry Directory* (Tom's River, NJ: Urner Barry Publications, 1987), 375.

223 "a large sum of money on this meat deal": Federal Bureau of Investigation, file of Dr. John Ackah Blay-Miezah.

223 "He made us make fools of ourselves": Gladys Blay-Hill, interview with author, 2018.

224 "You know the secrecy laws": Saline, "Out of Africa."

224 Amoako-Atta had died: *England & Wales, Civil Registration Death Index, 1916–2007* (United Kingdom: General Register Office), vol. 13, 1729.

224 "He never quit the job": Blay-Miezah, tape recording, June 17, 1989.

224 "Minister of Finance in the First Republic": "Kwasi [*sic*] Amoako-Atta Dies," *Guardian*, May 11, 1984.

224 claimed they spent $250,000: Commonwealth v. Ellis, Court of Common Pleas, April 8, 1987, 200.

224 "My beloved friend": Blay-Miezah, tape recording, June 17, 1989.

224 He was the only link: Saline, "Out of Africa."

225 "a bit of a field day": Rider, interview with author, 2019.

225 STS was pure British establishment: Jim Shortt, interview, April 2017, http://www.ibabodyguards.com/news.

226 "I don't really hold with any of that": Rider, interview with author, 2019.

226 "Rider is not being sincere": Blay-Miezah, tape recording, June 17, 1989.

227 "many corporations and other foundations": Charles Lowenthal, typescript letter, August 6, 1984, private collection.

228 "why this family": Commonwealth v. Ellis, Affidavit of Probable Cause, 22.

228 his former manager: *Philadelphia Inquirer*, April 14, 1998, 60.

228 "a couple of hundred million": Commonwealth v. Ellis, Court of Common Pleas, April 8, 1987, 238.

228 "to fool officials in Ghana": *Philadelphia Inquirer*, April 14, 1998, 60.

228 "false and all made up": Commonwealth v. Ellis, Court of Common Pleas, April 8, 1987, 238.

CHAPTER 20: AMERICAN GRIFTER

229 "used to help": Federal Bureau of Investigation, file of Dr. John Ackah Blay-Miezah.

229 in just a few months: Commonwealth v. Ellis, Affidavit of Probable Cause, 3.

230 $160 billion: Commonwealth v. Ellis, Affidavit of Probable Cause, 17.

230 $15 million: Commonwealth v. Ellis, Affidavit of Probable Cause, 5.

280 Gregory Frazier, of Detroit: Commonwealth v. Ellis, Affidavit of Probable Cause, 24.

230 totaled a billion dollars: Commonwealth v. Ellis, 53.

230 meeting with her in Accra: Samia Nkrumah, interview with author, 2018.

230 "assigned any rights": United States District Court for the Eastern District of Pennsylvania, Civil Action No. 87-778, Motion to Dismiss, 1.

230 twelve thousand dollars in one shopping trip: Saline, "Out of Africa."

231 A secretary was told: Federal Bureau of Investigation, file of Dr. John Ackah Blay-Miezah, Memorandum of Interview, March 1, 1989.

231 had to sell her engagement ring: "Nkrumah's Widow Starves," *Talking Drums* 1 (1983): 14.

231 "believing a story he never told": Richard C. Morais, "He Gave Off That Kind of Aura," *Forbes*, February 8, 1988.

232 "Governments use legitimization": Rider, interview with author, 2019.

232 too big to fail: The term came from a 1984 congressional hearing on Continental Illinois Bank: "If It's Too Big to Fail, Is It Too Big to Exist?" *New York Times*, June 20, 2009.

232 no books or ledgers: Commonwealth v. Ellis, Affidavit of Probable Cause, 9.

232 "no tax on borrowed money": Saline, "Out of Africa."

233 His telephone at the Dorchester: Robert Ellis, miscellaneous papers, private collection.

233 "attracting lots of attention": Saline, "Out of Africa."

234 secret tape recordings: United States District Court, Eastern District of Pennsylvania, Robert Shulman v. Vincent Mbrika, June 24, 2011, 10-CV-07035-RBS. For Mitchell and the Watergate tapes, see *New York Times*, May 18, 1974.

234 He eventually sold his share: Commonwealth v. Ellis, Court of Common Pleas, April 8, 1987, 207.

234 selling popcorn to make ends meet: Commonwealth v. Ellis, 206–7.

235 Ellis began to pursue: "Ghana Man Accused in $15 Million Scam Here," *Philadelphia Inquirer*, March 20, 1986.

235 David Ryland invested: Commonwealth v. Ellis, Affidavit of Probable Cause, 23.

235 "wined, dined and romanced": Claude Lewis, "The Mystery behind an Investment Scam," *Philadelphia Inquirer*, March 29, 1986.

235 She heard about the fund: "Ghanaian Bilked Investors of Millions," *Philadelphia Daily News*, March 20, 1986.

235 "for the first time in my life, I didn't have to worry": Claude Lewis, "Only the Con Men Came Out Ahead," *Philadelphia Inquirer*, February 6, 1989.

235 She gave him sixty-five thousand dollars: Federal Bureau of Investigation, file of Dr. John Ackah Blay-Miezah, Memorandum of Interview, March 1, 1989.

235 "I am destitute": Commonwealth v. Ellis, 175–77.

236 "to repatriate the millions": Quantson, *Ghana*, 286–87.

236 "you are an ex-convict": Quantson, *Ghana*, 288.

237 "The money is always there": Quantson, *Ghana*, 289.

237 "deep involvement in Blay-Miezah's affairs": National Archives (UK), FCO 65/4861.

238 "beaten up": Rider, interview with author, 2019.

238 The target: Phillip Knightley, "The History of the Honey Trap," *Foreign Policy*, March 12, 2010.

238 "C.I.A. operational plans": "C.I.A. Clerk and Ghanaian Charged in Espionage Case," *New York Times*, July 12, 1985.

238 "dissident groups being funded by the Americans": *New York Times*, August 7, 1985.

238 the CIA's entire network: *Finger Lakes Times*, December 6, 1985, 3.

238 reportedly murdered: "Officials Think Spying Led to Death of C.I.A. Informant In Ghana," *New York Times*, July 13, 1985.

238 charged Captain Tsikata: Gladys Blay-Hill, interview with author, 2018.

239 An office in an outbuilding: Quantson, *Ghana*, 284.

239 "History, indeed, will be our final arbiter": Blay-Miezah, tape recording, June 17, 1989.

240 "most precious documents": Commonwealth v. Ellis, 233.

240 signed by Nkrumah himself: United States District Court, Eastern District of Pennsylvania, Shulman v. Mbrika.

240 "a stack nearly four-feet high": Claude Lewis, "The Mystery behind an Investment Scam," *Philadelphia Inquirer*, March 29, 1986.

240 "a story you won't believe": Saline, "Out of Africa."

241 "exquisitely written letters": Lewis, "The Mystery behind an Investment Scam."

241 "several hundred photographs": Commonwealth v. Ellis, Court of Common Pleas, April 8, 1987, 231.

241 prosecutors added charge after charge: Commonwealth v. Ellis, Affidavit of Probable Cause, 7.

241 "the biggest fraud in the history of Philadelphia": "Doctor' Faces Ghanaian Capital Charges in $6M Bilking of Philadelphians," *Philadelphia Daily News*, March 20, 1986.

241 His passport was seized: "City Seeks a Trade with Ghana in $15m Fraud," *Philadelphia Inquirer*, April 15, 1986.

241 "Distribution of the fund": Commonwealth v. Ellis, Affidavit of Probable Cause, 21.

241 Blay-Miezah claimed that he was shocked: Rider, interview with author, 2019.

242 "considerable pain and discomfort": Blay-Miezah to investors, typescript letter, June 2, 1986, private collection.

243 It would not hold up in federal court: Saline, "Out of Africa."

243 "blinded by greed": "Philadelphia Orders Ghanaian's Arrest over Alleged $100 Million Fund Scam," *Wall Street Journal*, March 20, 1986.

243 "the first Black-owned disco": Michael A. Nutter, *Mayor: The Best Job in Politics* (Philadelphia: University of Pennsylvania Press, 2017), 13–14.

244 "one last time to get the money": Saline, "Out of Africa."

244 "I'll put the bullets in the chamber": Jacob V. Lamar Jr., "Out of Africa, Stung by a Ghanaian Smoothy," *Time* magazine, April 21, 1986.

244 to help pay his taxes: Federal Bureau of Investigation, file of Dr. John Ackah Blay-Miezah, Memorandum of Interview, March 1, 1989.

244 "a final conclusion": Commonwealth v. Ellis, Affidavit of Probable Cause, 18.

244 "a treasure map": "The Big Payoff: A Vision Fed on Promises," *Philadelphia Inquirer*, March 26, 1986.

245 as if they were going to war: Charles Abraham, "MOVE: Philadelphia's Forgotten Bombing," *James Madison Undergraduate Research Journal* 7, no. 1 (2020): 27–35.

245 drop a bomb on it: Gene Demby, "I'm from Philly. 30 Years Later, I'm Still Trying to Make Sense of the MOVE Bombing," NPR, May 13, 2015, https://www.npr.org/sections/codeswitch/2015/05/13/406243272/im-from-philly-30-years-later-im-still-trying-to-make-sense-of-the-move-bombing.

245 "all this was cloak and dagger stuff": Rigby, unpublished memoirs.

246 "blow the whistle": Rider, interview with author, 2019.

246 "he cannot look himself in the face": Elizabeth Ohene, "Dr Secretary, You Aren't Going . . . ?" *Talking Drums* 3.1-22 (1983): 10.

247 "We can see light": Rigby, unpublished memoirs.

247 "He took Ghana by storm": Bright Akwetey, interview with author, 2018.

247 "some of this money": Blay-Miezah, tape recording, June 17, 1989.

248 investigators could find no evidence: Akwetey, interview with author, 2018.

248 "Rawlings had withdrawn the requisite diplomatic passport": Rigby, unpublished memoirs.

248 The charges against him: *Philadelphia Inquirer*, March 26, 1986.

249 "'Yo, Abraham!'": "My Philadelphia Story: Lynne Abraham," *Philadelphia*, January 2, 2005.

249 "in support of Mr Ellis": Commonwealth v. Ellis, 5.

249 "these monies and accounts and places really exist": Commonwealth v. Ellis, 7.

249 "a one-to-one basis": Commonwealth v. Ellis, 43.

249 "private, personal business reasons": Commonwealth v. Ellis, 57.

250 "a chair and a whip": Commonwealth v. Ellis, 65.

CHAPTER 21: SOON PARTED

251 "welcome to Guernsey": Rigby, video footage.

251 "a mail-drop and a Telex machine": "The Con Men Are Always with Us," *Philadelphia Inquirer*, March 22, 1986.

252 "They ended up opening all the windows": Stephens, interview with author, 2018.

252 "It's become very awkward": Rigby, video footage.

252 a financial wizard: "Man Sentenced in Ghana Fraud Case," *Philadelphia Inquirer*, April 10, 1987.

253 "these sixteen banks": Rigby, video footage.

253 studied African history: Abraham, interview with author, 2019.

253 "either the greatest benefactor or the worst thief": Commonwealth v. Ellis, Opinion of Judge Lynne Abraham, July 14, 1987, 2.

254 "to maintain Dr Blay-Miezah": Commonwealth v. Ellis, 167.

255 "gold bars from the various countries": Oman Ghana Trust Deed, typescript, private collection.

257 "nothing to do with him": Commonwealth v. Ellis, 231.

257 "Nkrumah put Blay-Miezah in jail": Commonwealth v. Ellis, 229.

257 "always been in one spot": Commonwealth v. Ellis, 233–34.

257 "twenty to one": Commonwealth v. Ellis, 172–73.

257 without telling her husband: Commonwealth v. Ellis, 169.

257 "made a pain of himself": Commonwealth v. Ellis, 191–92.

257 "she was constantly criticizing her husband": Commonwealth v. Ellis, 201.

258 "Our wishes were not respected": Commonwealth v. Ellis, 252.

258 "doesn't mean a hill of beans": Commonwealth v. Ellis, 254.

258 a return of $4 million: Commonwealth v. Ellis, 317.

258 "I have seen the officials from Ghana": Commonwealth v. Ellis, 309–10.

258 "not so sophisticated": Commonwealth v. Ellis, 329–31.

258 "How could he haul all that gold?": Abraham, interview with author, 2019.

259 "a mammoth task": Commonwealth v. Ellis, 339.

259 "You have to give it back": Commonwealth v. Ellis, 351.

259 "I met and said hello to Mr. Tsikata": Commonwealth v. Ellis, 352.

260 "it's a quantum leap": Commonwealth v. Ellis, 353.

261 they would receive commendations: Rider, interview with author, 2019.

261 "Guilty": Commonwealth v. Ellis, 425–26.

261 "it should all prove out I was right": Commonwealth v. Ellis, 463.

261 "took, and took, and took some more": Commonwealth v. Ellis, Sentencing Memorandum, 3.

261 "Zimmers and townhouses": Commonwealth v. Ellis, Sentencing Memorandum, 5.

261 "My object all sublime": Commonwealth v. Ellis, Sentencing Memorandum, 5.

262 "three-fifty muffins": Commonwealth v. Ellis, 483.

262 "to keep people from being stupid": Commonwealth v. Ellis, 512.

262 "not less than five nor more than fifteen years": Commonwealth v. Ellis, 527.

CHAPTER 22: THE THRONE AND THE CHAIN

263 perfectly tailored: Morais, "He Gave Off That Kind of Aura."

264 "originated partly from Ghana": Kwesi Botchwey, typescript letter, April 24, 1988, private collection.

264   Another letter assured investors: Kwesi Botchwey, typescript letter, February 12, 1987, private collection.

264   "verifying the existence of huge sums of money": United States District Court, Eastern District of Pennsylvania, United States of America v. John Ackah Blay-Miezah, September 8, 1992.

264   "I forgive and forget": Blay-Miezah, tape recording, June 17, 1989.

264   "All that you have heard is basically untrue": "The Curious Case of Blay 'The Fat Man' Miezah," *New African*, June 1987, 19.

266   "an enormous lounge": Rigby, unpublished memoirs.

266   "I have no property": Blay-Miezah, tape recording, June 17, 1989.

267   "no question of confusing": "Doctor Accused of Killing Patient," *Guardian*, July 7, 1981.

267   "an obsessive psychopath": *Times* (London), April 1, 1993.

267   "we'd all go down the tubes": *Philadelphia Inquirer*, February 22, 1989.

267   clutched the cash, and disappeared: Rigby, unpublished memoirs.

268   "I am a tragic figure": Blay-Miezah, tape recording, June 17, 1989.

268   "I have to beg": Morais, "He Gave Off That Kind of Aura."

269   "I couldn't believe it": Dave Racher, "Victims Wave Con Man Off to Jail," *Philadelphia Daily News*, May 12, 1987.

269   "we just sent the indictment": Rider, interview with author, 2019.

270   "fully expectant of being paid": Rigby, unpublished memoirs.

270   "this job is delayed": Blay-Miezah, tape recording, June 17, 1989.

271   almost sixty-two billion dollars: Oman Ghana Trust Fund accounts, typescript, private collection.

271   "I can surface the funds": Blay-Miezah, tape recording, June 17, 1989.

271   "a large swimming pool": Rigby, interview with author, 2018–2022.

272   "complete with a throne": Rigby, unpublished memoirs.

273   he wasn't there: Zoe Ackah, "Corruption Comes Home," *Epoch Times*, April 30, 2008, 2.

273   "my mum sounded pretty upset": Mona Lisa Brookshire, unpublished memoirs, private collection.

273   a law firm in Norristown: Commonwealth v. Ellis, 15–16.

273   The paper looked old and weathered: Saline, "Out of Africa."

274   "the trust had been written by Nkrumah at the University of Pennsylvania": Commonwealth v. Ellis, 15–16.

274   he was not at liberty to say: Saline, "Out of Africa."

274   Marcos stole ten billion dollars: "The $10bn Question: What Happened to the Marcos Millions?" *Guardian*, May 7, 2016.

274   "Don't feel sorry for these people": Lamar Jr., "Out of Africa, Stung by a Ghanaian Smoothy."

274 a house in Woody Creek: "The Personal Side of Ed Bradley," CBS News, November 12, 2006, https://www.cbsnews.com/news/the-personal-side-of-ed-bradley/3/.

274 Bradley had covered: "Ed Bradley, TV Correspondent, Dies at 65," *New York Times*, November 10, 2006.

274 one of the top ten programs: "60 Minutes: Milestones," CBS News, August 20, 1999, https://www.cbsnews.com/news/60-minutes-milestones/.

274 "A crook doesn't believe he has made it as a crook": Jeff Fager, *Fifty Years of 60 Minutes: The Inside Story of Television's Most Influential News Broadcast* (New York: Simon and Schuster, 2017), 188.

275 "we had to find another source": Blay-Miezah, tape recording, June 17, 1989.

275 Butterfly House was lit up: Rigby, video footage.

277 "the requirements of the Trust had been met": Federal Bureau of Investigation, file of Dr. John Ackah Blay-Miezah, Civil Suit, September 1988, Plaintiffs v. John Ackah Blay-Miezah.

277 "not been in Philadelphia since the early 1970s": United States District Court, Eastern District of Pennsylvania, Civil Action No. 87-778, 3.

277 "undefined, unsupported, barely pleaded": United States District Court, Eastern District of Pennsylvania, Civil Action No. 87-778, Motion to Dismiss, 1.

277 "the vow to speak the truth": "The Ultimate Con Man."

278 "Who has reported missing money?": Blay-Miezah, tape recording, June 17, 1989.

CHAPTER 23: THE ULTIMATE CON MAN

279 calling in his debts: Rigby, unpublished memoirs.

280 Nobody wanted him to go back: Blay-Miezah, tape recording, June 17, 1989.

280 "What do you think I should do?": Rigby, unpublished memoirs.

280 A friend told her: Jeannine Blay-Miezah, interview with author, 2019.

280 "wouldn't embarrass the Queen": "The Ultimate Con Man."

280 "He lives like a king, and I don't have food": Lewis, "Only the Con Men Came Out Ahead."

282 "I would not like to be in Blay-Miezah's shoes": National Archives (UK), FCO 65/4861.

282 "the same old story": Blay-Miezah, tape recording, June 17, 1989.

283 It didn't work: Quantson, *Ghana*, 291.

284 "The firing squads": Adjei, *Death and Pain*, 277.

284 "has justice been done": "Judge Wants 'Killer Soldiers' Brought to Justice," BBC World Service, December 17, 1992, via Foreign Broadcast Information Service, FBIS-AFR-92-244.

284 "suddenly realized there was some merit in democracy": Adjei, *Death and Pain*, 312.

284 "multifarious problems": Quantson, *Ghana*, 291.

285 The facility had been named: S. Kojo Addae, *The Gold Coast and Achimota in the Second World War* (Accra: Sedco, 2004), 74.

286 "It simply has to be true": "Investors Are After a Con Man," *Philadelphia Inquirer*, February 22, 1989, 11.

286 almost complete: Federal Bureau of Investigation, file of Dr. John Ackah Blay-Miezah, Memorandum of Interview, April 25, 1988.

286 "not filing personal or corporate tax returns": *Philadelphia Inquirer*, April 15, 1992.

CHAPTER 24: ANANSI'S LAST TALE

287 "home to rest": George Shepperson and St. Clair Drake, "The Fifth Pan-African Conference," *Contributions in Black Studies* 8 (1986–1987): 63.

288 "face up to our history": *Daily Graphic*, June 30, 1992.

288 "suffering from massive palpitations": Kwesi Pratt Jnr, interview with author, 2018.

288 "They were having sex when he died": Gladys Blay-Hill, interview with author, 2018.

289 the American author Richard Wright: "Ellen Wright-Hervé," Entrée to Black Paris, January 3, 2019, https://www.entreetoblackparis.com/blog/black-paris -profiles-ii-ellen-wright-herve-part-1.

289 "We are laying Dr. Nkrumah's remains to rest": "Kwame Nkrumah Reburied with Full Military Honours, Flt. Lt. Rawlings Presides," Accra, June 1992, https://www.youtube.com/watch?v=UjYmucOVhGI.

289 "In the name of the people of Ghana": *West Africa* (1992): 1305.

289 "Rawlings urges all": "Rawlings Urges All to Continue Nkrumah's Battle," *Daily Graphic*, July 2, 1992.

289 "He is the father of us all": Milne, *Kwame Nkrumah*, 270.

289 When Quantson called: Quantson, *Ghana*, 203.

290 "to keep the fingerprints": Jackman, *Con Men*, 188.

290 "If convicted of all counts": Press Release, U.S. Attorney for the Eastern District of Pennsylvania, September 8, 1992.

290 "it is possible that he did not die": Kwesi Pratt Jnr, interview with author, 2018.

290 the full machinery of the junta: "Rawlings 'Wins' Ghana's Presidential Elections: Establishing a New Constitutional Order," *Africa Today* 39, no. 4 (1992): 70.

290 "continue the battle": "Rawlings Urges All to Continue Nkrumah's Battle."

290 a million new voters: "Rawlings 'Wins' Ghana's Presidential Elections," 70.

291 "perpetual indemnity": Baffour Ankomah, "Dictators' Last Chance," *New African*, May 1992, 16.

291 played for Blay-Miezah one last time: Rigby, video footage.

293 "not going to help me pay school fees": Gladys Blay-Hill, interview with author, 2018.

293 "It was the biggest transition": Mona Lisa Brookshire, unpublished memoirs, private collection.

294 He seemed to have made several wills: Supreme Court, Ghana, Dr John R. Kells and Joseph K. Whaja v. Dr E. Ako Adjei and 3 Others (2001), JELR 68294 (SC), 8/2000, October 24, 2001.

294 "whether he did indeed have all that": Supreme Court, Ghana, Dr John R. Kells and Joseph K. Whaja v. Dr E. Ako Adjei and 3 Others (2001).

294 "stands for nothing": "UBS Never Took Enough Interest in Its Risks," *Financial Times*, December 19, 2012.

294 messages on Blay-Miezah's letterhead: John Kells, typescript letter, July 26, 1998, private collection.

295 when he was put on trial in 1979: "Rawlings Bids Farewell to Adumua-Bossman; His Lead Counsel in 1979 Trial," *Ghanaweb*, January 19, 2018, https://www .ghanaweb.com/GhanaHomePage/NewsArchive/Rawlings-bids-farewell-to -Adumua-Bossman-his-lead-counsel-in-1979-trial-619177.

295 "closely associated with the abuses": National Reconciliation Commission, Ghana, October 2004, vol. 1, chap. 4.

295 "extract a single cent": "Controversy Unlimited: Blay-Miezah's Billions," *Ghanaweb*, July 1, 2009, https://www.ghanaweb.com/GhanaHomePage/features /Controversy-Unlimited-Blay-Miezah-s-Billions-164441.

295 "material misspellings": Supreme Court, Ghana, Dr John R. Kells and Joseph K. Whaja v. Dr E. Ako Adjei and 3 Others (2001).

295 "It's gone": "The Probe Dies with the Suspect," *Philadelphia Inquirer*, December 15, 1992.

EPILOGUE: THE REST IS HISTORY

298 "Our external debt would be a peanut": David Ampofo, "Time with David," interview with Gregory Frazier, Channel Two communications, 2001, https://vimeo .com/15272325.

298 "a group of Americans": "Ghana: Cadman Mills Pursues Blay-Miezah Money," *Ghanaian Chronicle*, June 12, 2009.

299 "he got corrupt, he conned people": Kobla Asamani, interview with author, 2016.

301 dusty and smudged: Rigby, interview with author, 2018–2022.

302 the biggest investment that the British made: Franklin Obeng-Odoom, *Oiling the Urban Economy: Land, Labour, Capital, and the State in Sekondi-Takoradi, Ghana* (New York: Routledge, 2014), 80.

ACKNOWLEDGMENTS

My first glimpse of John Ackah Blay-Miezah came in a WhatsApp message, containing a clip of his *60 Minutes* interview: low-resolution video from a decades-old television broadcast. Our man sat in his Louis Quinze chair, telling Ed Bradley about Ghana's hidden billions. The WhatsApp message was a question: Did I think Blay-Miezah was telling the truth? The more I looked into Blay-Miezah, the stranger his story became. Then one day in New York, I found *Hustlers and Con Men* by Jay Robert Nash sitting on the $2 stacks outside the Strand bookshop. A line on the contents page called to me: "The Inherited Billions." Here was the inheritance scam, one of the longest-running cons of all—and here was the blueprint for the Oman Ghana Trust Fund. The space between that first WhatsApp message, that day in New York, and this book has been filled by the expertise and infinite patience of countless people.

At Bloomsbury, my editor Ben Hyman simply got it: often, he understood the story I was trying to tell better than I did. He knew how to turn years of research, full of twists and turns, into a narrative. Barbara Darko, Jasmine Horsey, Morgan Jones, and Ian Marshall have been wonderfully supportive throughout this book's long and winding journey—and Nigel Newton has been a truly generous advocate for it.

Jin Auh at the Wylie Agency saw the potential in my ideas and helped me shape them into a proposal. She has been endlessly encouraging, kind, and understanding. Alba Ziegler-Bailey and Jessica Bullock at Wylie have been invaluable allies.

I am deeply grateful to all the librarians and archivists who have helped me piece this story together. In particular, I would like to thank, in the United

States, the Philadelphia Courts and the Office of Judicial Services, the Urban Archives at Temple University, the Union League of Philadelphia, the Federal Bureau of Investigation, and the U.S. National Archives—and, in the United Kingdom, the UK National Archives, the British Library, and the British Library's Endangered Archives Programme.

I would like to thank Peter Rigby, in the warmest possible terms, for giving me access to his personal archive, for all the amazing stories he told me, for sharing his research into Ghana and its history, and for cups of tea and spirited debates. The late Ben Hayford generously shared his encyclopedic knowledge of the world of this book. Bright Akwetey kindly gave me access to documents from his personal archive and let me glimpse what it was like investigating Blay-Miezah.

Many members of John Ackah Blay-Miezah's extended family shared their recollections, family lore, and fond memories, in particular Gladys "Auntie Naana" Blay-Hill, John Blay-Miezah Jr., Mona Lisa Brookshire, and Francis Kaku Mensah.

I am thankful to all the people who were generous with their time and expertise, and kindly answered my many, many questions over the last six years. In Ghana, Akyaaba Addai-Sebo, Ebenezer Moses Debrah, Samia Nkrumah, Kwesi Pratt Jnr, and Ezra D. M. Stephens. In America and Canada, Lynne Abraham, Zoe Ackah, Steven Burbank, Ben Bynum Jr., Carol Saline, Oliver St. Clair Franklin, Linn Washington, and Clark White. In the UK, Joseph Amamoo and Barry Rider. To them, to countless others, and to my other sources who asked not to be named, thank you.

James Barnor and his extensive archive provided me with a dazzling window into the past: the dinner-dances around independence, the fashions, the color of the light in Accra. It was truly an honor to view his work and hear his stories.

I would like to thank everybody who frequented the bar behind the coffee machine at Uncle Bobbie's Coffee & Books in Germantown, Philadelphia, and all the staff who make it such a special place to write and to have extensive debates. I am so grateful to my friends, who kept me sane as this book became wilder and wilder. To Jack Mirkinson, for reading countless versions of countless drafts, for reminding me that the story was what mattered, for all the rambling conversations that turned into moments of life-altering beauty, and for not wearing shoes in my house. To Jade Emily Bradford, and Donnie and Ricky Bradford, for bringing me joy, sanity, and sleepy tea, for making the world seem infinitely better, and for encouraging my most outrageous trains of thought. To Shanielle Joseph, for saying wonderful things, many times, and for doing wonderful things, many more times. To Kuukuwa Manful, for reading drafts and tracking sources down, and for her project "Building Early Accra: Preserving Historical Building Permits in Ghana" (British Library, EAP1161), which changed the way I thought about my research. To Marta Downer and Jo Gipson, for literally keeping me functional. To Dr. Tanya McDonnaugh, for helping me find a path. And to Lauren Alix Brown, who told me that this was a story worth chasing, whatever it took: rest in peace.

To my family: Bridget Agoe and Samuel Nii Obodai Mensah, thank you for doing the most important work, and for being bright during the darkest times, and to Kezier Naa Dromo Agoe, for being the brightest light of all, and for being as enthusiastic about stories as I am. To my sister, Mma Yeebo-Agoe. And to my parents, Belinda Agoe and Zaya Yeebo, without whom I would not exist.

And finally, to Edmund Richardson, who saved my life: Thank you.

INDEX

Note: Page numbers in italics refer to images.

A NOTE ON THE AUTHOR

Yepoka Yeebo is a British-Ghanaian journalist whose work has appeared in *Bloomberg Businessweek*, the *Guardian*, *Quartz*, PRI's *The World*, and other publications, and she has been interviewed on NPR's *All Things Considered*. A graduate of Columbia University's School of Journalism and the University of London, she divides her time between London, UK, and Accra, Ghana. *Anansi's Gold* is her first book.